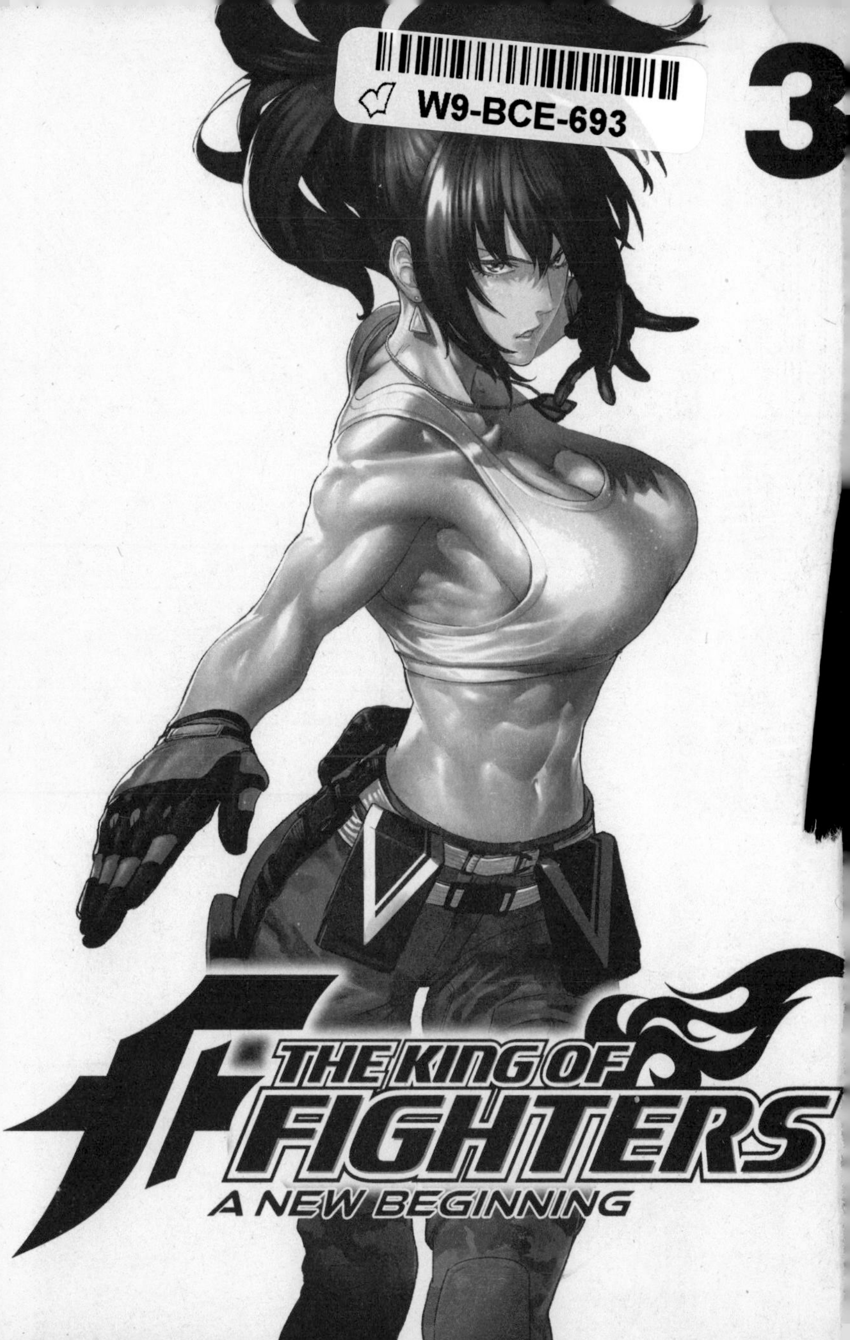
3
THE KING OF
FIGHTERS
A NEW BEGINNING

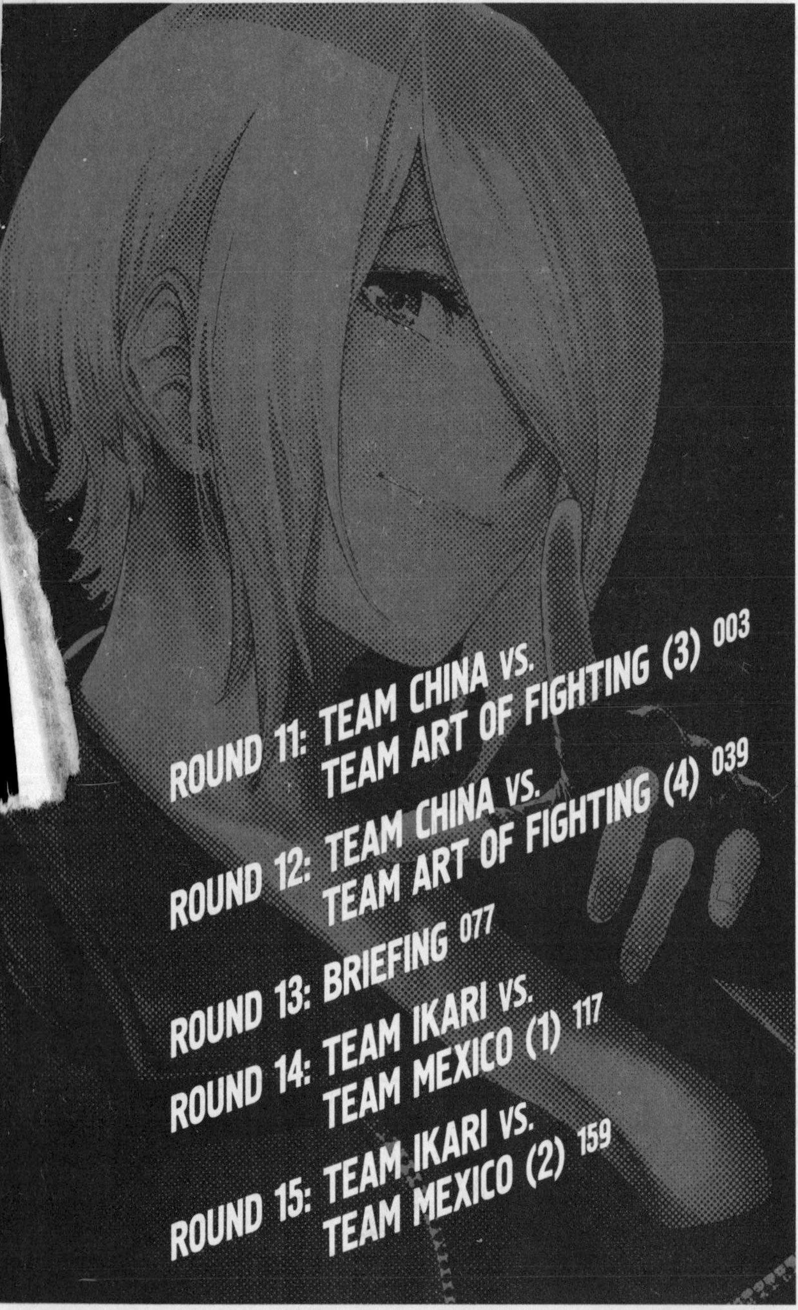

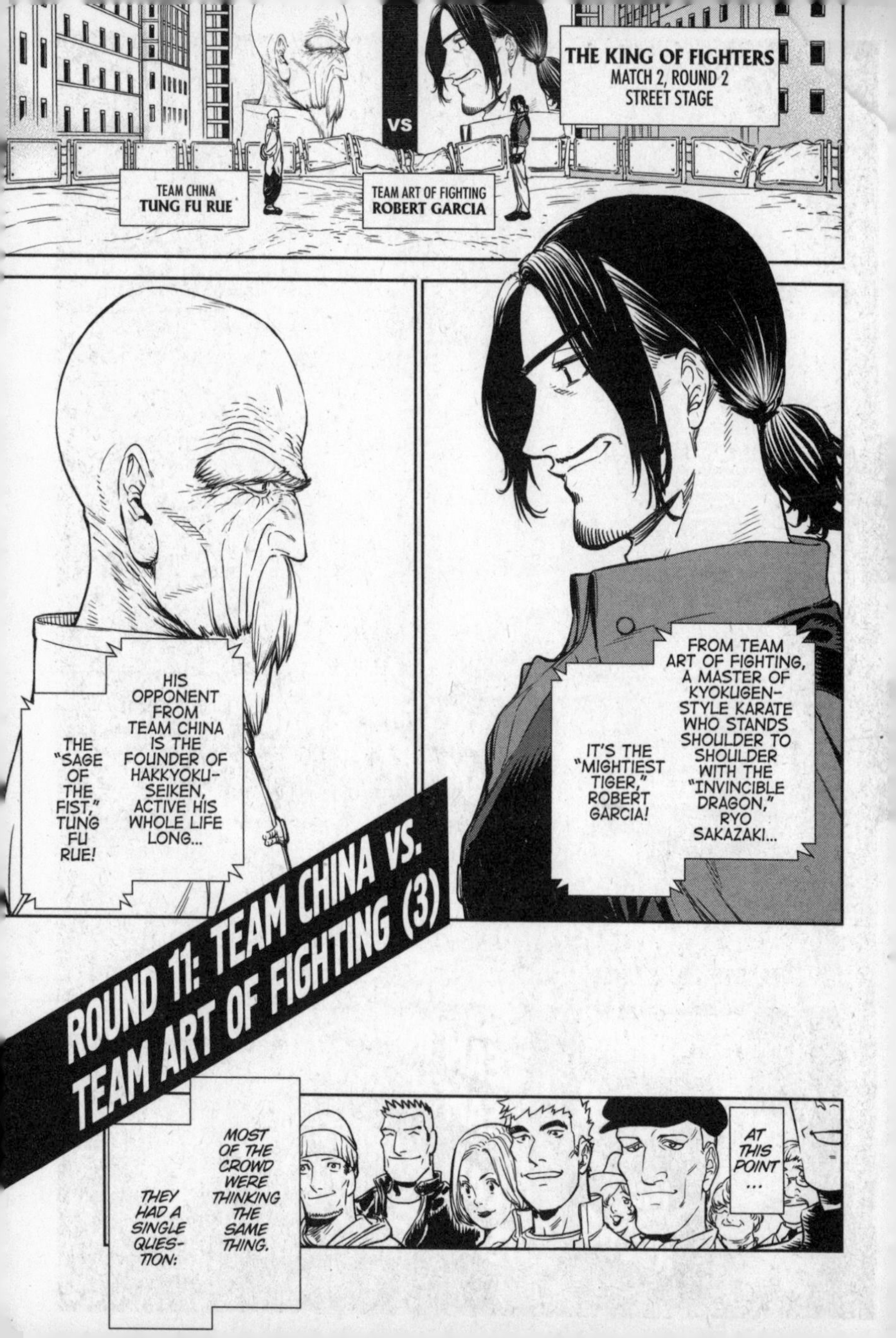
THE KING OF FIGHTERS MATCH 2, ROUND 2 STREET STAGE
VS
TEAM ART OF FIGHTING ROBERT GARCIA
TEAM CHINA TUNG FU RUE
FROM TEAM ART OF FIGHTING, A MASTER OF KYOKUGEN-STYLE KARATE WHO STANDS SHOULDER TO SHOULDER WITH THE "INVINCIBLE DRAGON," RYO SAKAZAKI...
IT'S THE "MIGHTIEST TIGER," ROBERT GARCIA!
HIS OPPONENT FROM TEAM CHINA IS THE FOUNDER OF HAKKYOKU-SEIKEN, ACTIVE HIS WHOLE LIFE LONG...
THE "SAGE OF THE FIST," TUNG FU RUE!
ROUND 11: TEAM CHINA VS. TEAM ART OF FIGHTING (3)
AT THIS POINT...
MOST OF THE CROWD WERE THINKING THE SAME THING.
THEY HAD A SINGLE QUES-TION:

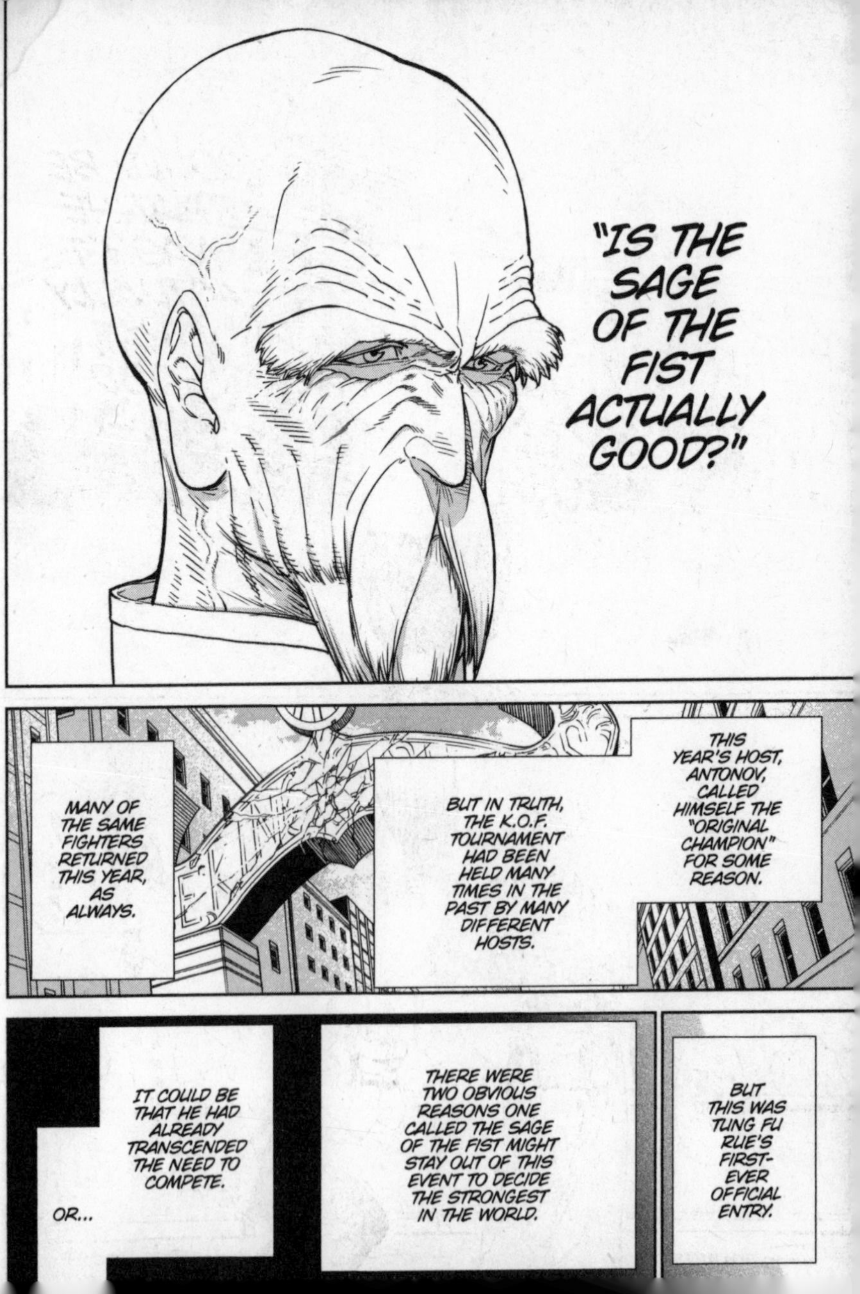
"IS THE SAGE OF THE FIST ACTUALLY GOOD?"
THIS YEAR'S HOST, ANTONOV, CALLED HIMSELF THE "ORIGINAL CHAMPION" FOR SOME REASON.
BUT IN TRUTH, THE K.O.F. TOURNAMENT HAD BEEN HELD MANY TIMES IN THE PAST BY MANY DIFFERENT HOSTS.
MANY OF THE SAME FIGHTERS RETURNED THIS YEAR, AS ALWAYS.
BUT THIS WAS TUNG FU RUE'S FIRST-EVER OFFICIAL ENTRY.
THERE WERE TWO OBVIOUS REASONS ONE CALLED THE SAGE OF THE FIST MIGHT STAY OUT OF THIS EVENT TO DECIDE THE STRONGEST IN THE WORLD.
IT COULD BE THAT HE HAD ALREADY TRANSCENDED THE NEED TO COMPETE.
OR...

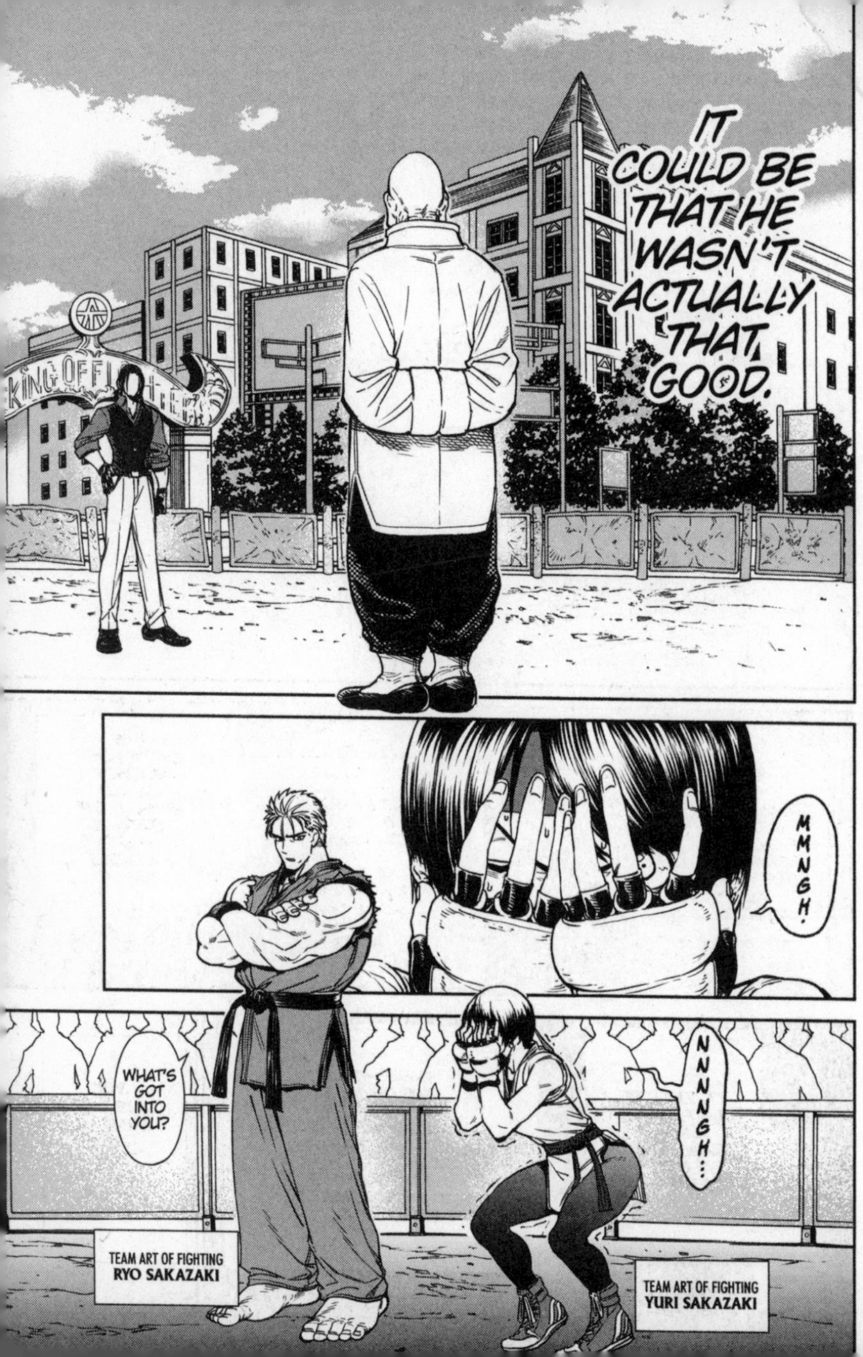
IT COULD BE THAT HE WASN'T ACTUALLY THAT GOOD.
MMNGH!
NNNNGH...
WHAT'S GOT INTO YOU?
TEAM ART OF FIGHTING
RYO SAKAZAKI
TEAM ART OF FIGHTING
YURI SAKAZAKI

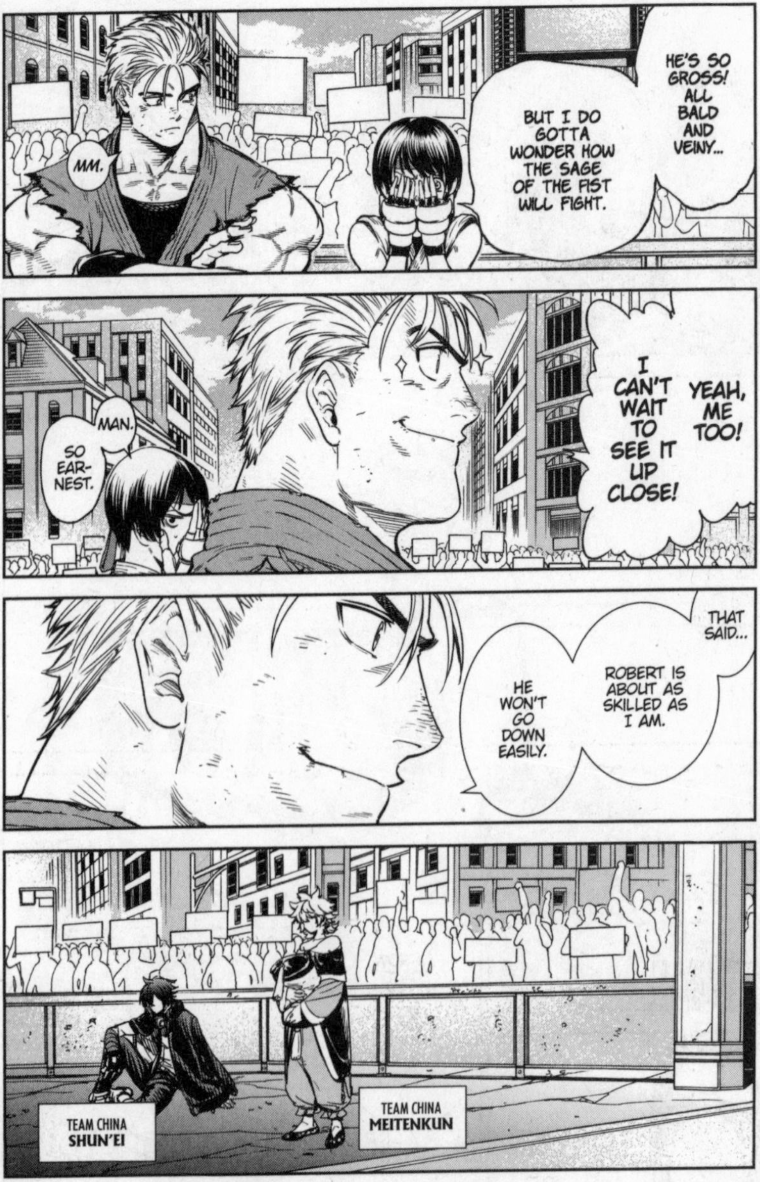
HE'S SO GROSS! ALL BALD AND VEINY...
BUT I DO GOTTA WONDER HOW THE SAGE OF THE FIST WILL FIGHT.
MM.
YEAH, ME TOO!
I CAN'T WAIT TO SEE IT UP CLOSE!
MAN.
SO EARNEST.
THAT SAID...
ROBERT IS ABOUT AS SKILLED AS I AM.
HE WON'T GO DOWN EASILY.
TEAM CHINA MEITENKUN
TEAM CHINA SHUN'EI

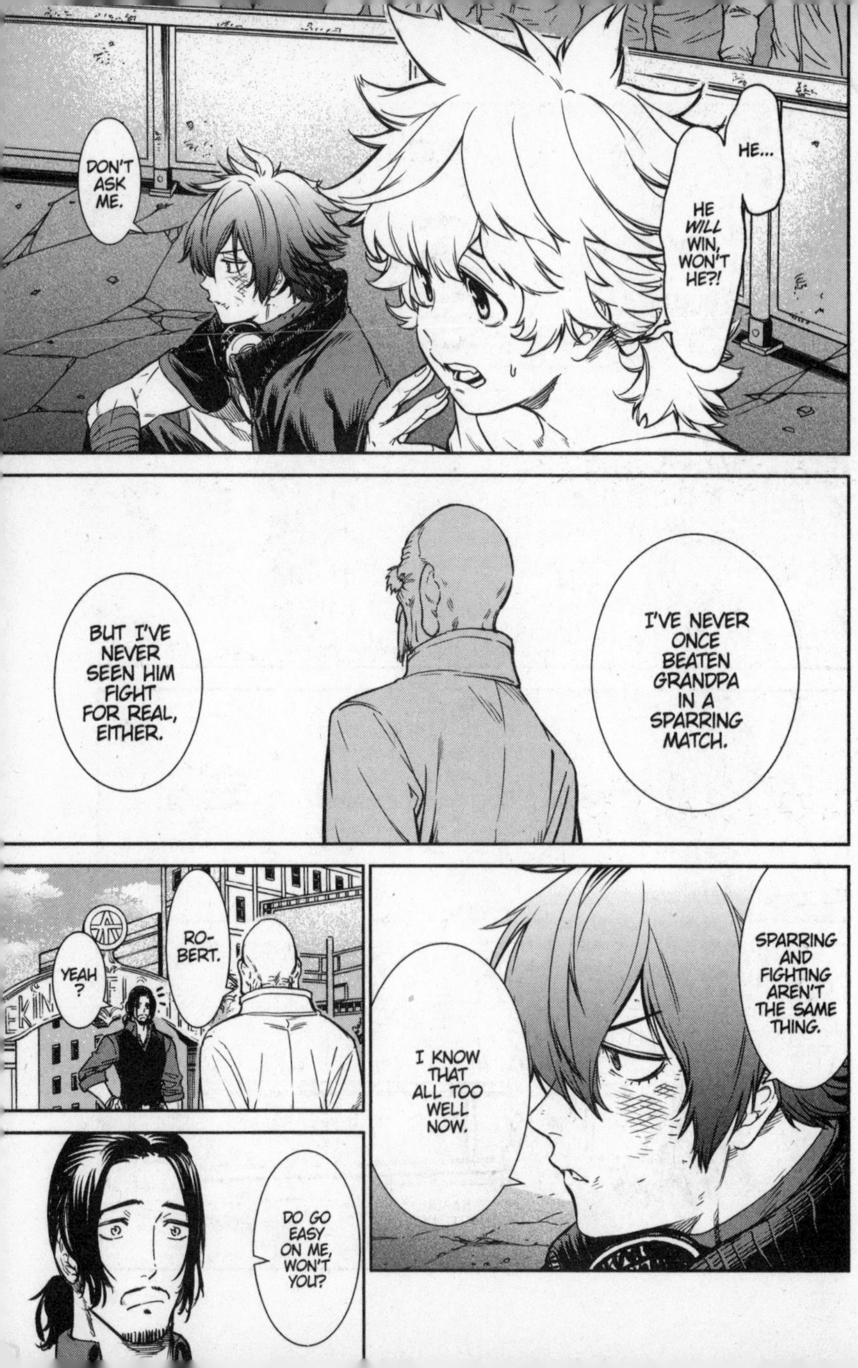
HE...
HE *WILL* WIN, WON'T HE?!
DON'T ASK ME.
I'VE NEVER ONCE BEATEN GRANDPA IN A SPARRING MATCH.
BUT I'VE NEVER SEEN HIM FIGHT FOR REAL, EITHER.
SPARRING AND FIGHTING AREN'T THE SAME THING.
I KNOW THAT ALL TOO WELL NOW.
RO-BERT.
YEAH?
DO GO EASY ON ME, WON'T YOU?

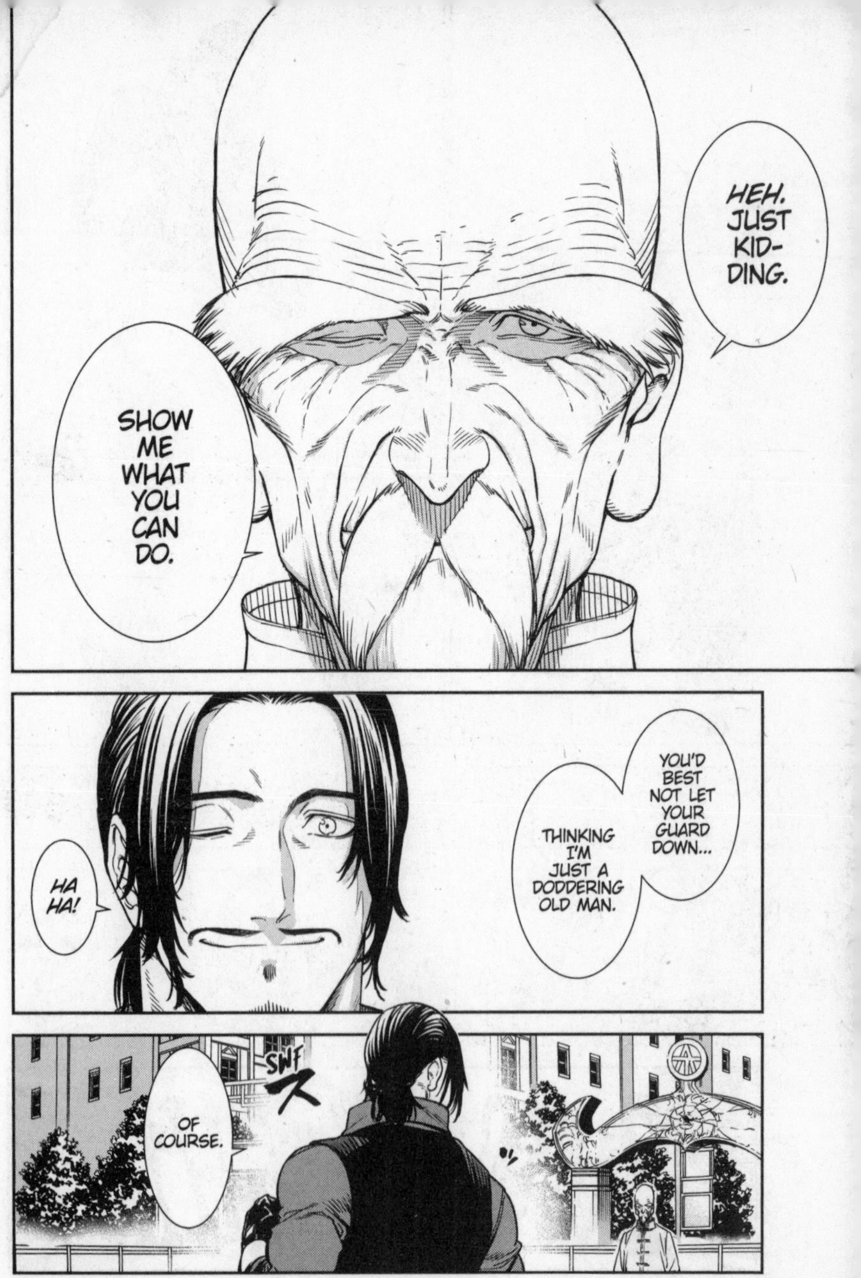
HEH. JUST KID-DING.
SHOW ME WHAT YOU CAN DO.
YOU'D BEST NOT LET YOUR GUARD DOWN...
THINKING I'M JUST A DODDERING OLD MAN.
HA HA!
SWF
OF COURSE.

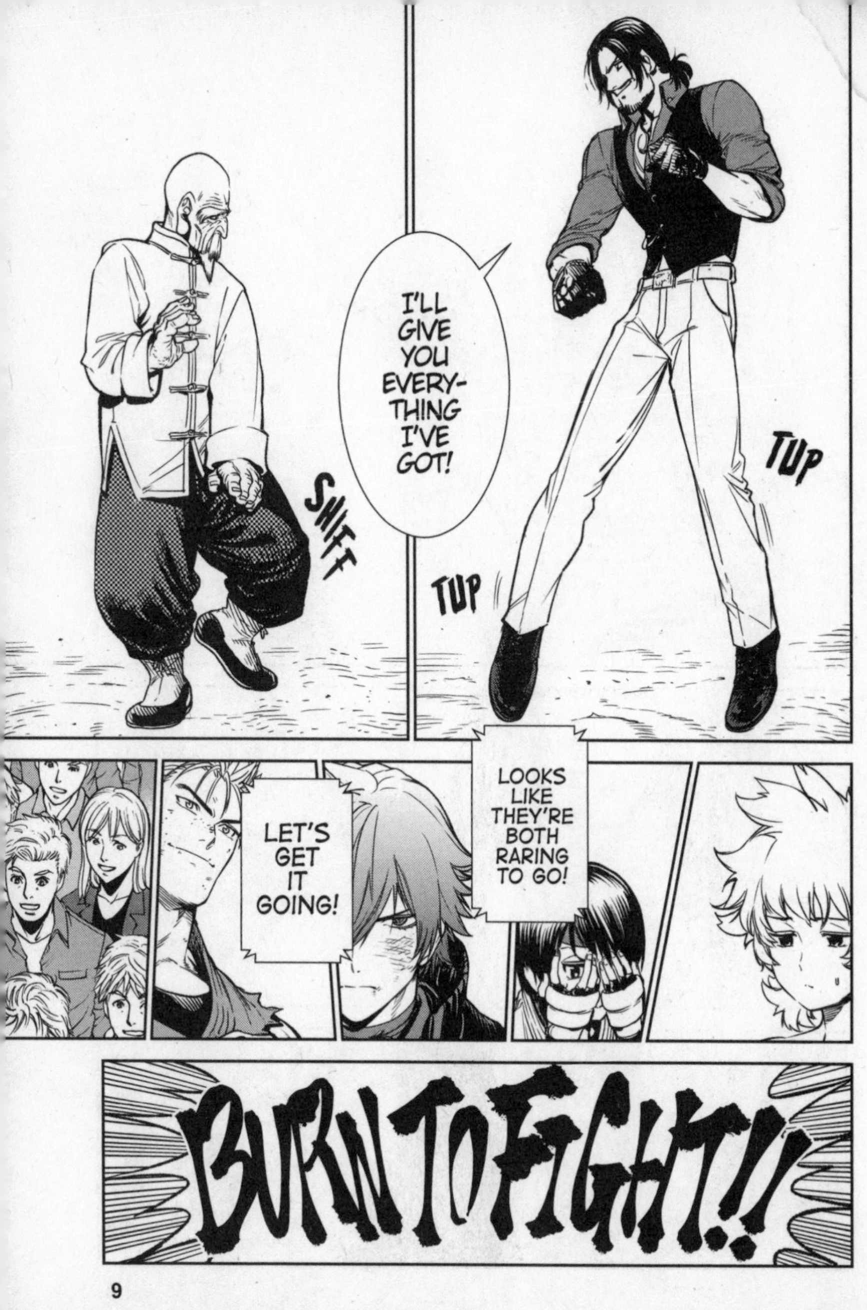
I'LL GIVE YOU EVERYTHING I'VE GOT!
TUP
TUP
SHIFF
LOOKS LIKE THEY'RE BOTH RARING TO GO!
LET'S GET IT GOING!
BURN TO FIGHT!!

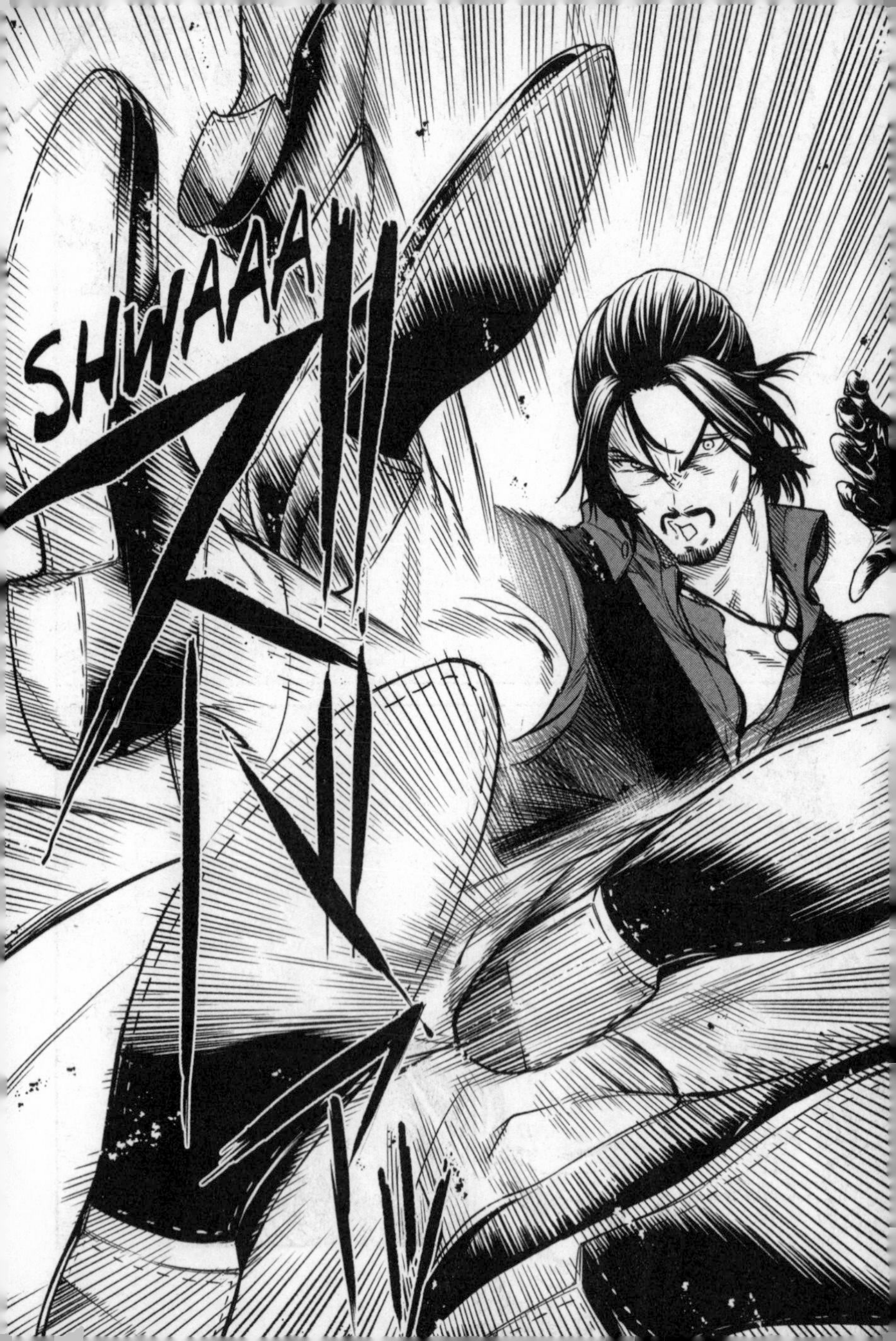
SHWAAA

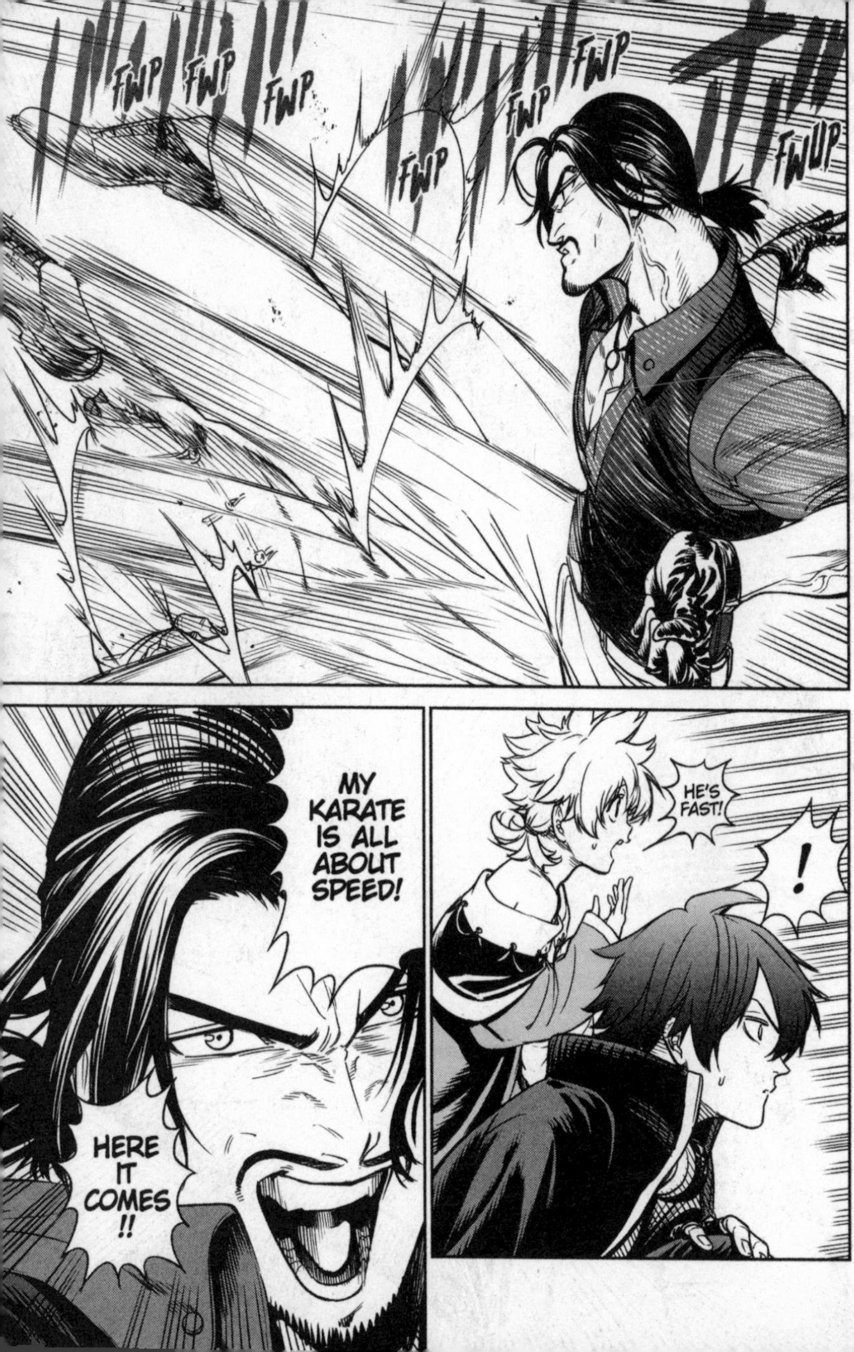
FWUP
FWP
FWP
FWP
FWP
FWP
FWP
HE'S FAST!
!
MY KARATE IS ALL ABOUT SPEED!
HERE IT COMES!!

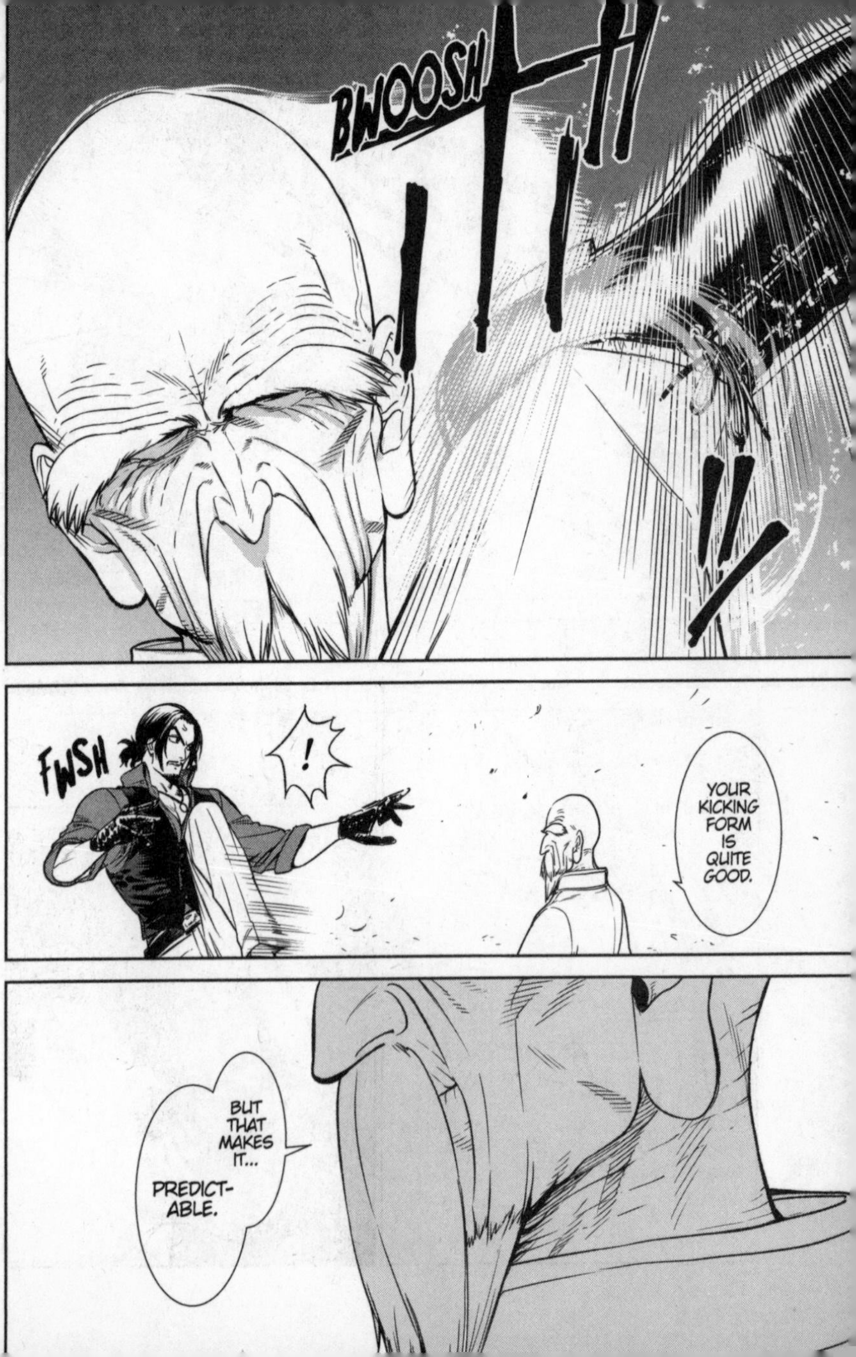
BWOOSH
FWSH
YOUR KICKING FORM IS QUITE GOOD.
!
BUT THAT MAKES IT...
PREDICT-ABLE.

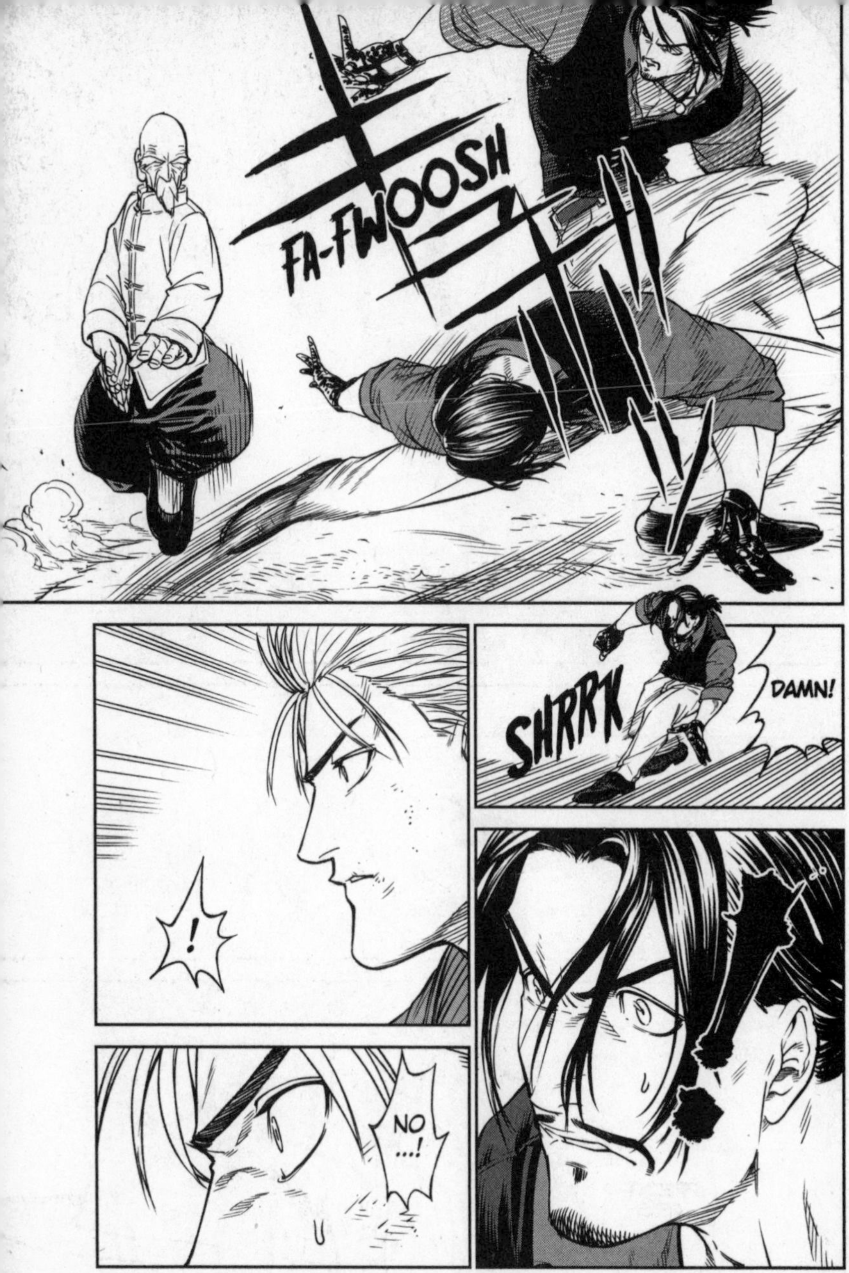
FA-FWOOSH
DAMN!
SHRRK
!
NO ...!

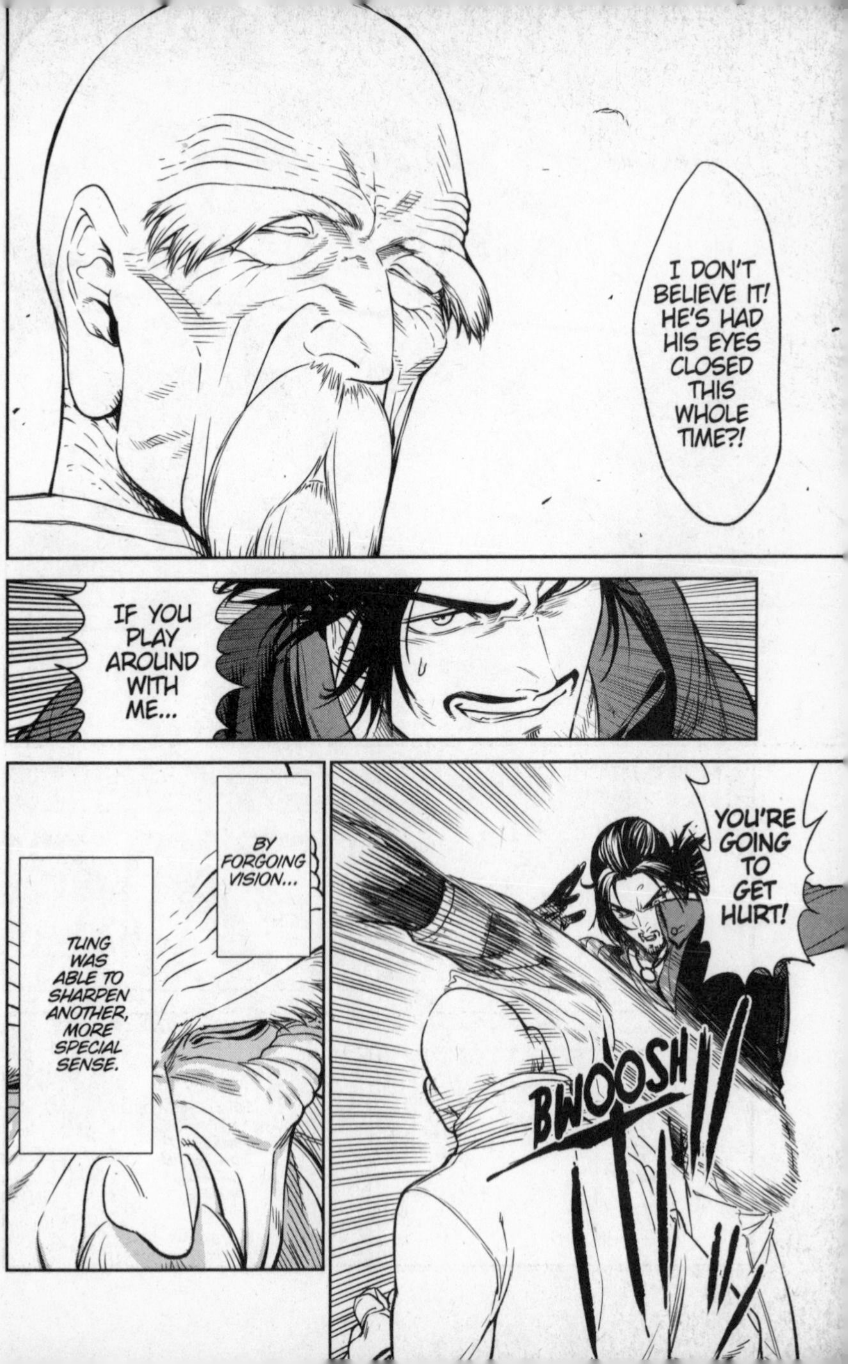

I DON'T BELIEVE IT! HE'S HAD HIS EYES CLOSED THIS WHOLE TIME?!
IF YOU PLAY AROUND WITH ME...
YOU'RE GOING TO GET HURT!
BWOOSH
BY FORGOING VISION...
TUNG WAS ABLE TO SHARPEN ANOTHER, MORE SPECIAL SENSE.

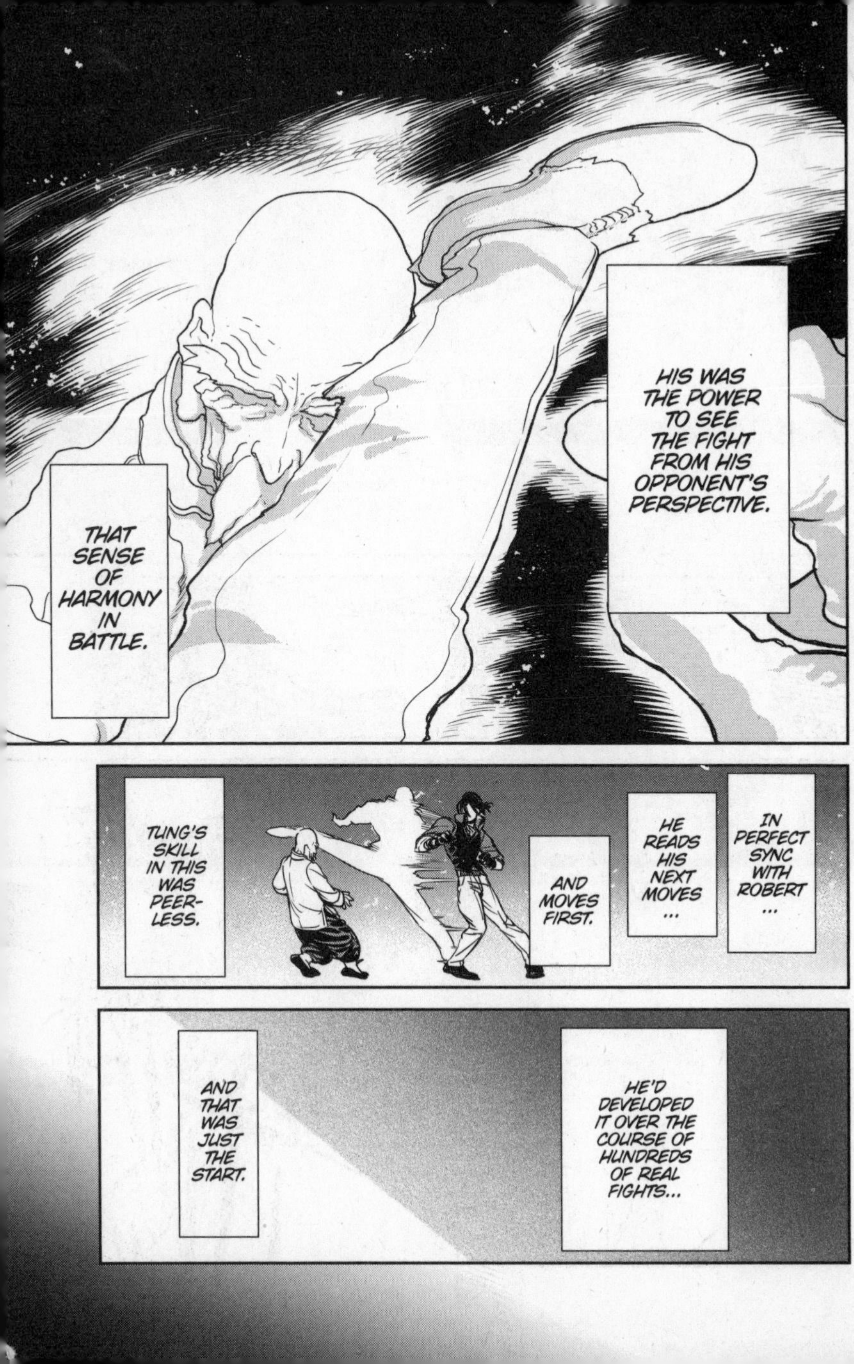
HIS WAS THE POWER TO SEE THE FIGHT FROM HIS OPPONENT'S PERSPECTIVE.
THAT SENSE OF HARMONY IN BATTLE.
IN PERFECT SYNC WITH ROBERT...
HE READS HIS NEXT MOVES...
AND MOVES FIRST.
TUNG'S SKILL IN THIS WAS PEER-LESS.
HE'D DEVELOPED IT OVER THE COURSE OF HUNDREDS OF REAL FIGHTS...
AND THAT WAS JUST THE START.

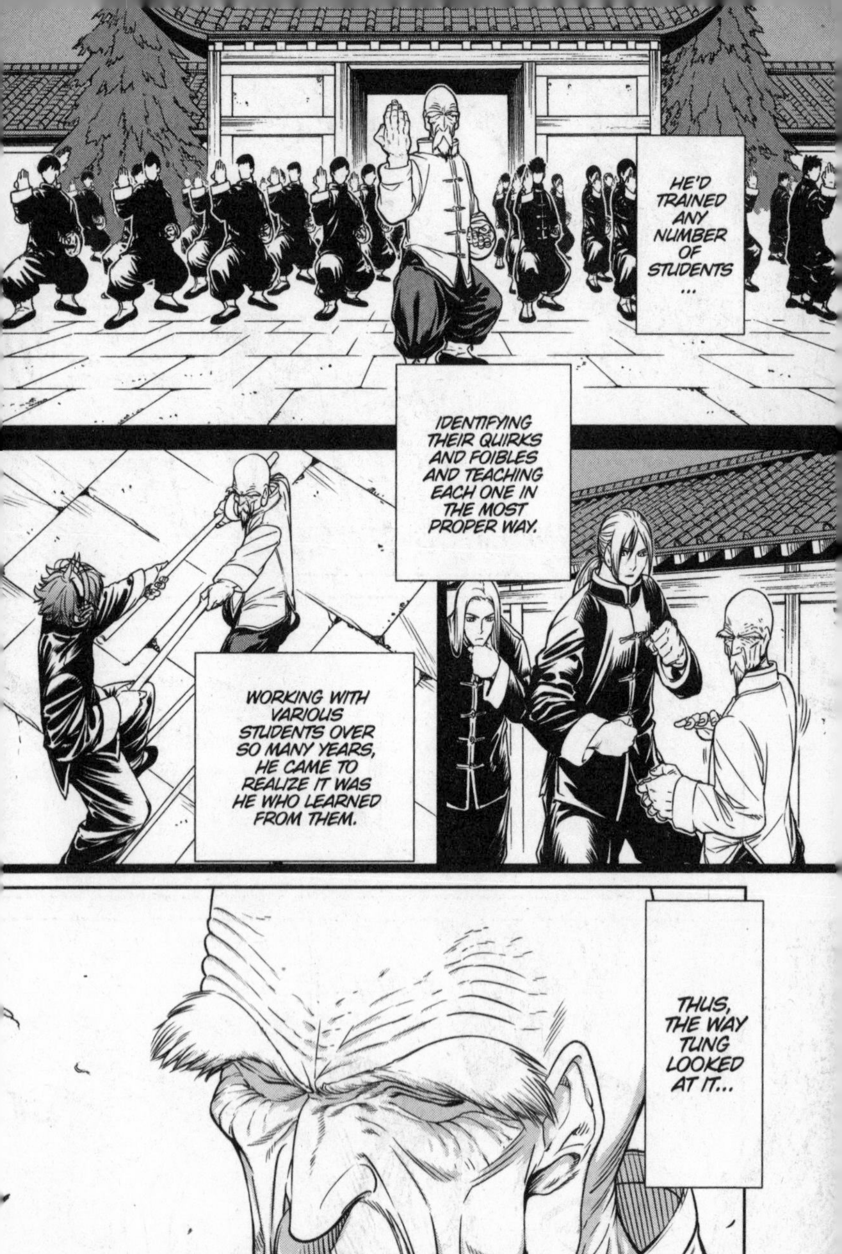
HE'D TRAINED ANY NUMBER OF STUDENTS...
IDENTIFYING THEIR QUIRKS AND FOIBLES AND TEACHING EACH ONE IN THE MOST PROPER WAY.
WORKING WITH VARIOUS STUDENTS OVER SO MANY YEARS, HE CAME TO REALIZE IT WAS HE WHO LEARNED FROM THEM.
THUS, THE WAY TUNG LOOKED AT IT...

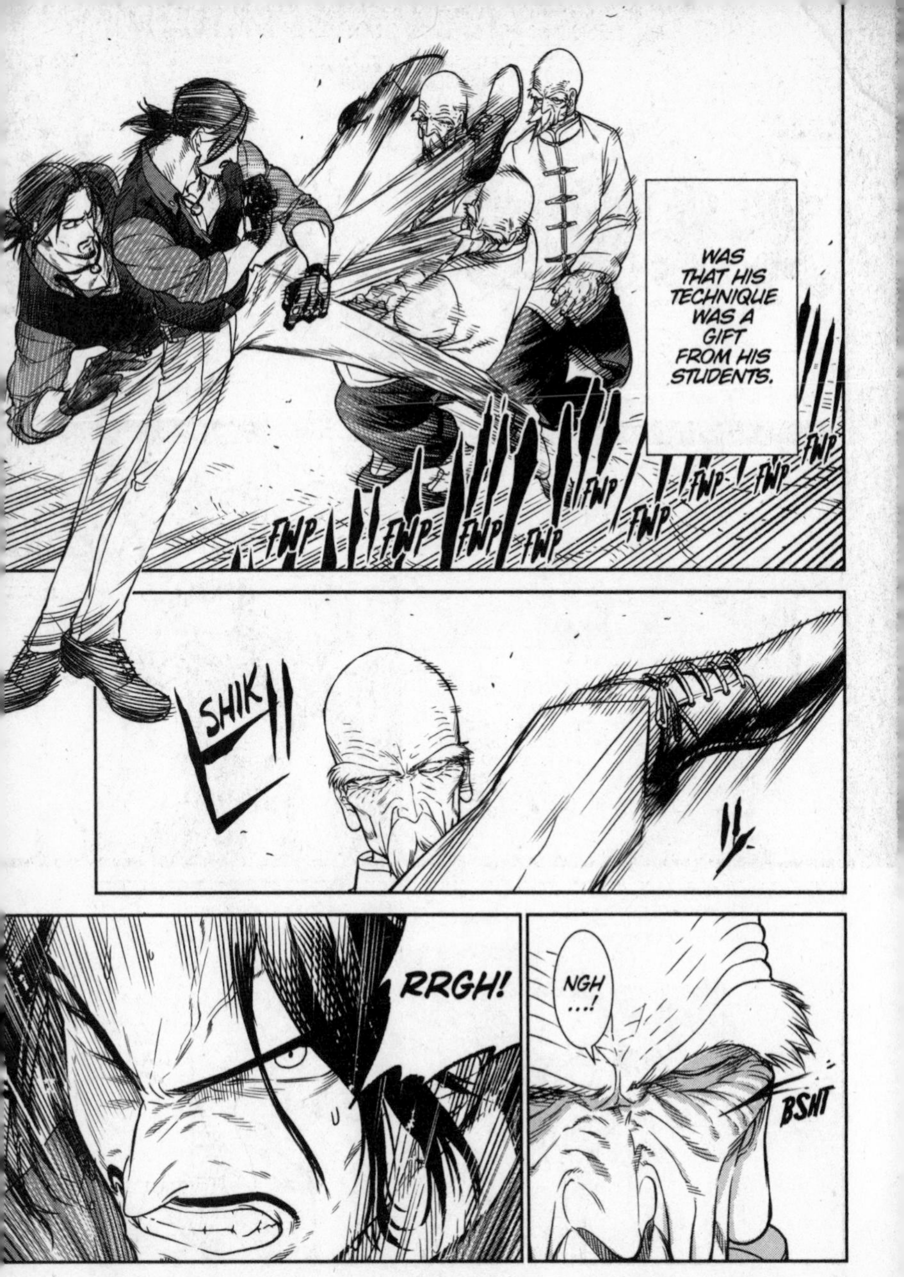
WAS THAT HIS TECHNIQUE WAS A GIFT FROM HIS STUDENTS.
FWP FWP FWP FWP FWP FWP FWP FWP FWP FWP
SHIK
NGH ...!
BSHT
RRGH!

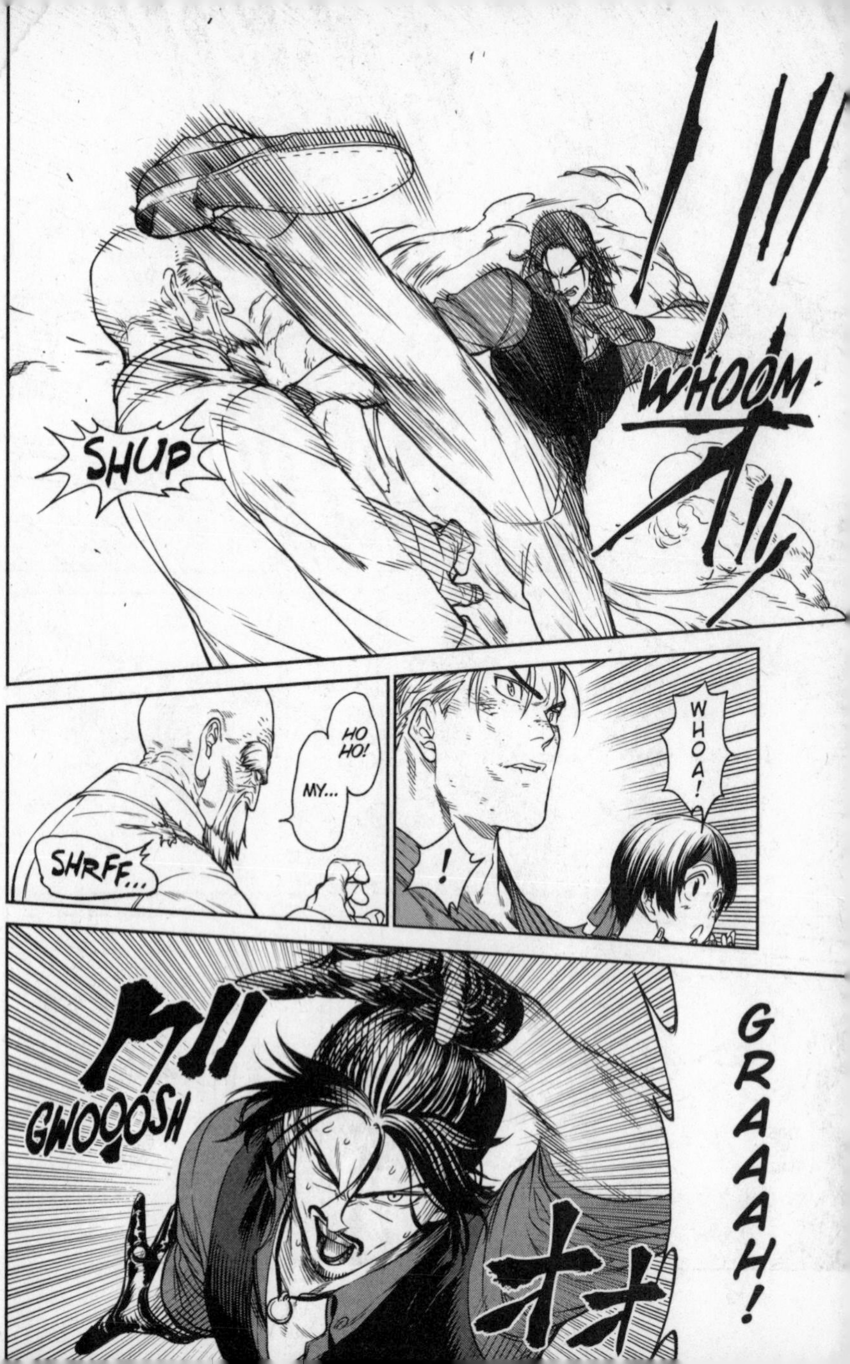
WHOOM
SHUP
WHOA!
!
HO HO!
MY...
SHRFF...
GRAAAH!
GWOOOSH

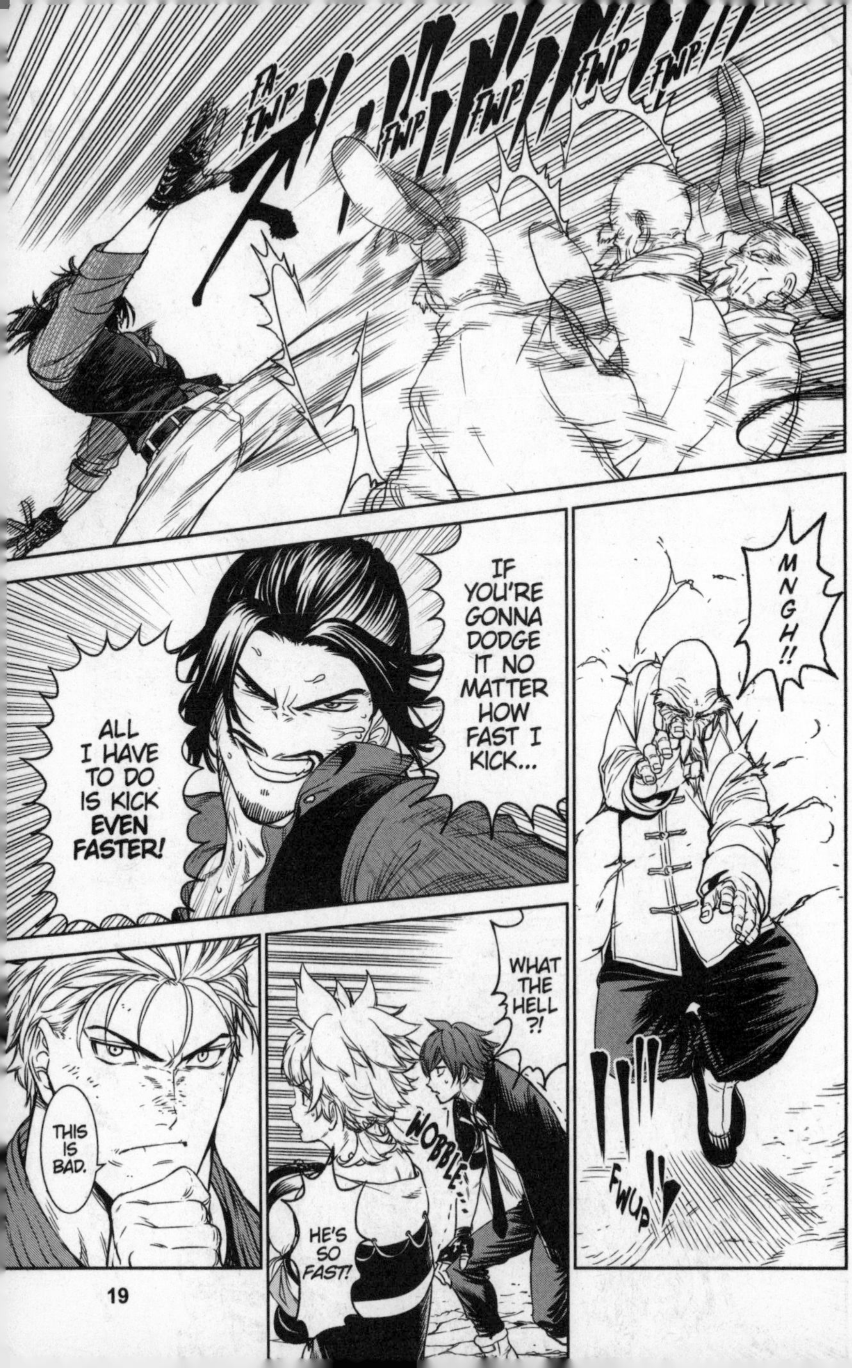
FA-FWIP
FWIP
FWIP
FWIP
FWIP
FWIP
MNGH!!
FWUP!!
IF YOU'RE GONNA DODGE IT NO MATTER HOW FAST I KICK...
ALL I HAVE TO DO IS KICK EVEN FASTER!
WHAT THE HELL?!
WOBBLE...
HE'S SO FAST!
THIS IS BAD.

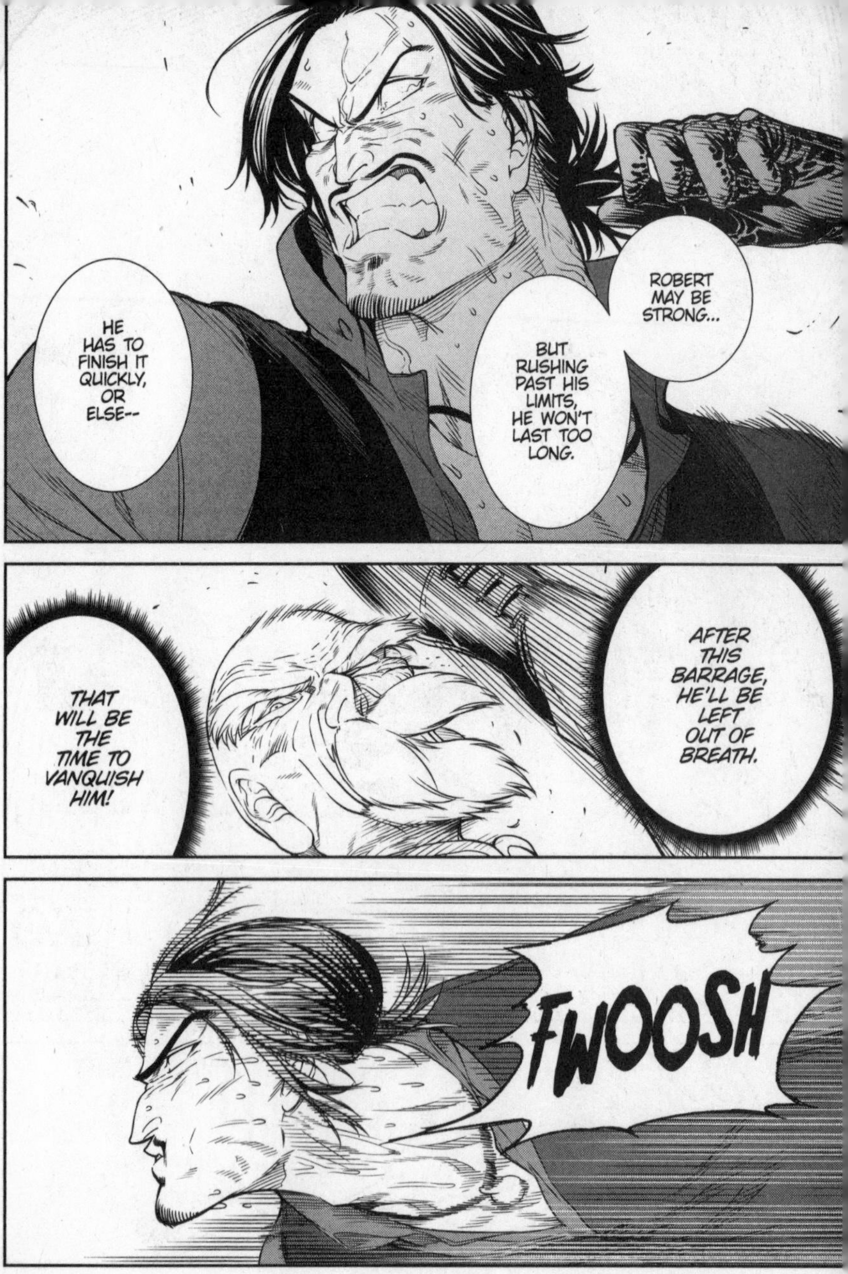
ROBERT MAY BE STRONG...
BUT RUSHING PAST HIS LIMITS, HE WON'T LAST TOO LONG.
HE HAS TO FINISH IT QUICKLY, OR ELSE--
AFTER THIS BARRAGE, HE'LL BE LEFT OUT OF BREATH.
THAT WILL BE THE TIME TO VANQUISH HIM!
FWOOSH

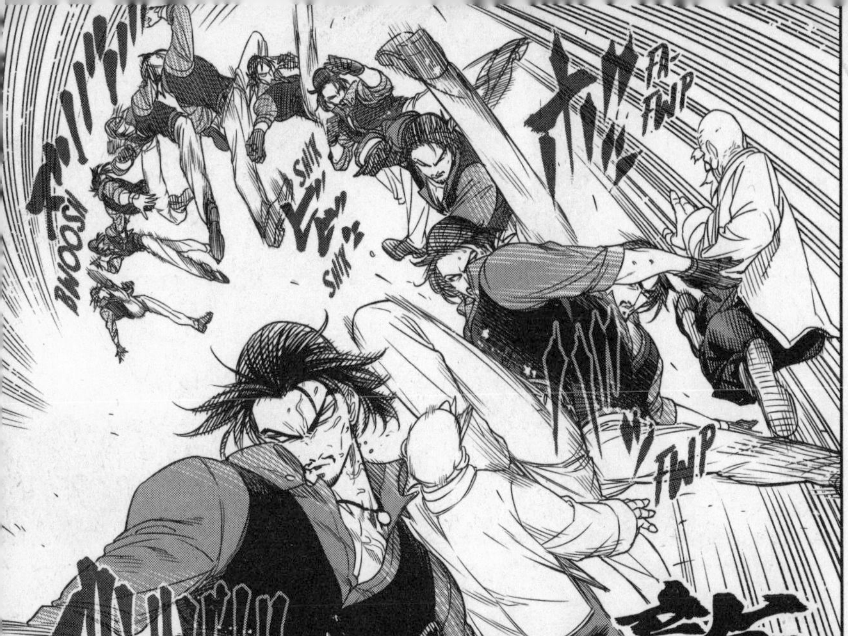
FA-FWIP
SHIK
SHIK
BWOOSH
FWIP
RYUUKO RANBU!
PA PA PA
WHA-

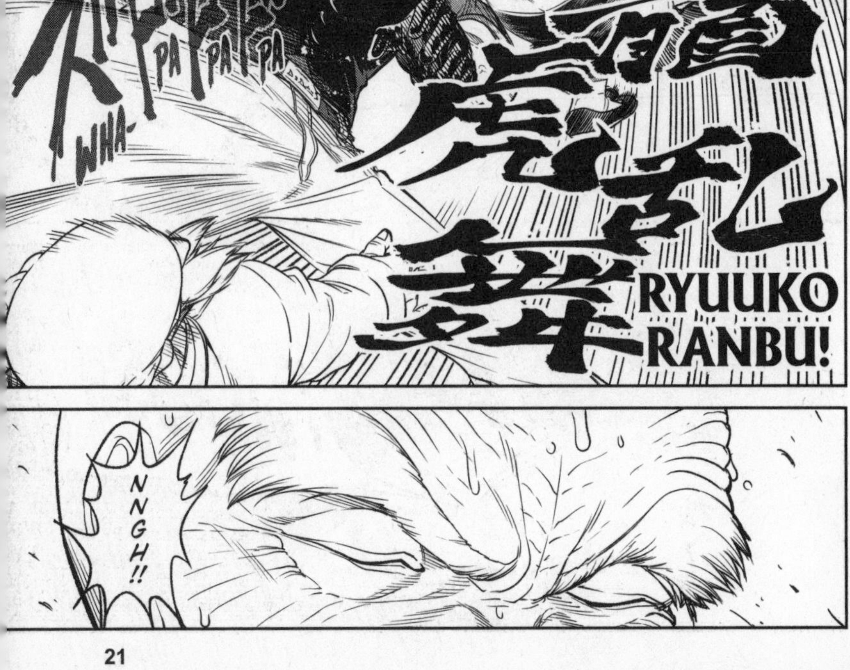
NNGH!!

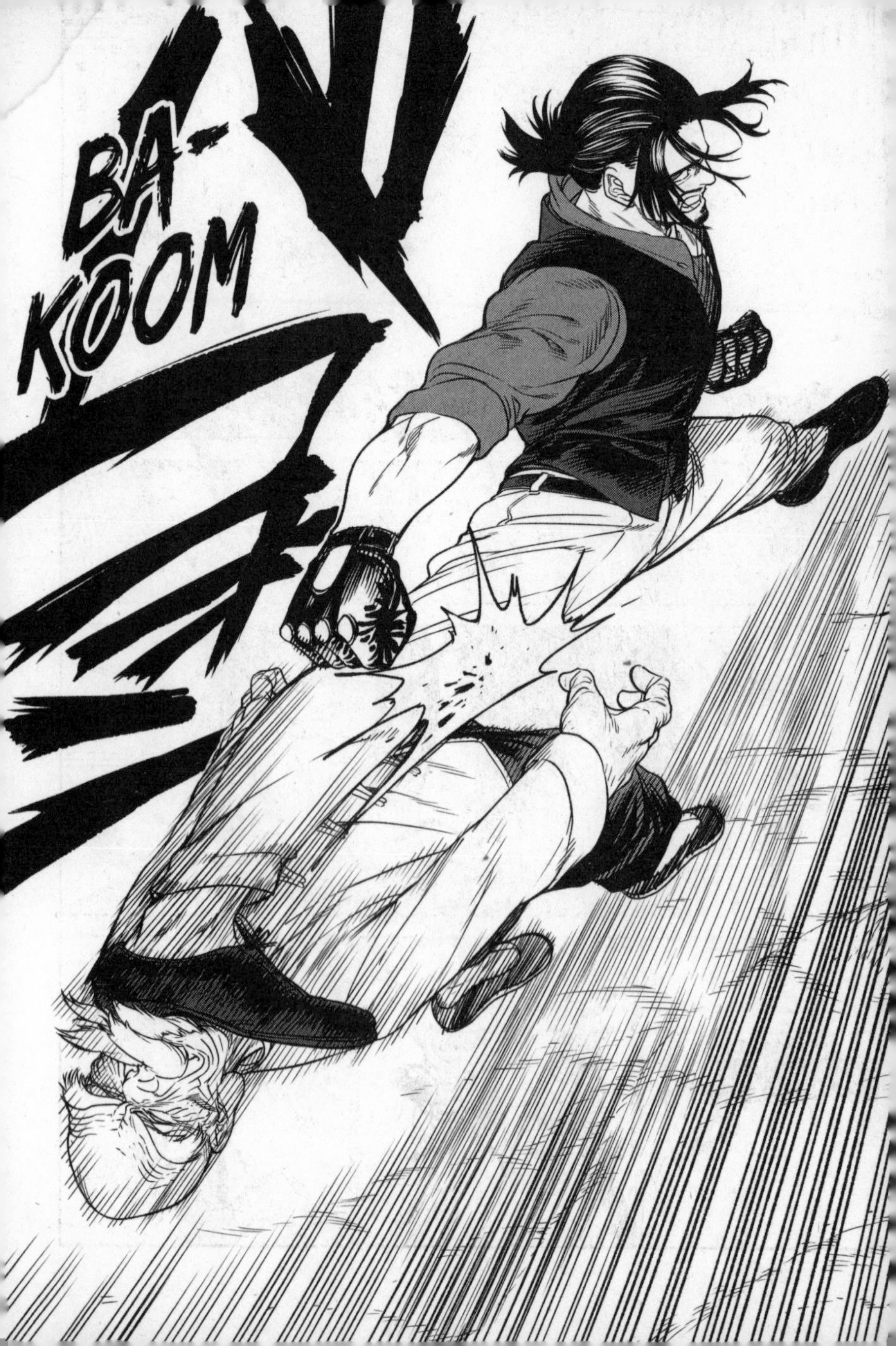
BA-KOOM

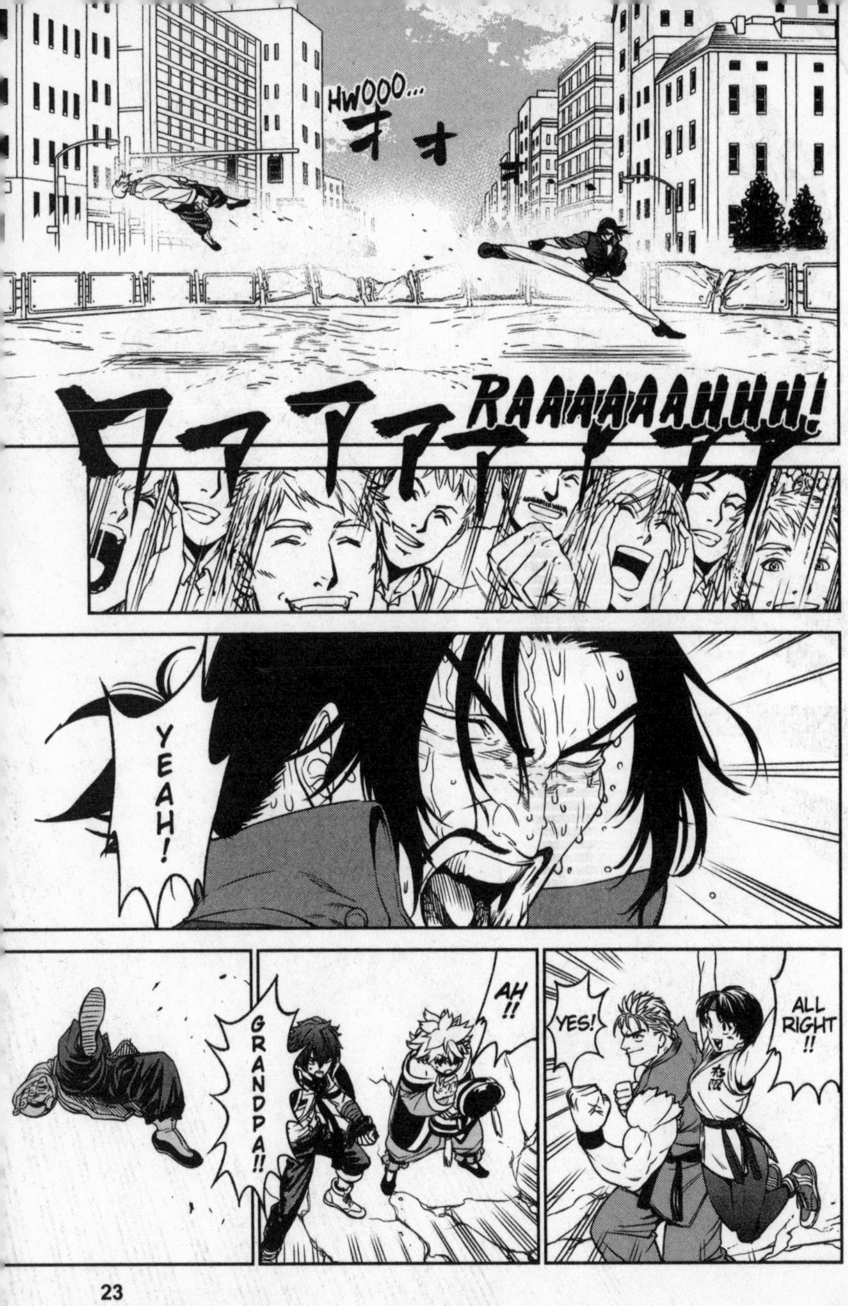
HWOOO...
オオ
RAAAAAAHHH!
YEAH!
ALL RIGHT!!
YES!
AH!!
GRANDPA!!

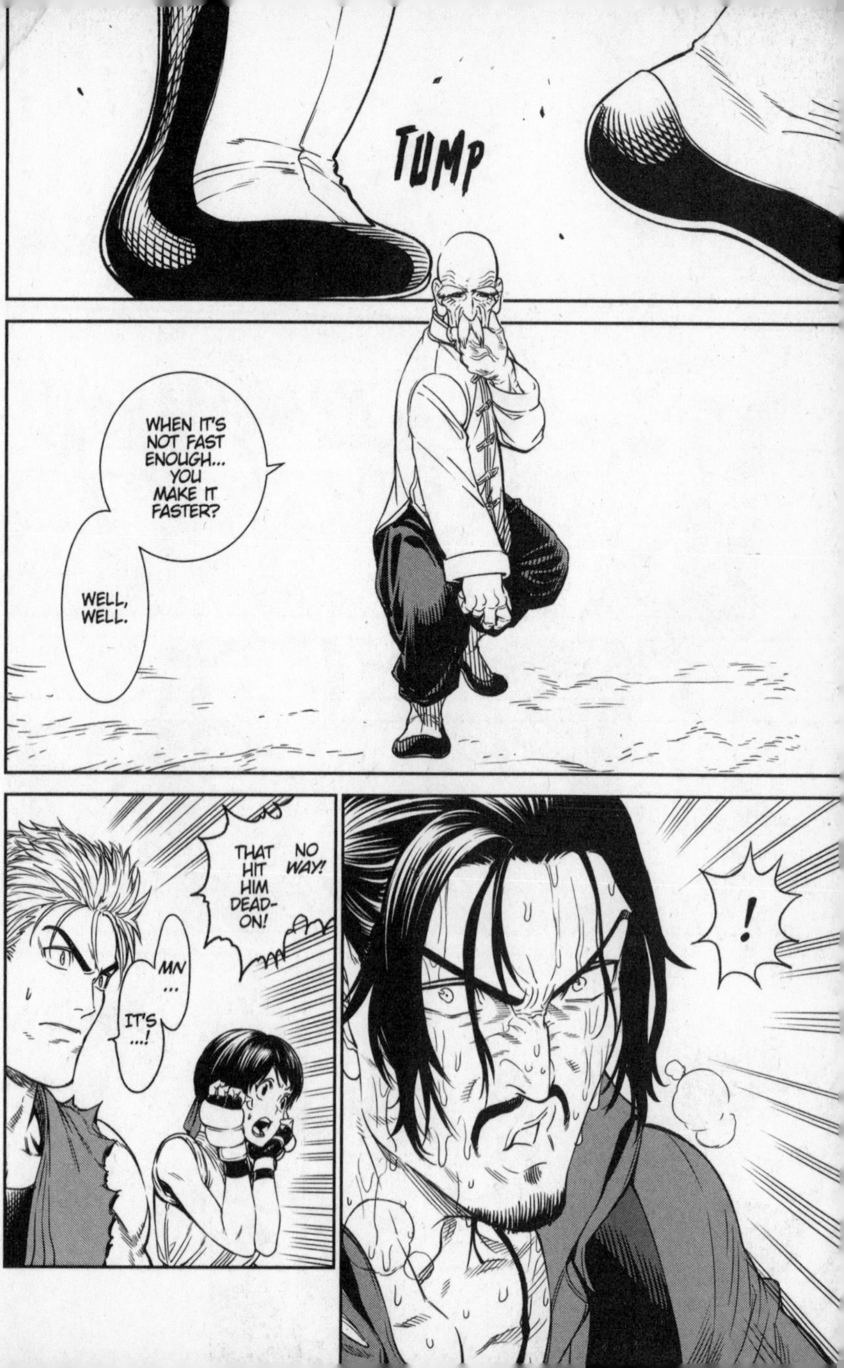
TUMP
WHEN IT'S NOT FAST ENOUGH... YOU MAKE IT FASTER?
WELL, WELL.
!
NO WAY!
THAT HIT HIM DEAD-ON!
MN... IT'S...!

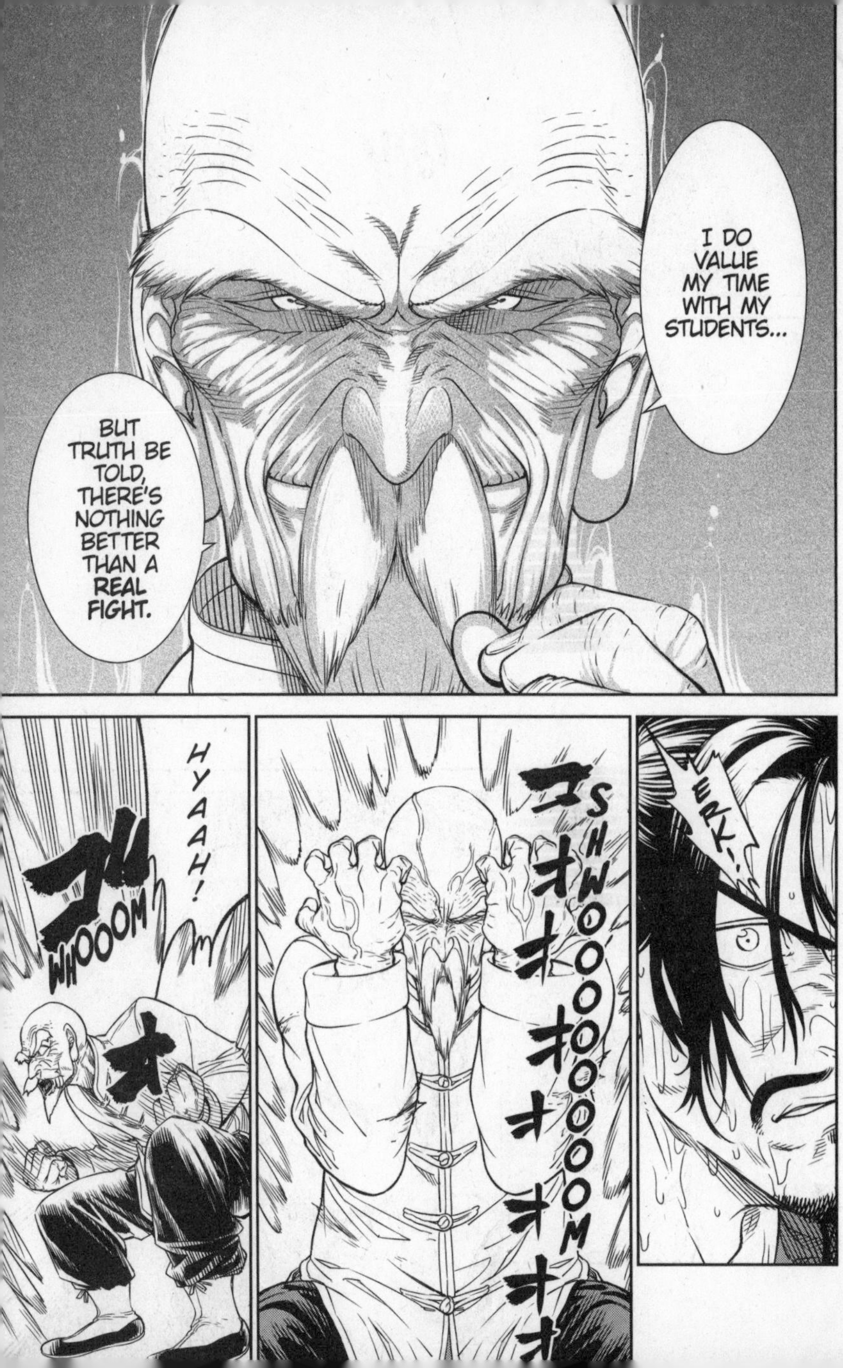
I DO VALUE MY TIME WITH MY STUDENTS...
BUT TRUTH BE TOLD, THERE'S NOTHING BETTER THAN A REAL FIGHT.
ERK...!
SHWOOOOOOOOOOOM
HYAAAH!
WHOOOM

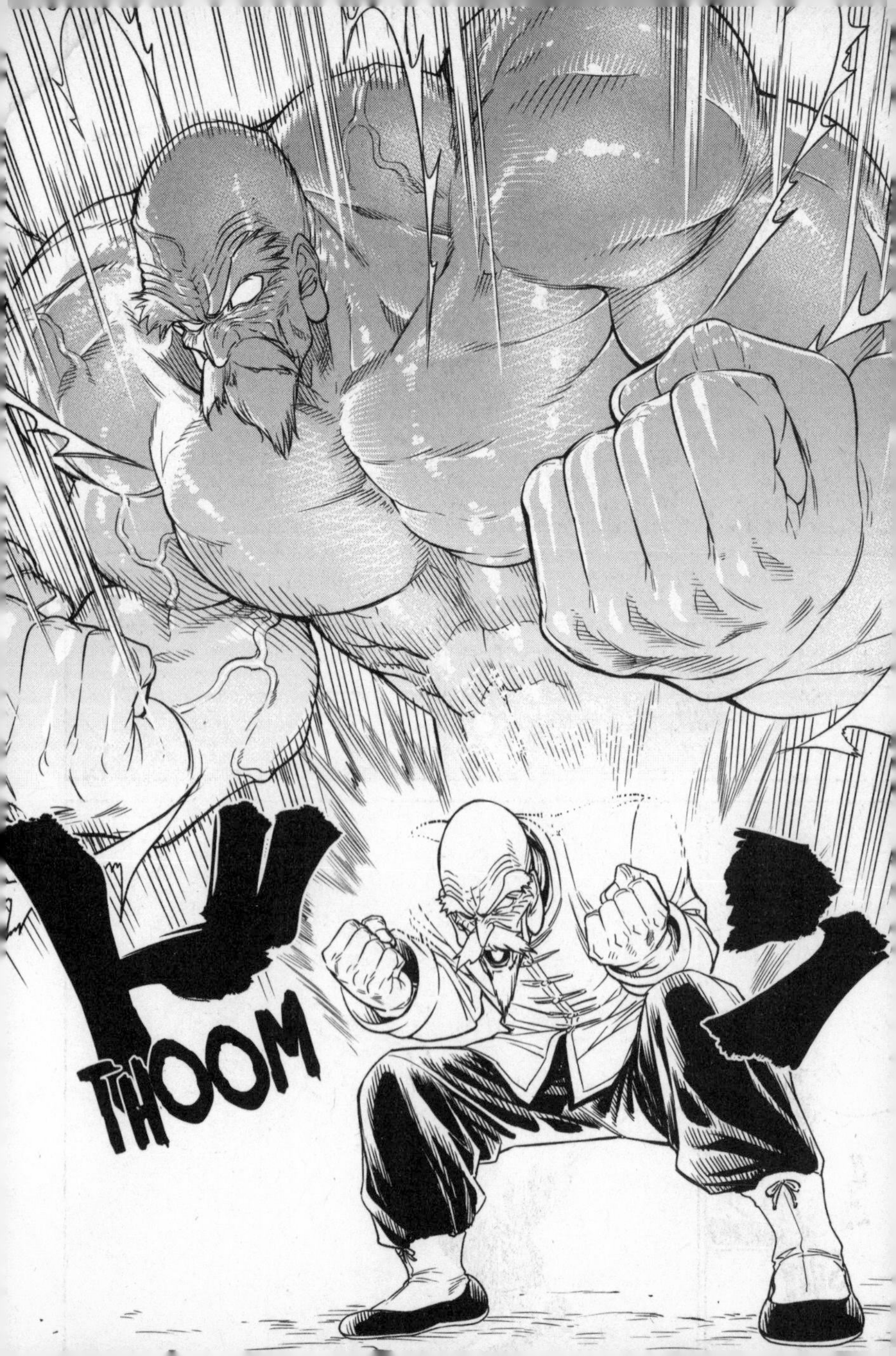
THOOM

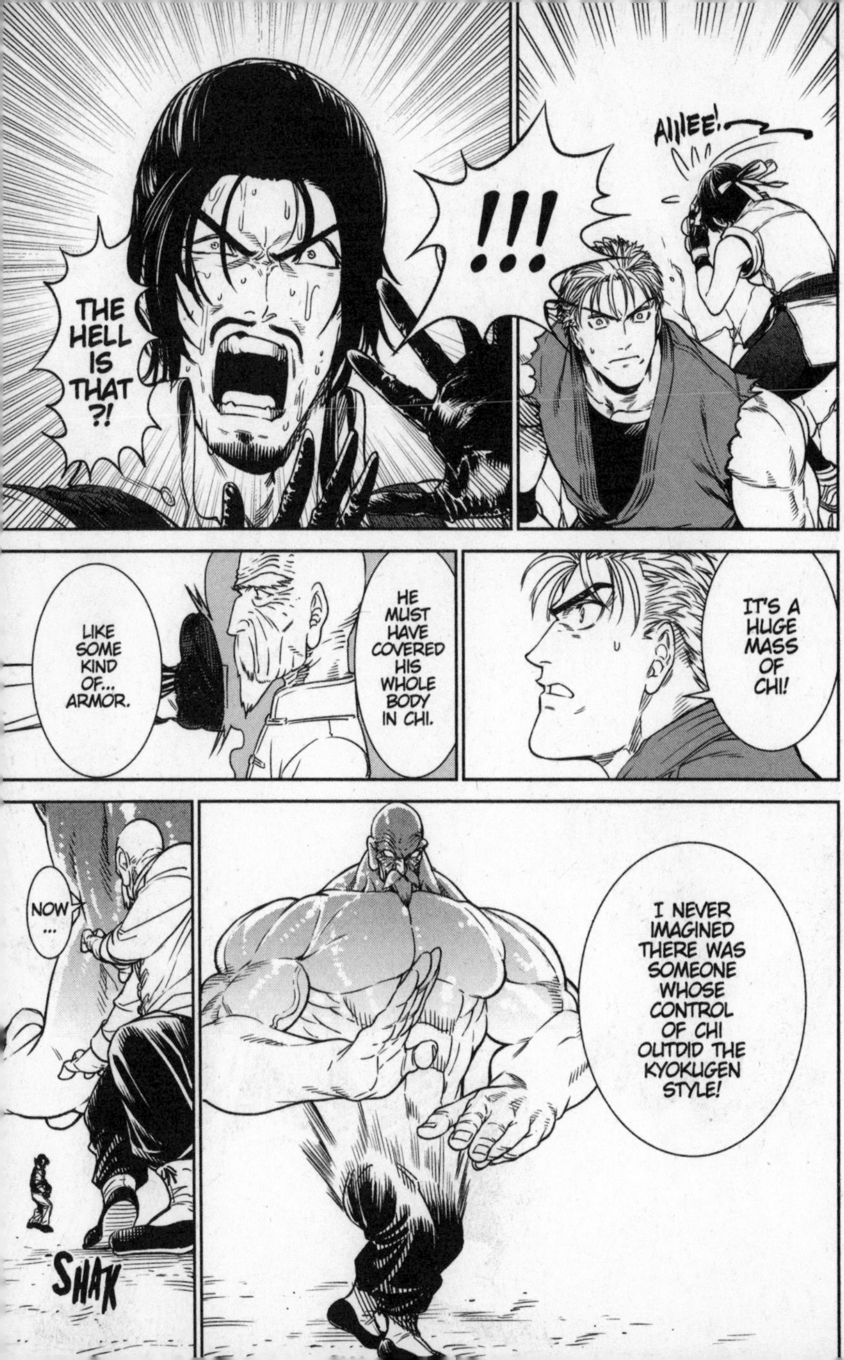
AIIIEE!
!!!
THE HELL IS THAT?!
IT'S A HUGE MASS OF CHI!
HE MUST HAVE COVERED HIS WHOLE BODY IN CHI.
LIKE SOME KIND OF... ARMOR.
I NEVER IMAGINED THERE WAS SOMEONE WHOSE CONTROL OF CHI OUTDID THE KYOKUGEN STYLE!
NOW...
SHAK

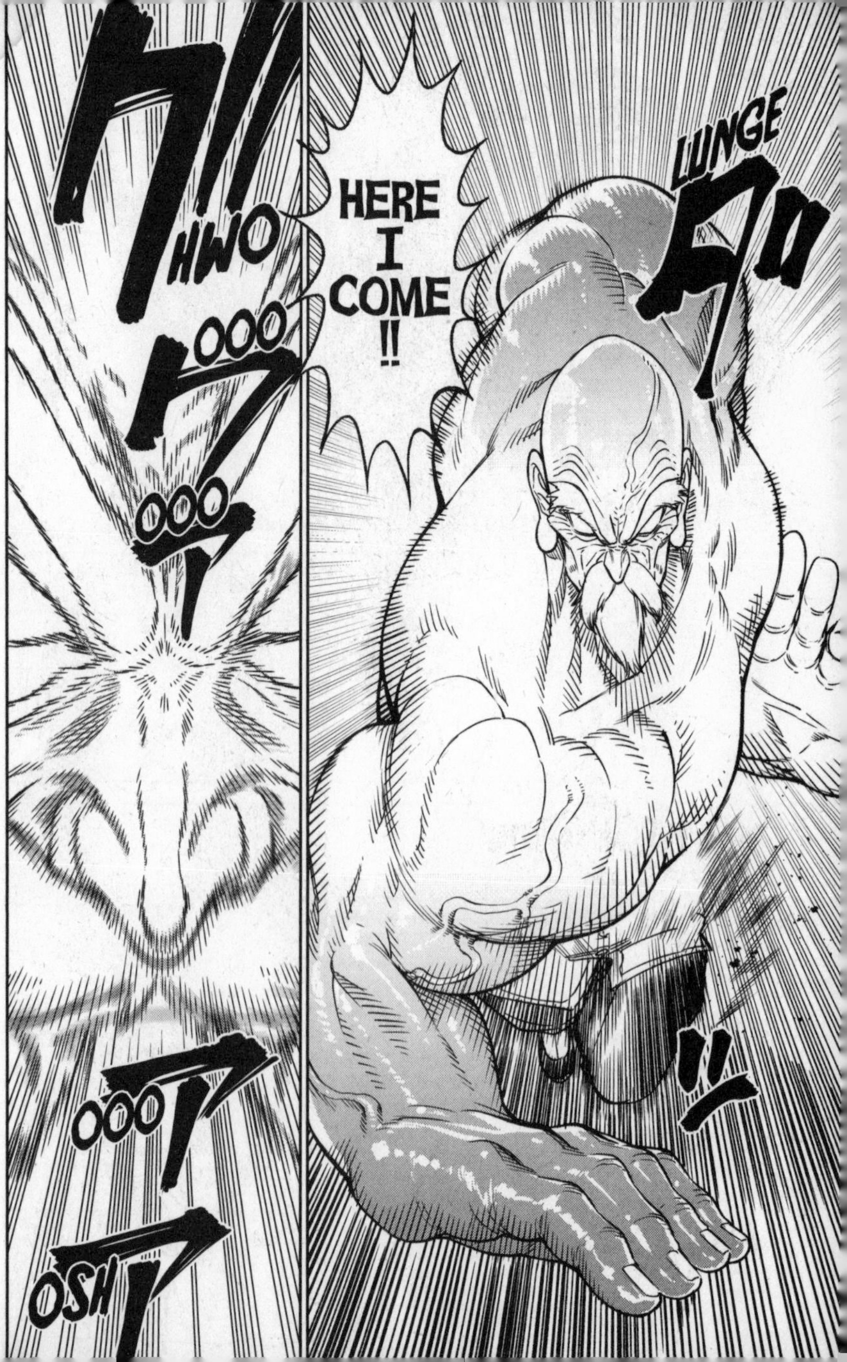
HERE I COME!!
LUNGE
HWO
OOO
OOO
OOO
OSH

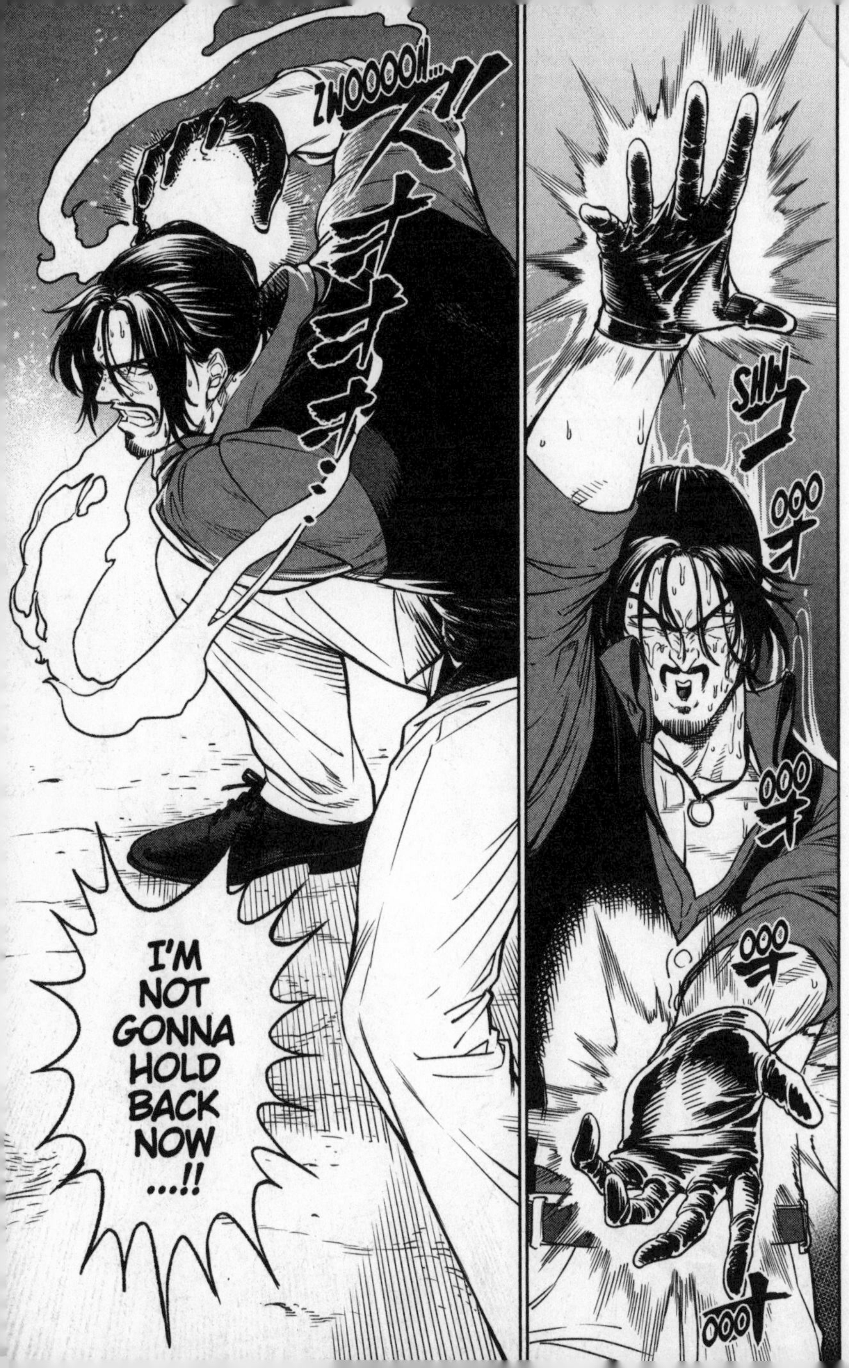
SHW
ooo
ooo
ooo
ooo
ZWOOOOH...!!
I'M NOT GONNA HOLD BACK NOW ...!!

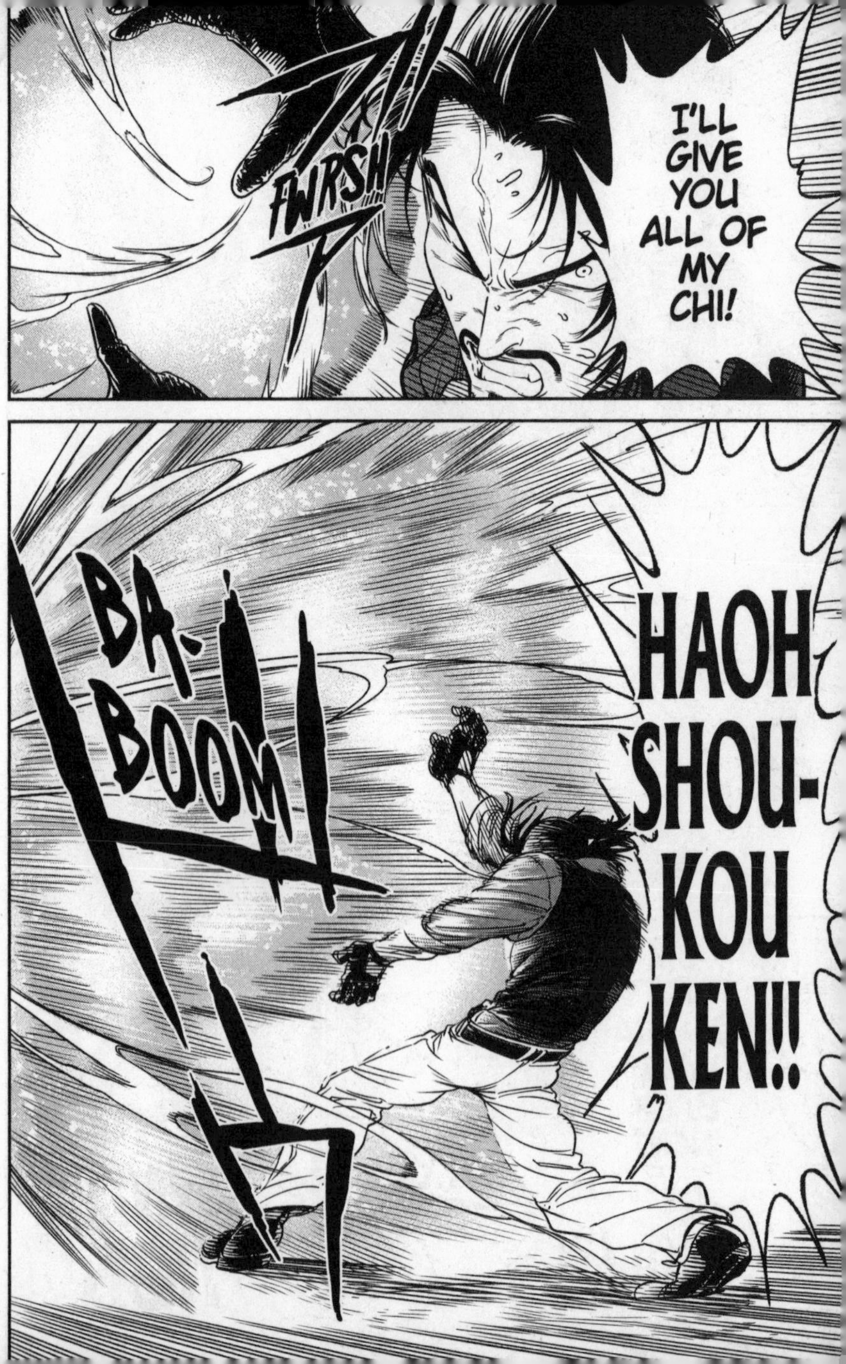
I'LL GIVE YOU ALL OF MY CHI!
FWRSH
HAOH SHOU-KOU KEN!!
BA-BOOM!

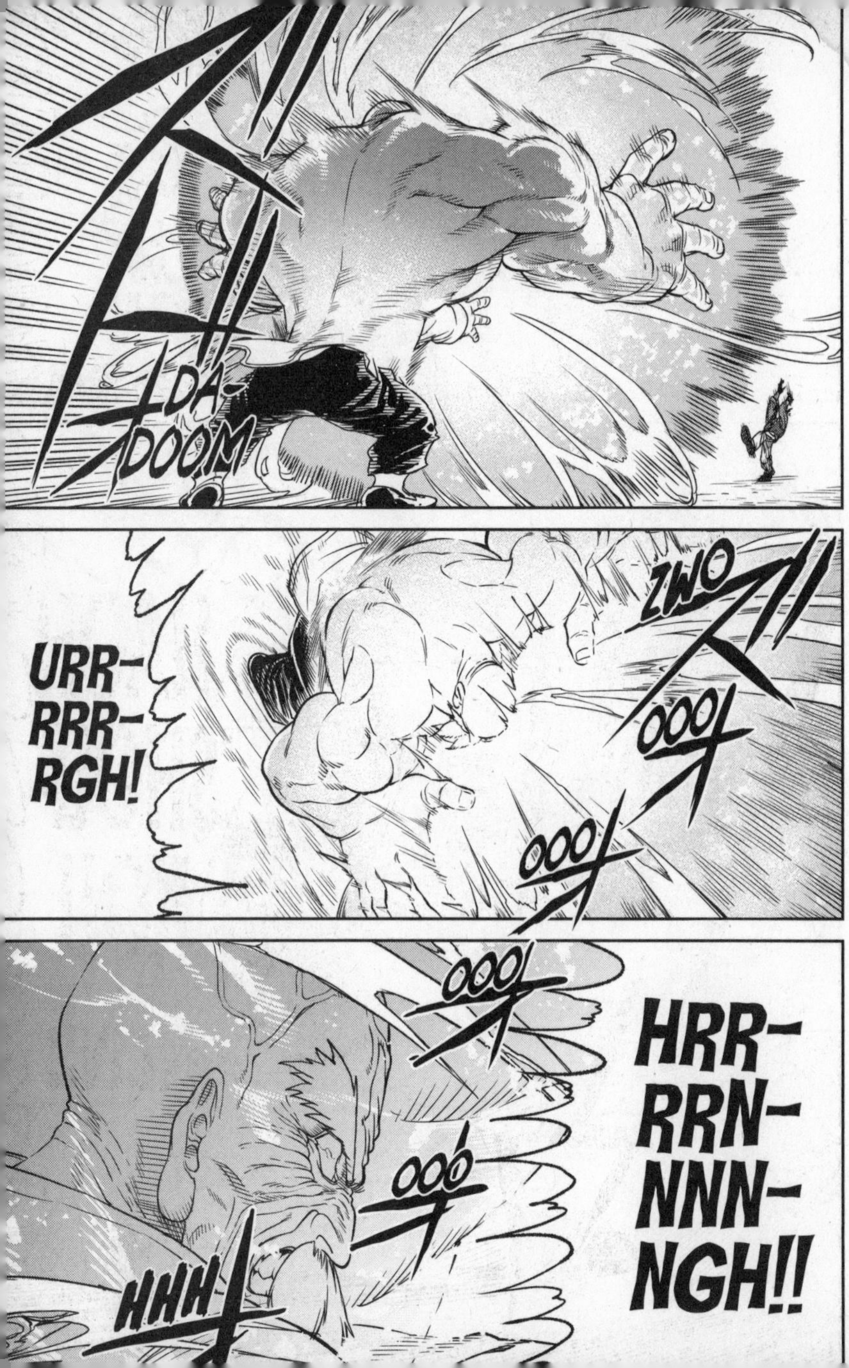
DA-DOOM
ZWO
OOO
OOO
URR-RRR-RGH!
HRR-RRN-NNN-NGH!!
OOO
OOO
HHH

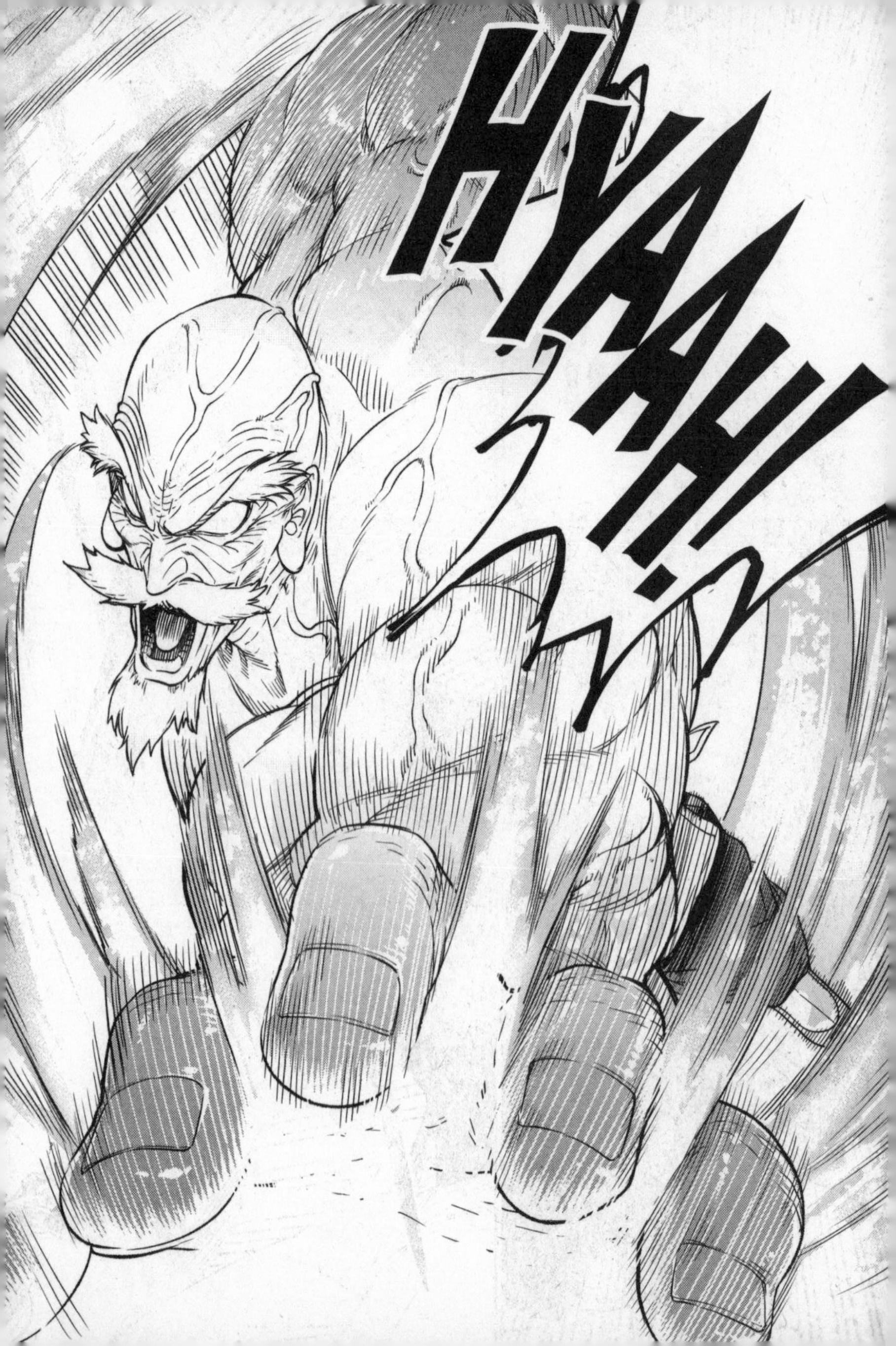
HYAAH!!

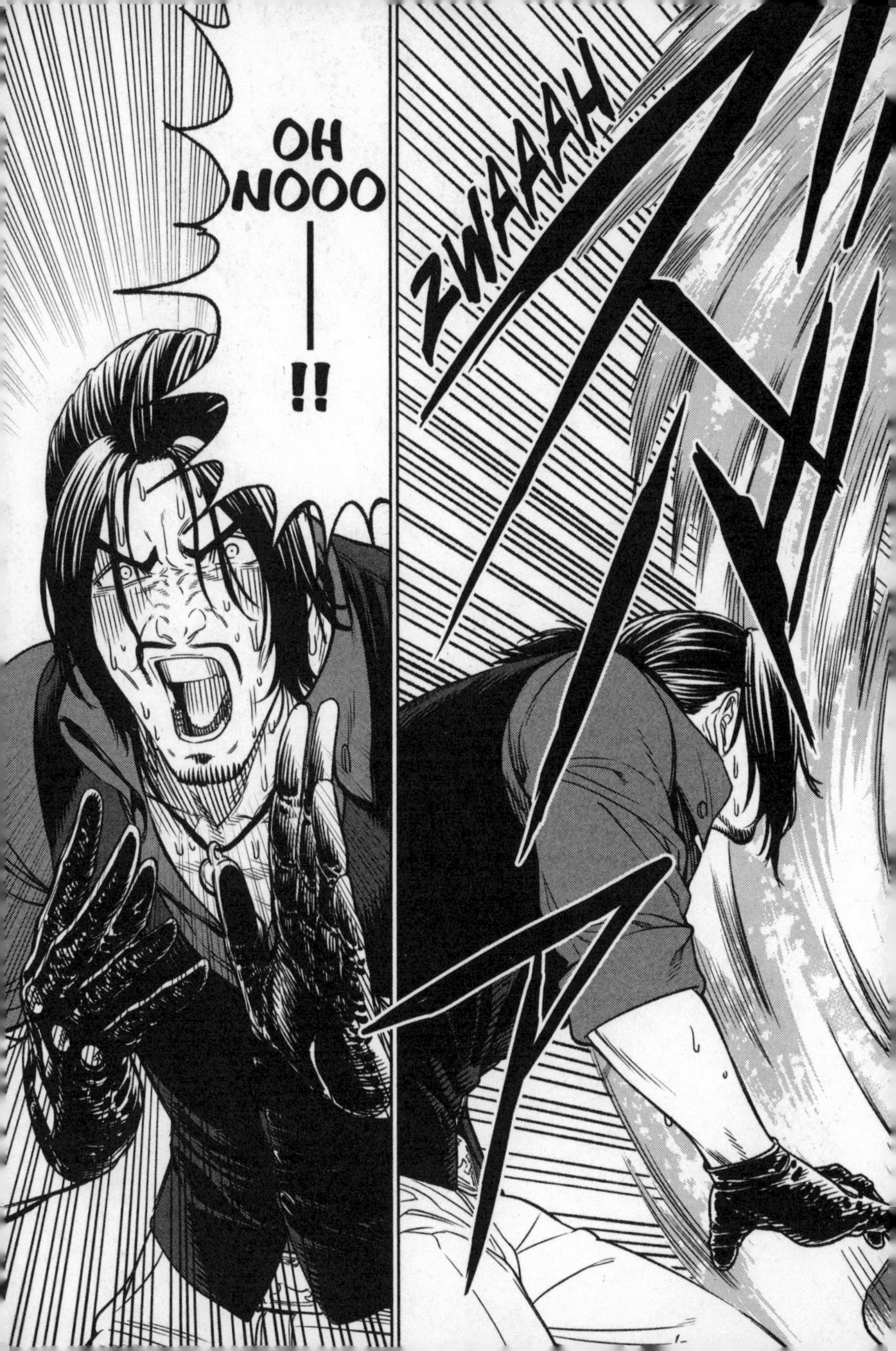
ZWAAAH
OH NOOO—!!

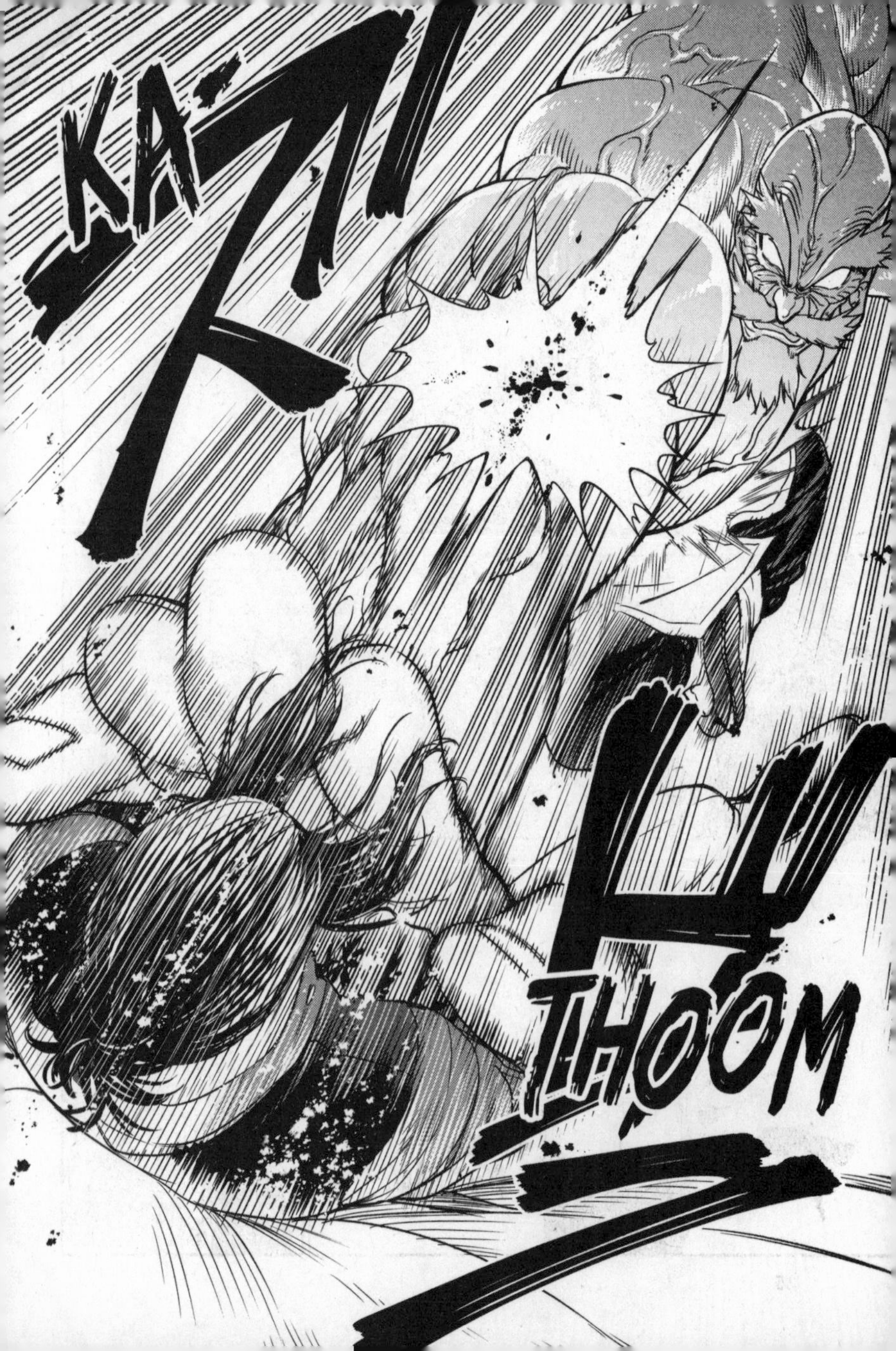
KA-
THOOM

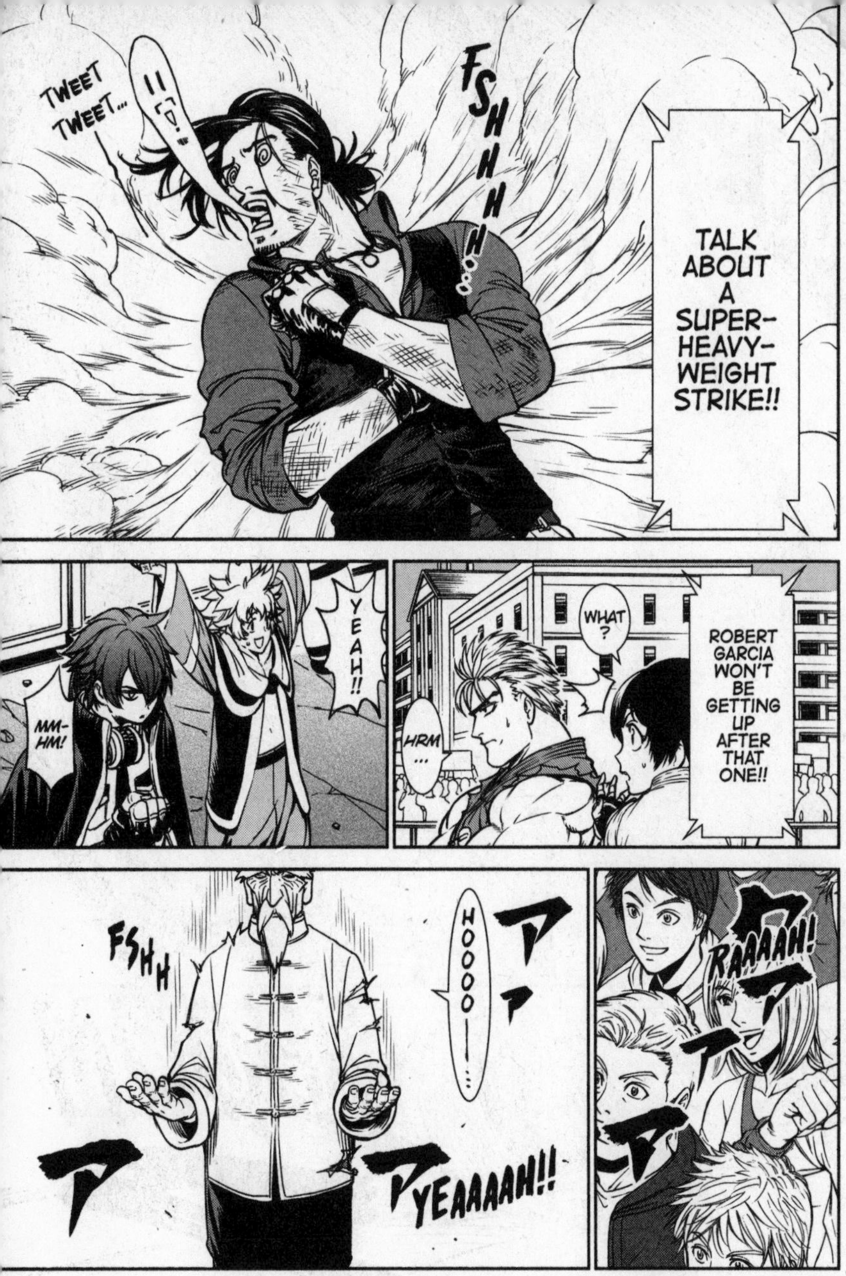
TALK ABOUT A SUPER-HEAVY-WEIGHT STRIKE!!
FSHHHHH...
!!?
TWEET TWEET...
ROBERT GARCIA WON'T BE GETTING UP AFTER THAT ONE!!
WHAT?
HRM...
YEAH!!
MM-HM!
RAAAAH!
HOOOO—...!
FSHH
YEAAAAH!!

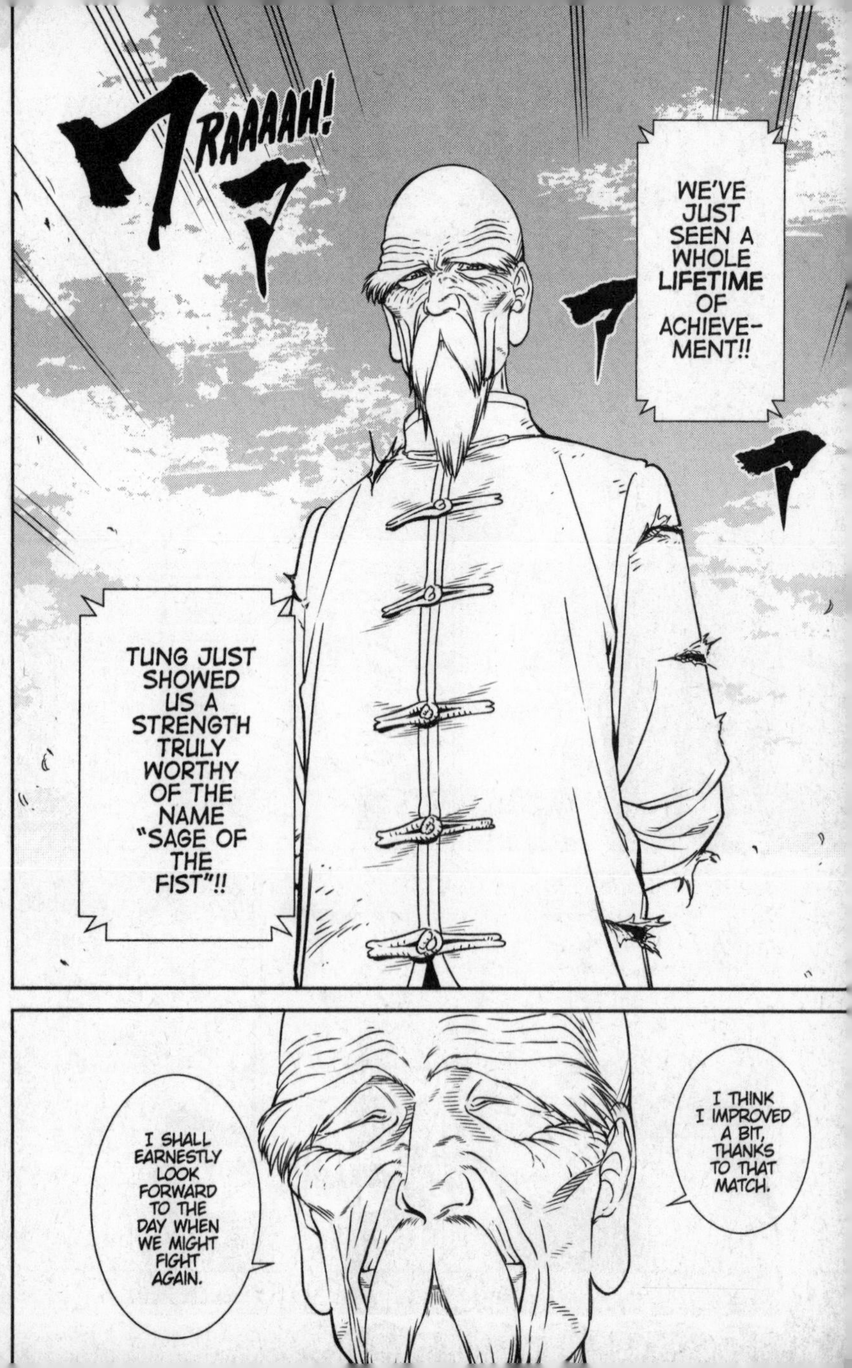
WE'VE JUST SEEN A WHOLE LIFETIME OF ACHIEVE-MENT!!
RAAAAH!
TUNG JUST SHOWED US A STRENGTH TRULY WORTHY OF THE NAME "SAGE OF THE FIST"!!
I THINK I IMPROVED A BIT, THANKS TO THAT MATCH.
I SHALL EARNESTLY LOOK FORWARD TO THE DAY WHEN WE MIGHT FIGHT AGAIN.

MOVE LIST

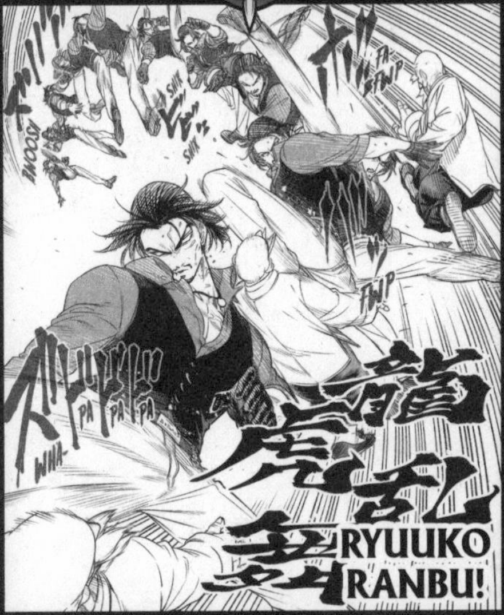

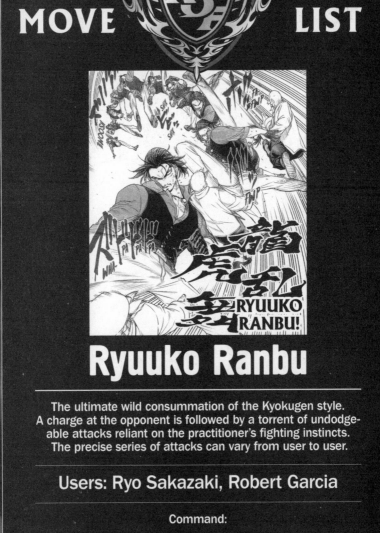

龍虎乱舞
RYUUKO RANBU!
WHA-
PA PA PA PA

Ryuuko Ranbu

The ultimate wild consummation of the Kyokugen style. A charge at the opponent is followed by a torrent of undodgeable attacks reliant on the practitioner's fighting instincts. The precise series of attacks can vary from user to user.

Users: Ryo Sakazaki, Robert Garcia

Command:

↓↘→↘↓↙← + LP or HP

MOVE LIST

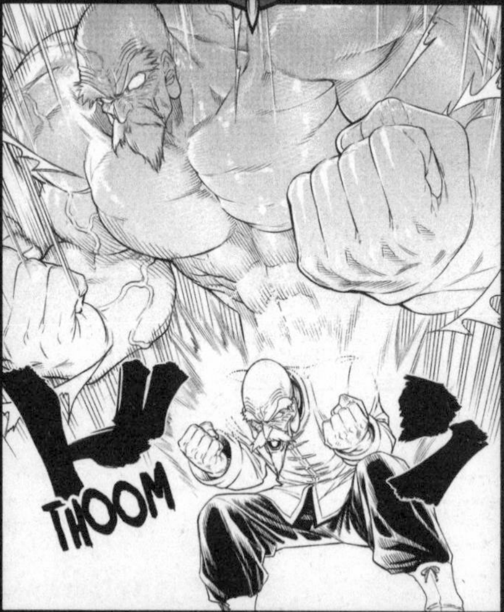
THOOM

Kyoku · Koureishin

Covers the body with a mass of chi, enacting a transformation into a brawny giant. The ultimate art of Hakkyokuseiken, exclusive to Tung, who has been working to refine his chi for years and years. Improves speed, power, and defense explosively.

User: Tung Fu Rue

Command:

↓↘→↓↘→ + LP + HP

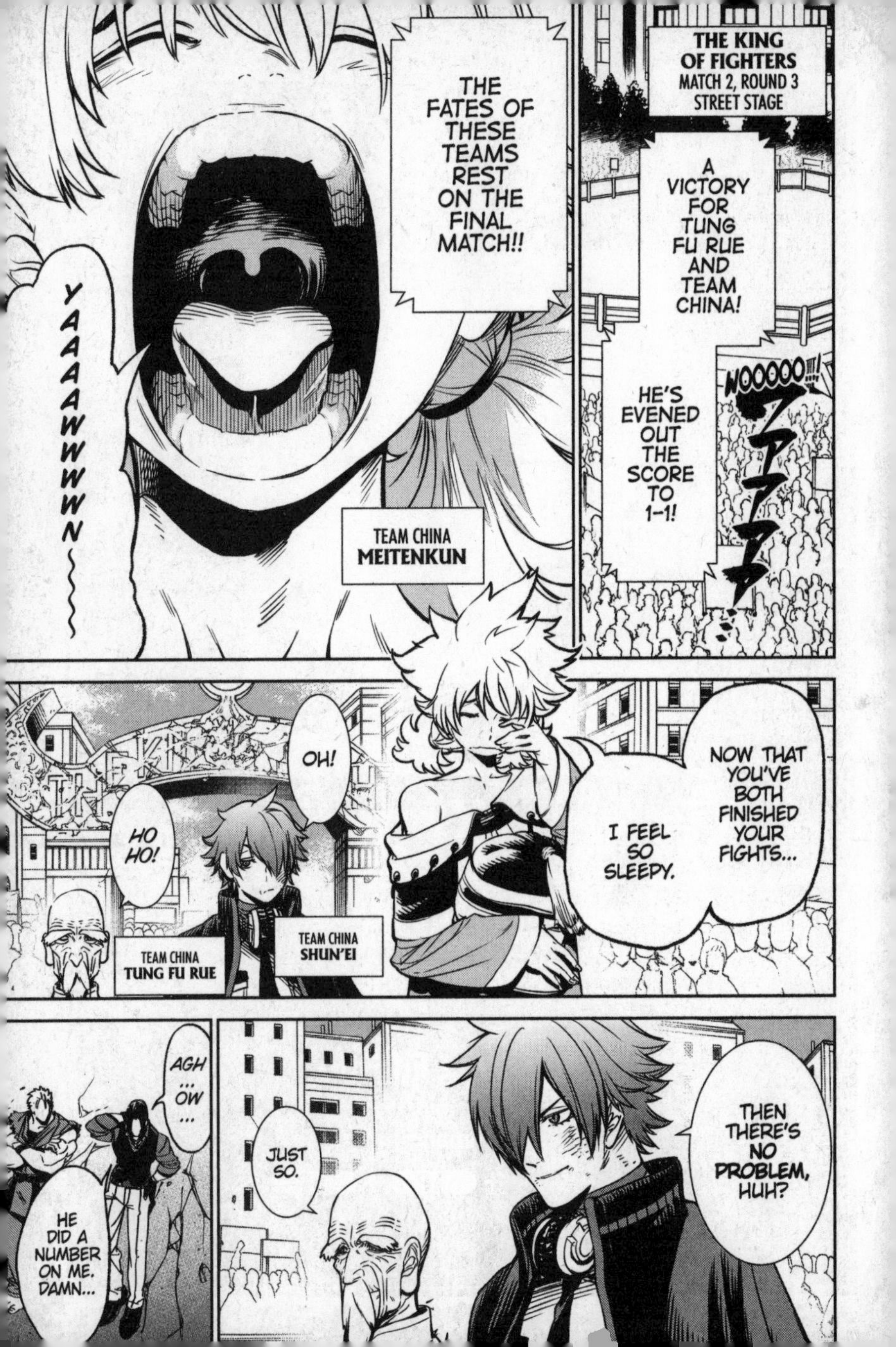
THE KING OF FIGHTERS
MATCH 2, ROUND 3
STREET STAGE
A VICTORY FOR TUNG FU RUE AND TEAM CHINA!
HE'S EVENED OUT THE SCORE TO 1-1!
WOOOOO!!!
THE FATES OF THESE TEAMS REST ON THE FINAL MATCH!!
TEAM CHINA
MEITENKUN
YAAAAAWWWWWN~~~
NOW THAT YOU'VE BOTH FINISHED YOUR FIGHTS...
I FEEL SO SLEEPY.
OH!
HO HO!
TEAM CHINA
SHUN'EI
TEAM CHINA
TUNG FU RUE
THEN THERE'S NO PROBLEM, HUH?
JUST SO.
AGH... OW...
HE DID A NUMBER ON ME. DAMN...

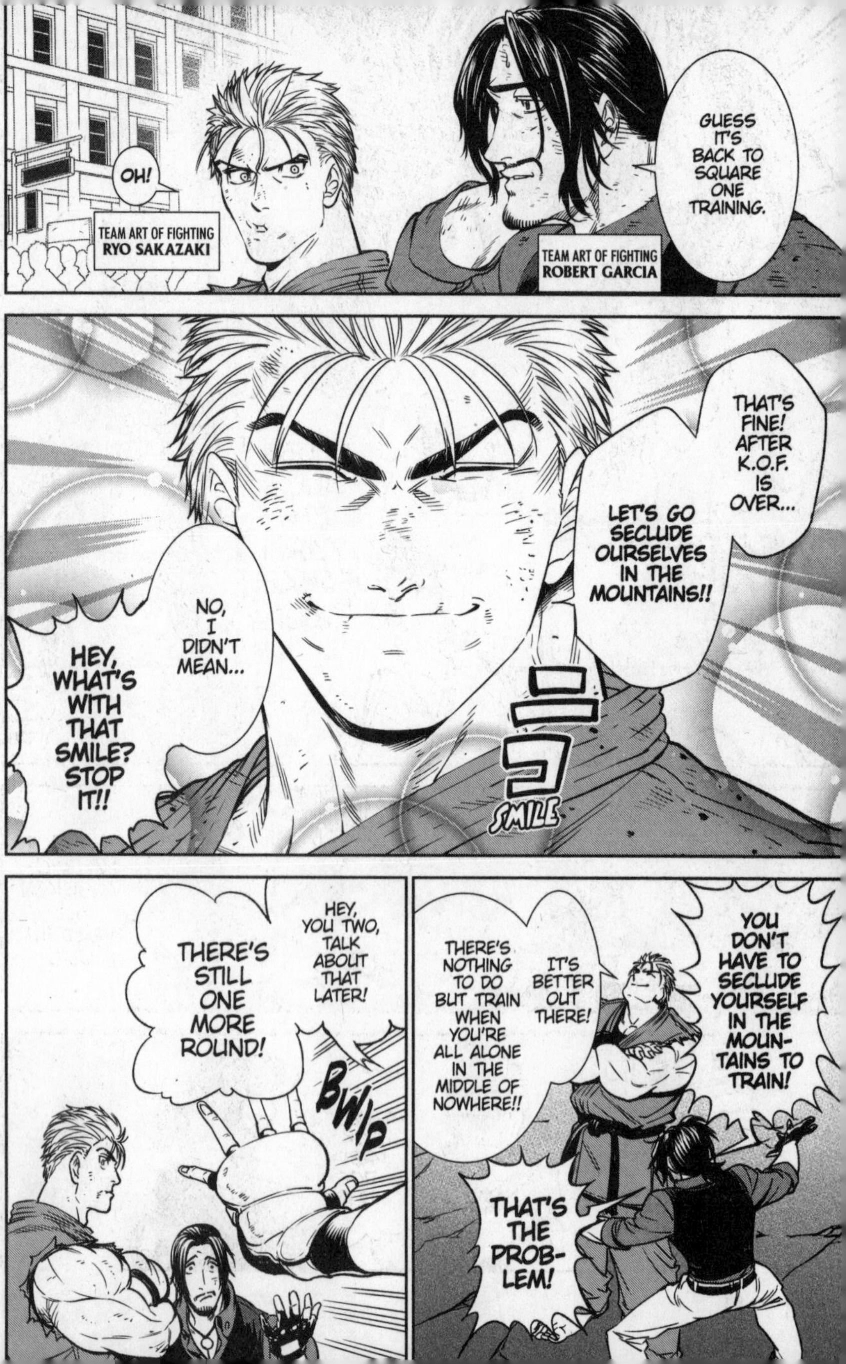
GUESS IT'S BACK TO SQUARE ONE TRAINING.
TEAM ART OF FIGHTING ROBERT GARCIA
OH!
TEAM ART OF FIGHTING RYO SAKAZAKI
THAT'S FINE! AFTER K.O.F. IS OVER...
LET'S GO SECLUDE OURSELVES IN THE MOUNTAINS!!
SMILE
NO, I DIDN'T MEAN...
HEY, WHAT'S WITH THAT SMILE? STOP IT!!
YOU DON'T HAVE TO SECLUDE YOURSELF IN THE MOUN-TAINS TO TRAIN!
IT'S BETTER OUT THERE!
THERE'S NOTHING TO DO BUT TRAIN WHEN YOU'RE ALL ALONE IN THE MIDDLE OF NOWHERE!!
THAT'S THE PROB-LEM!
HEY, YOU TWO, TALK ABOUT THAT LATER!
BWIP
THERE'S STILL ONE MORE ROUND!

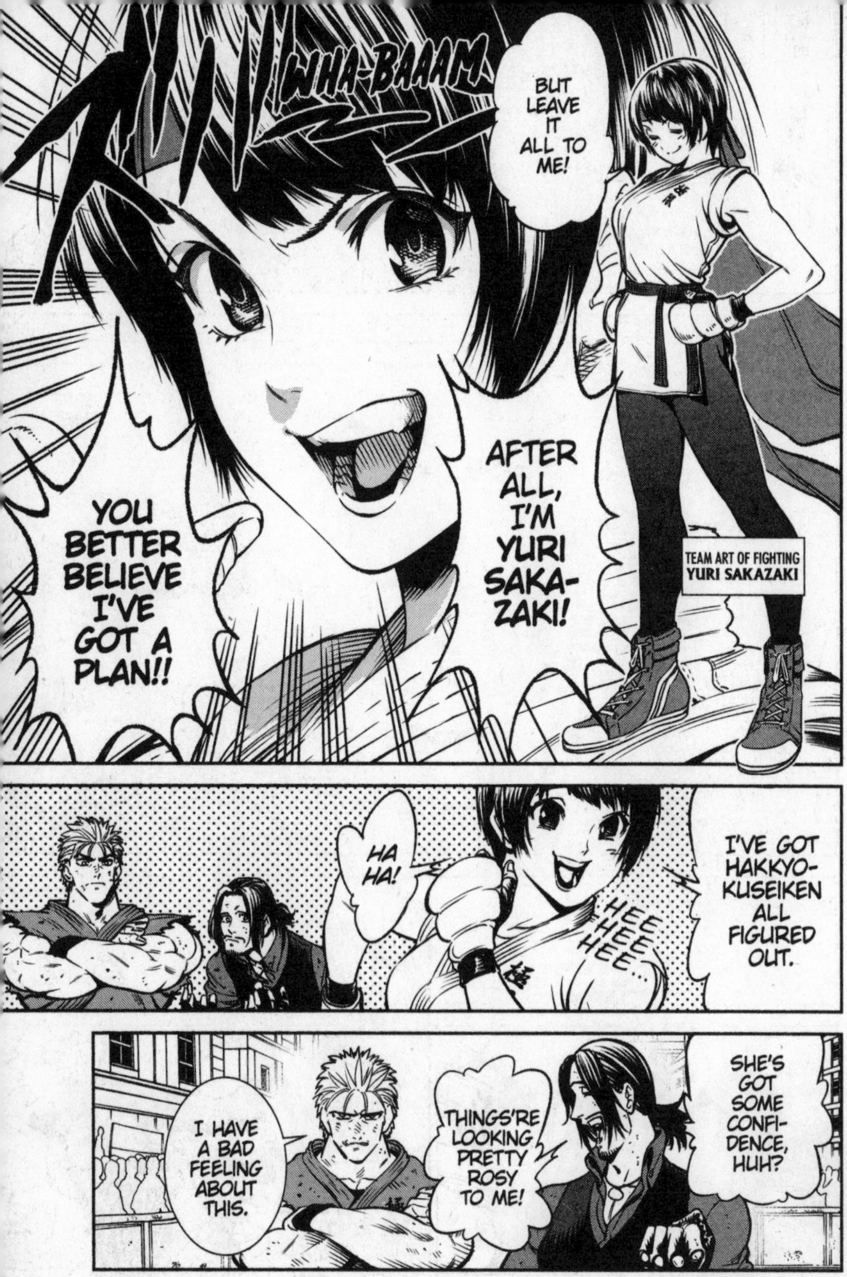
BUT LEAVE IT ALL TO ME!
WHA-BAAAM
AFTER ALL, I'M YURI SAKAZAKI!
TEAM ART OF FIGHTING YURI SAKAZAKI
YOU BETTER BELIEVE I'VE GOT A PLAN!!
I'VE GOT HAKKYO-KUSEIKEN ALL FIGURED OUT.
HEE HEE HEE...
HA HA!
SHE'S GOT SOME CONFI-DENCE, HUH?
THINGS'RE LOOKING PRETTY ROSY TO ME!
I HAVE A BAD FEELING ABOUT THIS.

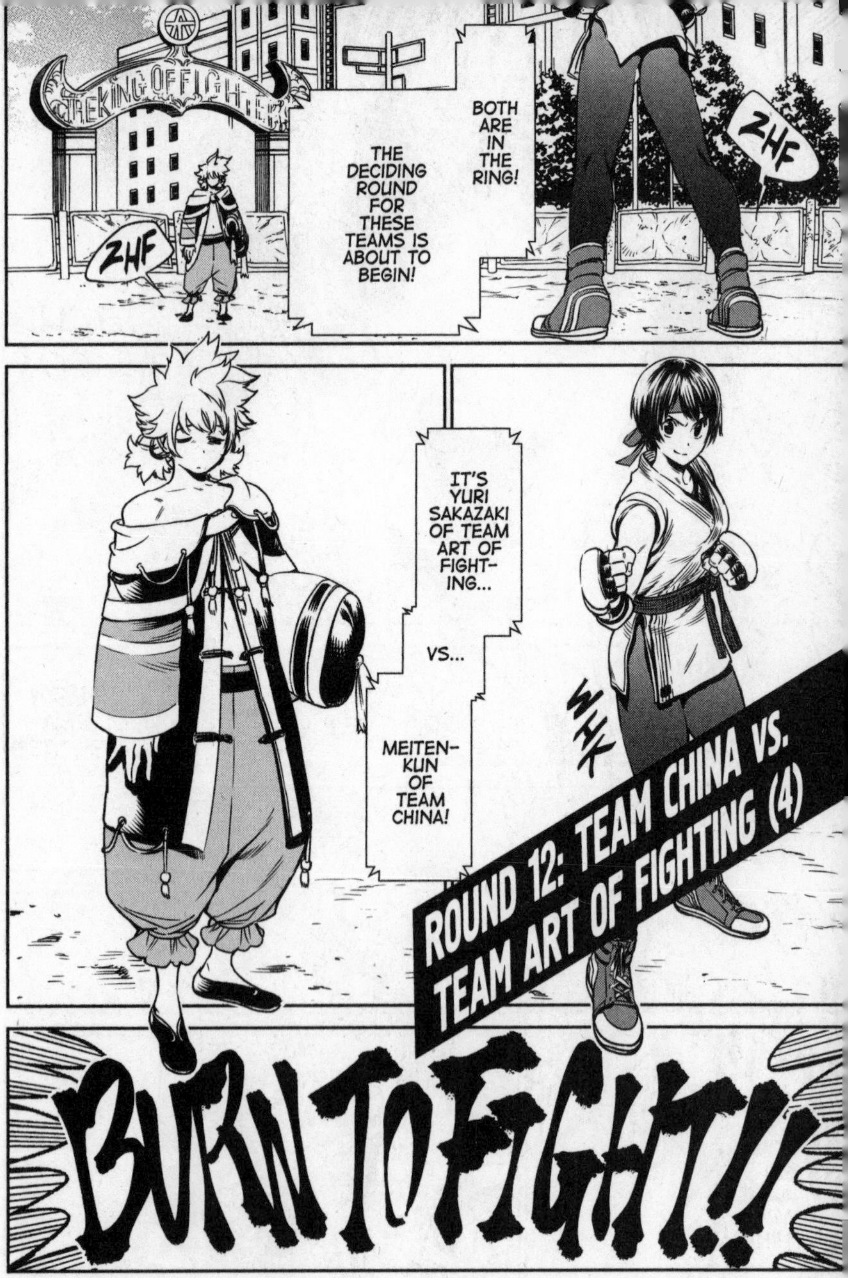
ZHF
BOTH ARE IN THE RING!
THE DECIDING ROUND FOR THESE TEAMS IS ABOUT TO BEGIN!
ZHF
IT'S YURI SAKAZAKI OF TEAM ART OF FIGHTING...
VS...
MEITEN-KUN OF TEAM CHINA!
ROUND 12: TEAM CHINA VS. TEAM ART OF FIGHTING (4)
BURN TO FIGHT!!

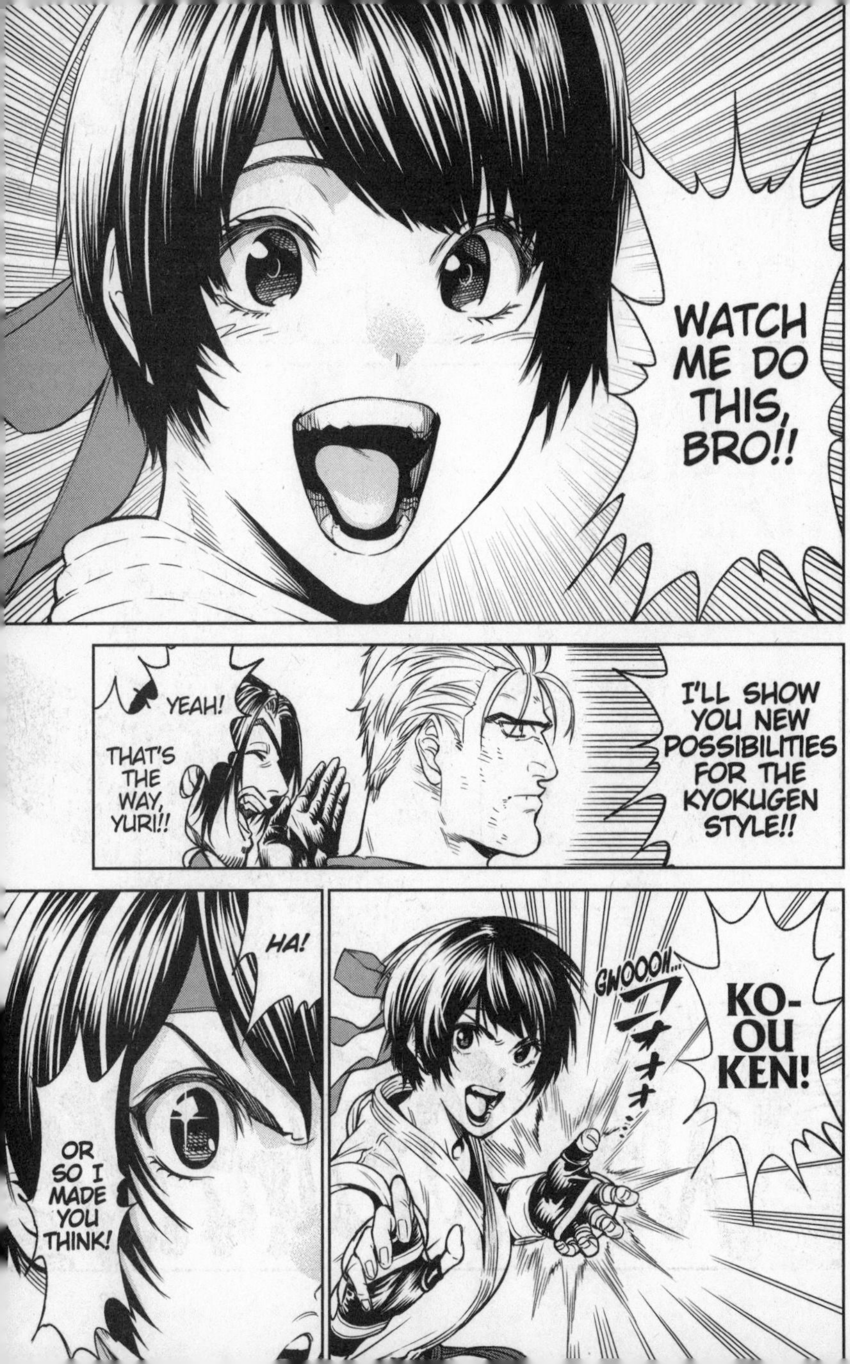
WATCH ME DO THIS, BRO!!
I'LL SHOW YOU NEW POSSIBILITIES FOR THE KYOKUGEN STYLE!!
YEAH!
THAT'S THE WAY, YURI!!
KO-OU KEN!
GWOOOH...
HA!
OR SO I MADE YOU THINK!

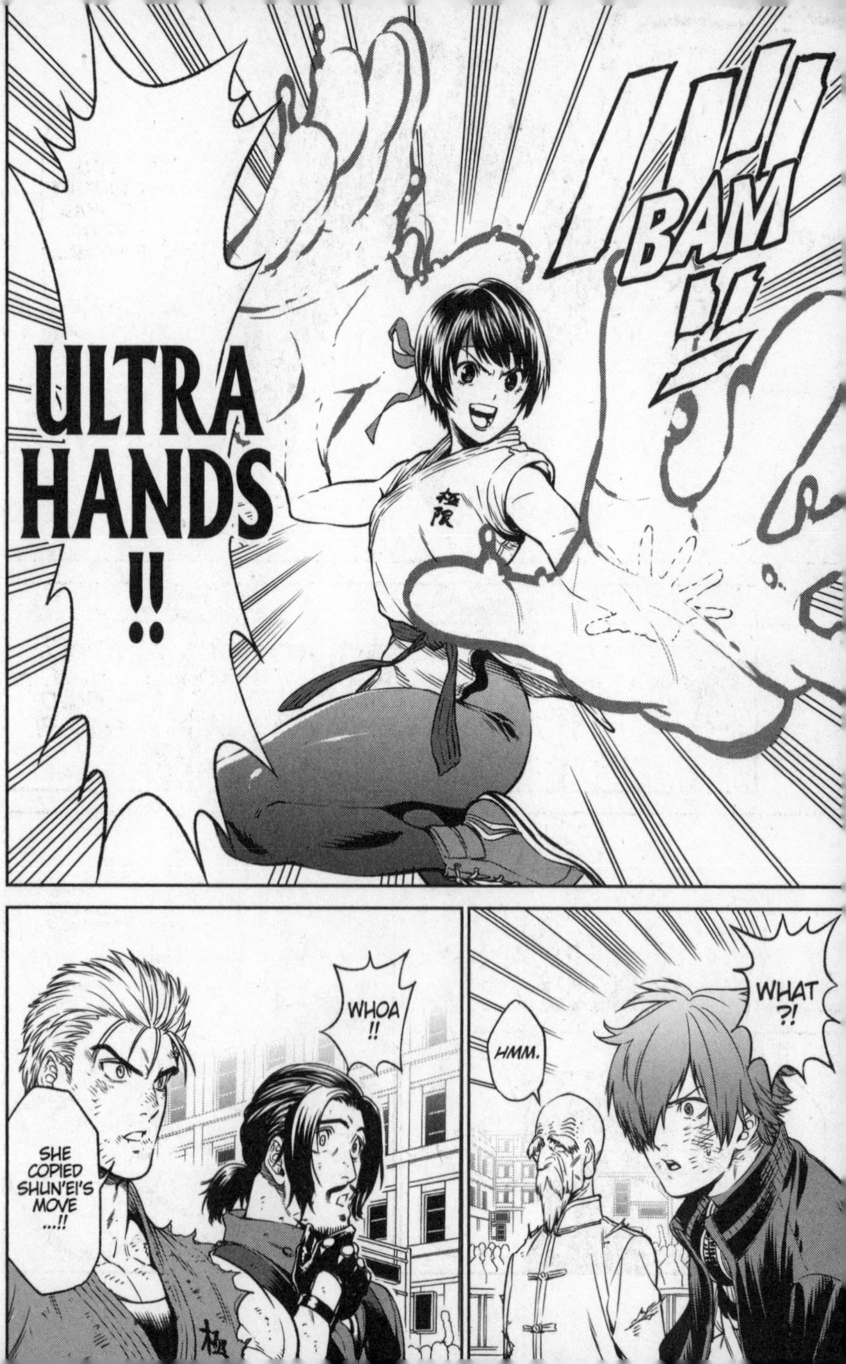
BAM!!
ULTRA HANDS!!
WHAT?!
HMM.
WHOA!!
SHE COPIED SHUN'EI'S MOVE ...!!

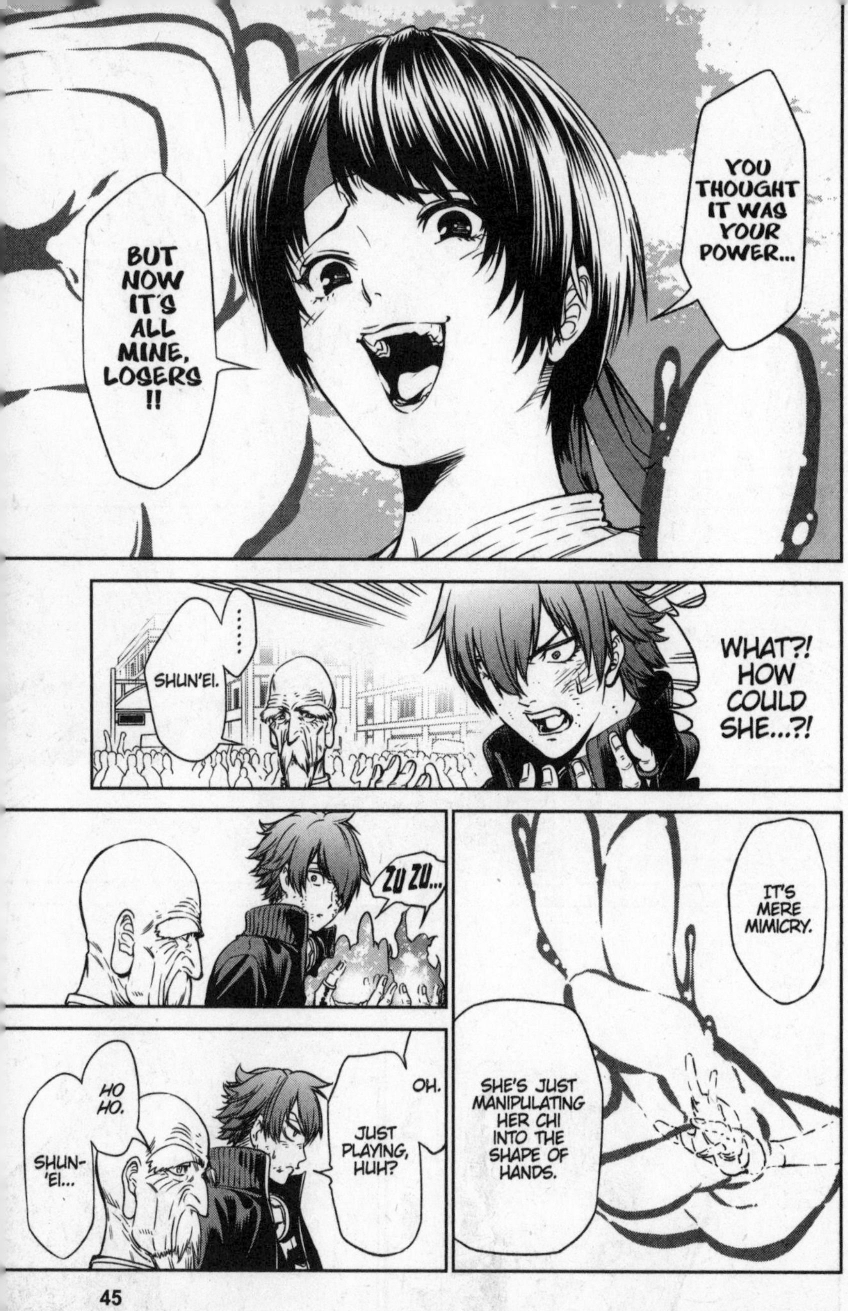
YOU THOUGHT IT WAS YOUR POWER...
BUT NOW IT'S ALL MINE, LOSERS!!
WHAT?! HOW COULD SHE...?!
......
SHUN'EI.
IT'S MERE MIMICRY.
SHE'S JUST MANIPULATING HER CHI INTO THE SHAPE OF HANDS.
ZU ZU...
OH.
JUST PLAYING, HUH?
HO HO.
SHUN-'EI...

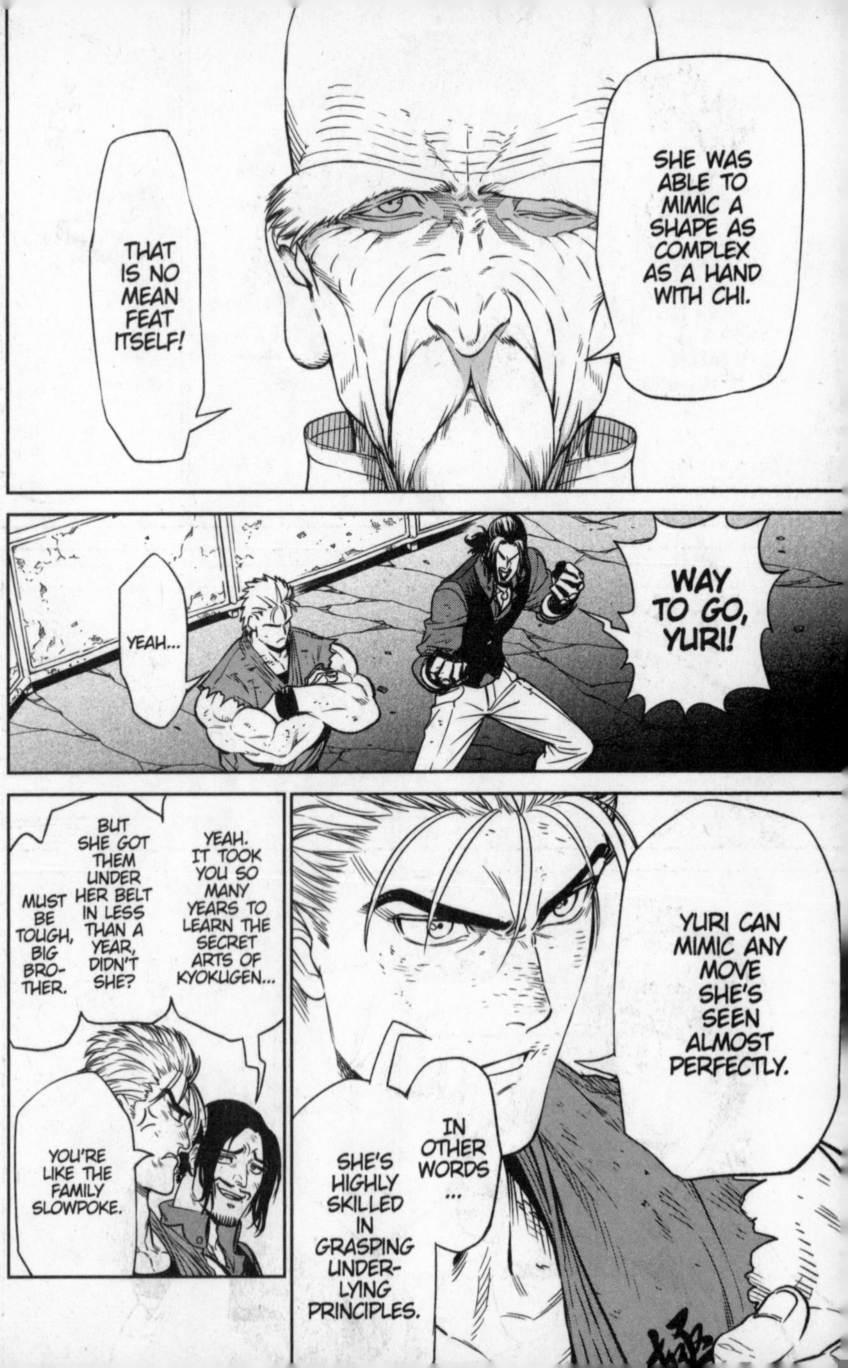
SHE WAS ABLE TO MIMIC A SHAPE AS COMPLEX AS A HAND WITH CHI.
THAT IS NO MEAN FEAT ITSELF!
WAY TO GO, YURI!
YEAH...
YURI CAN MIMIC ANY MOVE SHE'S SEEN ALMOST PERFECTLY.
IN OTHER WORDS...
SHE'S HIGHLY SKILLED IN GRASPING UNDERLYING PRINCIPLES.
YEAH. IT TOOK YOU SO MANY YEARS TO LEARN THE SECRET ARTS OF KYOKUGEN...
BUT SHE GOT THEM UNDER HER BELT IN LESS THAN A YEAR, DIDN'T SHE?
MUST BE TOUGH, BIG BROTHER.
YOU'RE LIKE THE FAMILY SLOWPOKE.

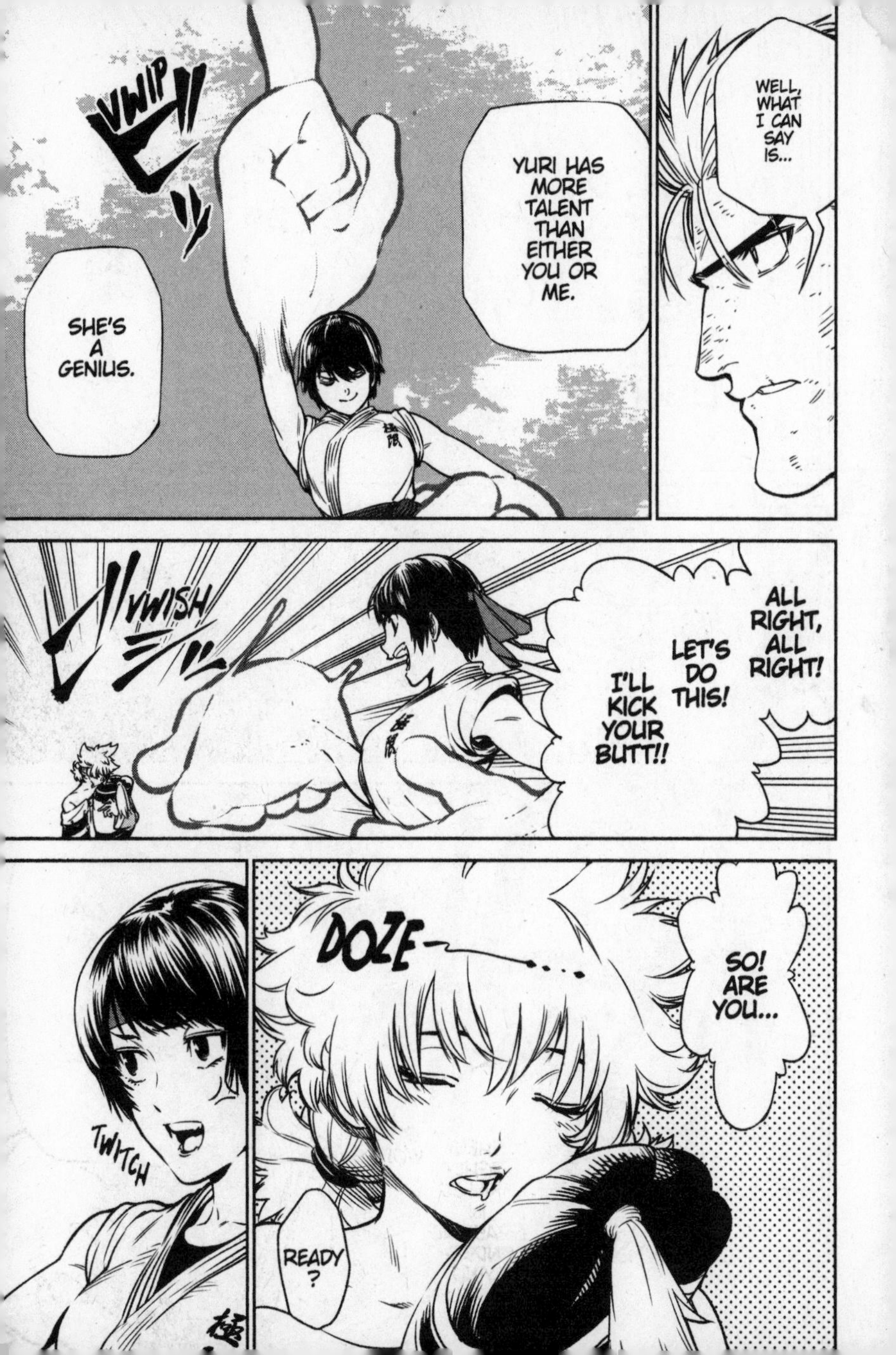

WELL, WHAT I CAN SAY IS...
YURI HAS MORE TALENT THAN EITHER YOU OR ME.
VWIP
SHE'S A GENIUS.
ALL RIGHT, ALL RIGHT!
LET'S DO THIS!
I'LL KICK YOUR BUTT!!
VWISH
SO! ARE YOU...
DOZE-
READY?
TWITCH

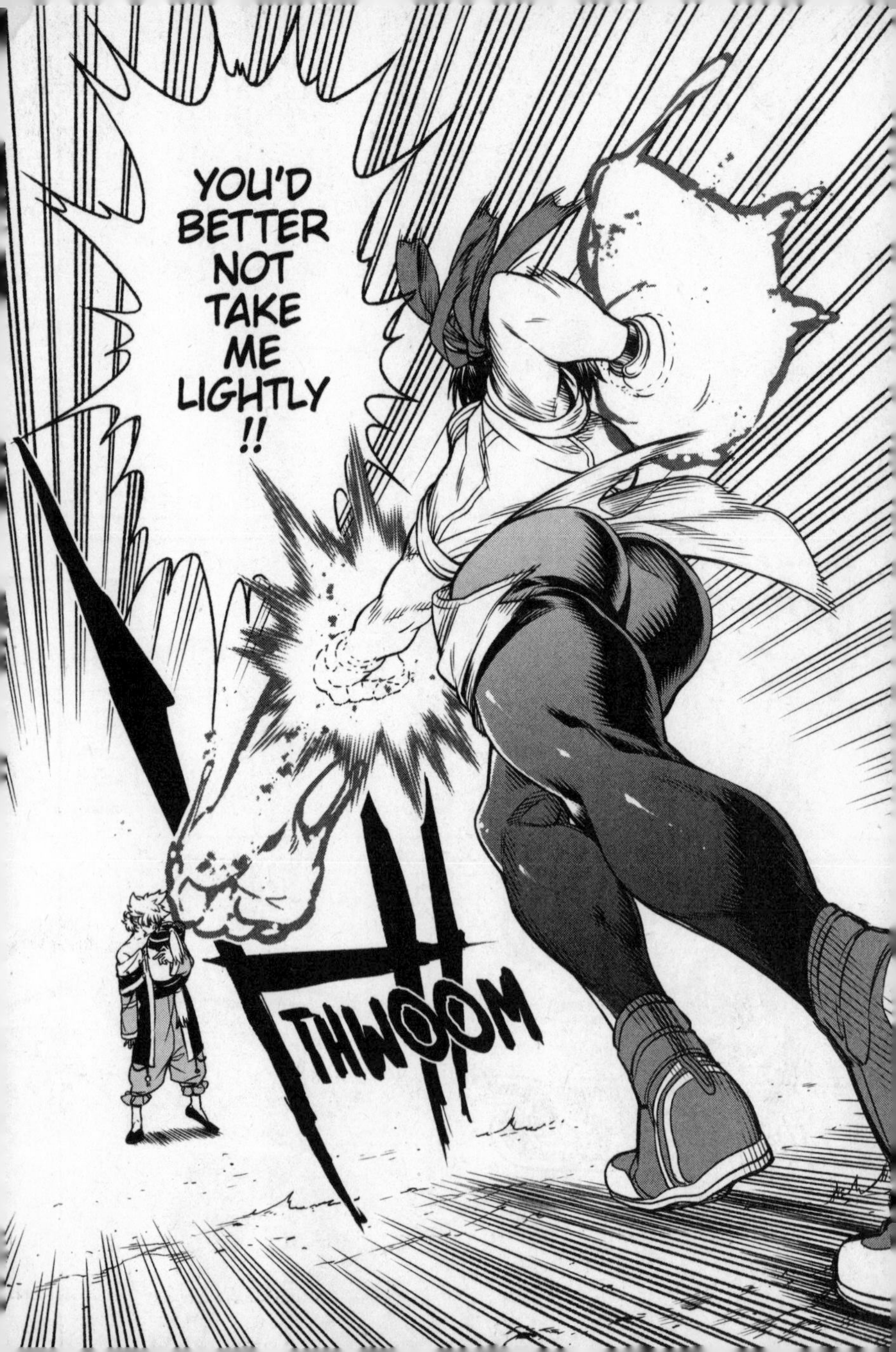
YOU'D BETTER NOT TAKE ME LIGHTLY !!
THWOOM

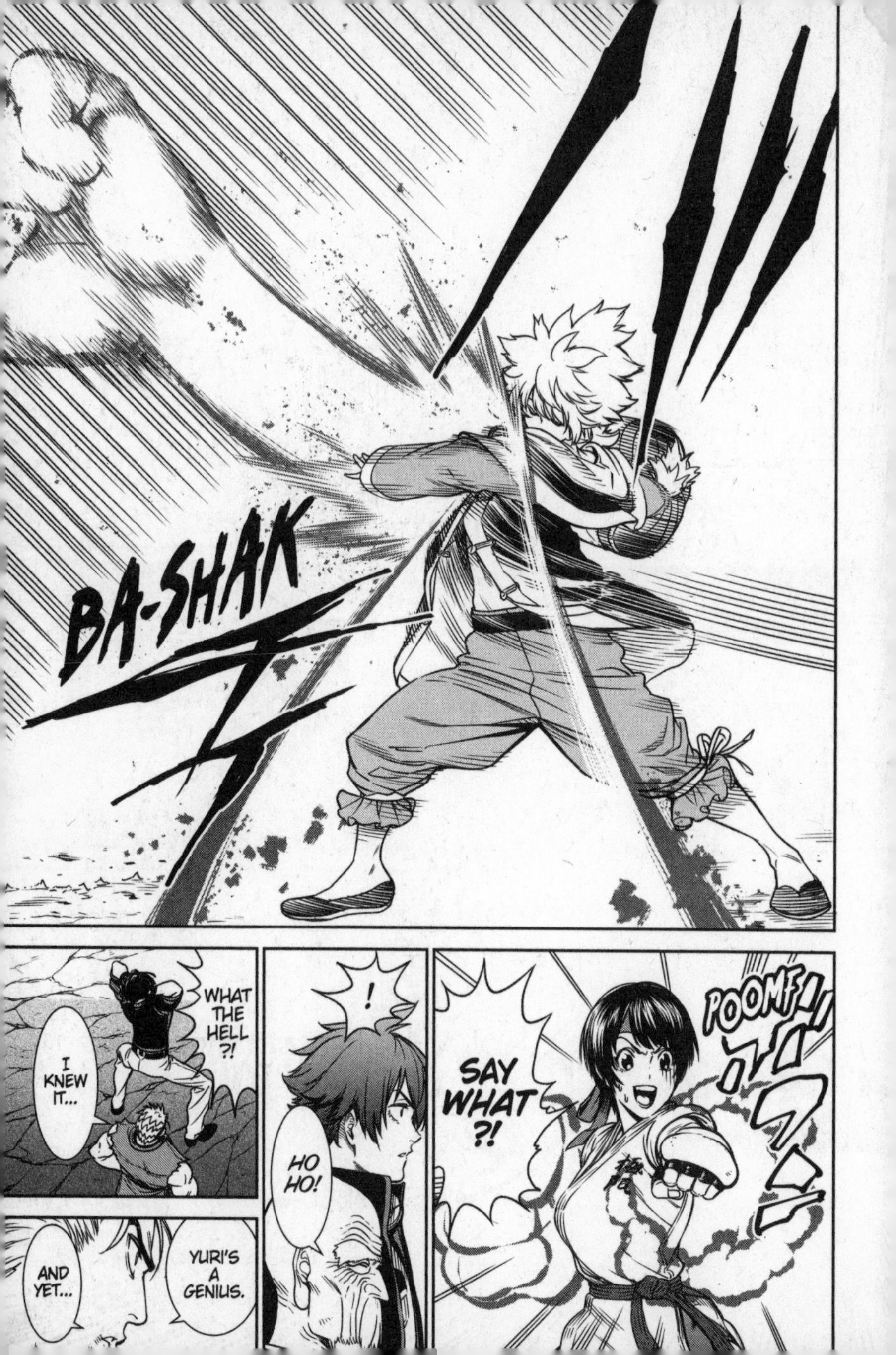
BA-SHAK
POOMF
SAY WHAT?!
!
HO HO!
WHAT THE HELL?!
I KNEW IT...
YURI'S A GENIUS.
AND YET...

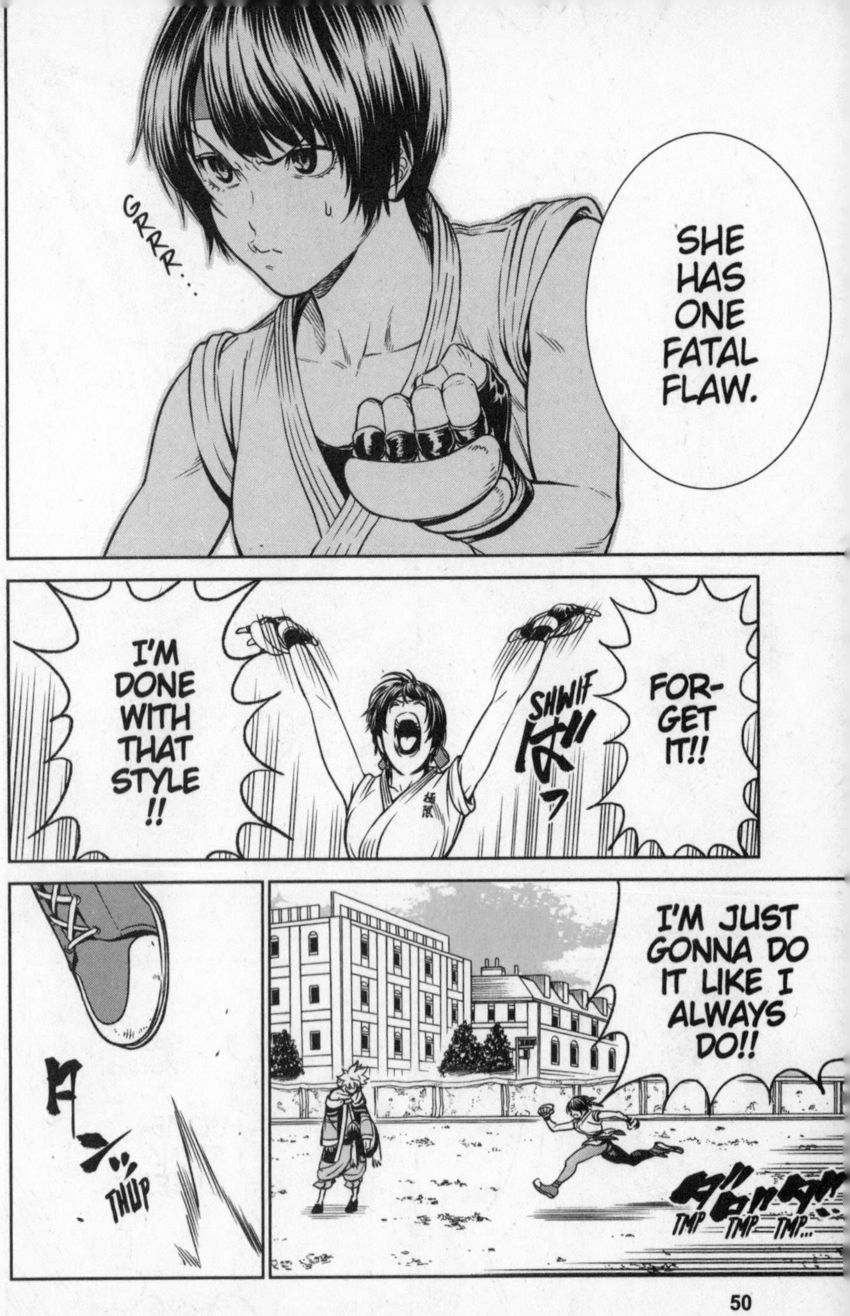
SHE HAS ONE FATAL FLAW.
GRRR...
FOR-GET IT!!
SHWIF
I'M DONE WITH THAT STYLE!!
I'M JUST GONNA DO IT LIKE I ALWAYS DO!!
TMP TMP TMP...
THUP

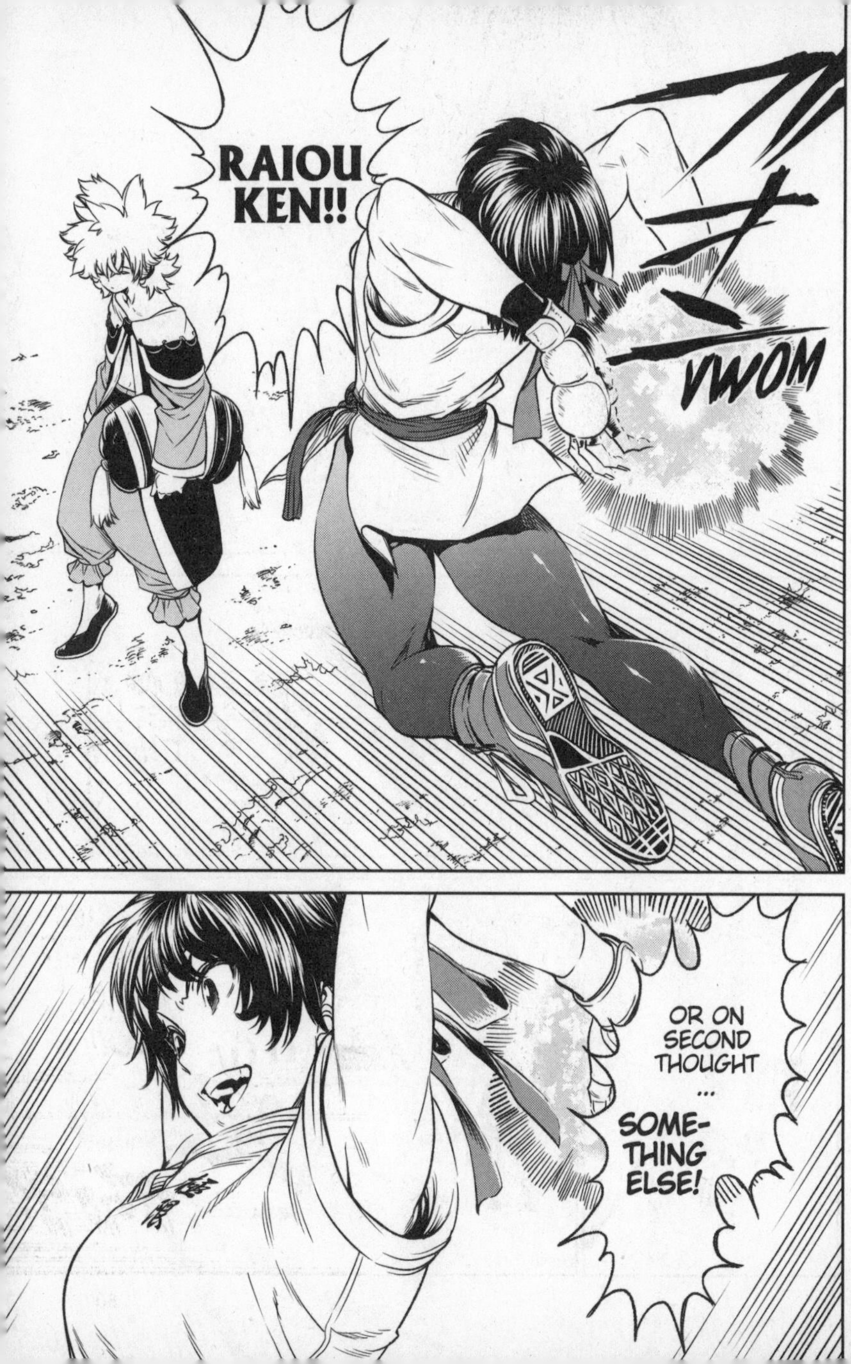
VWOM
RAIOU KEN!!
OR ON SECOND THOUGHT ...
SOME-THING ELSE!

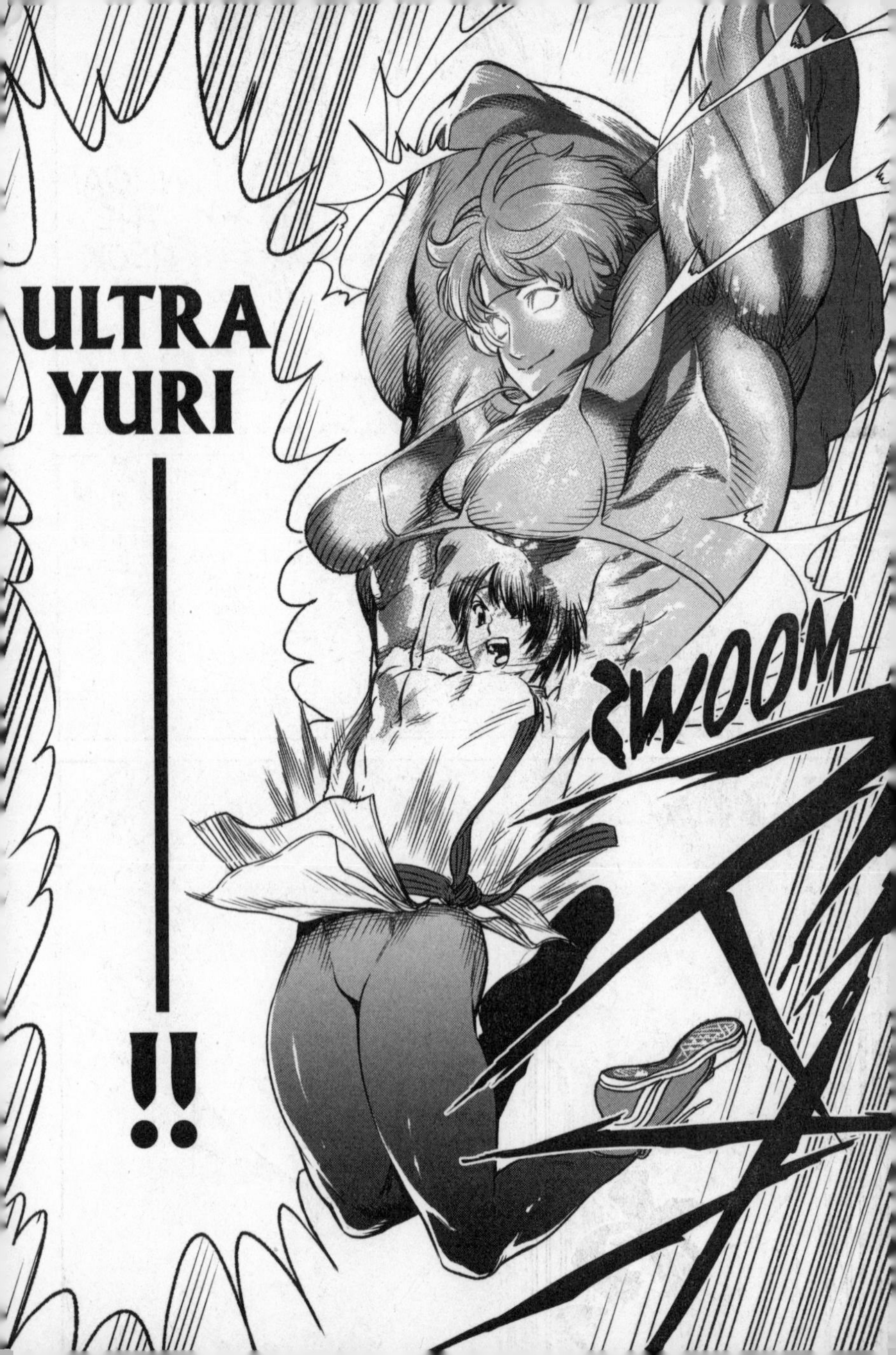
ULTRA YURI——!!
ZWOOM

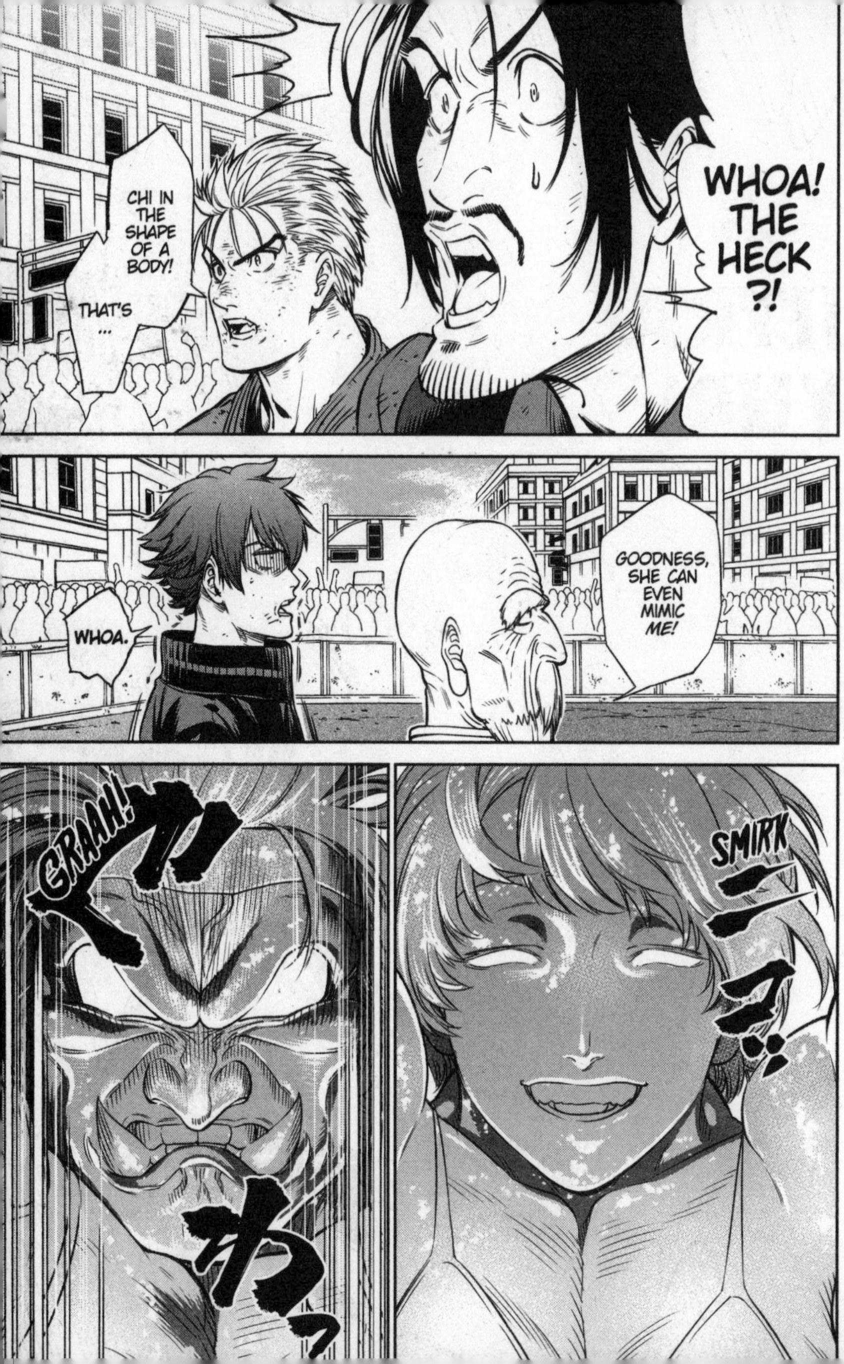
WHOA! THE HECK?!
CHI IN THE SHAPE OF A BODY!
THAT'S ...
GOODNESS, SHE CAN EVEN MIMIC ME!
WHOA.
SMIRK
GRAAH!

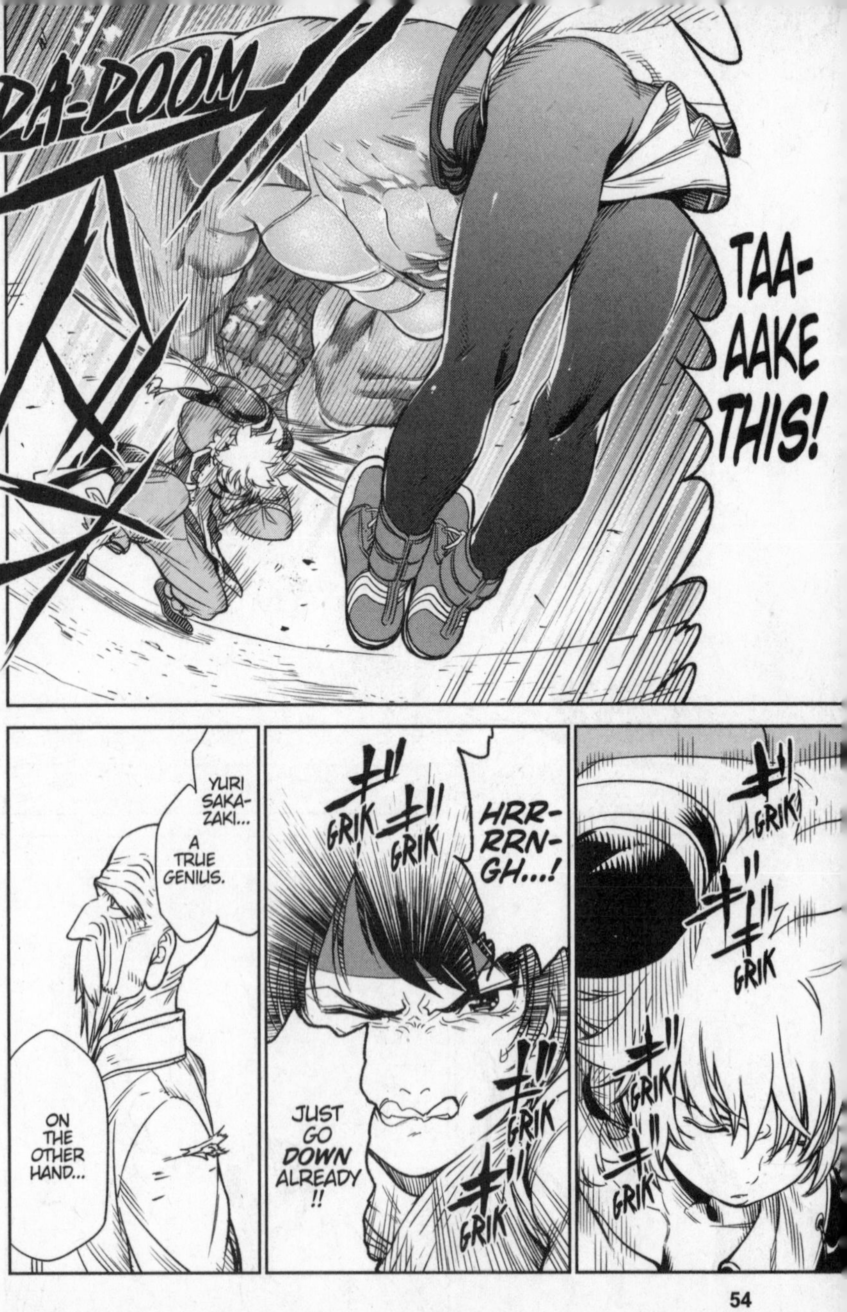
DA-DOOM
TAAAKE THIS!
ギ GRIK
ギ GRIK
ギ GRIK
ギ GRIK
ギ GRIK
HRR-RRN-GH...!
ギ GRIK
ギ GRIK
JUST GO DOWN ALREADY!!
ギ GRIK
ギ GRIK
YURI SAKAZAKI...
A TRUE GENIUS.
ON THE OTHER HAND...

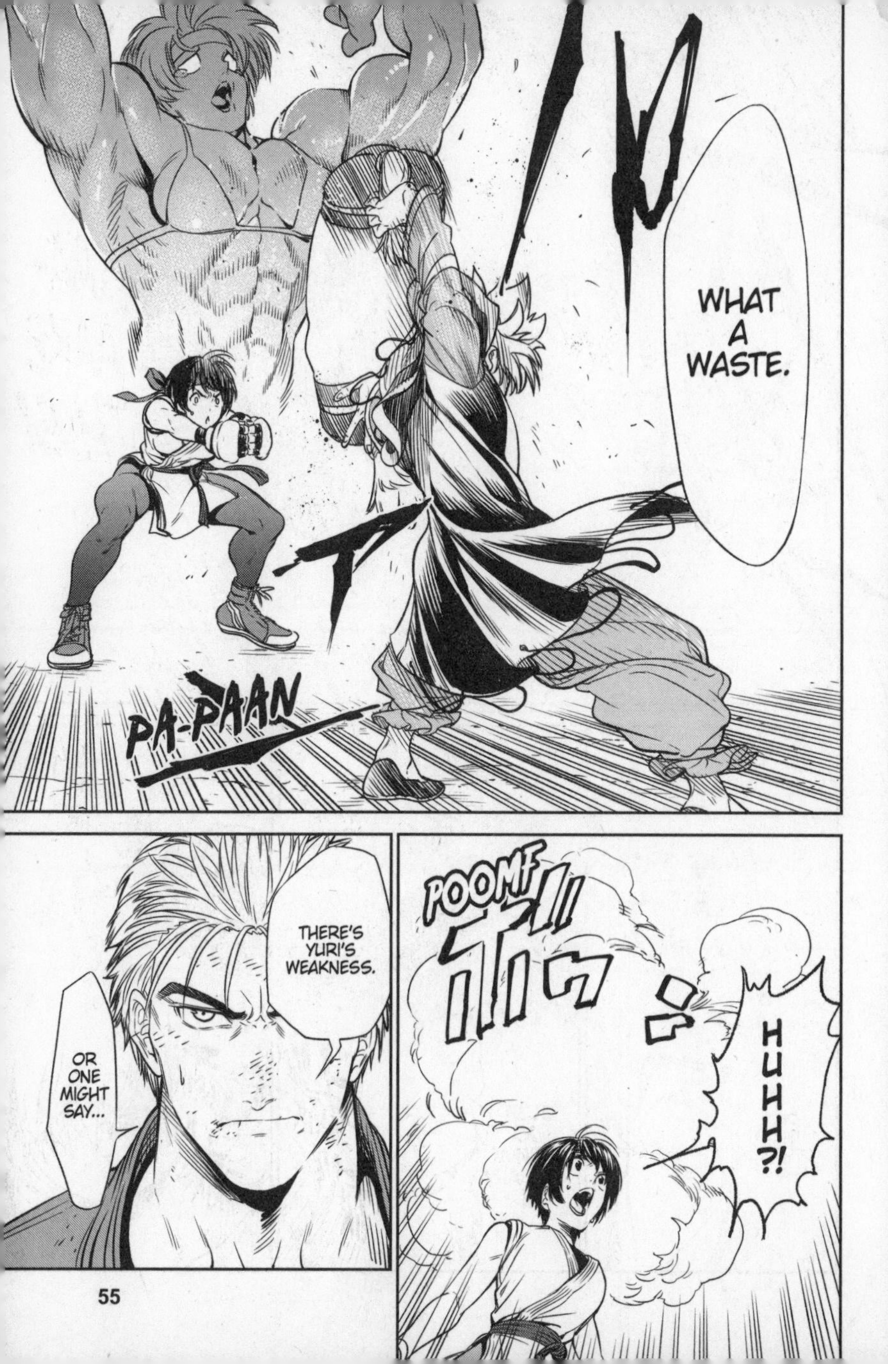
WHAT A WASTE.
PA-PAAN
POOMF
HUHH?!
THERE'S YURI'S WEAKNESS.
OR ONE MIGHT SAY...

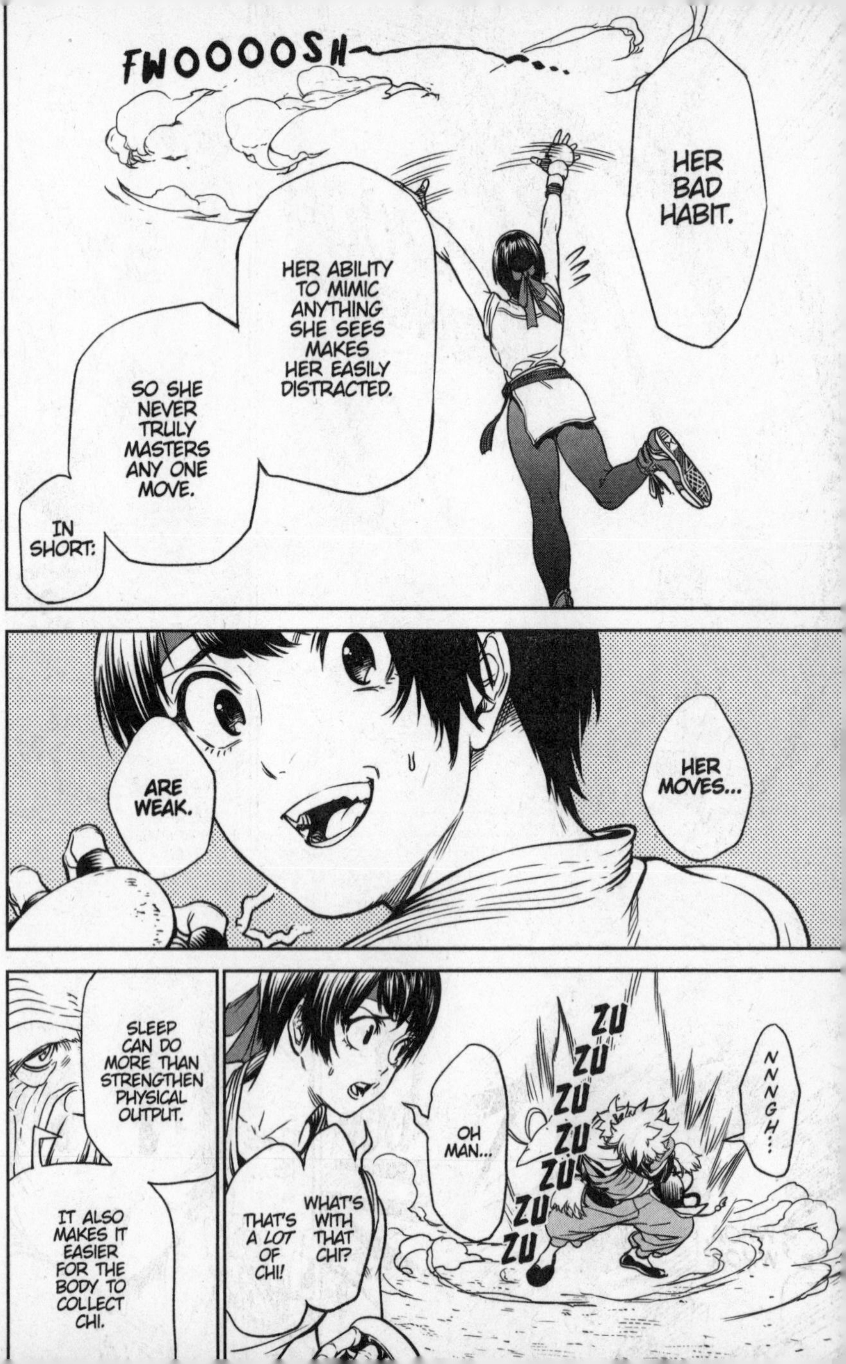
HER BAD HABIT.
FWOOOOSH
HER ABILITY TO MIMIC ANYTHING SHE SEES MAKES HER EASILY DISTRACTED.
SO SHE NEVER TRULY MASTERS ANY ONE MOVE.
IN SHORT:
HER MOVES...
ARE WEAK.
NNNGH...
ZU ZU ZU ZU ZU ZU ZU
OH MAN...
WHAT'S WITH THAT CHI?
THAT'S A *LOT* OF CHI!
SLEEP CAN DO MORE THAN STRENGTHEN PHYSICAL OUTPUT.
IT ALSO MAKES IT EASIER FOR THE BODY TO COLLECT CHI.

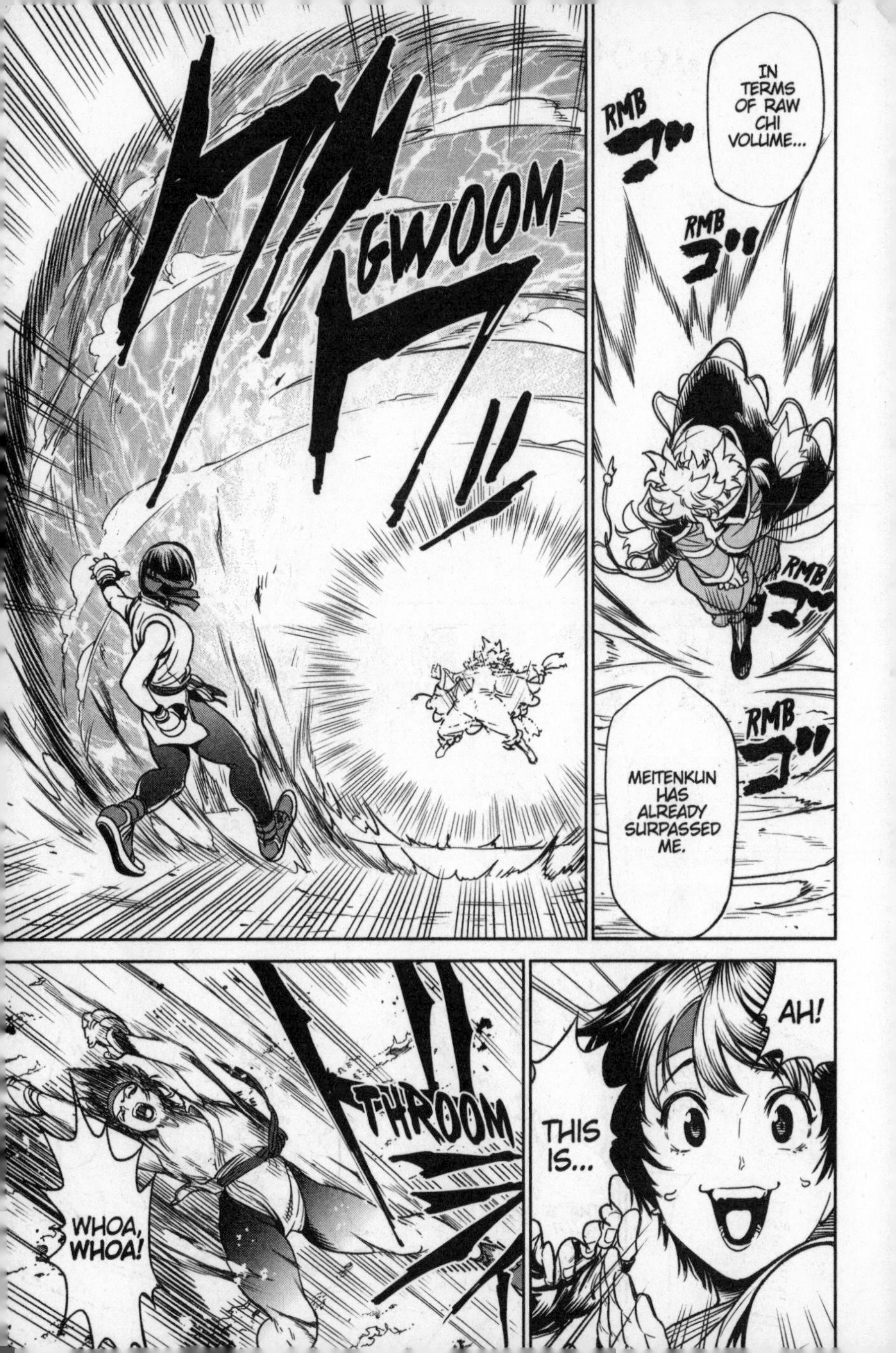
IN TERMS OF RAW CHI VOLUME...
RMB
RMB
RMB
RMB
MEITENKUN HAS ALREADY SURPASSED ME.
GWOOM
AH!
THIS IS...
THROOM
WHOA, WHOA!

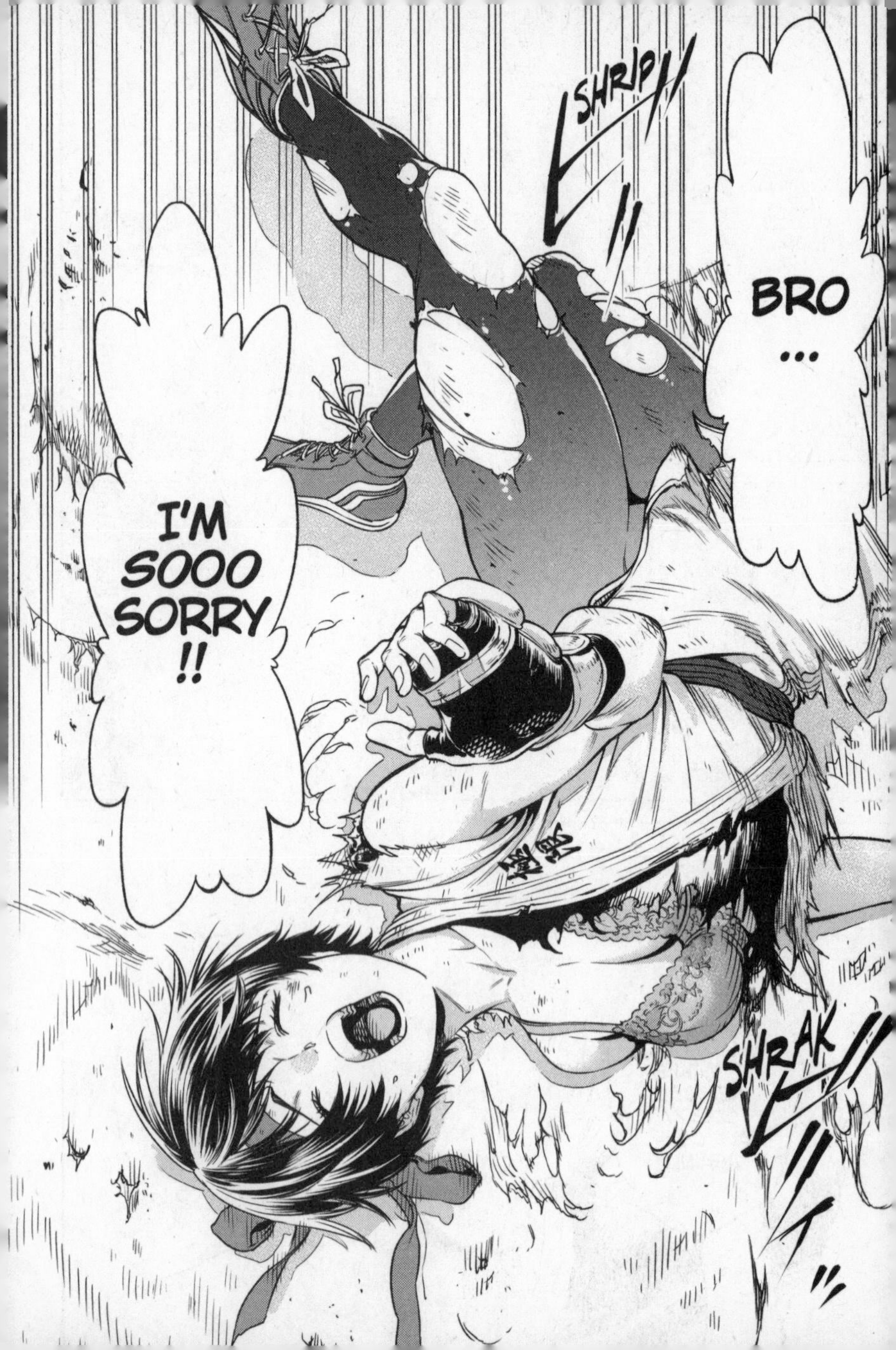
SHRIP!!
BRO ...
I'M SOOO SORRY!!
SHRAK!!

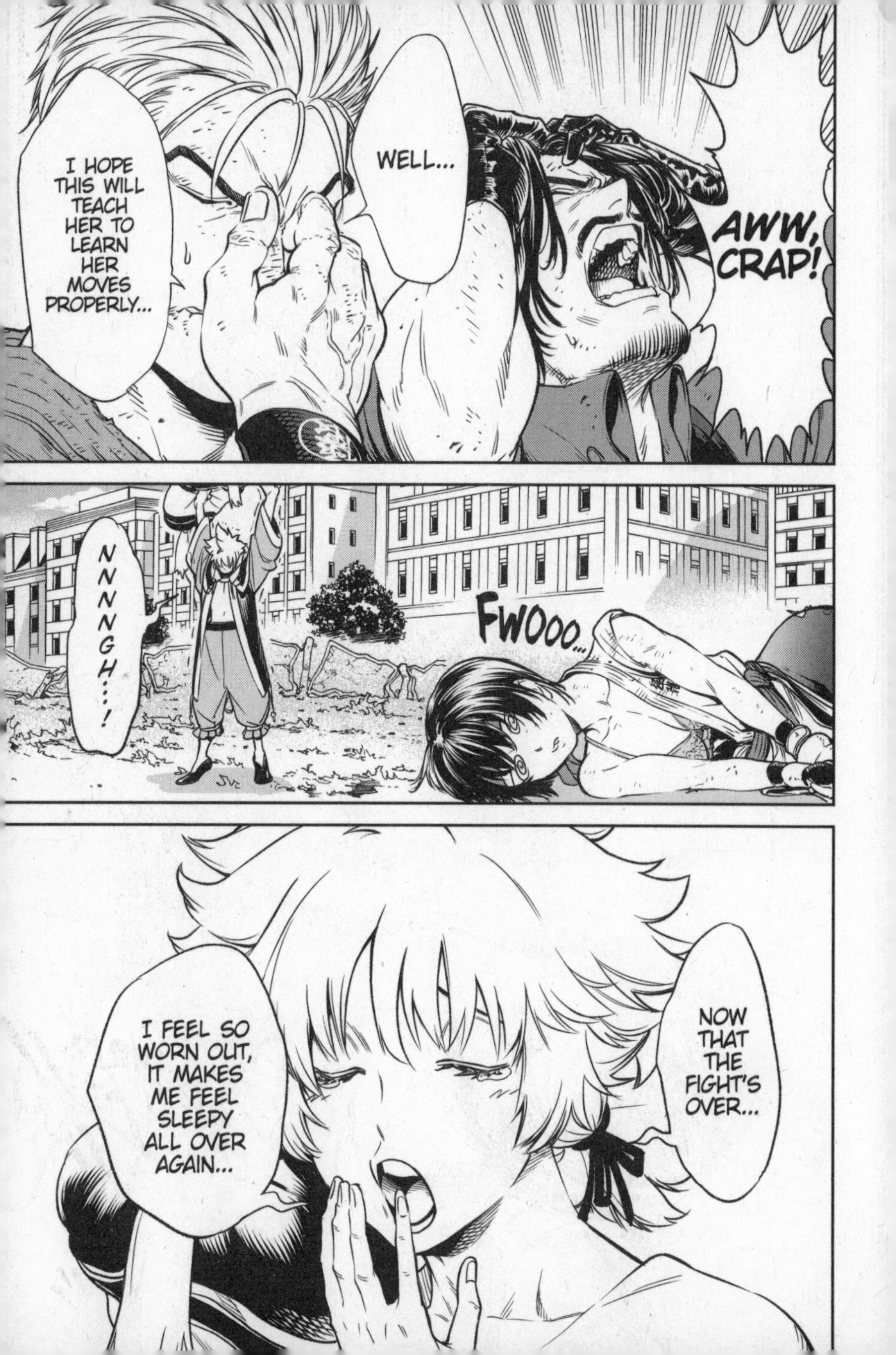
AWW, CRAP!
WELL...
I HOPE THIS WILL TEACH HER TO LEARN HER MOVES PROPERLY...
FWOOO...
NNNNNGH...!
NOW THAT THE FIGHT'S OVER...
I FEEL SO WORN OUT, IT MAKES ME FEEL SLEEPY ALL OVER AGAIN...

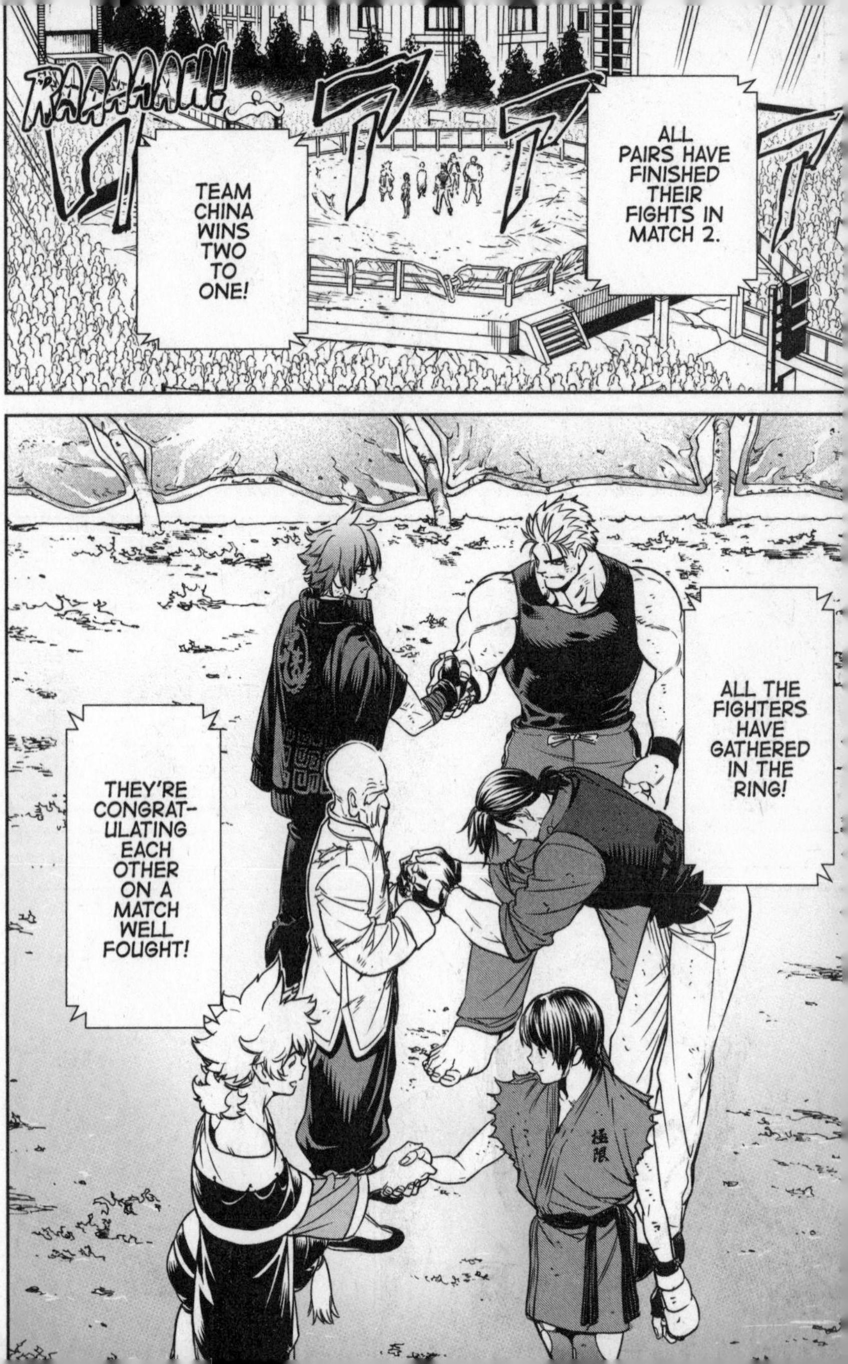
ALL PAIRS HAVE FINISHED THEIR FIGHTS IN MATCH 2.
RAAAAAH!
TEAM CHINA WINS TWO TO ONE!
ALL THE FIGHTERS HAVE GATHERED IN THE RING!
THEY'RE CONGRAT-ULATING EACH OTHER ON A MATCH WELL FOUGHT!

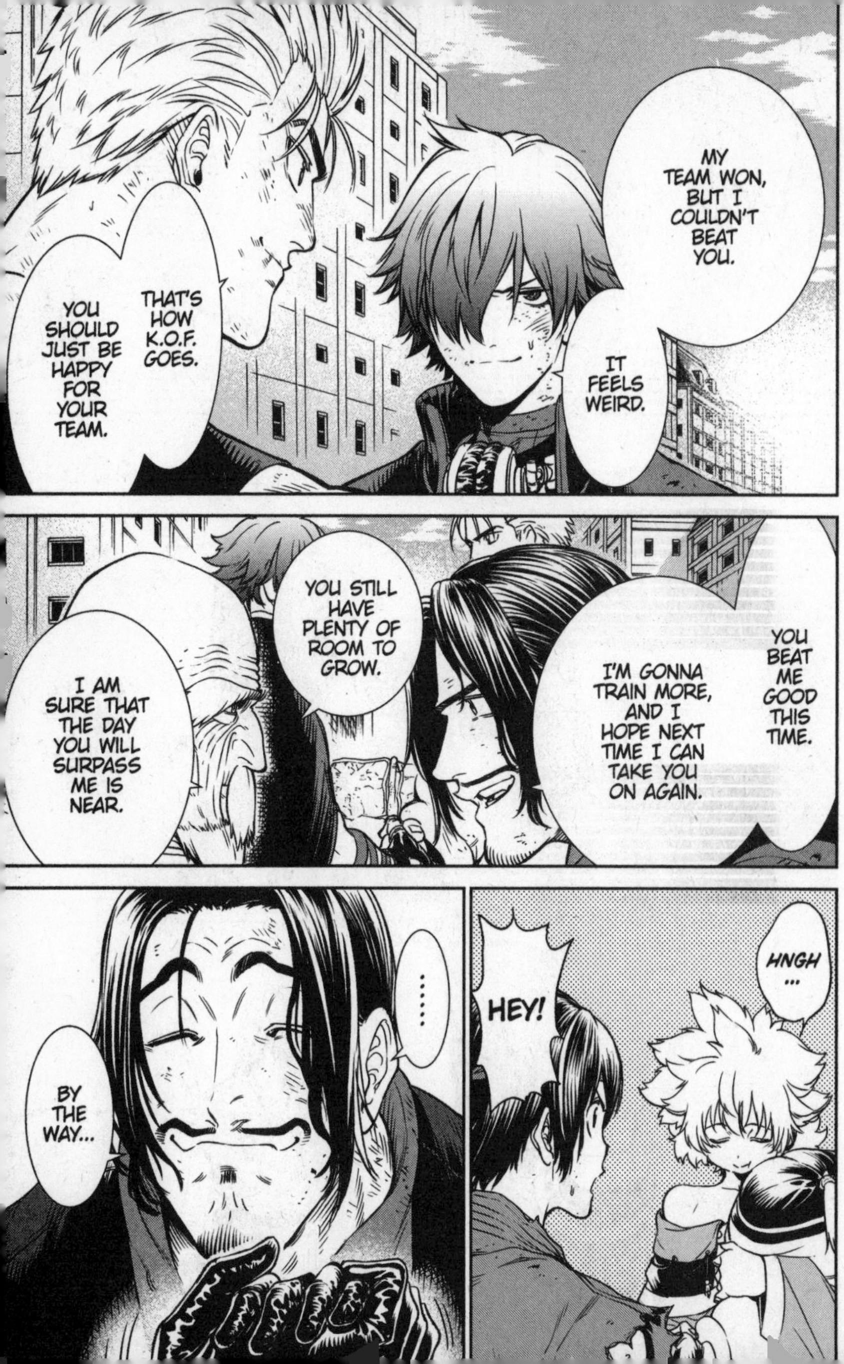
MY TEAM WON, BUT I COULDN'T BEAT YOU.
IT FEELS WEIRD.
THAT'S HOW K.O.F. GOES.
YOU SHOULD JUST BE HAPPY FOR YOUR TEAM.
YOU BEAT ME GOOD THIS TIME.
I'M GONNA TRAIN MORE, AND I HOPE NEXT TIME I CAN TAKE YOU ON AGAIN.
YOU STILL HAVE PLENTY OF ROOM TO GROW.
I AM SURE THAT THE DAY YOU WILL SURPASS ME IS NEAR.
HNGH ...
HEY!
......
BY THE WAY...

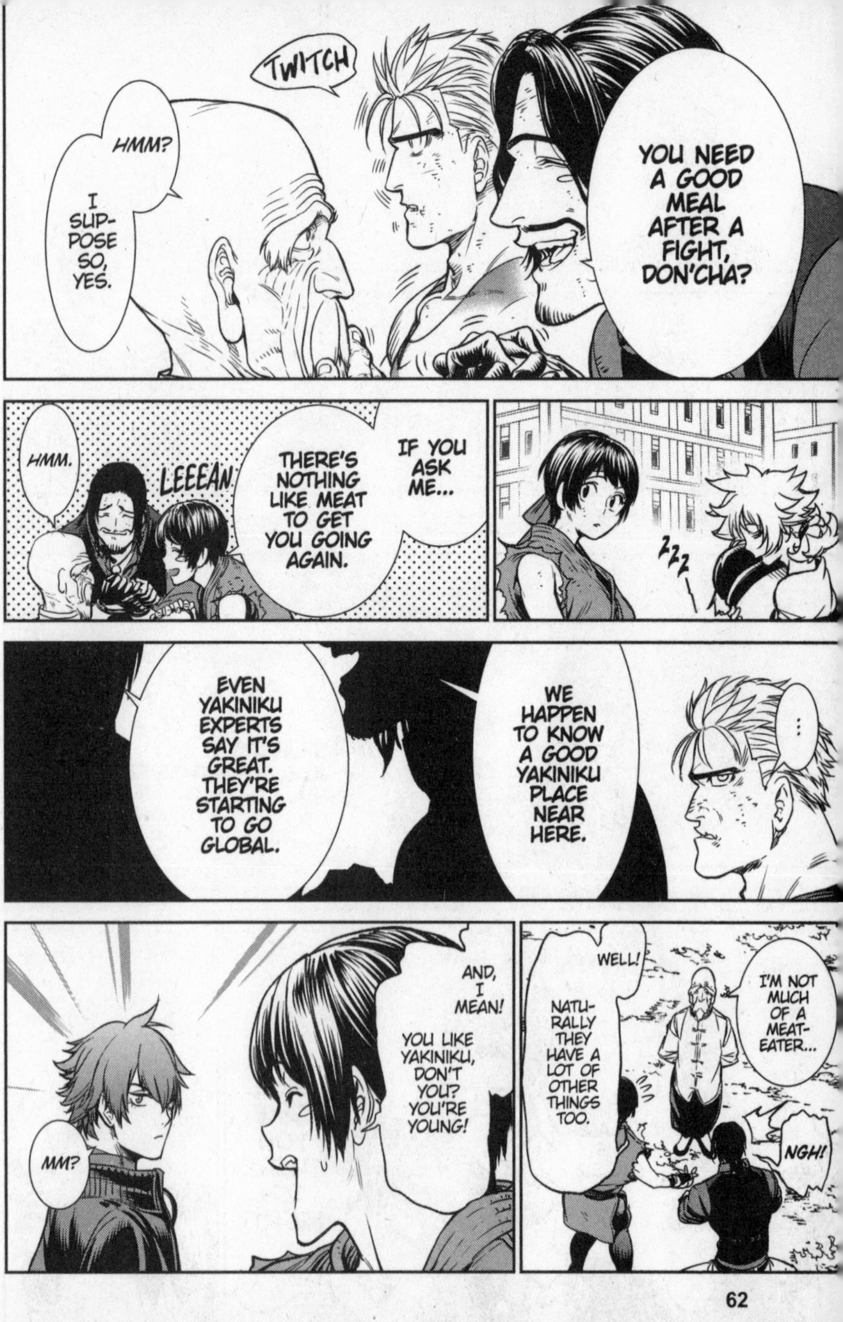
YOU NEED A GOOD MEAL AFTER A FIGHT, DON'CHA?
TWITCH
HMM?
I SUPPOSE SO, YES.
ZZZ
IF YOU ASK ME...
THERE'S NOTHING LIKE MEAT TO GET YOU GOING AGAIN.
LEEEAN
HMM.
...
WE HAPPEN TO KNOW A GOOD YAKINIKU PLACE NEAR HERE.
EVEN YAKINIKU EXPERTS SAY IT'S GREAT. THEY'RE STARTING TO GO GLOBAL.
I'M NOT MUCH OF A MEAT-EATER...
WELL!
NATURALLY THEY HAVE A LOT OF OTHER THINGS TOO.
NGH!
AND, I MEAN!
YOU LIKE YAKINIKU, DON'T YOU? YOU'RE YOUNG!
MM?

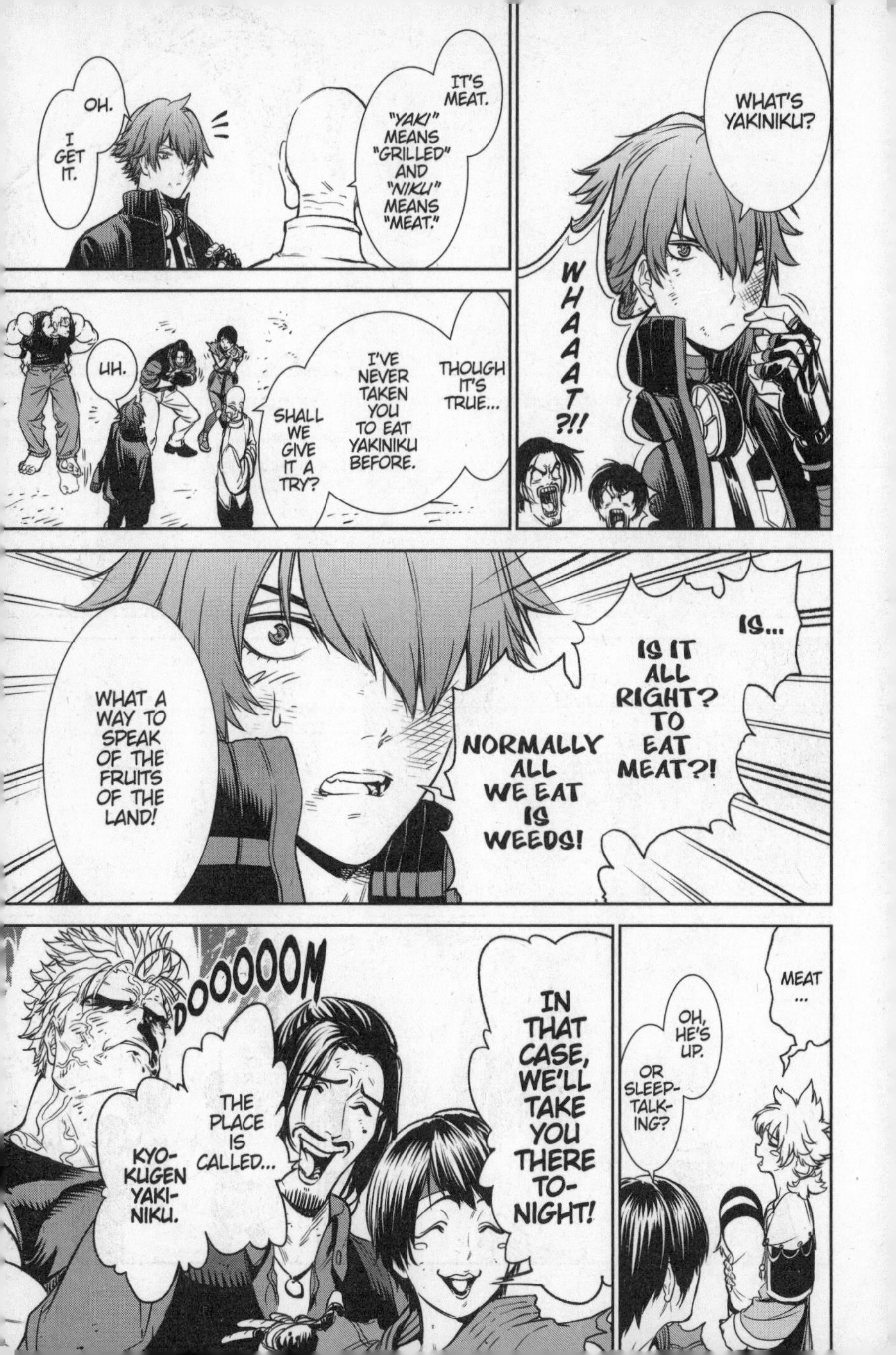
WHAT'S YAKINIKU?
WHAAAAT?!!
IT'S MEAT.
"YAKI" MEANS "GRILLED" AND "NIKU" MEANS "MEAT."
OH.
I GET IT.
THOUGH IT'S TRUE...
I'VE NEVER TAKEN YOU TO EAT YAKINIKU BEFORE.
SHALL WE GIVE IT A TRY?
UH.
IS...
IS IT ALL RIGHT? TO EAT MEAT?!
NORMALLY ALL WE EAT IS WEEDS!
WHAT A WAY TO SPEAK OF THE FRUITS OF THE LAND!
MEAT...
OH, HE'S UP.
OR SLEEP-TALKING?
IN THAT CASE, WE'LL TAKE YOU THERE TO-NIGHT!
DOOOOOM
THE PLACE IS CALLED...
KYO-KUGEN YAKI-NIKU.

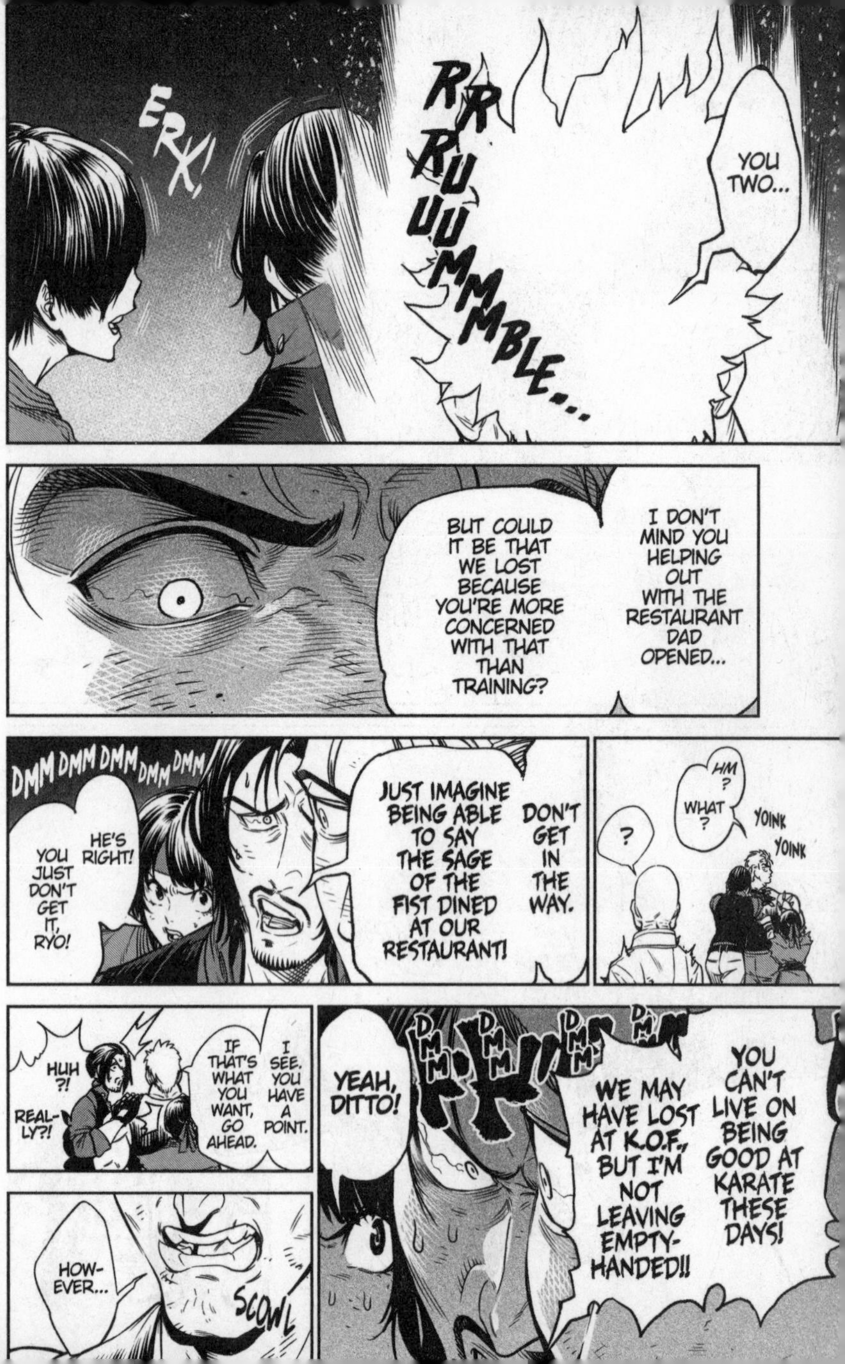
YOU TWO...
RRRUUMMMBLE...
ERK!
I DON'T MIND YOU HELPING OUT WITH THE RESTAURANT DAD OPENED...
BUT COULD IT BE THAT WE LOST BECAUSE YOU'RE MORE CONCERNED WITH THAT THAN TRAINING?
HM? WHAT?
YOINK
YOINK
?
DON'T GET IN THE WAY.
JUST IMAGINE BEING ABLE TO SAY THE SAGE OF THE FIST DINED AT OUR RESTAURANT!
HE'S RIGHT!
YOU JUST DON'T GET IT, RYO!
DMM DMM DMM DMM DMM
YOU CAN'T LIVE ON BEING GOOD AT KARATE THESE DAYS!
WE MAY HAVE LOST AT K.O.F., BUT I'M NOT LEAVING EMPTY-HANDED!!
YEAH, DITTO!
DMM DMM DMM DMM DMM
I SEE. YOU HAVE A POINT.
IF THAT'S WHAT YOU WANT, GO AHEAD.
HUH?!
REAL-LY?!
HOW-EVER...
SCOWL

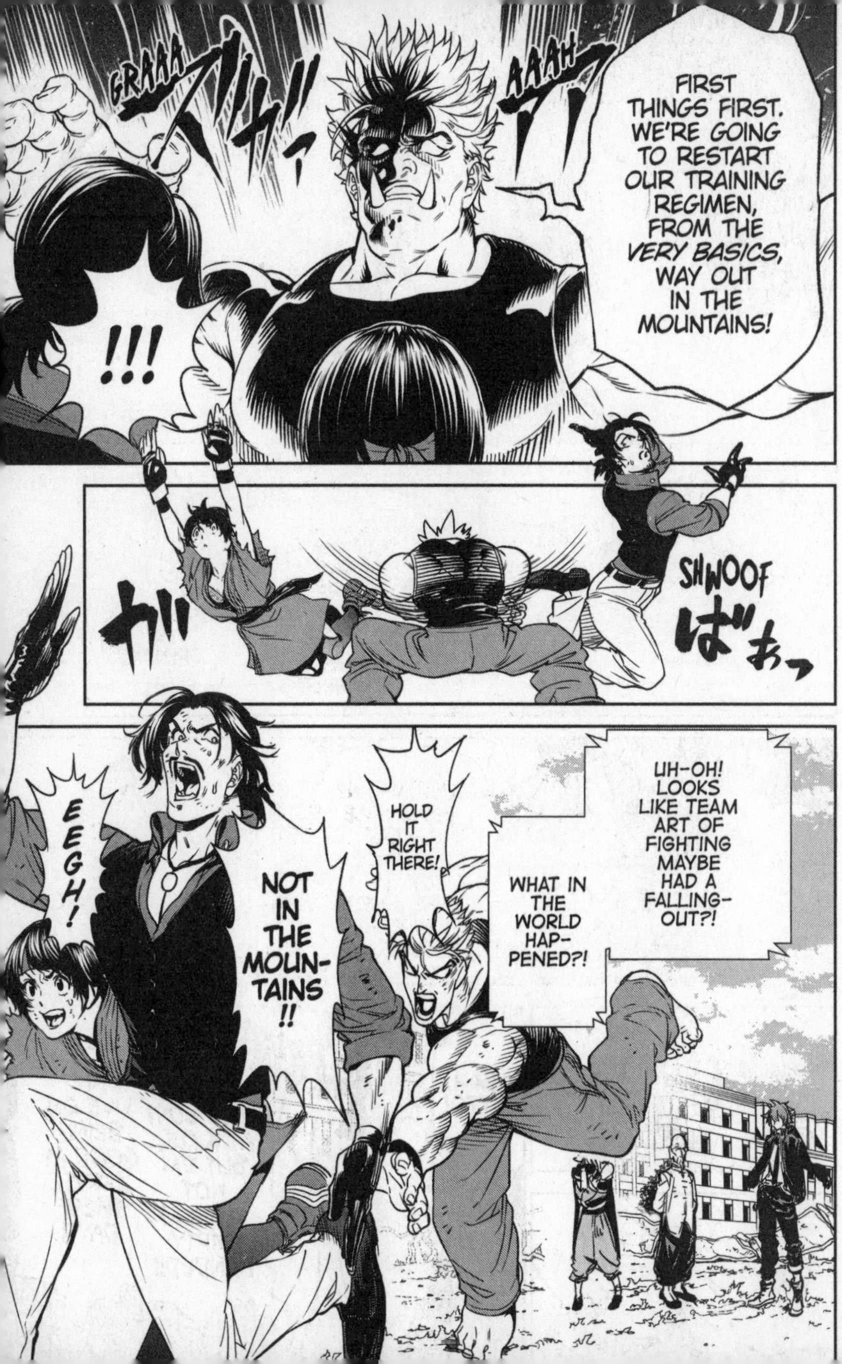
FIRST THINGS FIRST. WE'RE GOING TO RESTART OUR TRAINING REGIMEN, FROM THE *VERY BASICS*, WAY OUT IN THE MOUNTAINS!
AAAH
GRAAA
!!!
SHWOOF
UH-OH! LOOKS LIKE TEAM ART OF FIGHTING MAYBE HAD A FALLING-OUT?!
WHAT IN THE WORLD HAPPENED?!
HOLD IT RIGHT THERE!
NOT IN THE MOUNTAINS!!
EEGH!

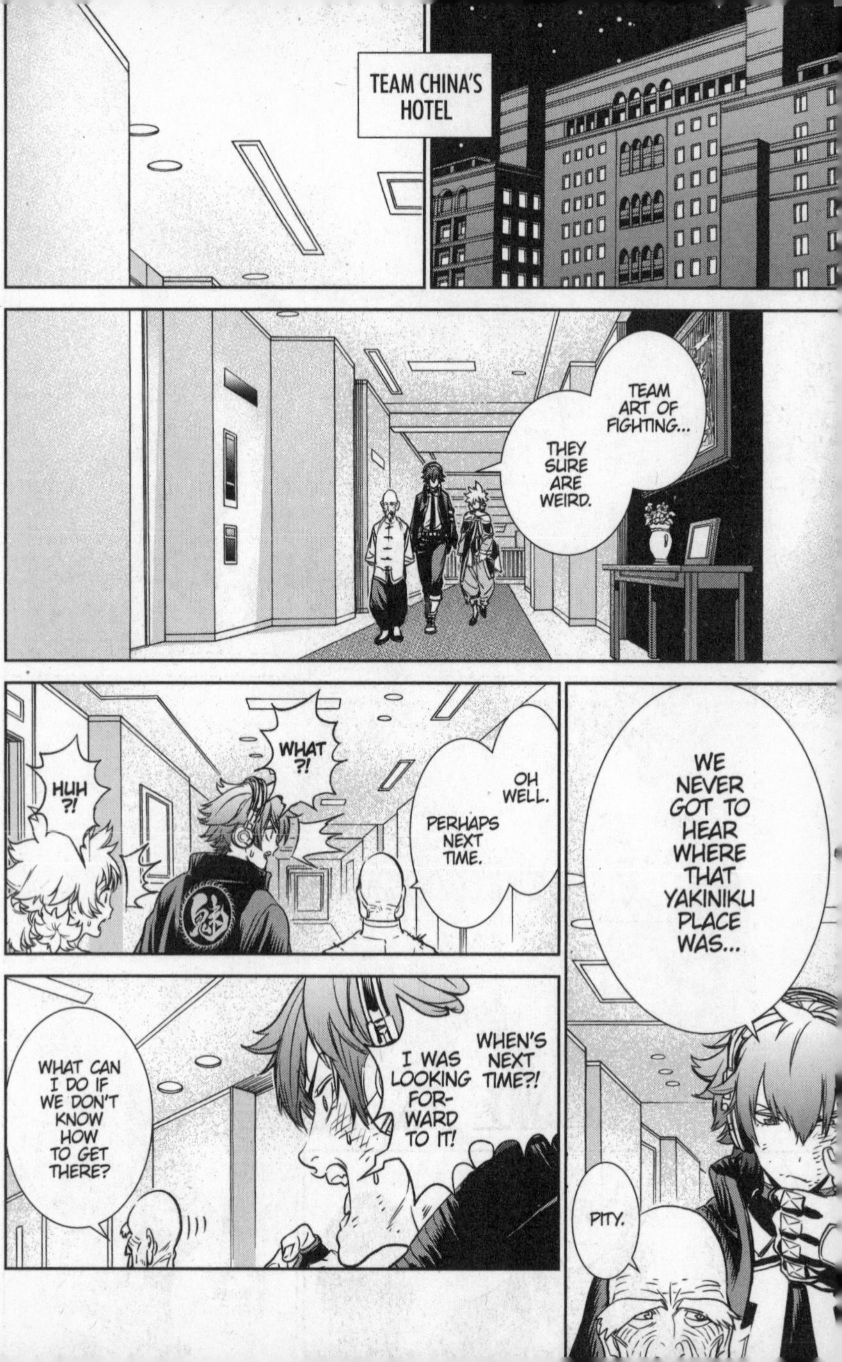
TEAM CHINA'S HOTEL
TEAM ART OF FIGHTING...
THEY SURE ARE WEIRD.
WE NEVER GOT TO HEAR WHERE THAT YAKINIKU PLACE WAS...
PITY.
OH WELL.
PERHAPS NEXT TIME.
WHAT?!
HUH?!
WHEN'S NEXT TIME?!
I WAS LOOKING FOR-WARD TO IT!
WHAT CAN I DO IF WE DON'T KNOW HOW TO GET THERE?

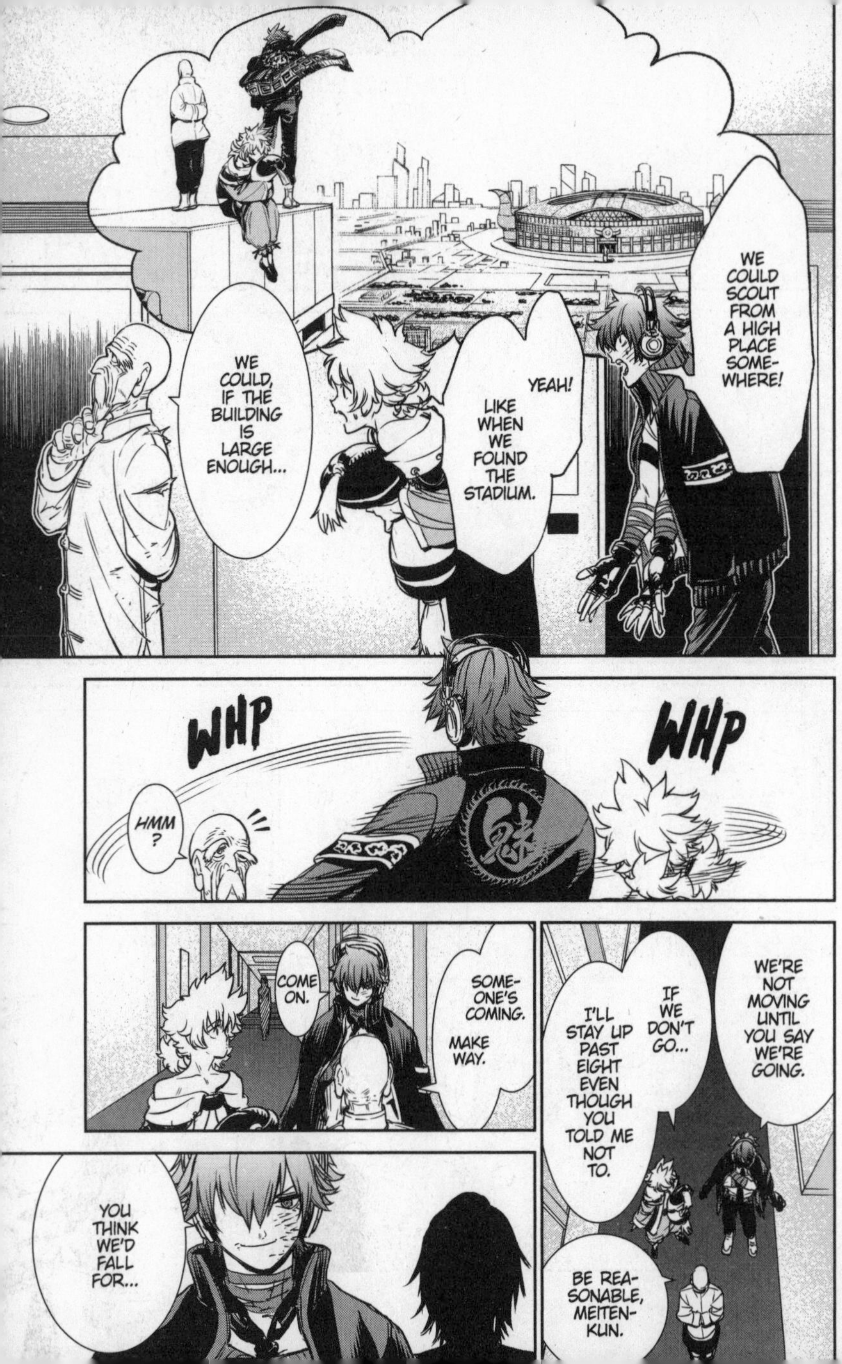
WE COULD SCOUT FROM A HIGH PLACE SOME-WHERE!
YEAH!
LIKE WHEN WE FOUND THE STADIUM.
WE COULD, IF THE BUILDING IS LARGE ENOUGH...
WHP
WHP
HMM?
WE'RE NOT MOVING UNTIL YOU SAY WE'RE GOING.
IF WE DON'T GO...
I'LL STAY UP PAST EIGHT EVEN THOUGH YOU TOLD ME NOT TO.
BE REA-SONABLE, MEITEN-KUN.
SOME-ONE'S COMING.
MAKE WAY.
COME ON.
YOU THINK WE'D FALL FOR...

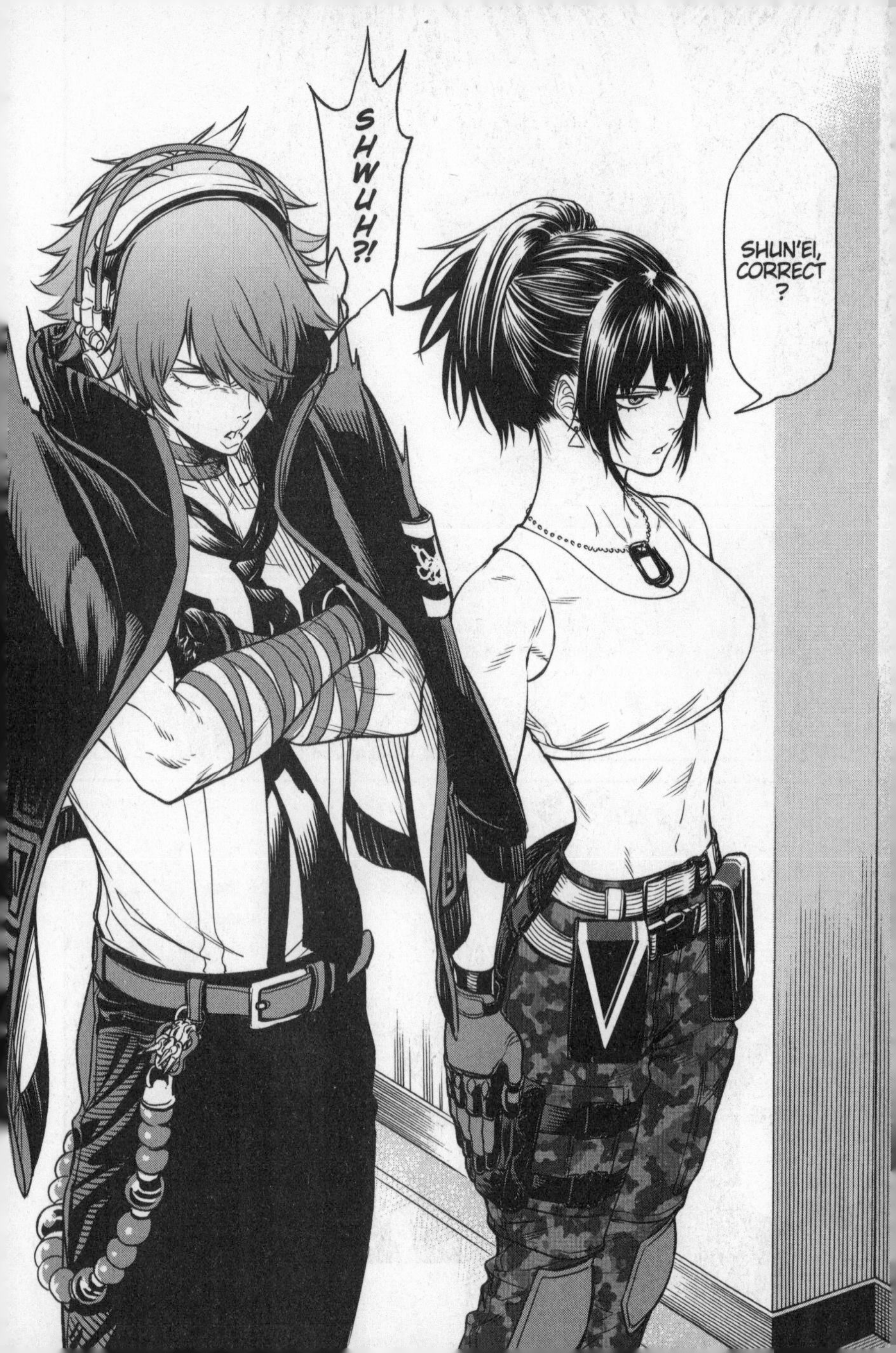
SHUN'EI, CORRECT?
SHWUH?!

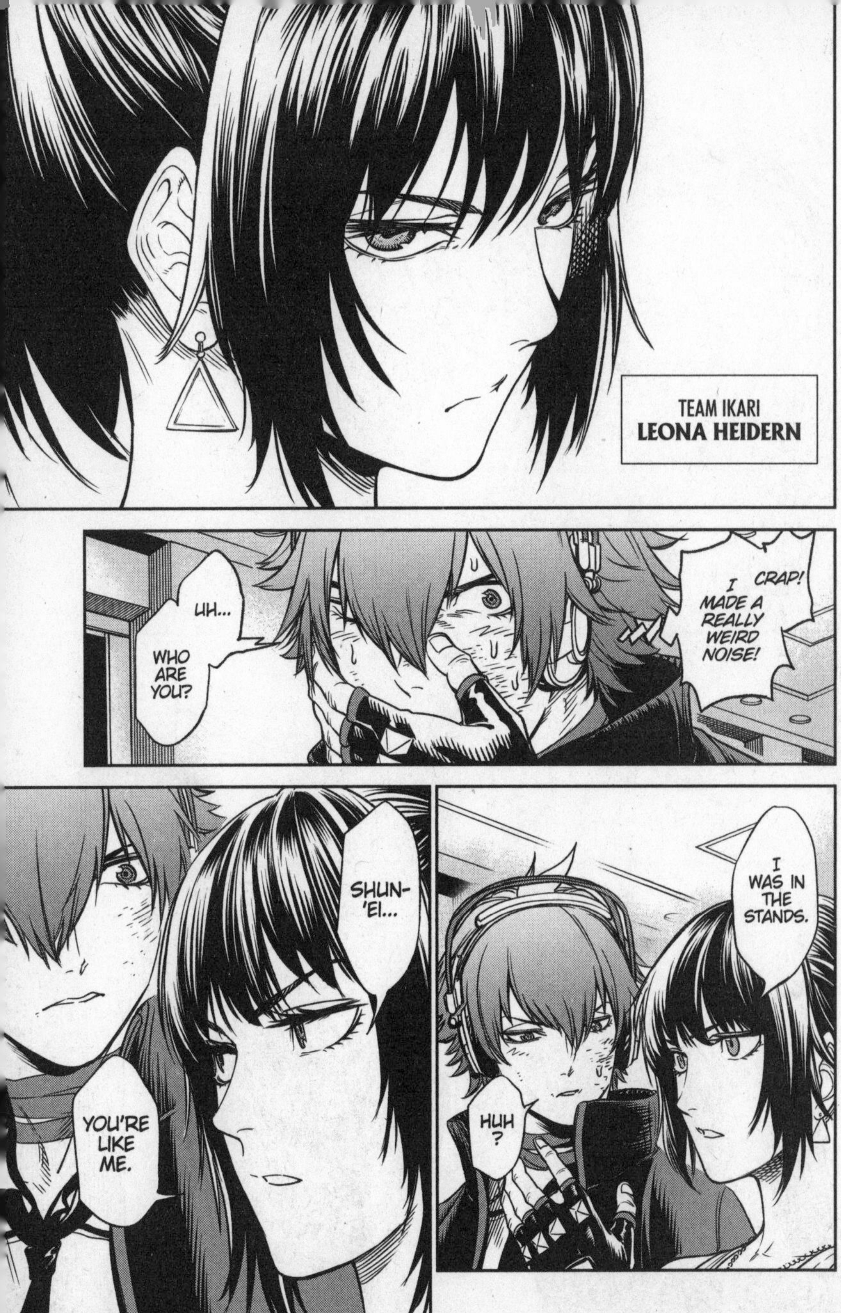
TEAM IKARI
LEONA HEIDERN
CRAP! I MADE A REALLY WEIRD NOISE!
UH...
WHO ARE YOU?
I WAS IN THE STANDS.
HUH?
SHUN-'EI...
YOU'RE LIKE ME.

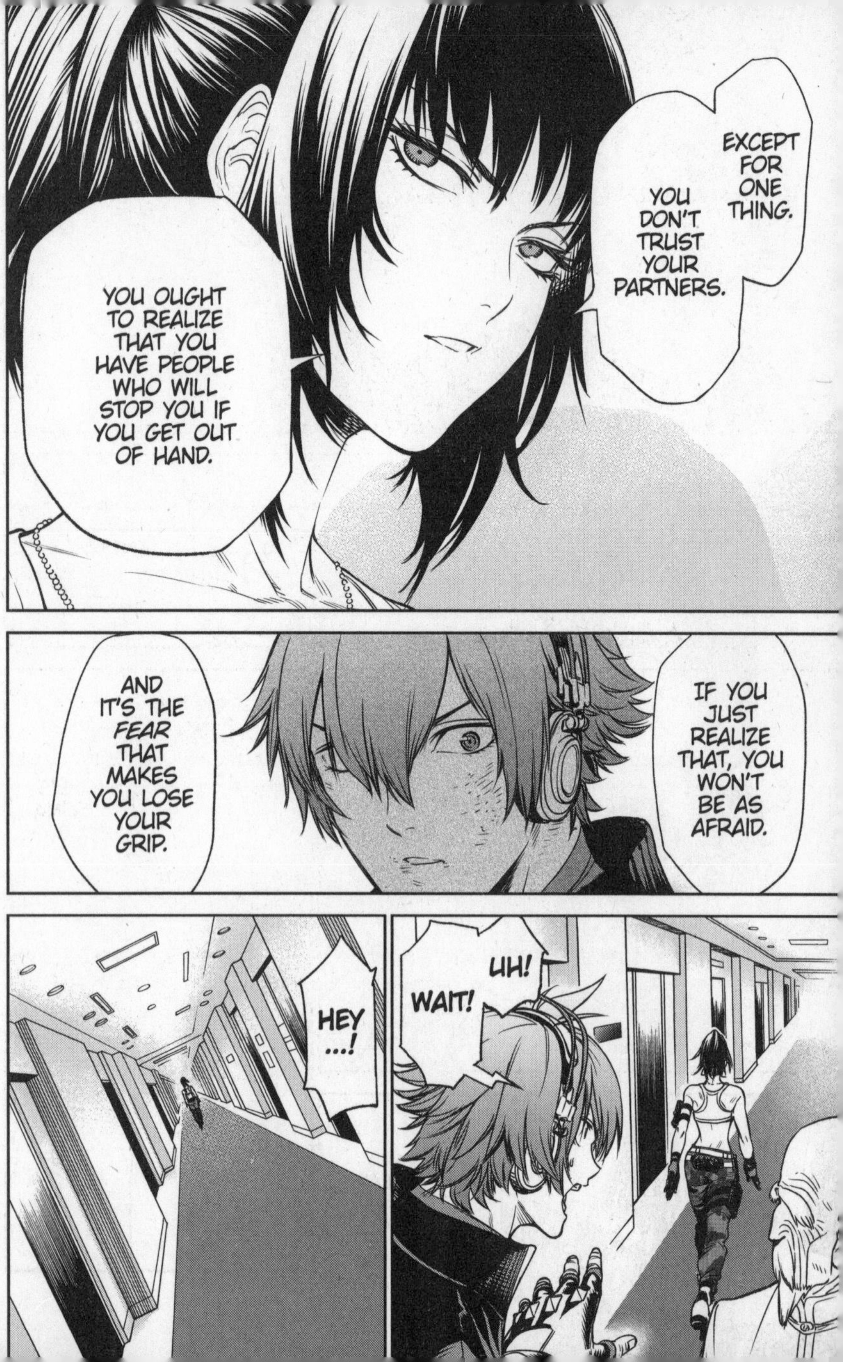
EXCEPT FOR ONE THING.
YOU DON'T TRUST YOUR PARTNERS.
YOU OUGHT TO REALIZE THAT YOU HAVE PEOPLE WHO WILL STOP YOU IF YOU GET OUT OF HAND.
IF YOU JUST REALIZE THAT, YOU WON'T BE AS AFRAID.
AND IT'S THE *FEAR* THAT MAKES YOU LOSE YOUR GRIP.
UH!
WAIT!
HEY ...!

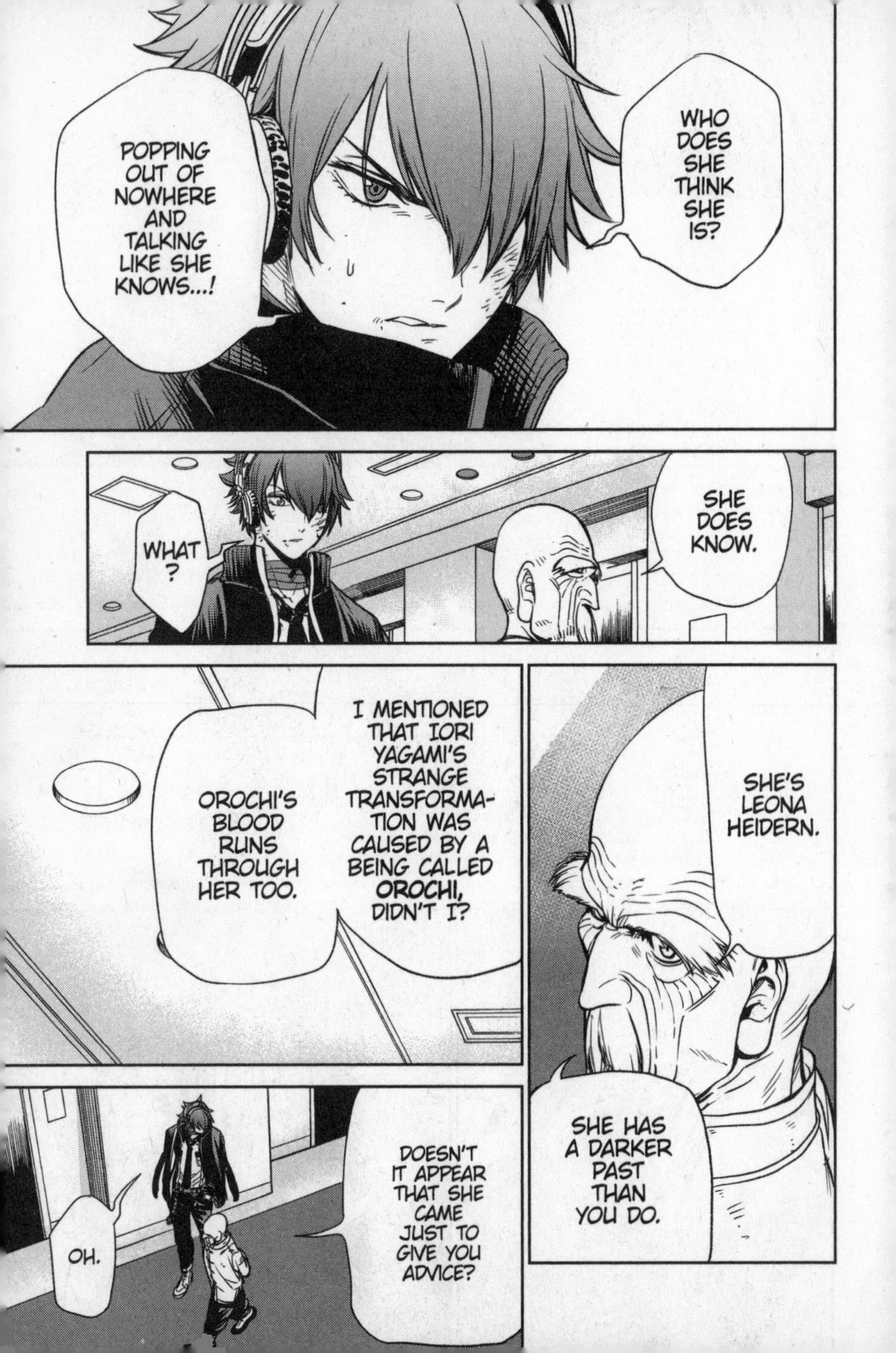
WHO DOES SHE THINK SHE IS?
POPPING OUT OF NOWHERE AND TALKING LIKE SHE KNOWS...!
SHE DOES KNOW.
WHAT?
SHE'S LEONA HEIDERN.
SHE HAS A DARKER PAST THAN YOU DO.
I MENTIONED THAT IORI YAGAMI'S STRANGE TRANSFORMATION WAS CAUSED BY A BEING CALLED OROCHI, DIDN'T I?
OROCHI'S BLOOD RUNS THROUGH HER TOO.
DOESN'T IT APPEAR THAT SHE CAME JUST TO GIVE YOU ADVICE?
OH.

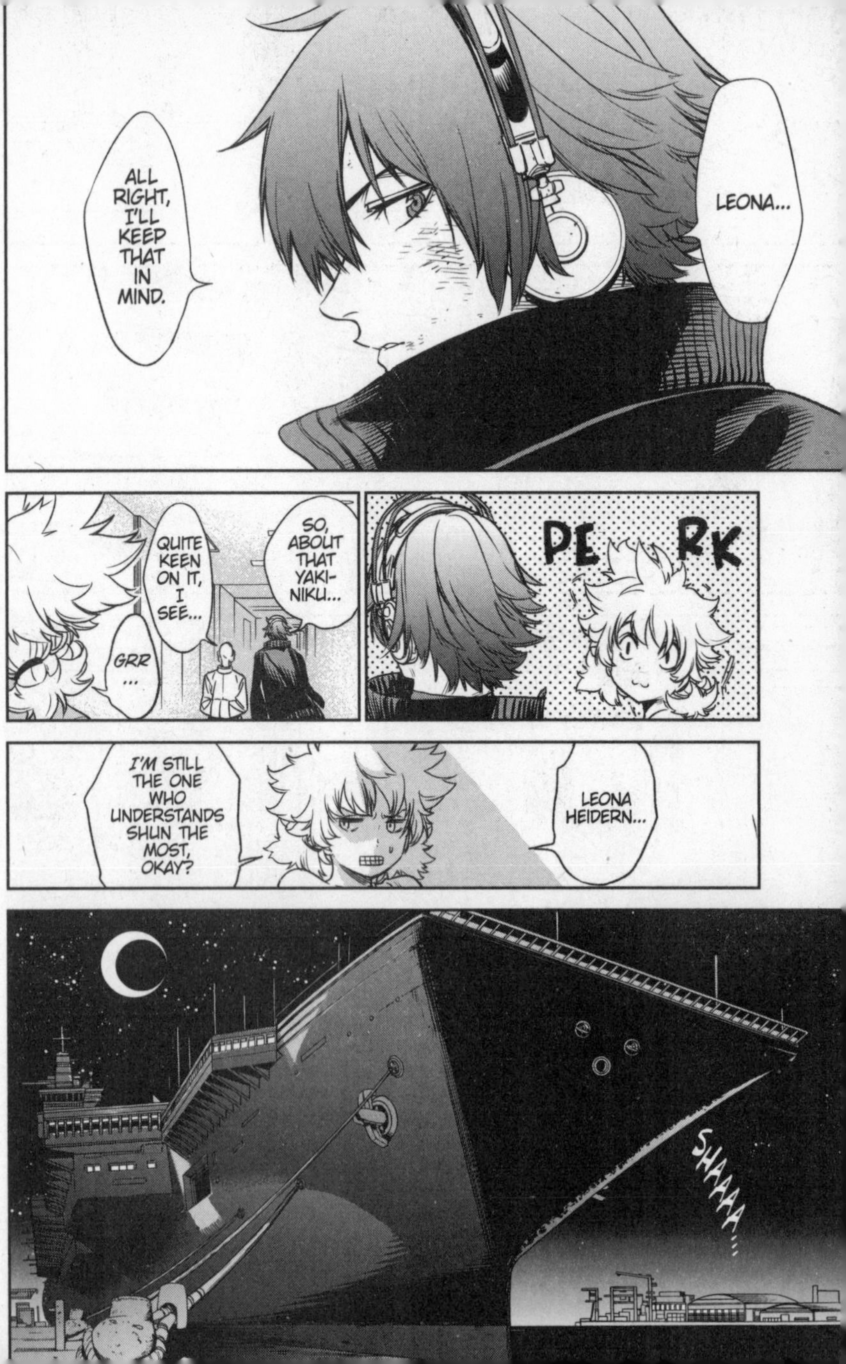
LEONA...
ALL RIGHT, I'LL KEEP THAT IN MIND.
PE RK
SO, ABOUT THAT YAKI-NIKU...
QUITE KEEN ON IT, I SEE...
GRR...
LEONA HEIDERN...
I'M STILL THE ONE WHO UNDERSTANDS SHUN THE MOST, OKAY?
SHAAAA...

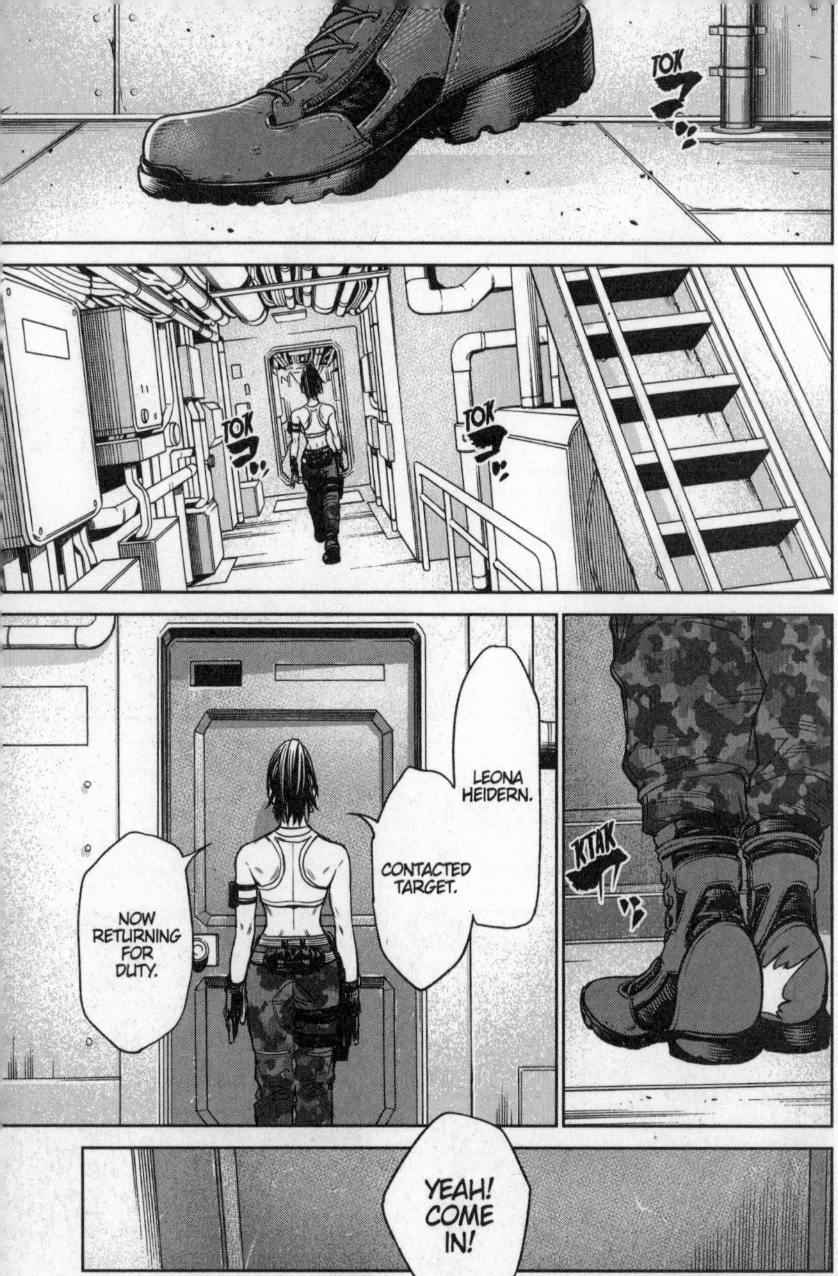
TOK
TOK
TOK
KTAK
LEONA HEIDERN.
CONTACTED TARGET.
NOW RETURNING FOR DUTY.
YEAH! COME IN!

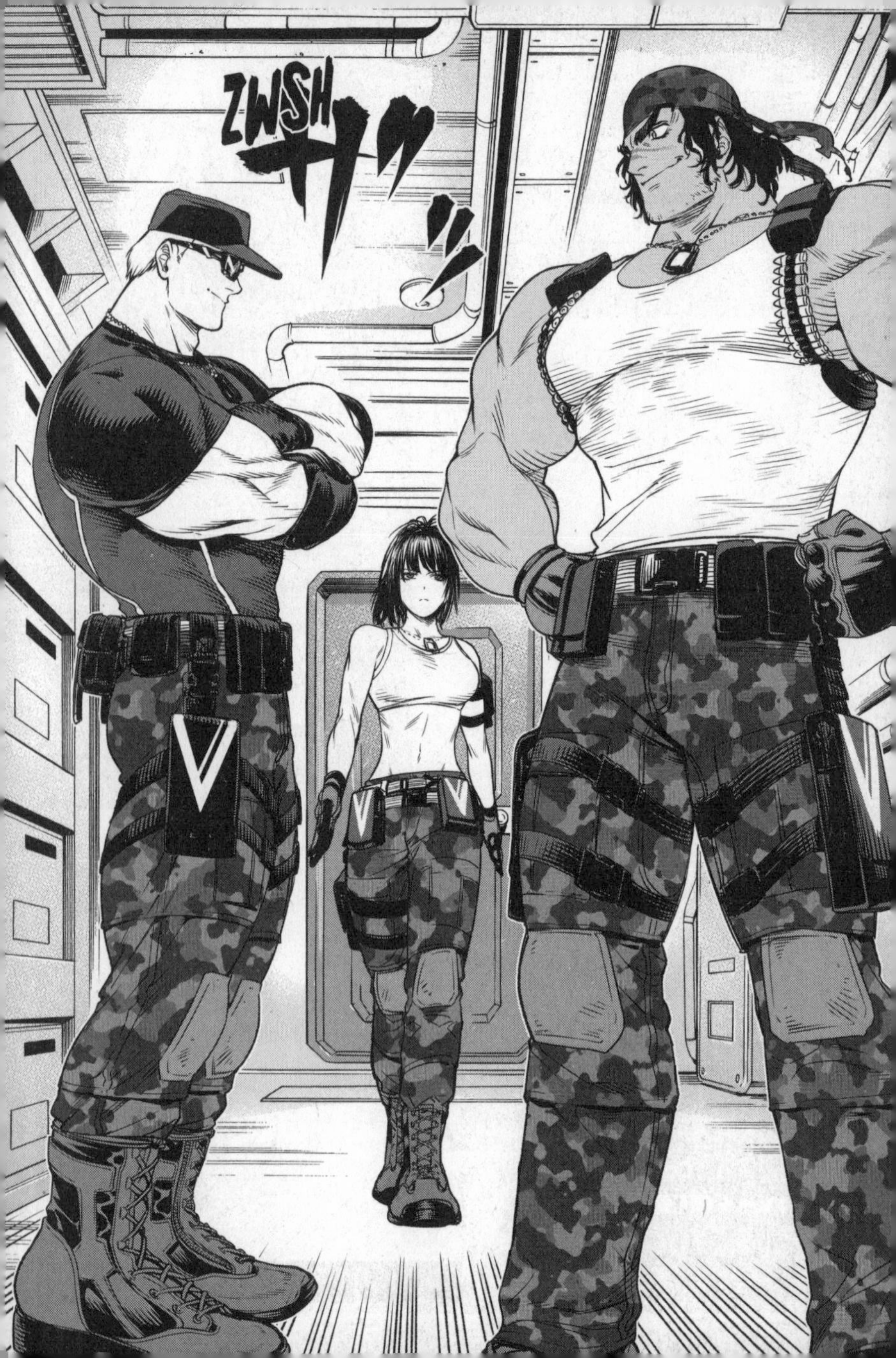
ZWSH

MOVE LIST

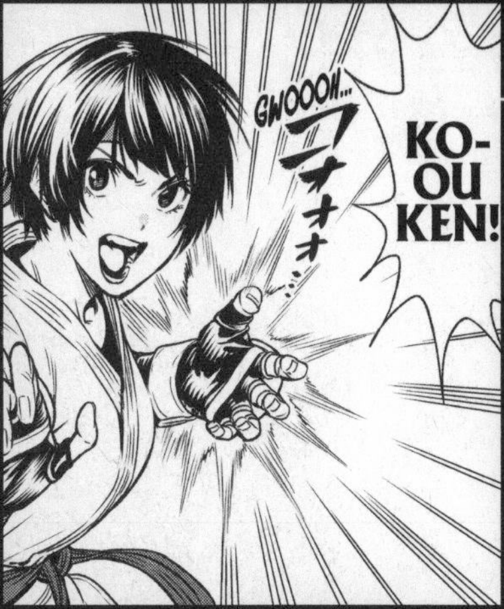

GWOOOH...
KO-OU KEN!!

Ko-Ou Ken

Gathers chi in the heel of the hand before striking it outward. Depending on the user, the chi may then take the form of a projectile or a shock wave. In the story, Yuri adjusts it to form "Ultra Hands."

Users:
Ryo Sakazaki, Yuri Sakazaki

Command:
↓↘→ + LP or HP

Raiou Ken

A projectile Ko-Ou Ken launched from the air. In the story, Yuri develops it into "Ultra Yuri," an imitation of Kyoku • Koureishin, by covering her whole body with chi. The disadvantage is that it exhausts her stamina.

User: Yuri Sakazaki

Command:
↓↘→ + LK or HK ※(in the air)

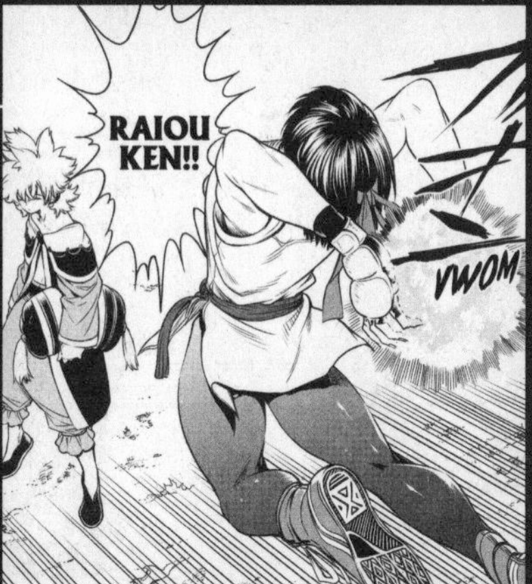

RAIOU KEN!!
VWOM

Chou Geki Hou

A secret art of Hakkyokuminminken that blasts out chi pooled in the sleeping body. Because the chi goes in all directions, it makes the user briefly invincible.

User: Meitenkun

Command:
↓↘→↓↘→ + LP or HP

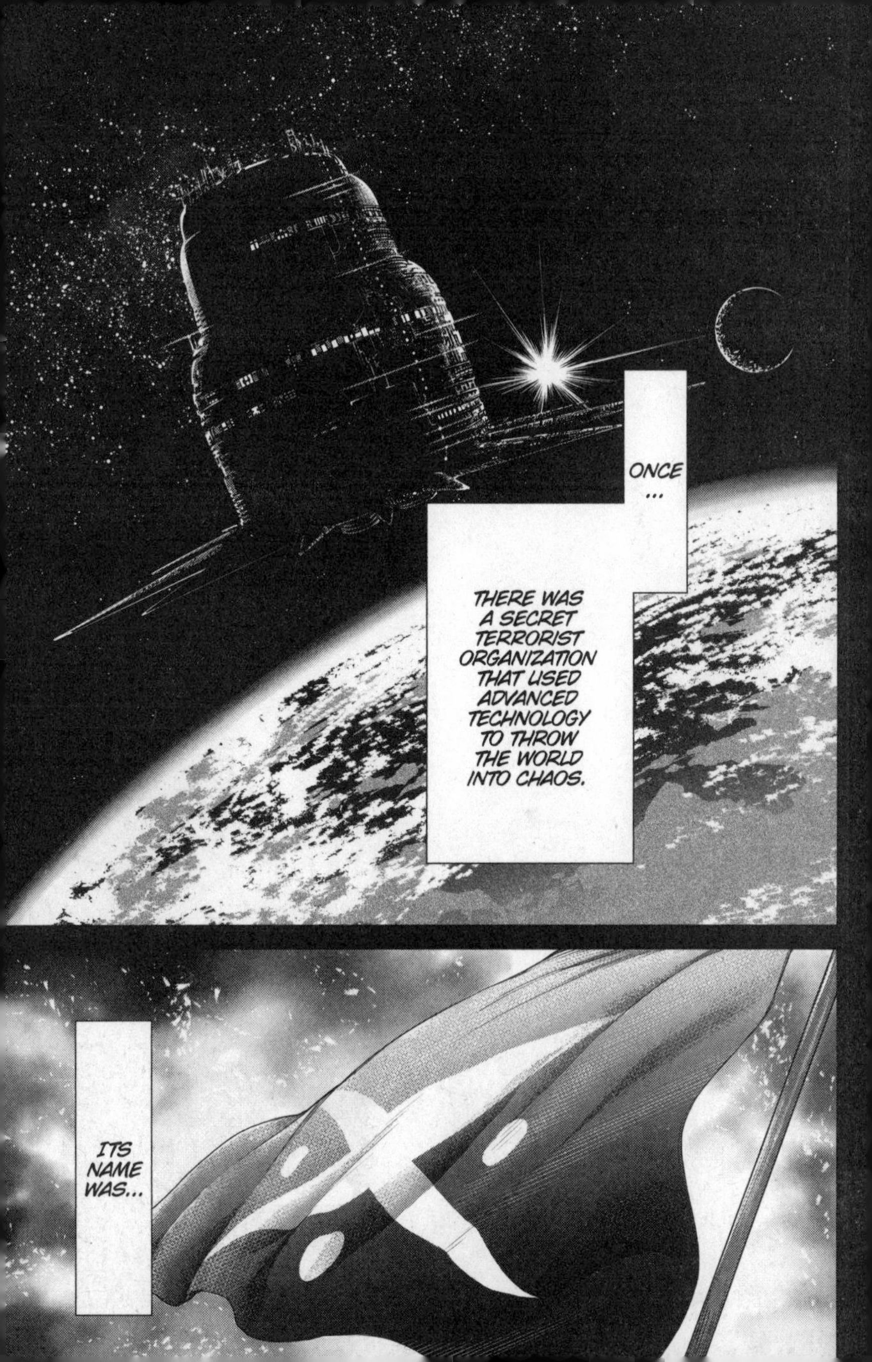
ONCE ...
THERE WAS A SECRET TERRORIST ORGANIZATION THAT USED ADVANCED TECHNOLOGY TO THROW THE WORLD INTO CHAOS.
ITS NAME WAS...

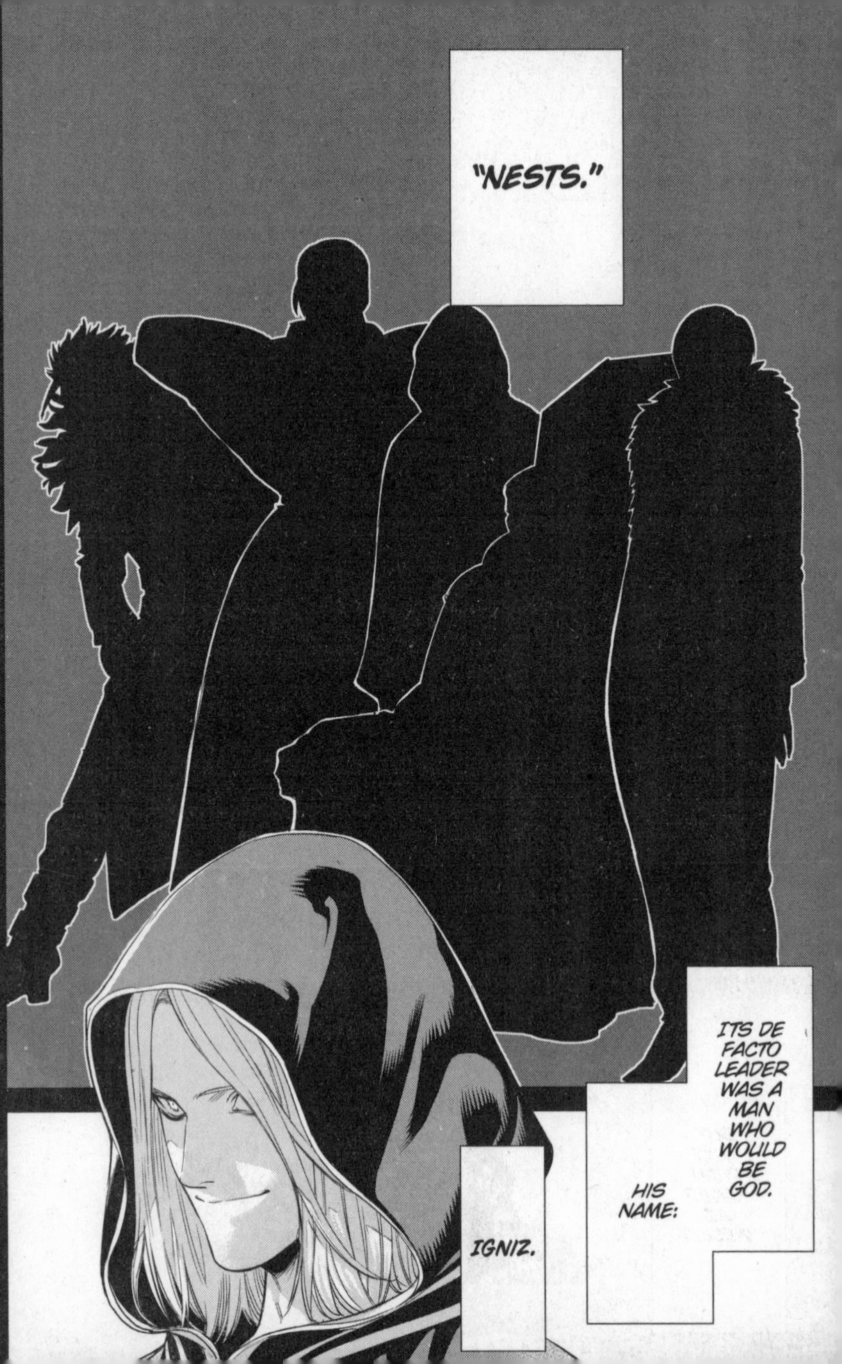
"NESTS."
ITS DE FACTO LEADER WAS A MAN WHO WOULD BE GOD.
HIS NAME:
IGNIZ.

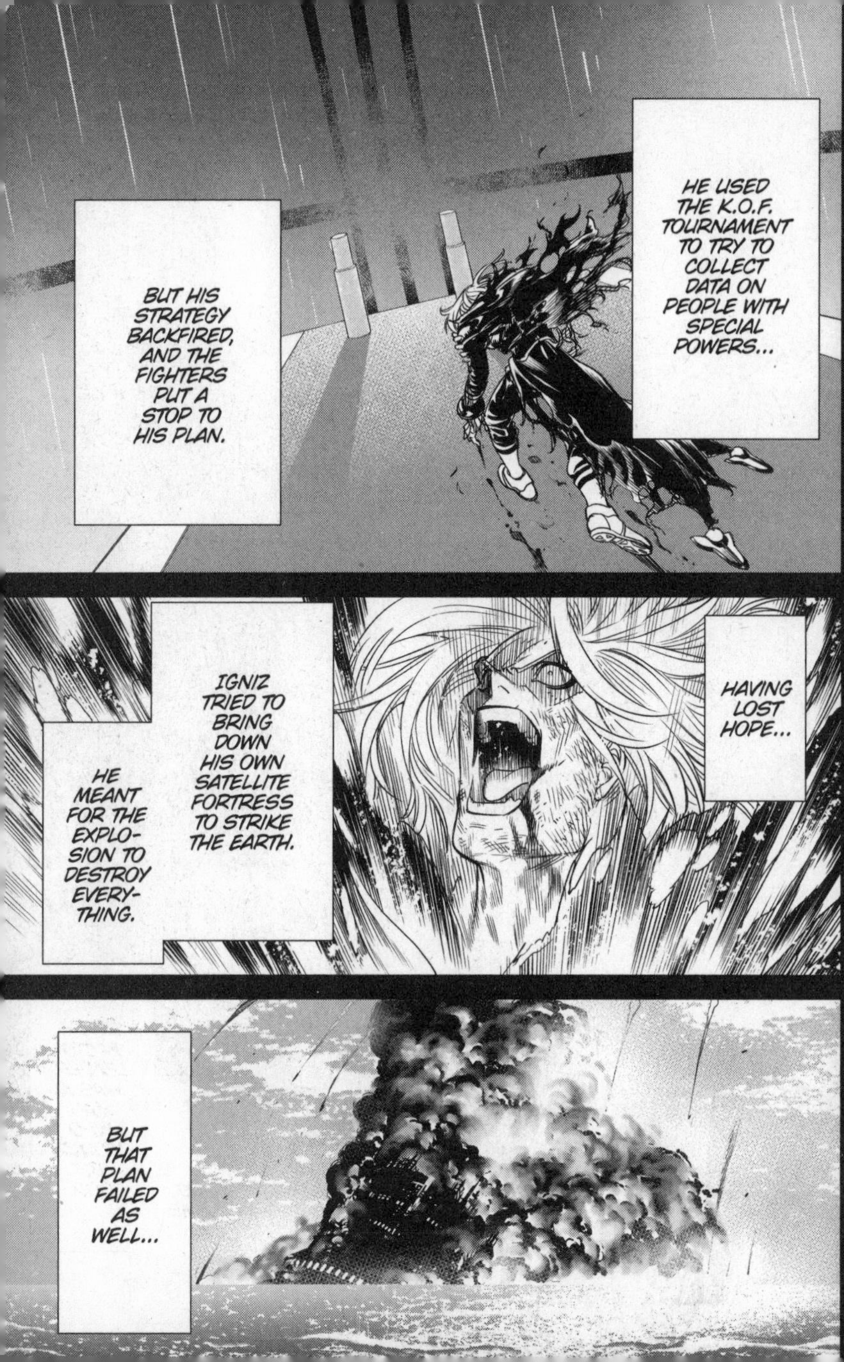
HE USED THE K.O.F. TOURNAMENT TO TRY TO COLLECT DATA ON PEOPLE WITH SPECIAL POWERS...
BUT HIS STRATEGY BACKFIRED, AND THE FIGHTERS PUT A STOP TO HIS PLAN.
HAVING LOST HOPE...
IGNIZ TRIED TO BRING DOWN HIS OWN SATELLITE FORTRESS TO STRIKE THE EARTH.
HE MEANT FOR THE EXPLOSION TO DESTROY EVERYTHING.
BUT THAT PLAN FAILED AS WELL...

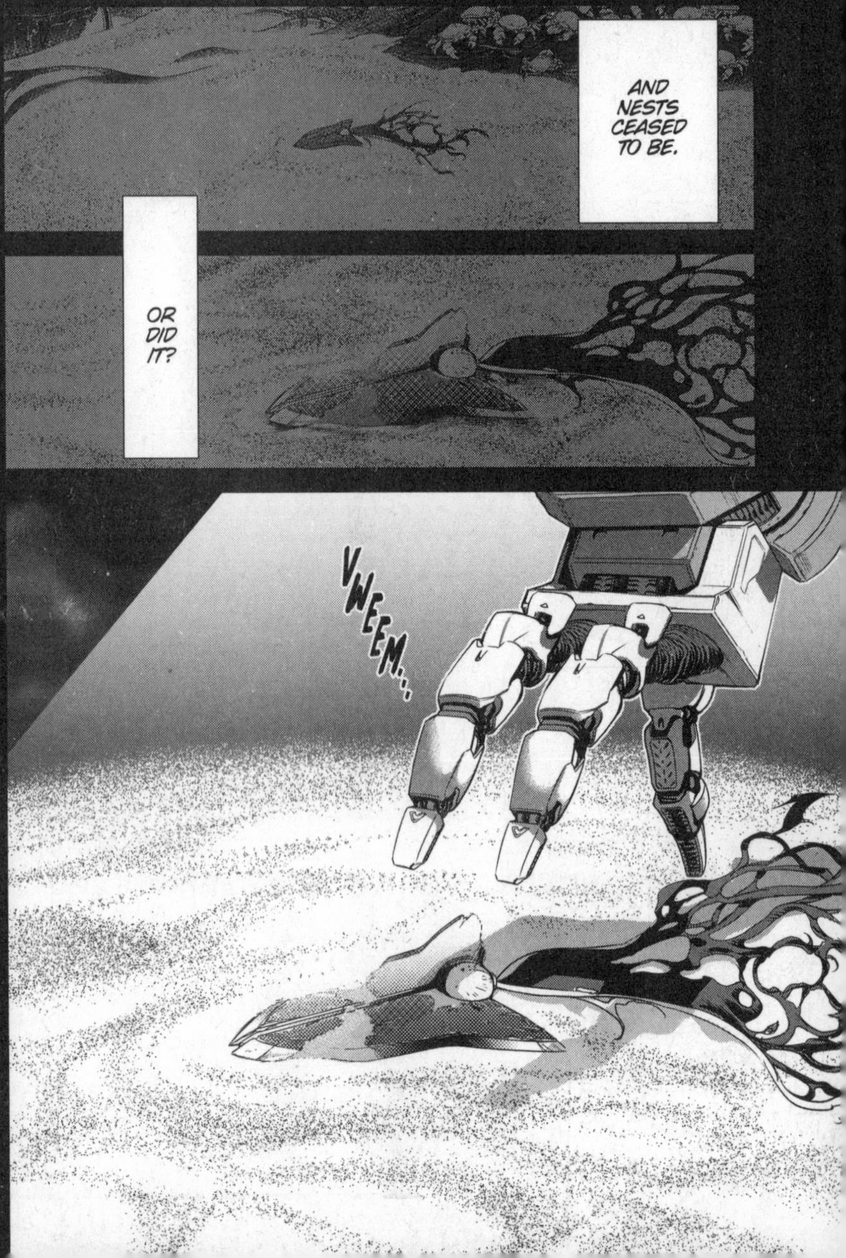
AND NESTS CEASED TO BE.
OR DID IT?
VWEEM...

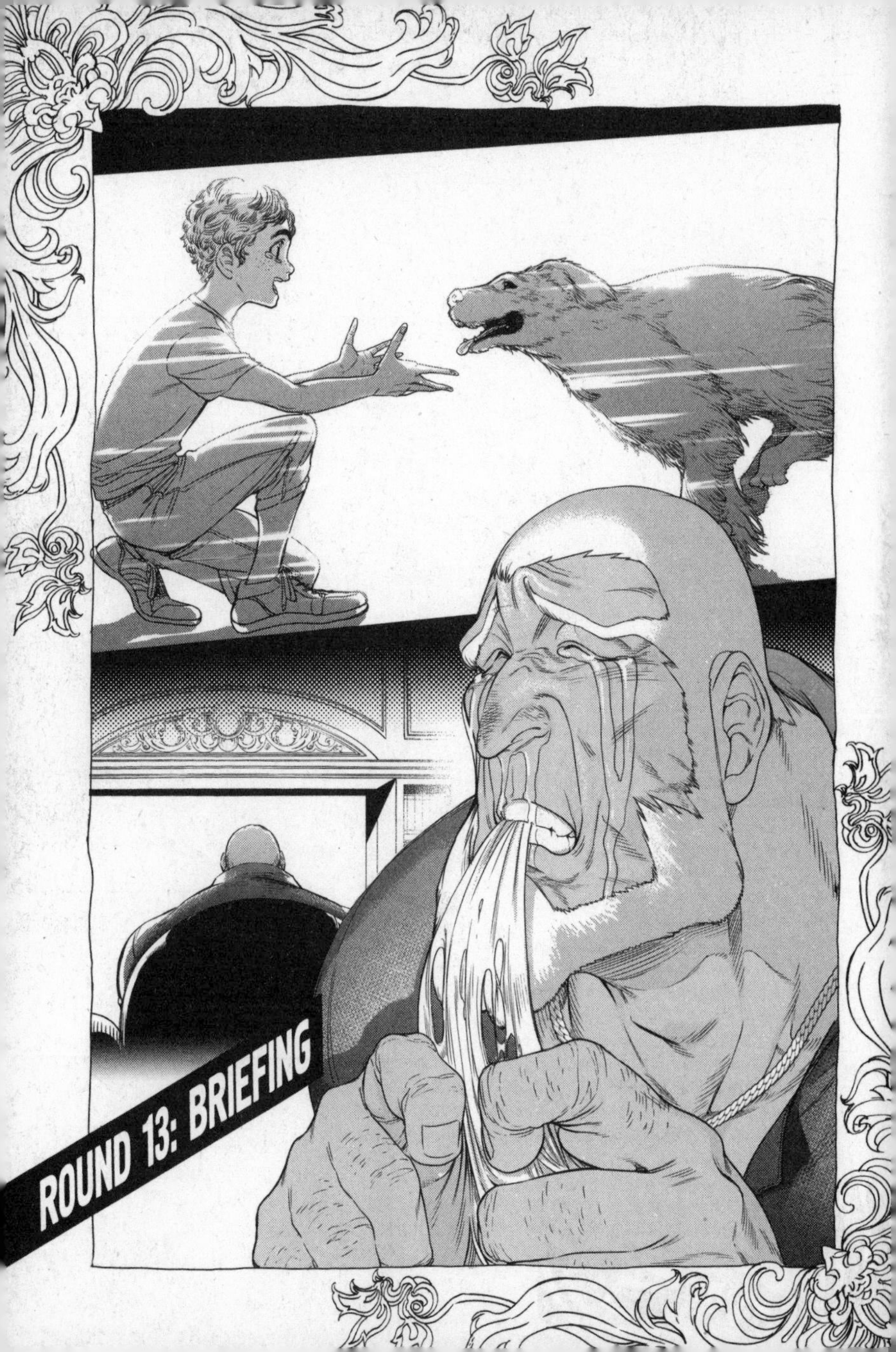
ROUND 13: BRIEFING

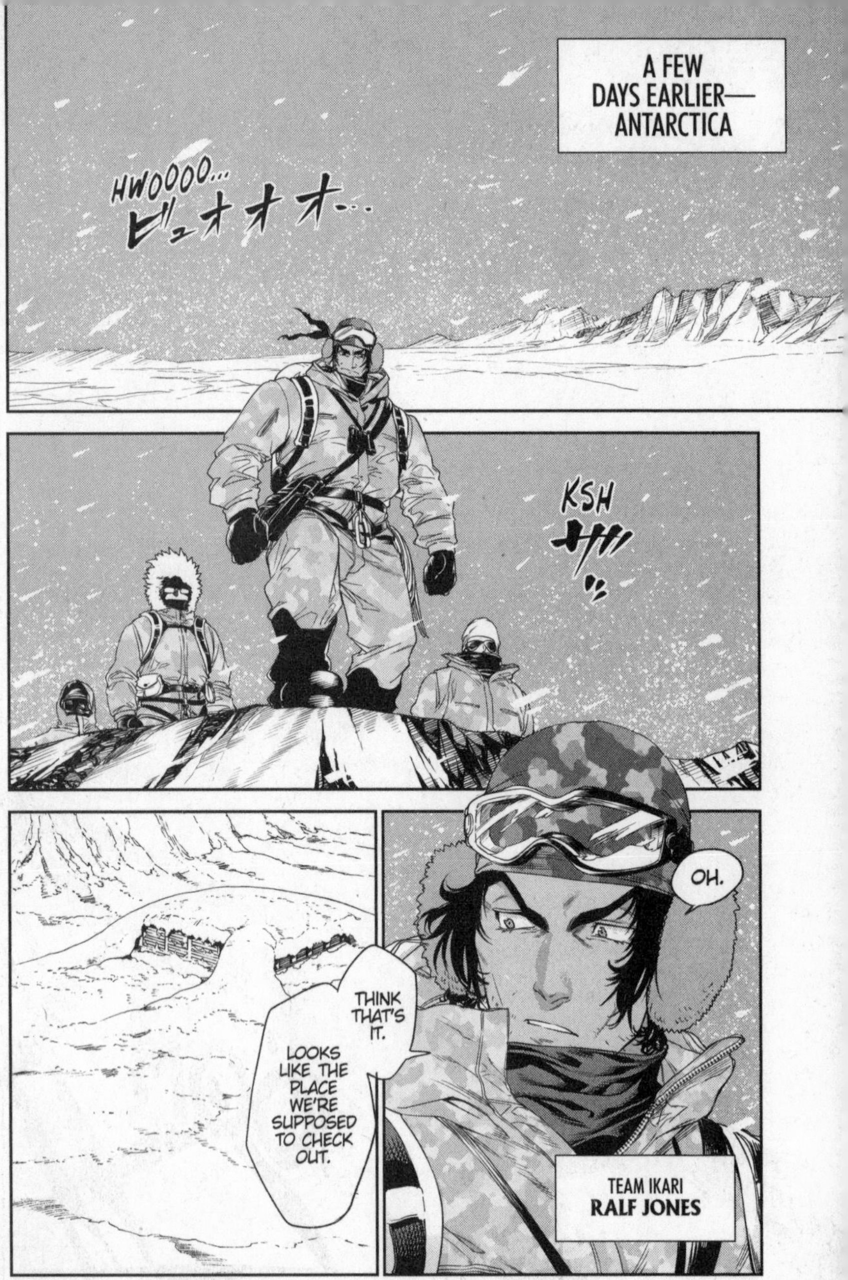
A FEW DAYS EARLIER— ANTARCTICA
HWOOOO...
ビュオオオー...
KSH
ザッ
OH.
TEAM IKARI
RALF JONES
THINK THAT'S IT.
LOOKS LIKE THE PLACE WE'RE SUPPOSED TO CHECK OUT.

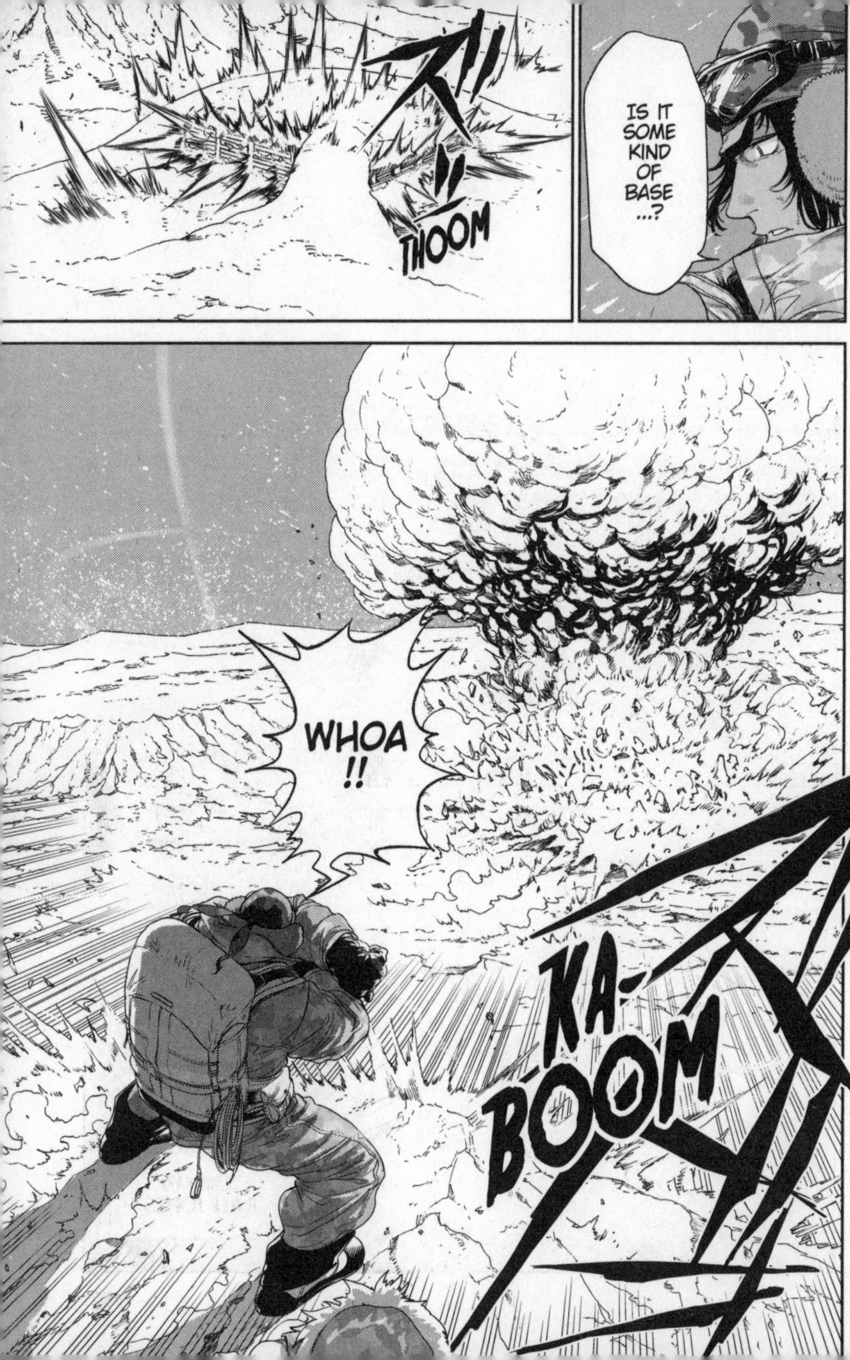
IS IT SOME KIND OF BASE ...?
THOOM
WHOA !!
KA-BOOM

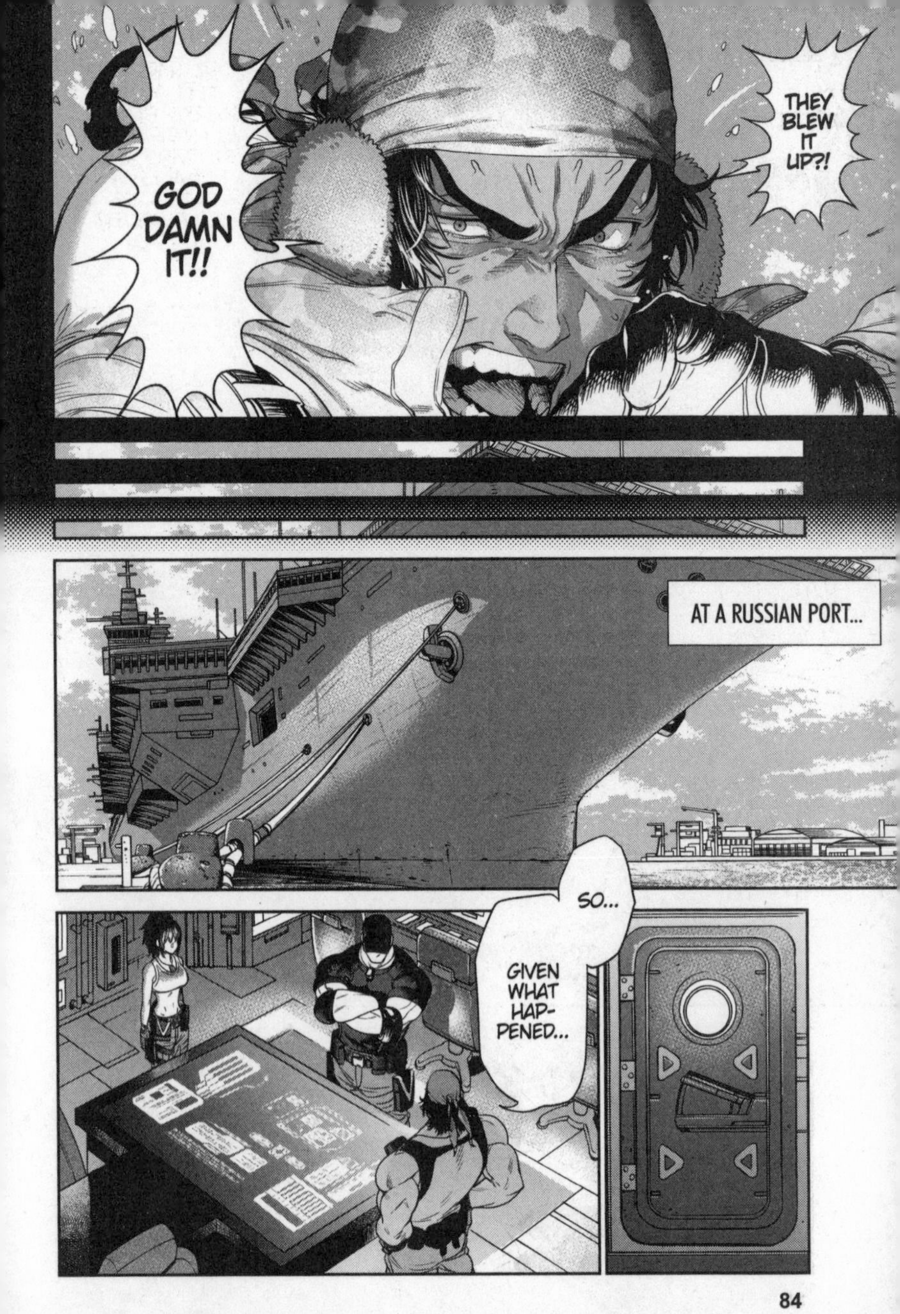
THEY BLEW IT UP?!
GOD DAMN IT!!
AT A RUSSIAN PORT...
SO...
GIVEN WHAT HAP-PENED...

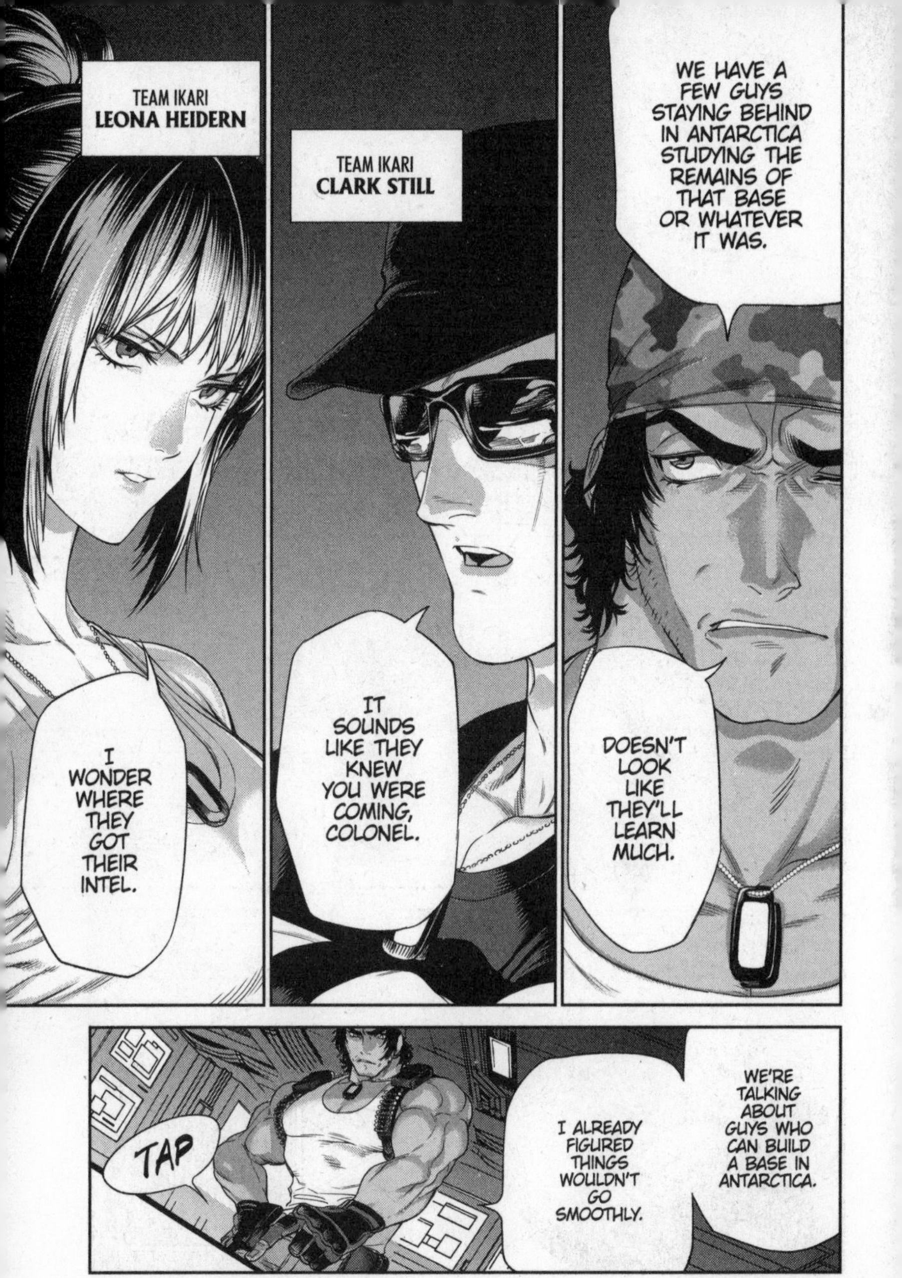
WE HAVE A FEW GUYS STAYING BEHIND IN ANTARCTICA STUDYING THE REMAINS OF THAT BASE OR WHATEVER IT WAS.
DOESN'T LOOK LIKE THEY'LL LEARN MUCH.
TEAM IKARI CLARK STILL
IT SOUNDS LIKE THEY KNEW YOU WERE COMING, COLONEL.
TEAM IKARI LEONA HEIDERN
I WONDER WHERE THEY GOT THEIR INTEL.
WE'RE TALKING ABOUT GUYS WHO CAN BUILD A BASE IN ANTARCTICA.
I ALREADY FIGURED THINGS WOULDN'T GO SMOOTHLY.
TAP

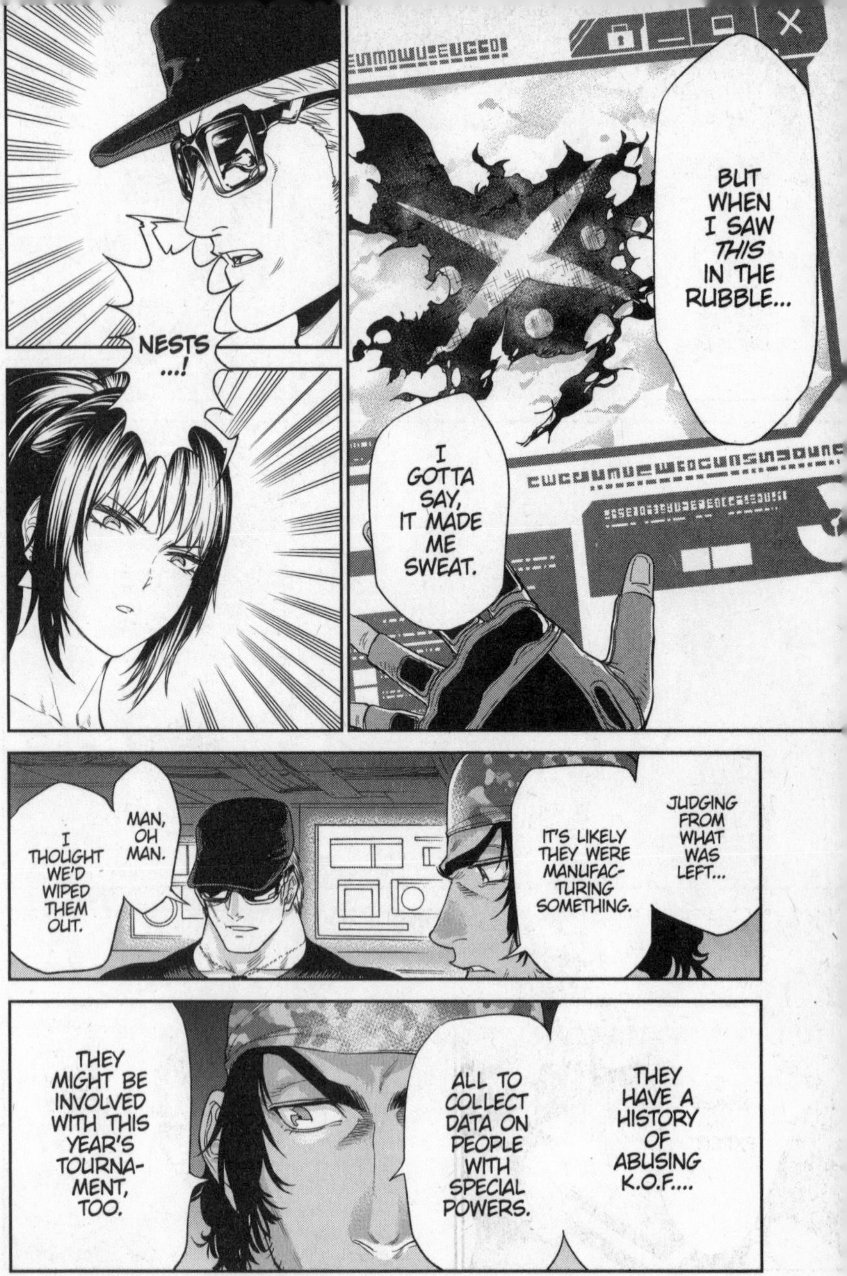
BUT WHEN I SAW *THIS* IN THE RUBBLE...
I GOTTA SAY, IT MADE ME SWEAT.
NESTS ...!
JUDGING FROM WHAT WAS LEFT...
IT'S LIKELY THEY WERE MANUFAC-TURING SOMETHING.
MAN, OH MAN.
I THOUGHT WE'D WIPED THEM OUT.
THEY HAVE A HISTORY OF ABUSING K.O.F....
ALL TO COLLECT DATA ON PEOPLE WITH SPECIAL POWERS.
THEY MIGHT BE INVOLVED WITH THIS YEAR'S TOURNA-MENT, TOO.

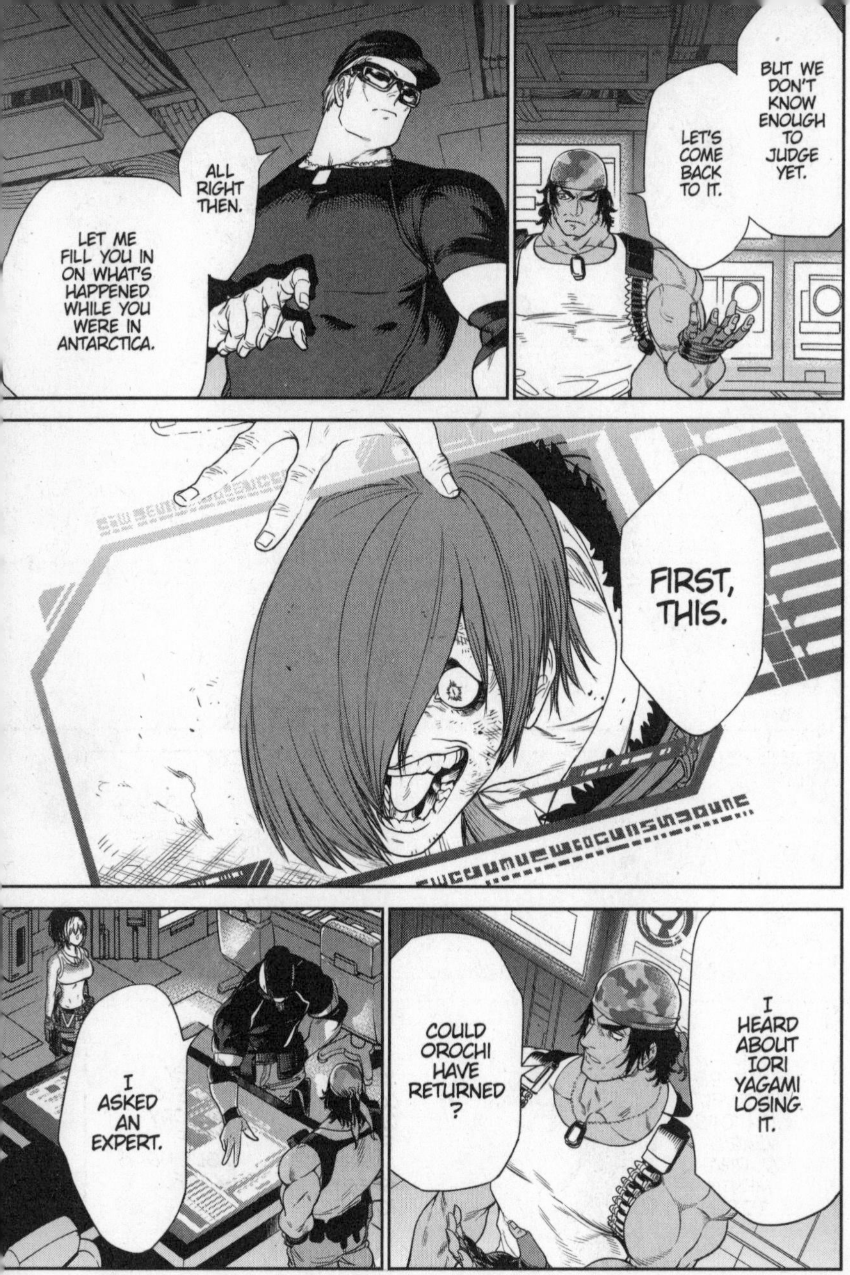
BUT WE DON'T KNOW ENOUGH TO JUDGE YET.
LET'S COME BACK TO IT.
ALL RIGHT THEN.
LET ME FILL YOU IN ON WHAT'S HAPPENED WHILE YOU WERE IN ANTARCTICA.
FIRST, THIS.
I HEARD ABOUT IORI YAGAMI LOSING IT.
COULD OROCHI HAVE RETURNED?
I ASKED AN EXPERT.

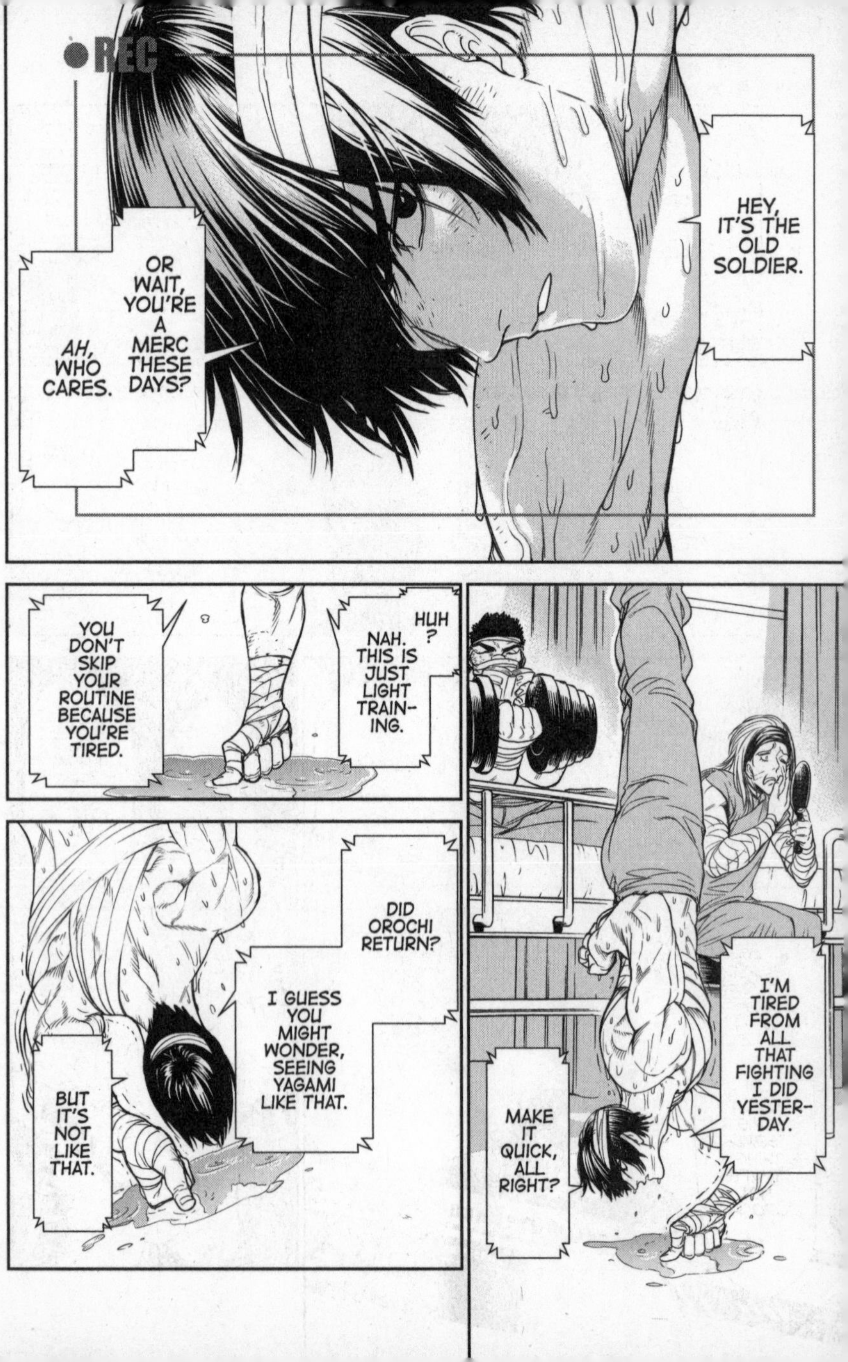
●REC
HEY, IT'S THE OLD SOLDIER.
OR WAIT, YOU'RE A MERC THESE DAYS?
AH, WHO CARES.
I'M TIRED FROM ALL THAT FIGHTING I DID YESTER-DAY.
MAKE IT QUICK, ALL RIGHT?
HUH?
NAH. THIS IS JUST LIGHT TRAIN-ING.
YOU DON'T SKIP YOUR ROUTINE BECAUSE YOU'RE TIRED.
DID OROCHI RETURN?
I GUESS YOU MIGHT WONDER, SEEING YAGAMI LIKE THAT.
BUT IT'S NOT LIKE THAT.

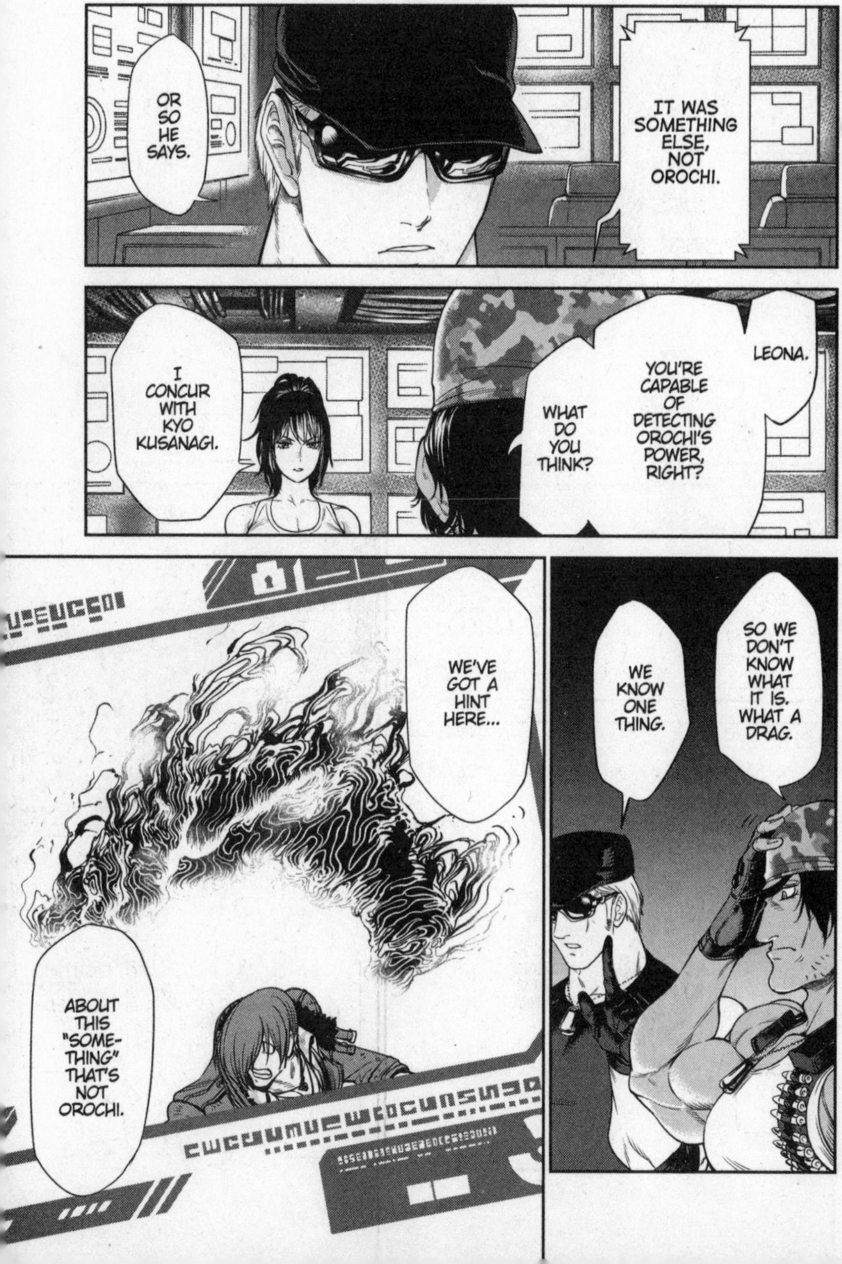
IT WAS SOMETHING ELSE, NOT OROCHI.
OR SO HE SAYS.
LEONA.
YOU'RE CAPABLE OF DETECTING OROCHI'S POWER, RIGHT?
WHAT DO YOU THINK?
I CONCUR WITH KYO KUSANAGI.
SO WE DON'T KNOW WHAT IT IS. WHAT A DRAG.
WE KNOW ONE THING.
WE'VE GOT A HINT HERE...
ABOUT THIS "SOME-THING" THAT'S NOT OROCHI.

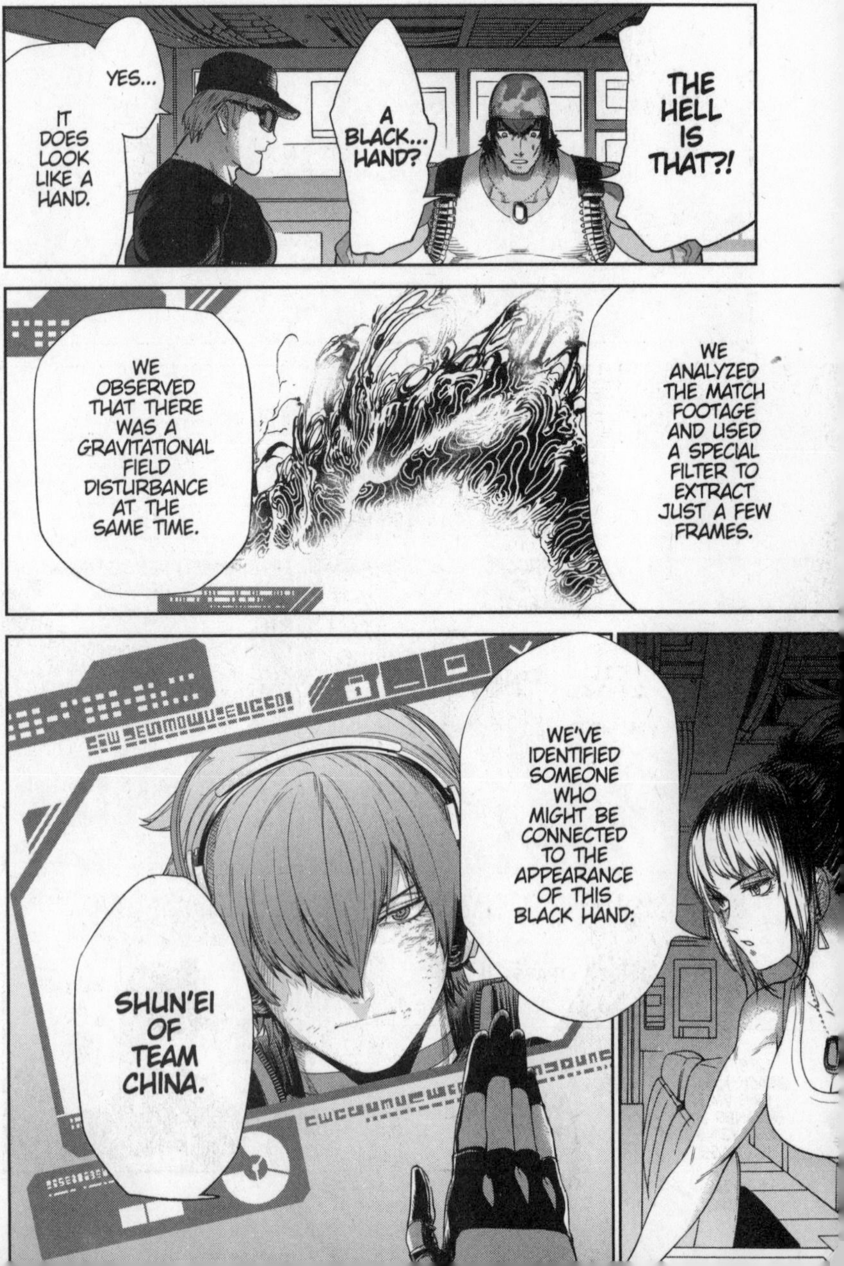
THE HELL IS THAT?!
A BLACK... HAND?
YES...
IT DOES LOOK LIKE A HAND.
WE ANALYZED THE MATCH FOOTAGE AND USED A SPECIAL FILTER TO EXTRACT JUST A FEW FRAMES.
WE OBSERVED THAT THERE WAS A GRAVITATIONAL FIELD DISTURBANCE AT THE SAME TIME.
WE'VE IDENTIFIED SOMEONE WHO MIGHT BE CONNECTED TO THE APPEARANCE OF THIS BLACK HAND:
SHUN'EI OF TEAM CHINA.

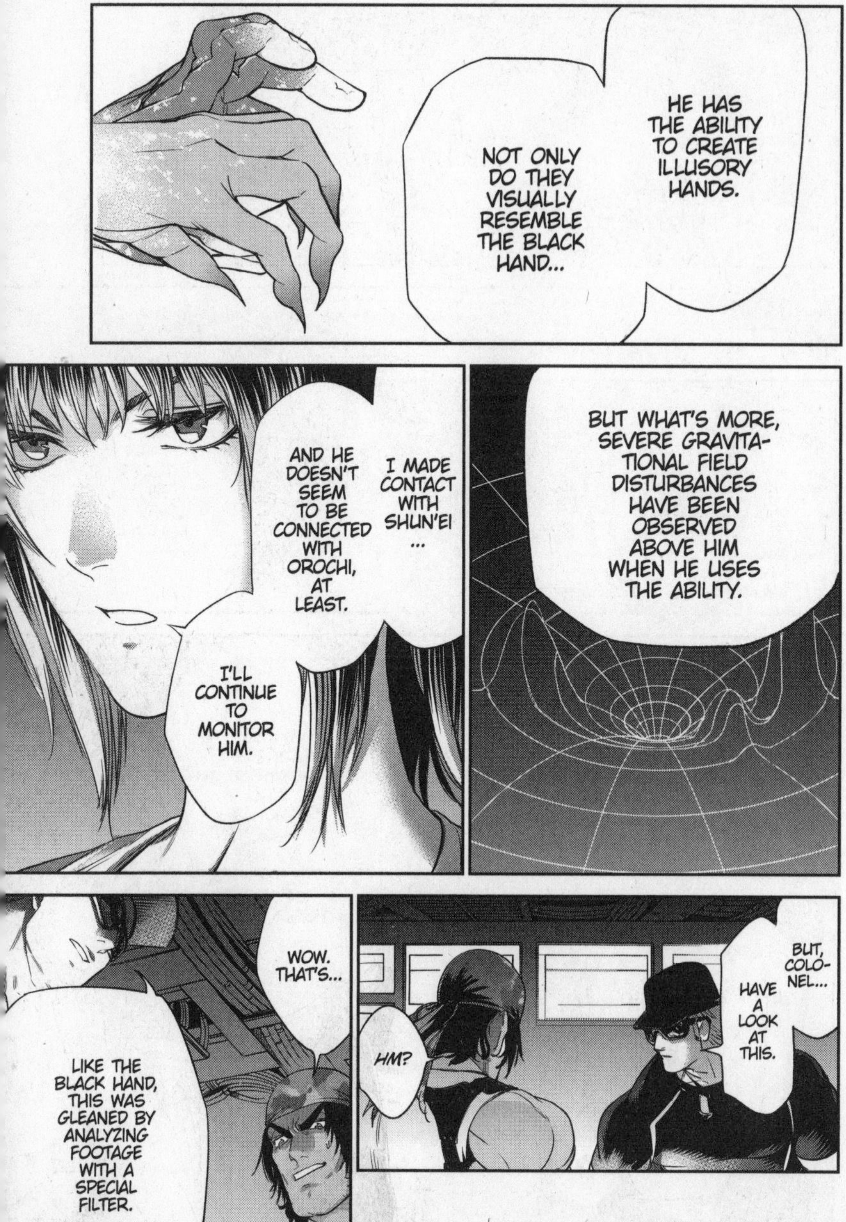
HE HAS THE ABILITY TO CREATE ILLUSORY HANDS.
NOT ONLY DO THEY VISUALLY RESEMBLE THE BLACK HAND...
BUT WHAT'S MORE, SEVERE GRAVITATIONAL FIELD DISTURBANCES HAVE BEEN OBSERVED ABOVE HIM WHEN HE USES THE ABILITY.
I MADE CONTACT WITH SHUN'EI ...
AND HE DOESN'T SEEM TO BE CONNECTED WITH OROCHI, AT LEAST.
I'LL CONTINUE TO MONITOR HIM.
BUT, COLONEL...
HAVE A LOOK AT THIS.
HM?
WOW. THAT'S...
LIKE THE BLACK HAND, THIS WAS GLEANED BY ANALYZING FOOTAGE WITH A SPECIAL FILTER.

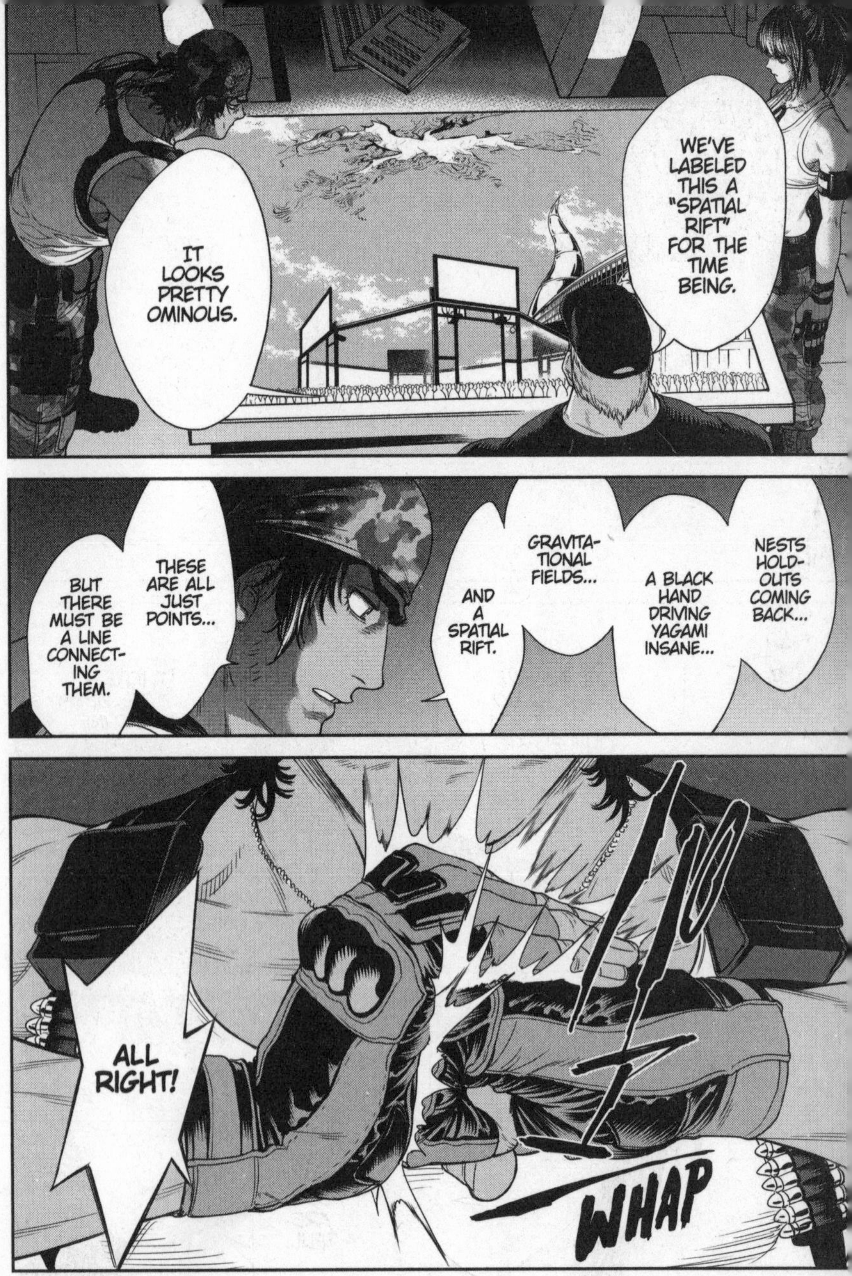
WE'VE LABELED THIS A "SPATIAL RIFT" FOR THE TIME BEING.
IT LOOKS PRETTY OMINOUS.
NESTS HOLDOUTS COMING BACK...
A BLACK HAND DRIVING YAGAMI INSANE...
GRAVITATIONAL FIELDS...
AND A SPATIAL RIFT.
THESE ARE ALL JUST POINTS...
BUT THERE MUST BE A LINE CONNECTING THEM.
WHAP
ALL RIGHT!

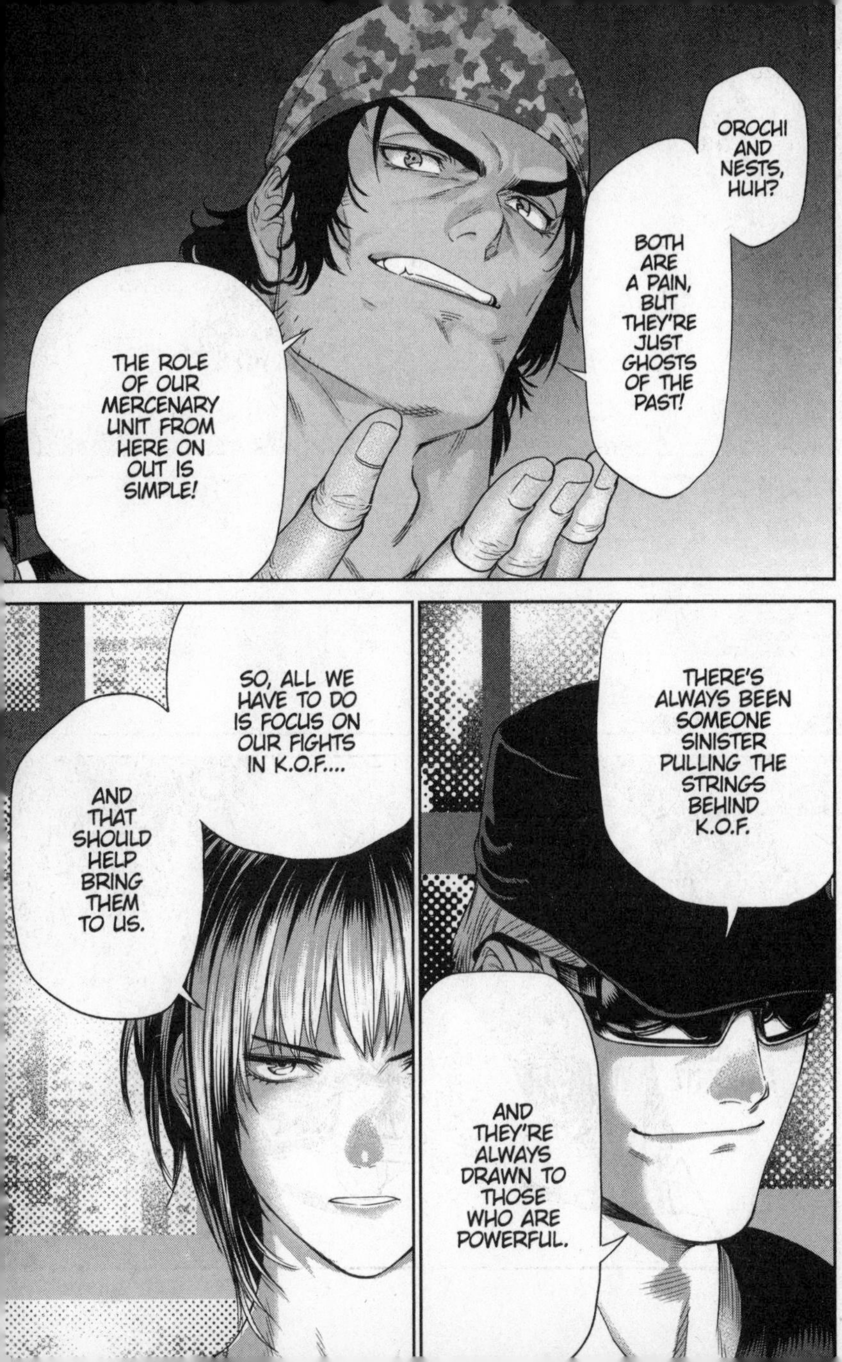
OROCHI AND NESTS, HUH?
BOTH ARE A PAIN, BUT THEY'RE JUST GHOSTS OF THE PAST!
THE ROLE OF OUR MERCENARY UNIT FROM HERE ON OUT IS SIMPLE!
THERE'S ALWAYS BEEN SOMEONE SINISTER PULLING THE STRINGS BEHIND K.O.F.
AND THEY'RE ALWAYS DRAWN TO THOSE WHO ARE POWERFUL.
SO, ALL WE HAVE TO DO IS FOCUS ON OUR FIGHTS IN K.O.F....
AND THAT SHOULD HELP BRING THEM TO US.

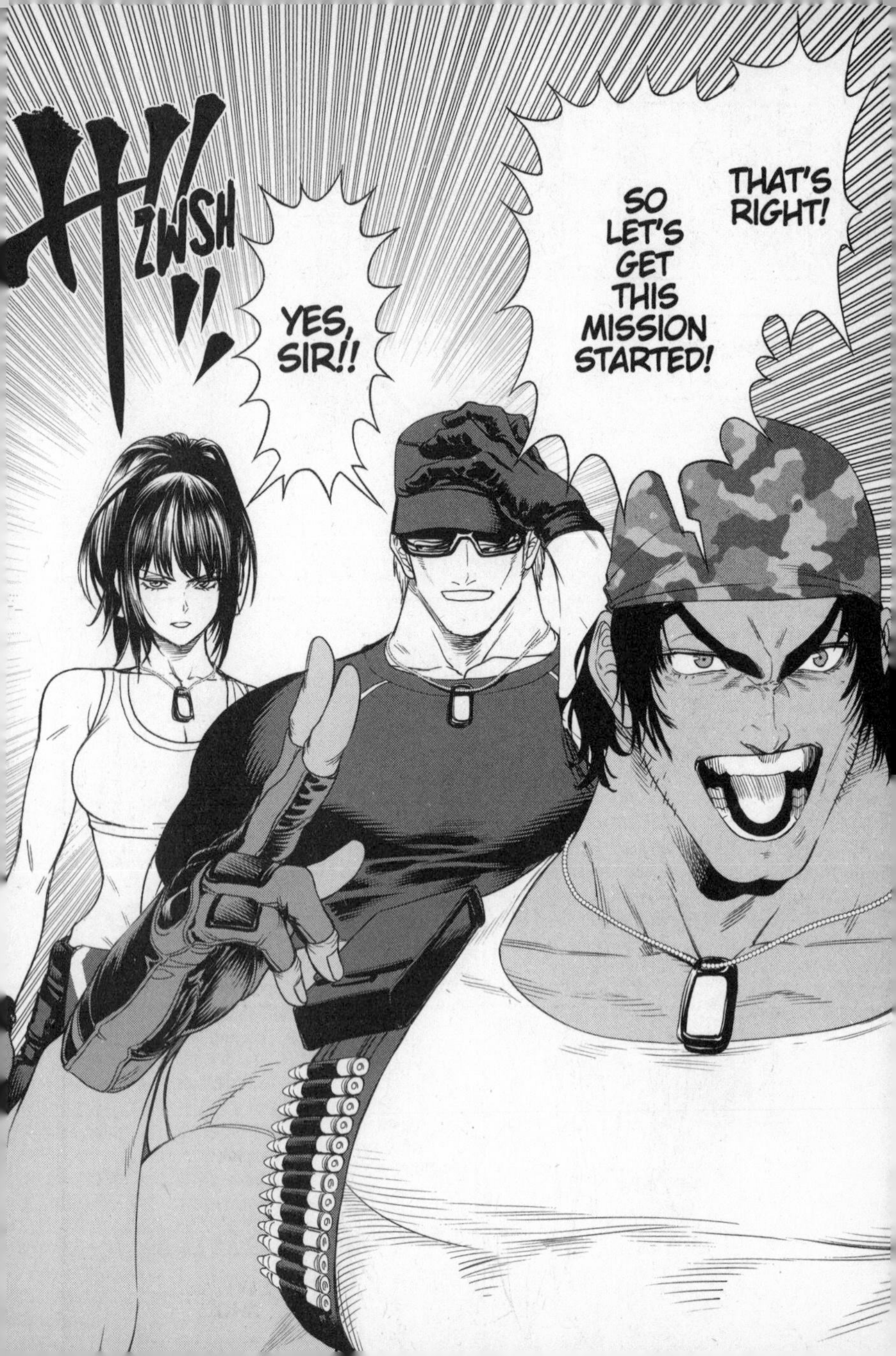
THAT'S RIGHT!
SO LET'S GET THIS MISSION STARTED!
YES, SIR!!
ZWSH

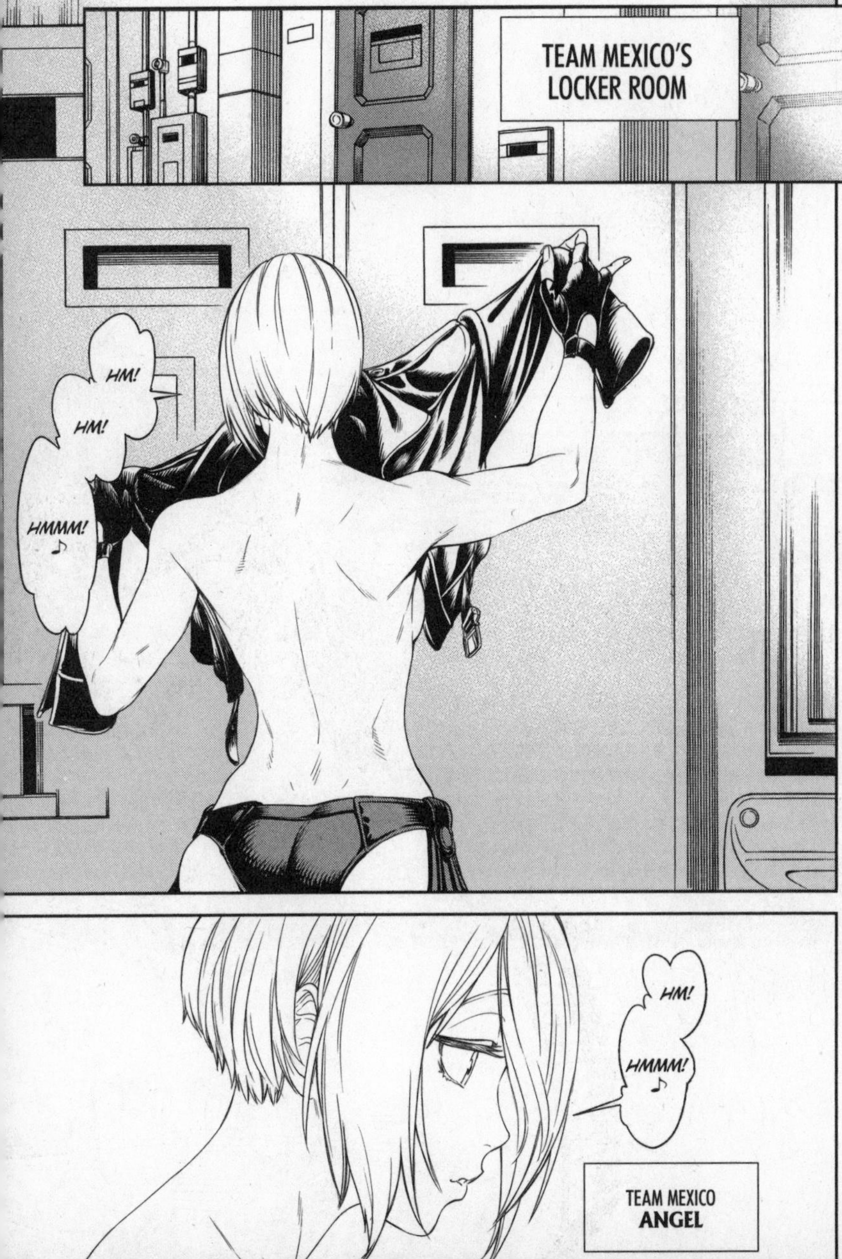
TEAM MEXICO'S LOCKER ROOM
HM! HM! HMMM! ♪
HM! HMMM! ♪
TEAM MEXICO
ANGEL

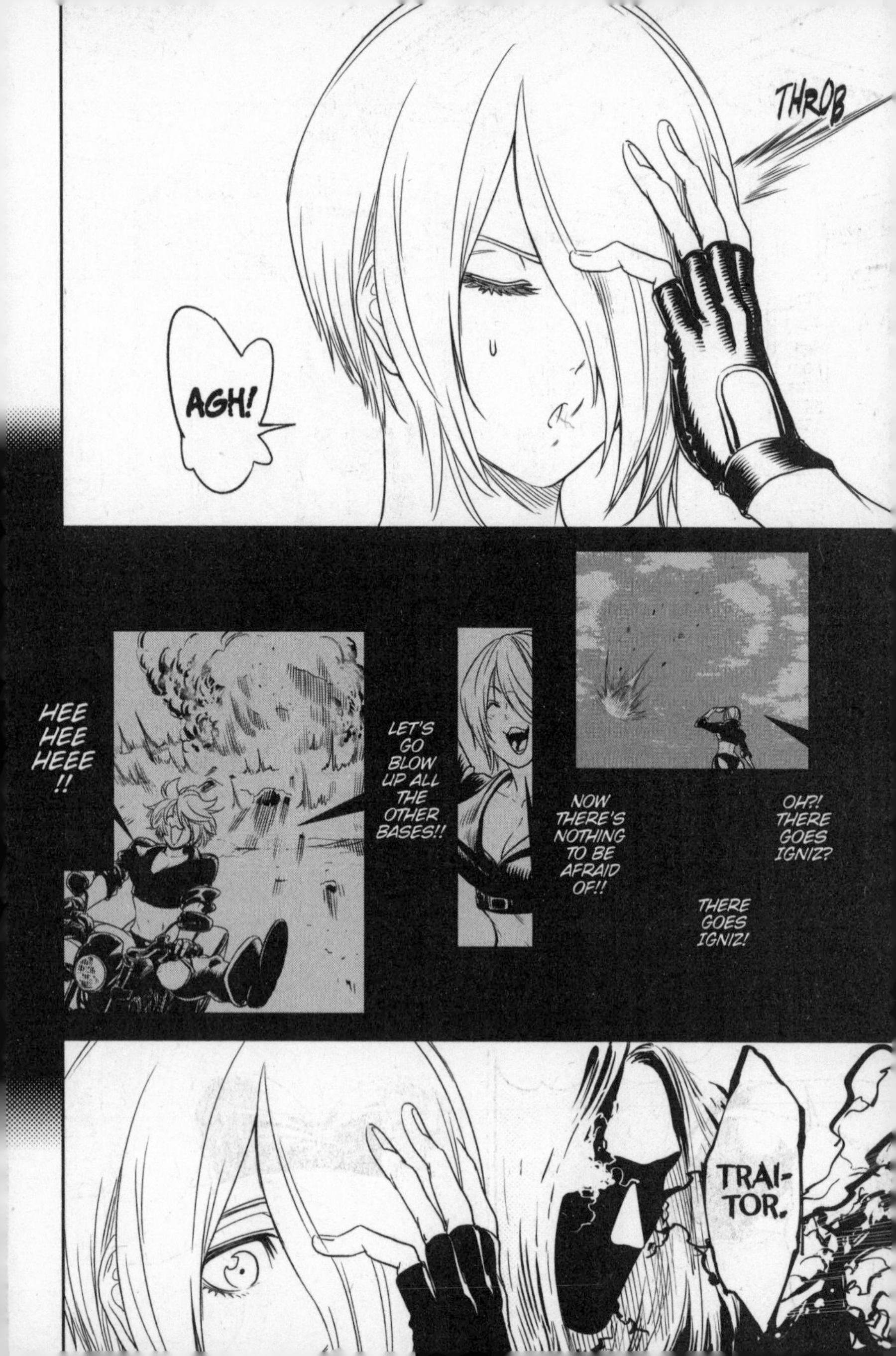
THROB
AGH!
OH?! THERE GOES IGNIZ?
THERE GOES IGNIZ!
NOW THERE'S NOTHING TO BE AFRAID OF!!
LET'S GO BLOW UP ALL THE OTHER BASES!!
HEE HEE HEEE !!
TRAI-TOR.

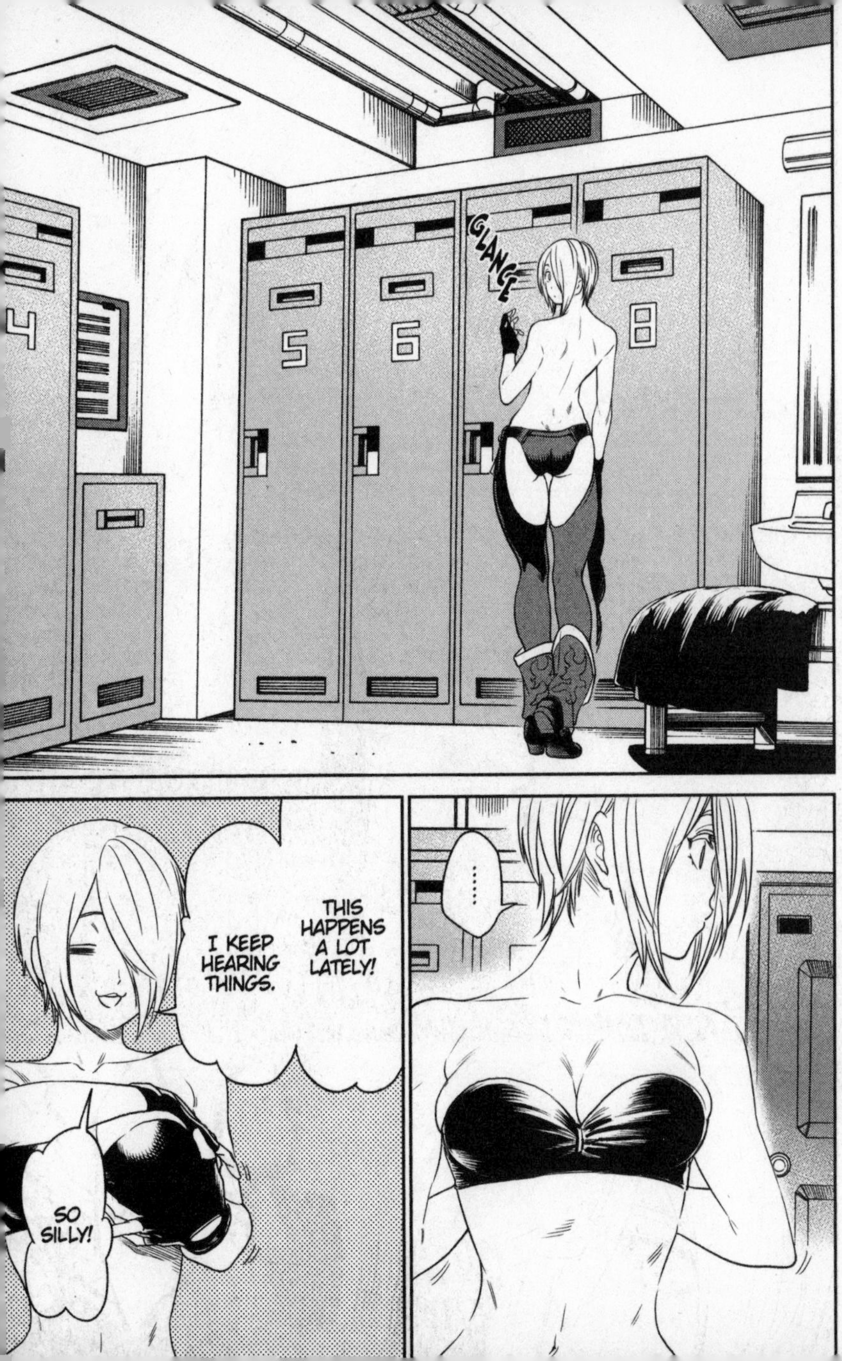
GLANCE
......
THIS HAPPENS A LOT LATELY!
I KEEP HEARING THINGS.
SO SILLY!

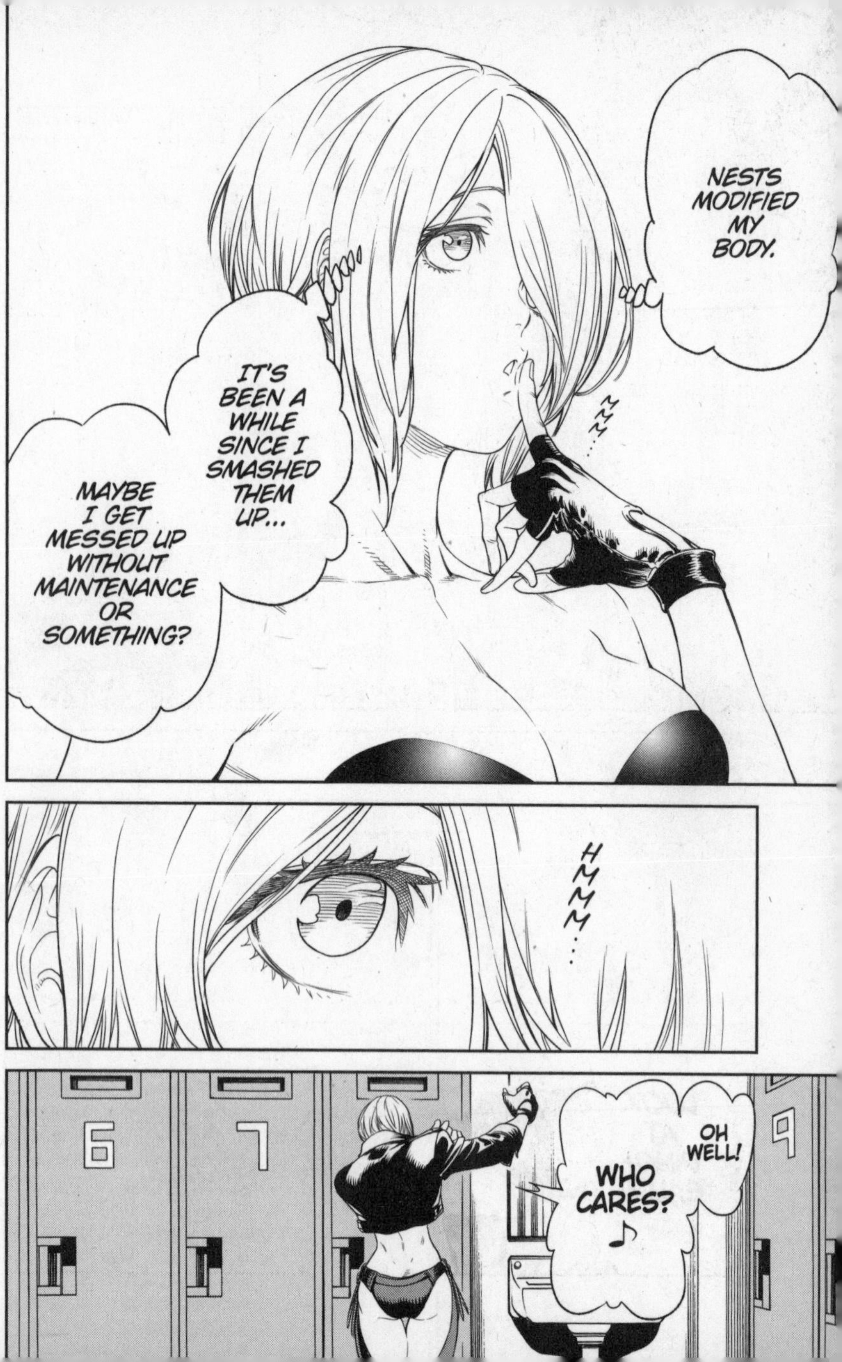
NESTS MODIFIED MY BODY.
MMM...
IT'S BEEN A WHILE SINCE I SMASHED THEM UP...
MAYBE I GET MESSED UP WITHOUT MAINTENANCE OR SOMETHING?
HMMM...
OH WELL!
WHO CARES? ♪

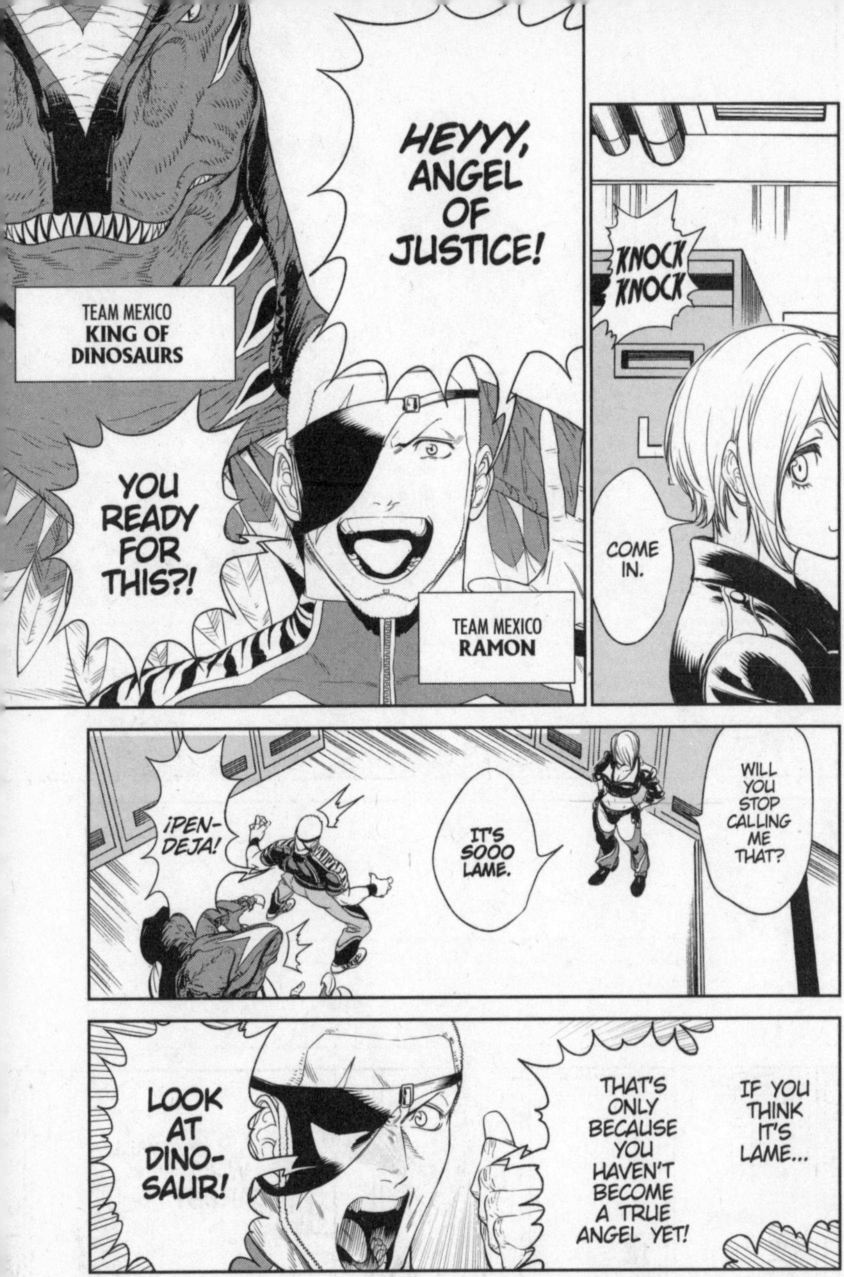
KNOCK KNOCK
COME IN.
HEYYY, ANGEL OF JUSTICE!
TEAM MEXICO KING OF DINOSAURS
YOU READY FOR THIS?!
TEAM MEXICO RAMON
WILL YOU STOP CALLING ME THAT?
IT'S SOOO LAME.
¡PEN-DEJA!
IF YOU THINK IT'S LAME...
THAT'S ONLY BECAUSE YOU HAVEN'T BECOME A TRUE ANGEL YET!
LOOK AT DINO-SAUR!

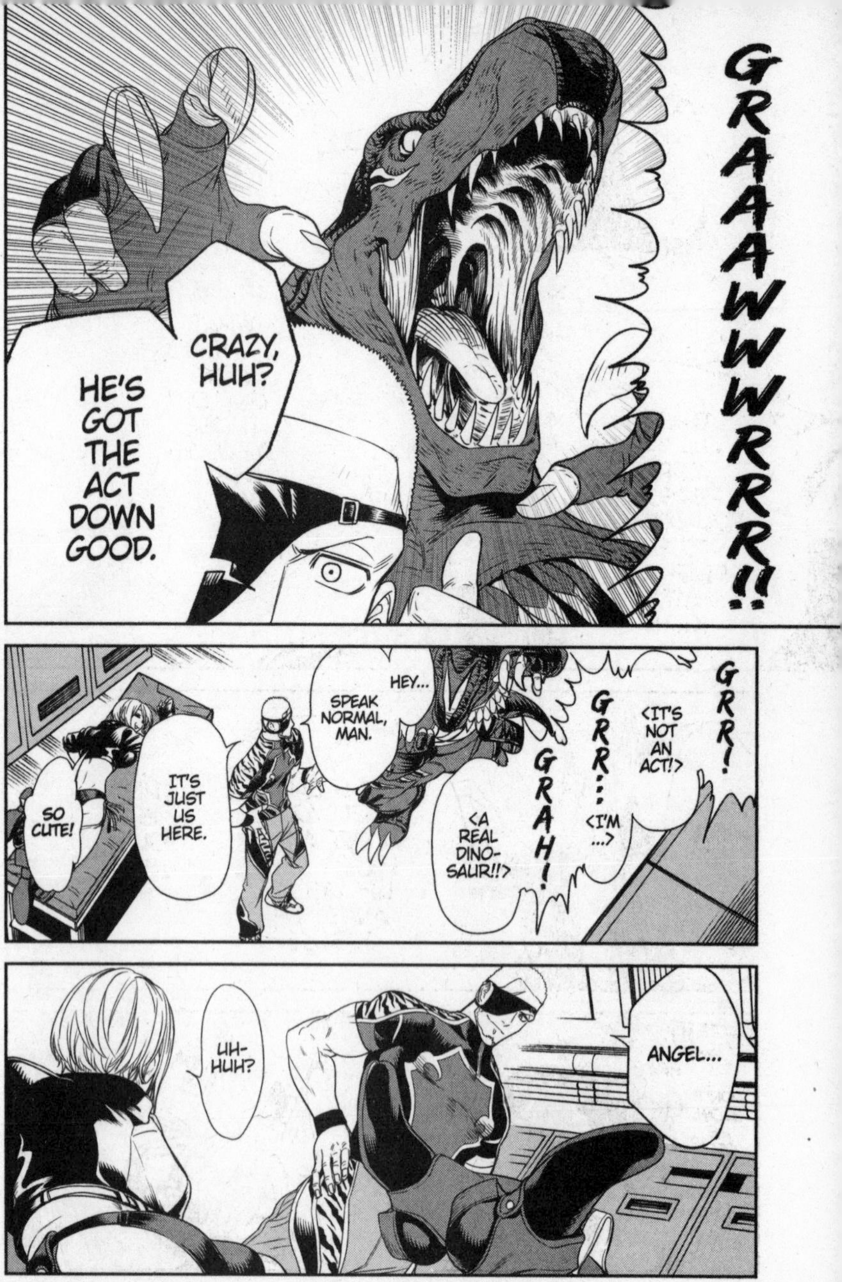
GRAAAWWWRRR!!
CRAZY, HUH?
HE'S GOT THE ACT DOWN GOOD.
GRR!
<IT'S NOT AN ACT!>
GRR...
<I'M ...>
GRAH!
<A REAL DINO-SAUR!!>
HEY... SPEAK NORMAL, MAN.
IT'S JUST US HERE.
SO CUTE!
ANGEL...
UH-HUH?

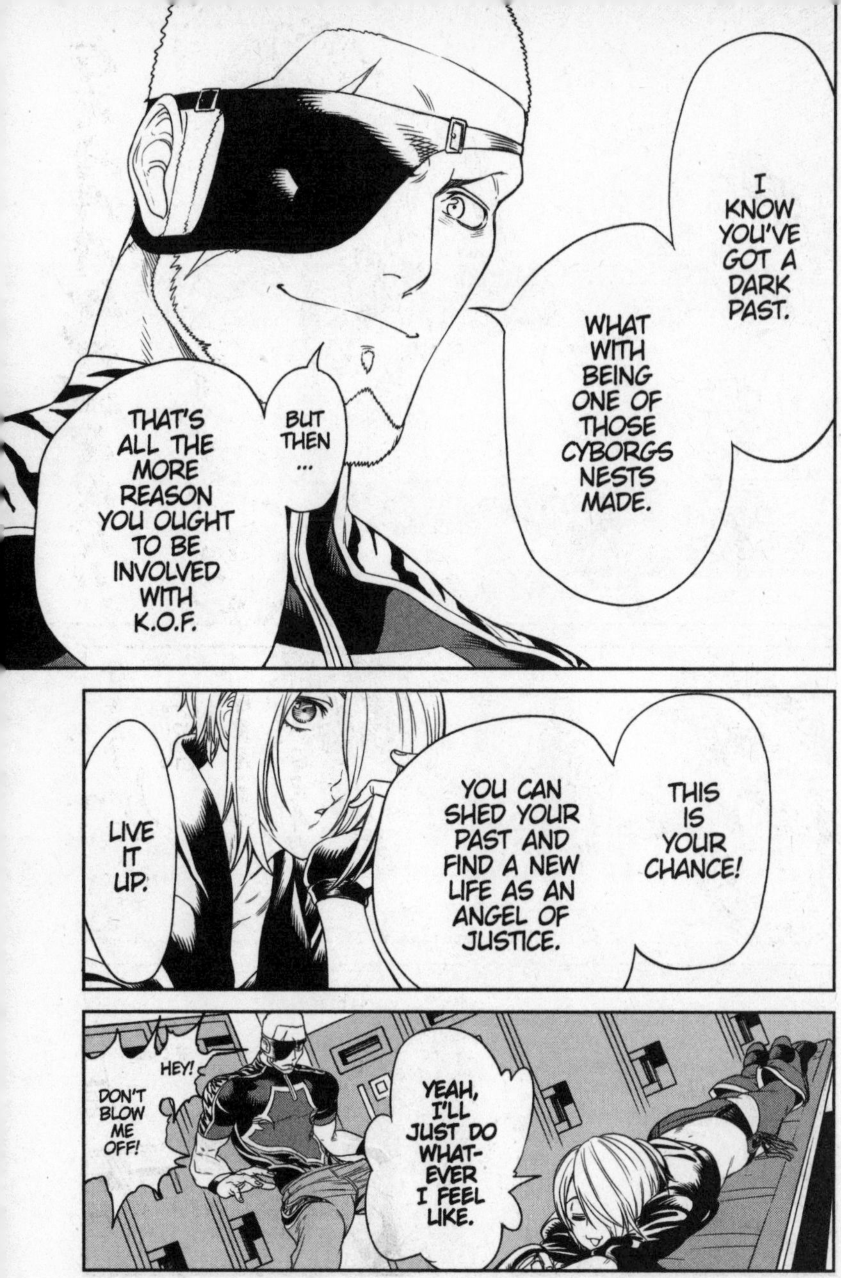
I KNOW YOU'VE GOT A DARK PAST.
WHAT WITH BEING ONE OF THOSE CYBORGS NESTS MADE.
BUT THEN ...
THAT'S ALL THE MORE REASON YOU OUGHT TO BE INVOLVED WITH K.O.F.
THIS IS YOUR CHANCE!
YOU CAN SHED YOUR PAST AND FIND A NEW LIFE AS AN ANGEL OF JUSTICE.
LIVE IT UP.
YEAH, I'LL JUST DO WHAT-EVER I FEEL LIKE.
HEY!
DON'T BLOW ME OFF!

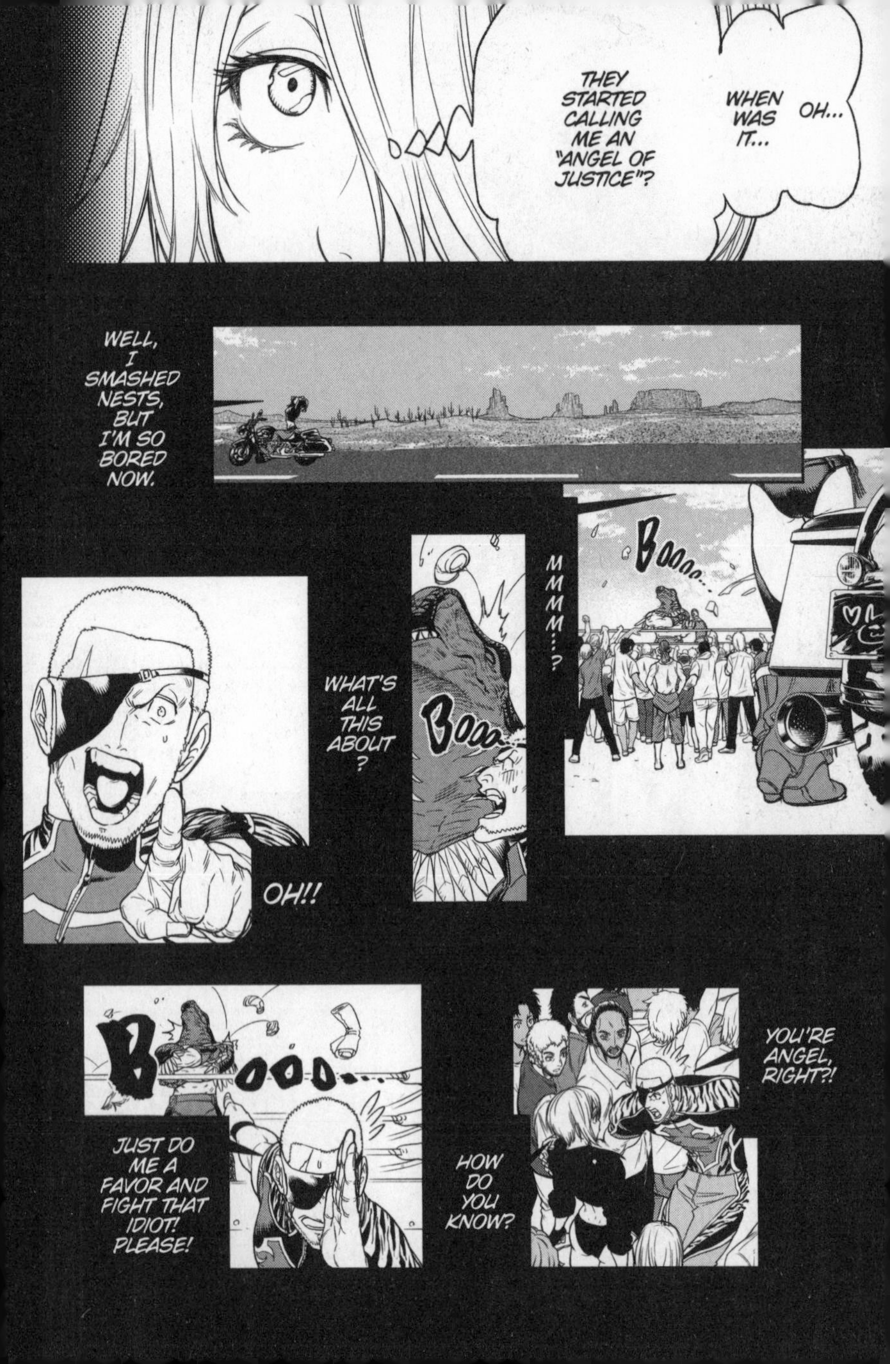
OH...
WHEN WAS IT...
THEY STARTED CALLING ME AN "ANGEL OF JUSTICE"?
WELL, I SMASHED NESTS, BUT I'M SO BORED NOW.
Boooo...
MMMM...?
Booo...
WHAT'S ALL THIS ABOUT?
OH!!
YOU'RE ANGEL, RIGHT?!
HOW DO YOU KNOW?
Booo...
JUST DO ME A FAVOR AND FIGHT THAT IDIOT! PLEASE!

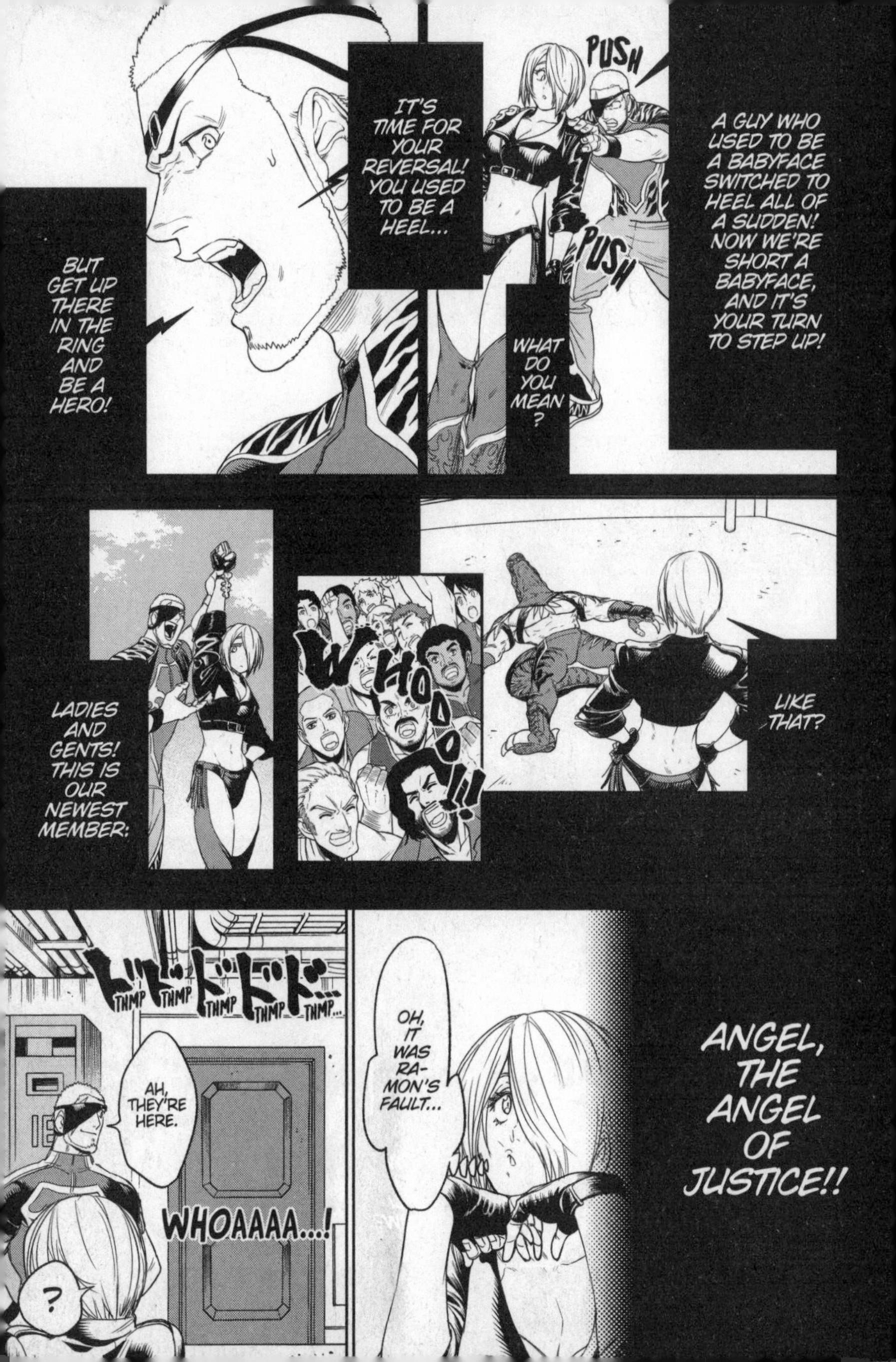

A GUY WHO USED TO BE A BABYFACE SWITCHED TO HEEL ALL OF A SUDDEN! NOW WE'RE SHORT A BABYFACE, AND IT'S YOUR TURN TO STEP UP!
PUSH
PUSH
WHAT DO YOU MEAN?
IT'S TIME FOR YOUR REVERSAL! YOU USED TO BE A HEEL...
BUT GET UP THERE IN THE RING AND BE A HERO!
LIKE THAT?
WHOOOO!!!
LADIES AND GENTS! THIS IS OUR NEWEST MEMBER:
ANGEL, THE ANGEL OF JUSTICE!!
OH, IT WAS RA-MON'S FAULT...
THMP THMP THMP THMP THMP...
AH, THEY'RE HERE.
WHOAAAA...!
?

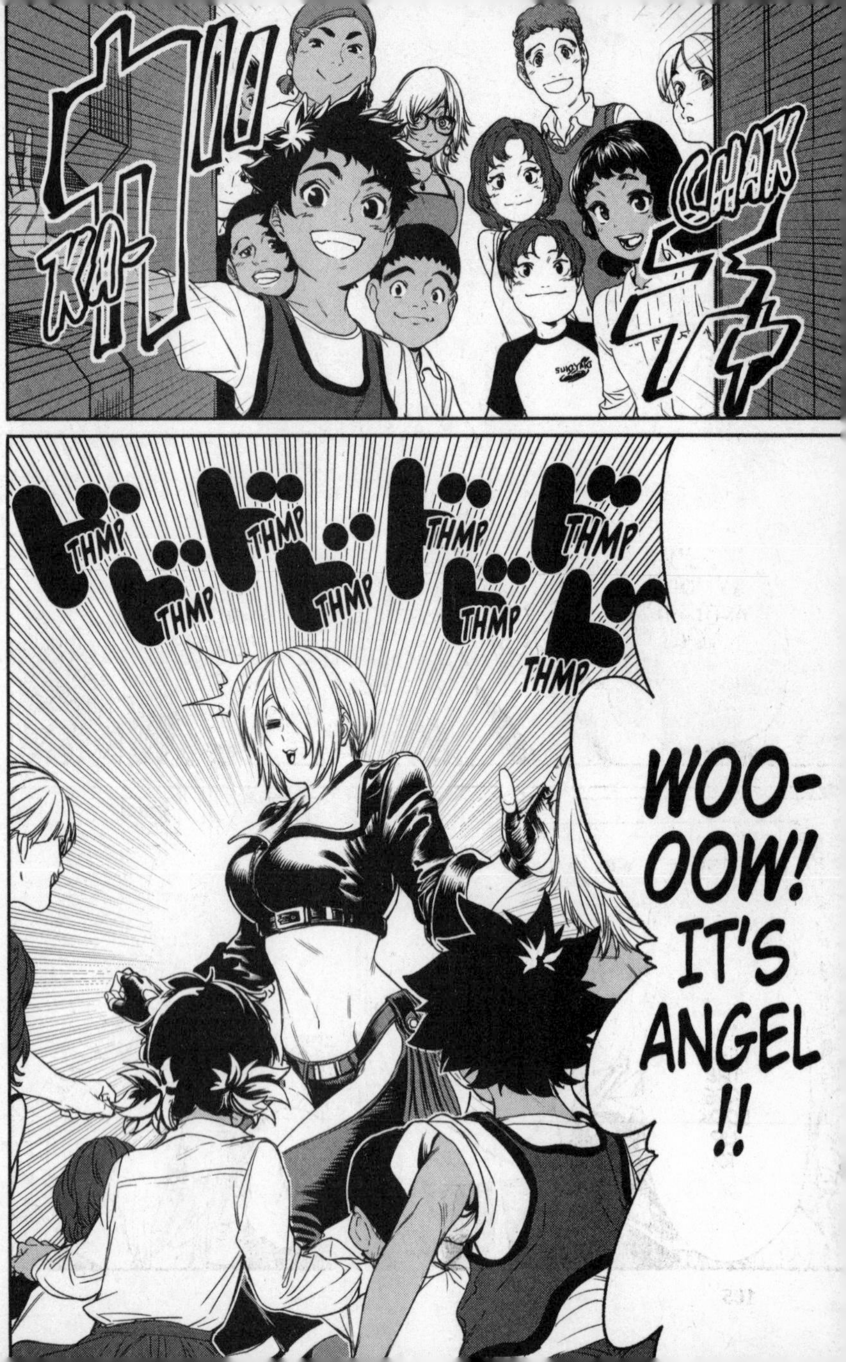
KA-
CHAK
THMP THMP THMP THMP THMP THMP THMP THMP
WOO-OOW! IT'S ANGEL!!

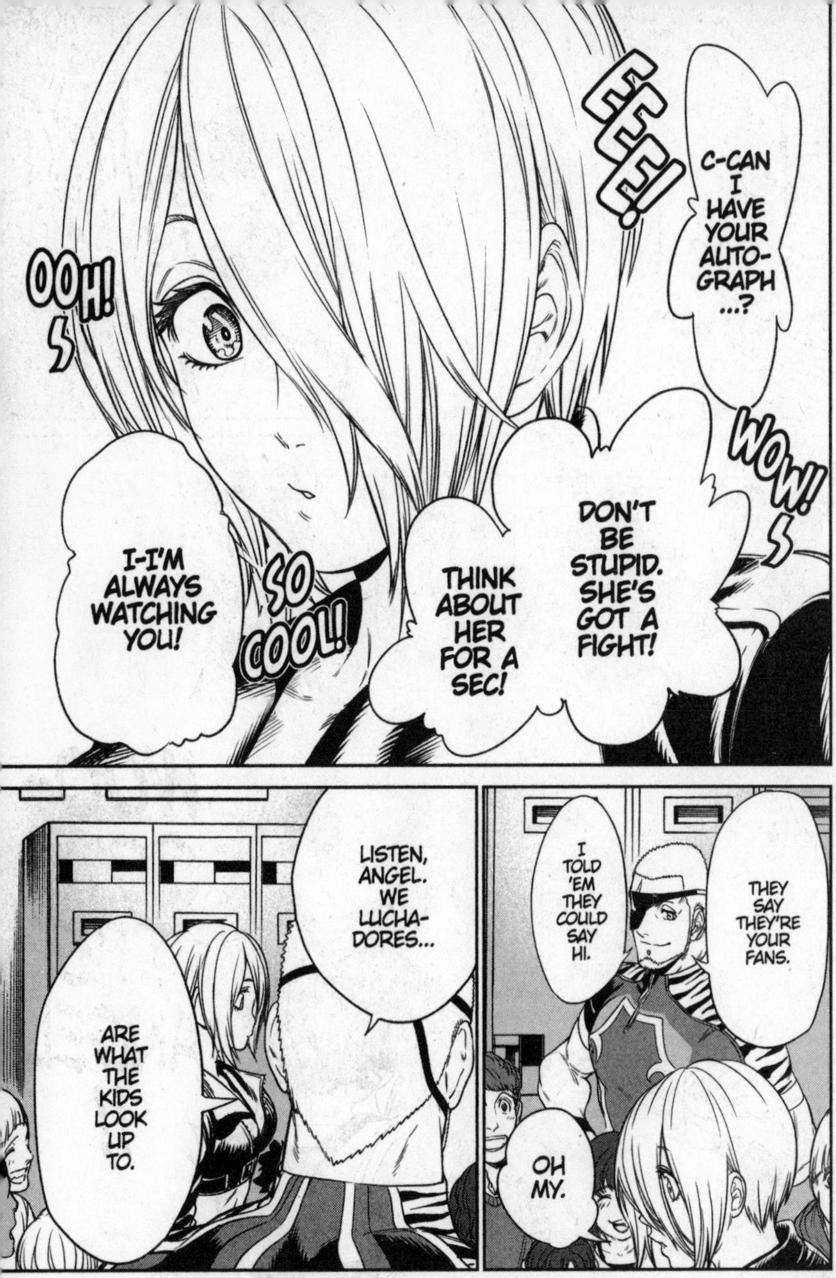
C-CAN I HAVE YOUR AUTOGRAPH ...?
EEEE!
WOW!
DON'T BE STUPID. SHE'S GOT A FIGHT!
THINK ABOUT HER FOR A SEC!
SO COOL!
I-I'M ALWAYS WATCHING YOU!
OOH!
THEY SAY THEY'RE YOUR FANS.
I TOLD 'EM THEY COULD SAY HI.
OH MY.
LISTEN, ANGEL. WE LUCHA-DORES...
ARE WHAT THE KIDS LOOK UP TO.

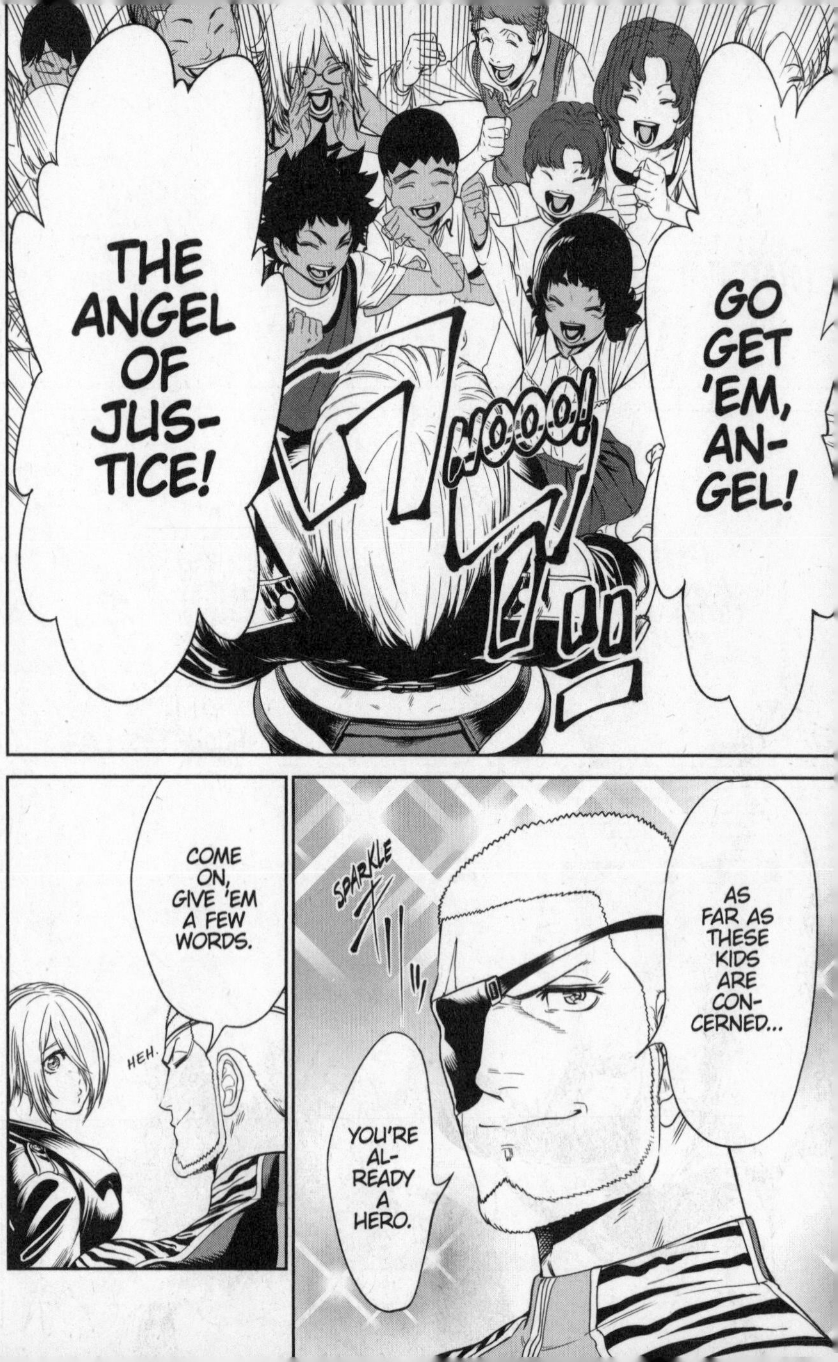
GO GET 'EM, ANGEL!
WOOO!
THE ANGEL OF JUSTICE!
AS FAR AS THESE KIDS ARE CONCERNED...
SPARKLE
YOU'RE ALREADY A HERO.
COME ON, GIVE 'EM A FEW WORDS.
HEH.

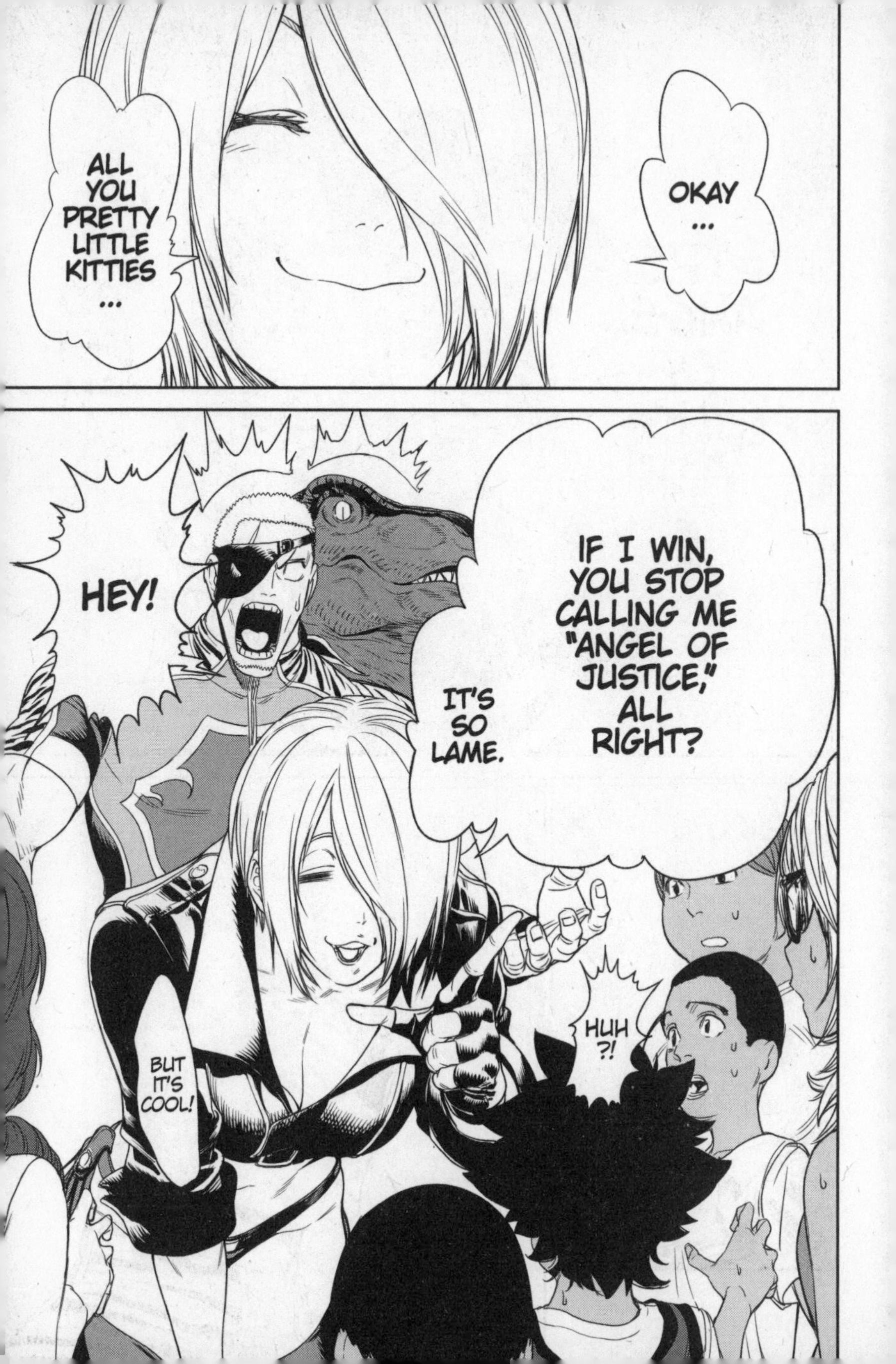
OKAY ...
ALL YOU PRETTY LITTLE KITTIES ...
IF I WIN, YOU STOP CALLING ME "ANGEL OF JUSTICE," ALL RIGHT?
IT'S SO LAME.
HEY!
HUH ?!
BUT IT'S COOL!

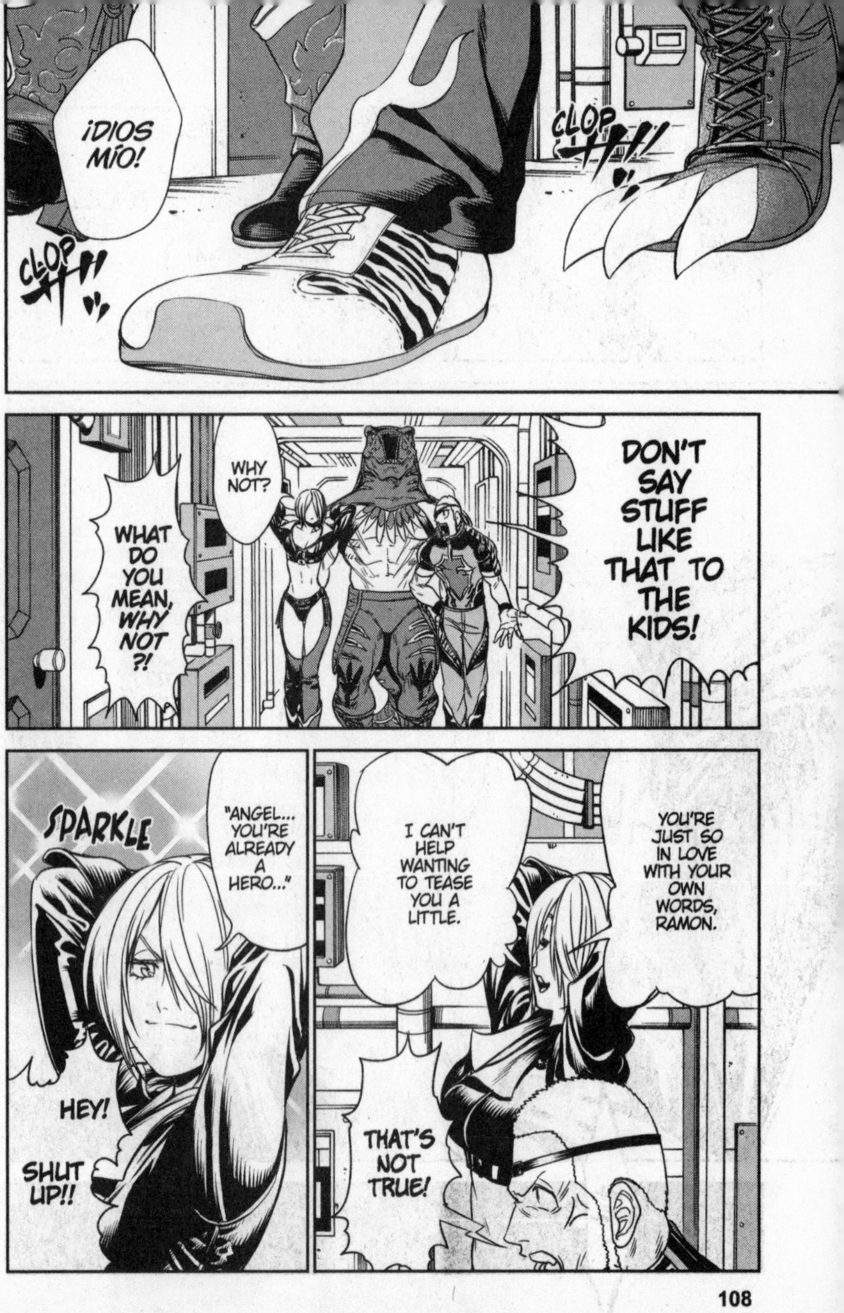
CLOP
¡DIOS MÍO!
CLOP
DON'T SAY STUFF LIKE THAT TO THE KIDS!
WHY NOT?
WHAT DO YOU MEAN, WHY NOT?!
YOU'RE JUST SO IN LOVE WITH YOUR OWN WORDS, RAMON.
I CAN'T HELP WANTING TO TEASE YOU A LITTLE.
THAT'S NOT TRUE!
"ANGEL... YOU'RE ALREADY A HERO..."
SPARKLE
HEY!
SHUT UP!!

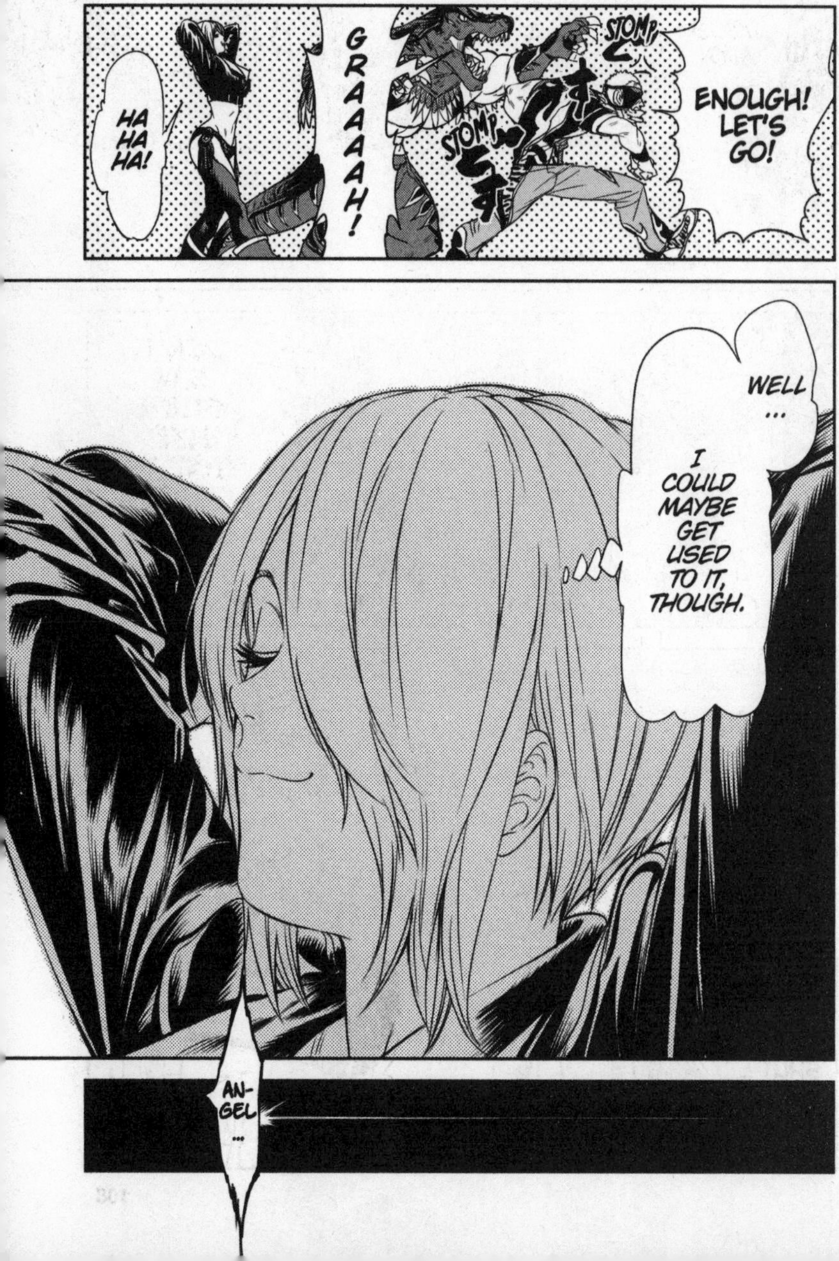
ENOUGH! LET'S GO!
STOMP
STOMP
GRAAAAAH!
HA HA HA!
WELL ...
I COULD MAYBE GET USED TO IT, THOUGH.
AN-GEL ...

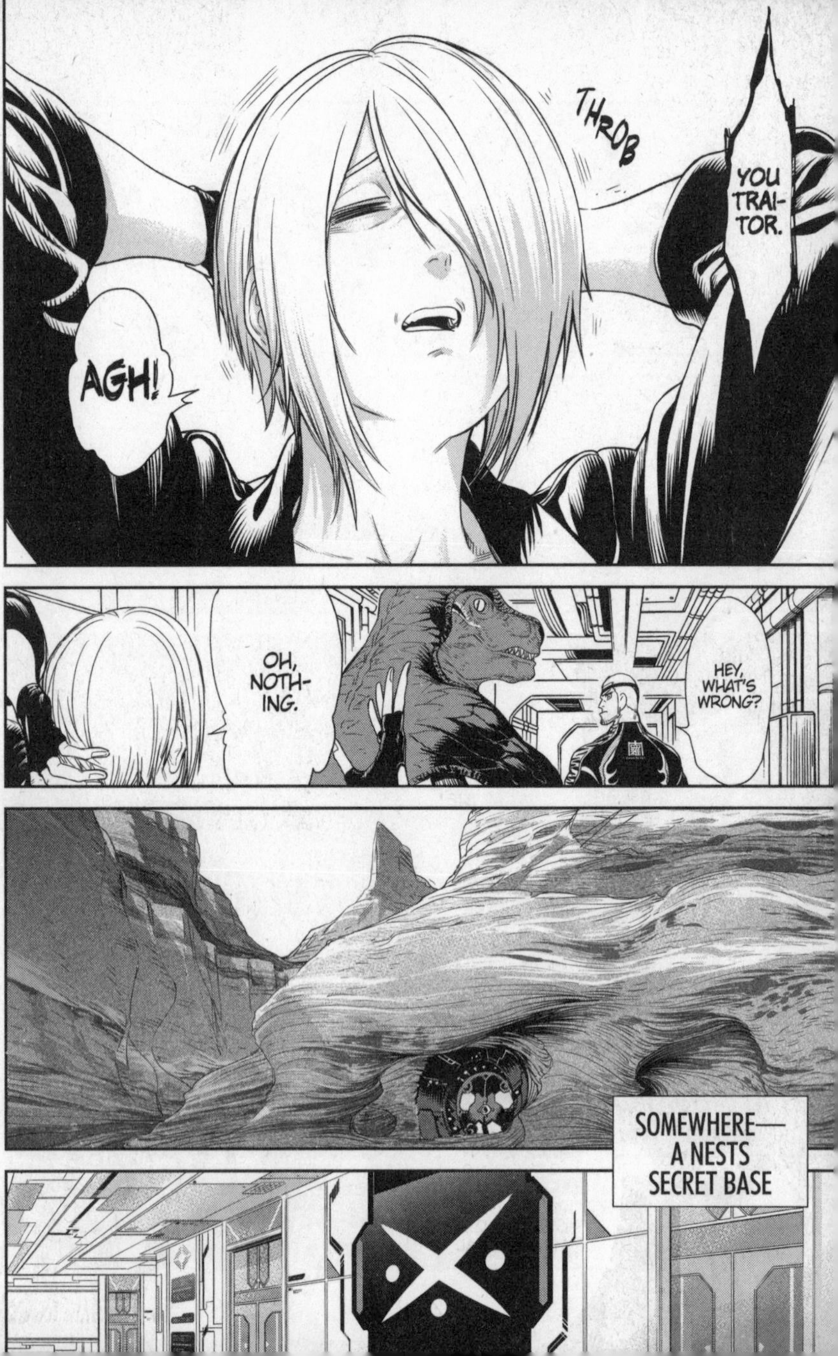
YOU TRAI-TOR.
THROB
AGH!
HEY, WHAT'S WRONG?
OH, NOTH-ING.
SOMEWHERE— A NESTS SECRET BASE

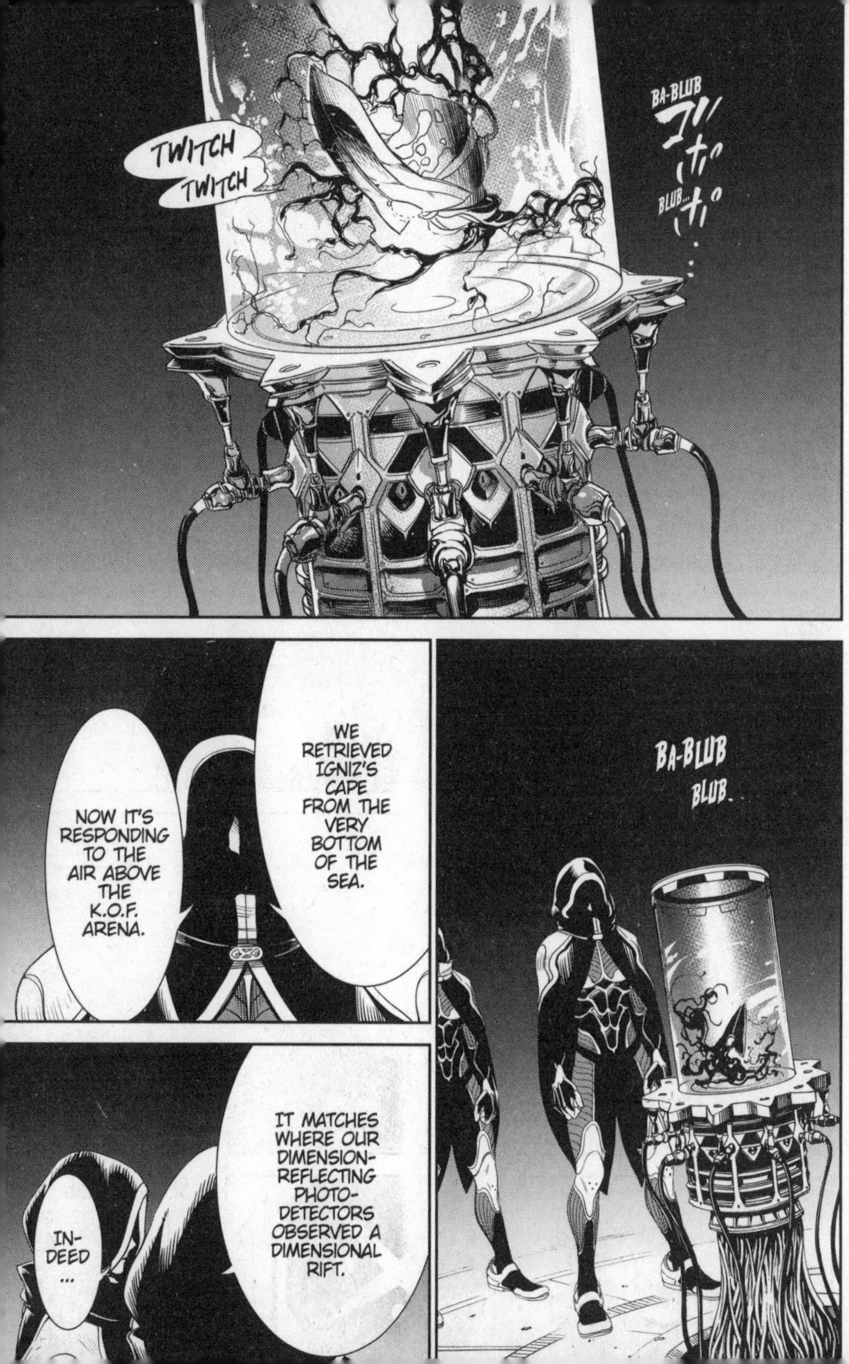
BA-BLUB
BLUB...
TWITCH TWITCH
BA-BLUB BLUB...
WE RETRIEVED IGNIZ'S CAPE FROM THE VERY BOTTOM OF THE SEA.
NOW IT'S RESPONDING TO THE AIR ABOVE THE K.O.F. ARENA.
IT MATCHES WHERE OUR DIMENSION-REFLECTING PHOTO-DETECTORS OBSERVED A DIMENSIONAL RIFT.
IN-DEED...

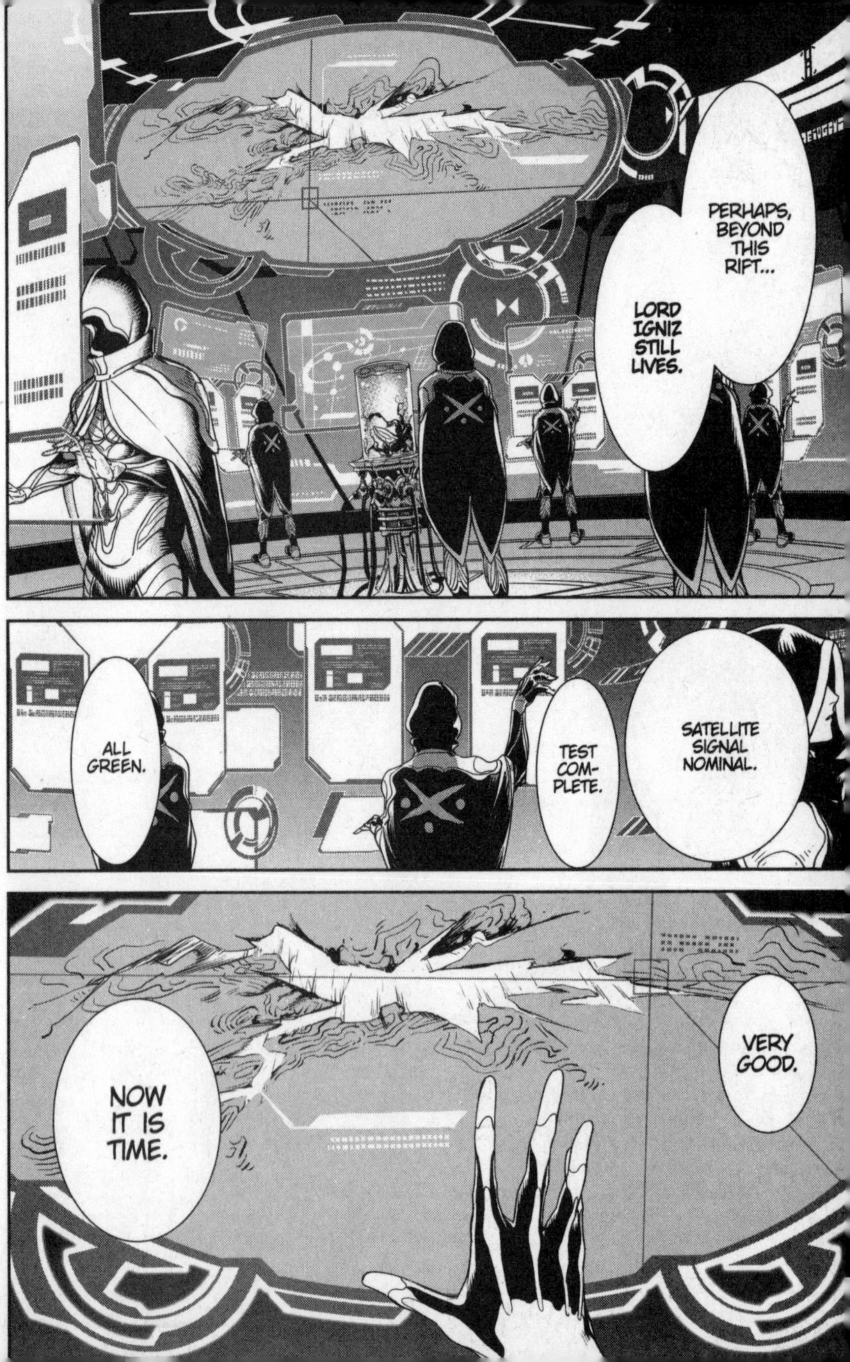
PERHAPS, BEYOND THIS RIFT...
LORD IGNIZ STILL LIVES.
SATELLITE SIGNAL NOMINAL.
TEST COM-PLETE.
ALL GREEN.
VERY GOOD.
NOW IT IS TIME.

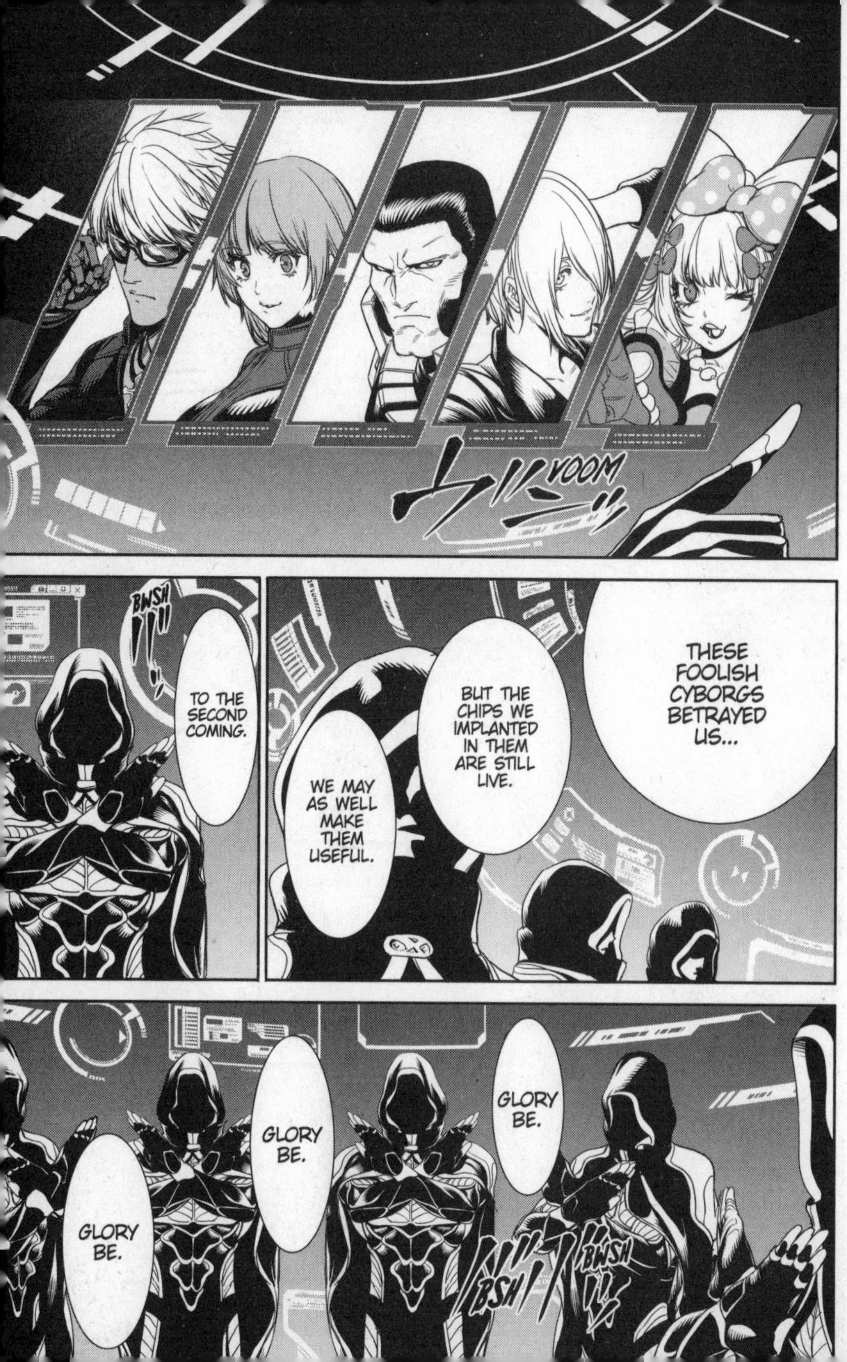
VOOM
THESE FOOLISH CYBORGS BETRAYED US...
BUT THE CHIPS WE IMPLANTED IN THEM ARE STILL LIVE.
WE MAY AS WELL MAKE THEM USEFUL.
BWSH
TO THE SECOND COMING.
GLORY BE.
GLORY BE.
GLORY BE.
BWSH
BSH

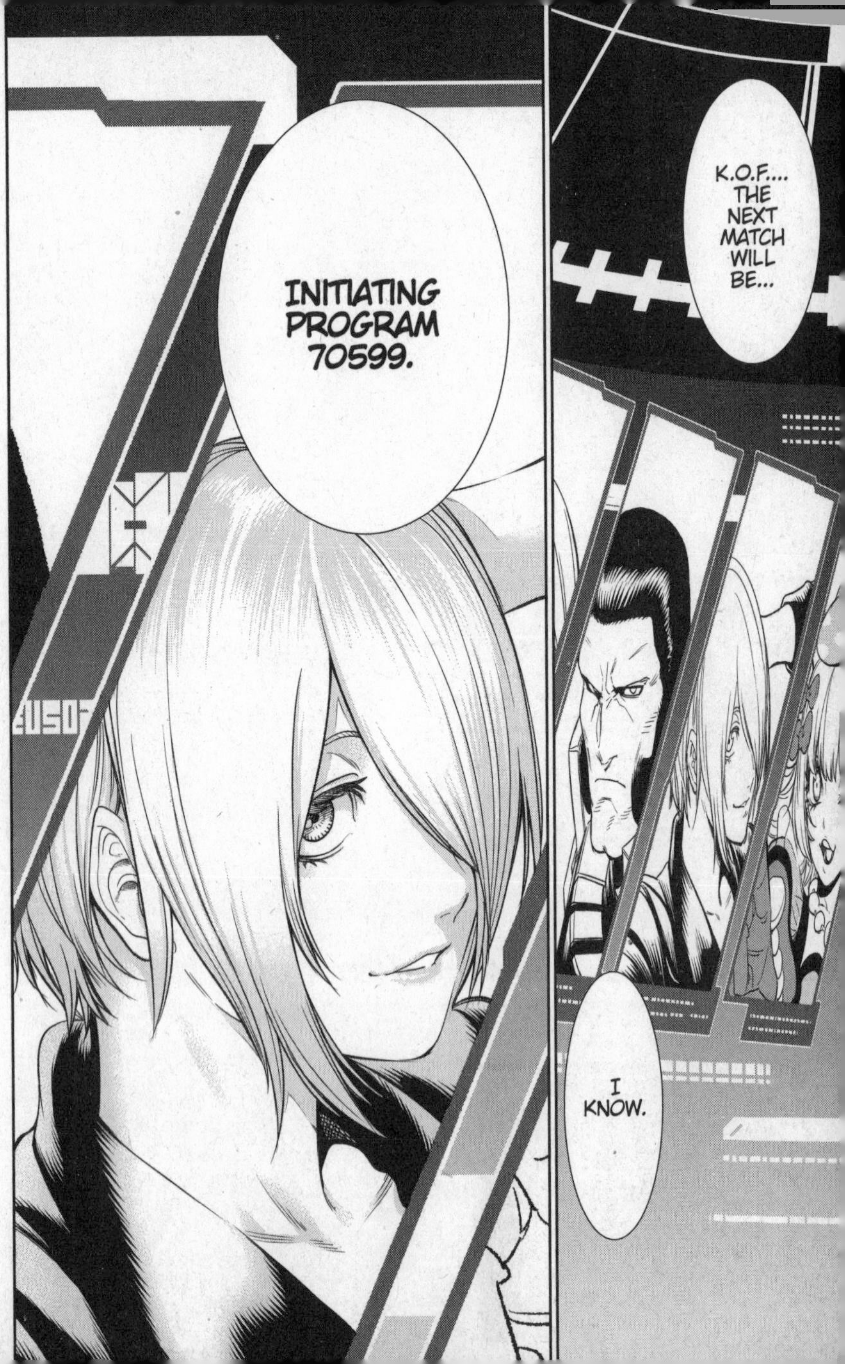
K.O.F.... THE NEXT MATCH WILL BE...
I KNOW.
INITIATING PROGRAM 70599.

THE KING OF FIGHTERS
A NEW BEGINNING

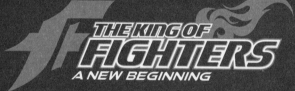

THE KING OF FIGHTERS

A NEW BEGINNING

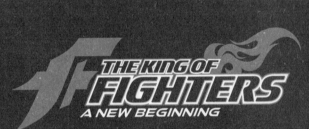

ROUND 14: TEAM IKARI VS. TEAM MEXICO (1)

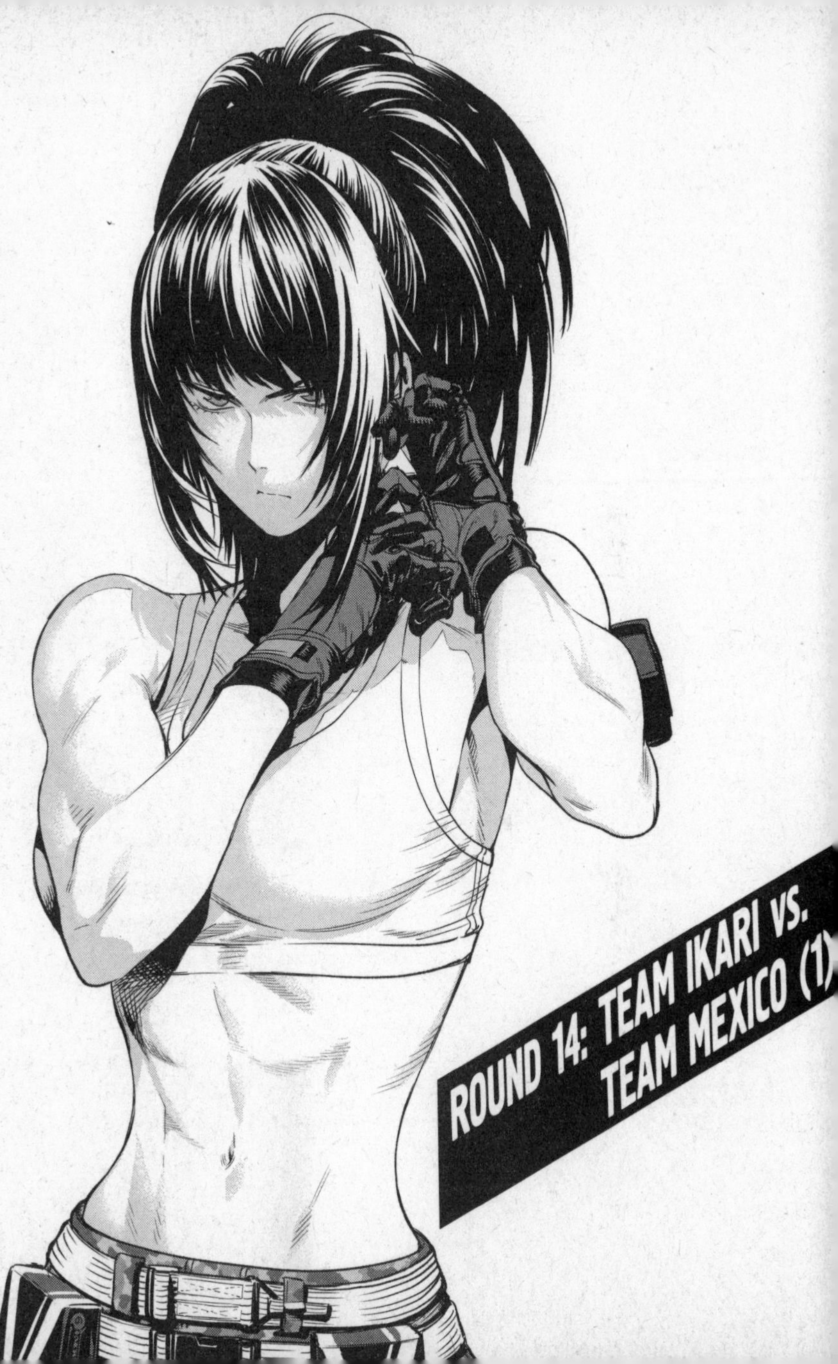

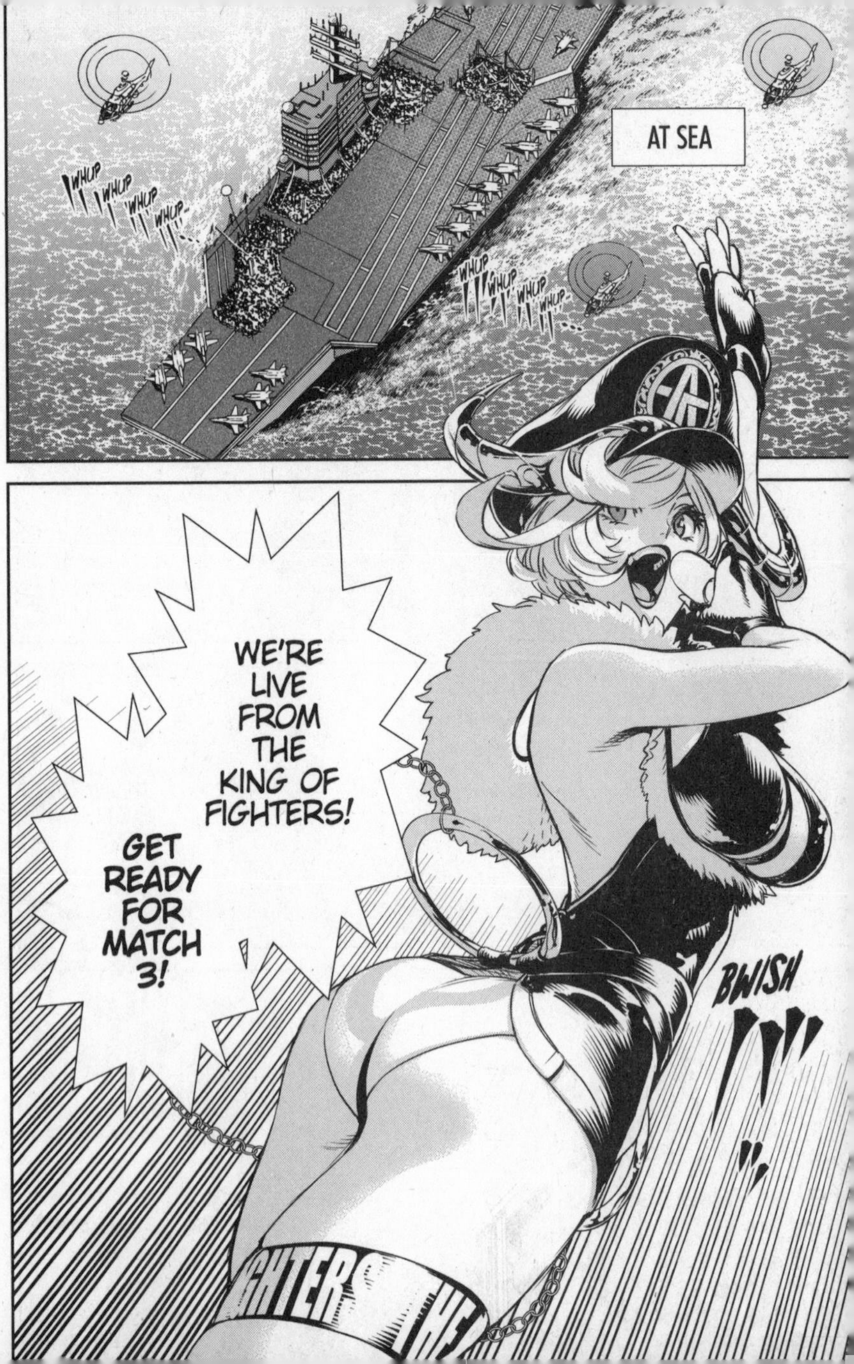
AT SEA
WHUP WHUP WHUP WHUP...
WHUP WHUP WHUP WHUP...
WE'RE LIVE FROM THE KING OF FIGHTERS!
GET READY FOR MATCH 3!
BWISH

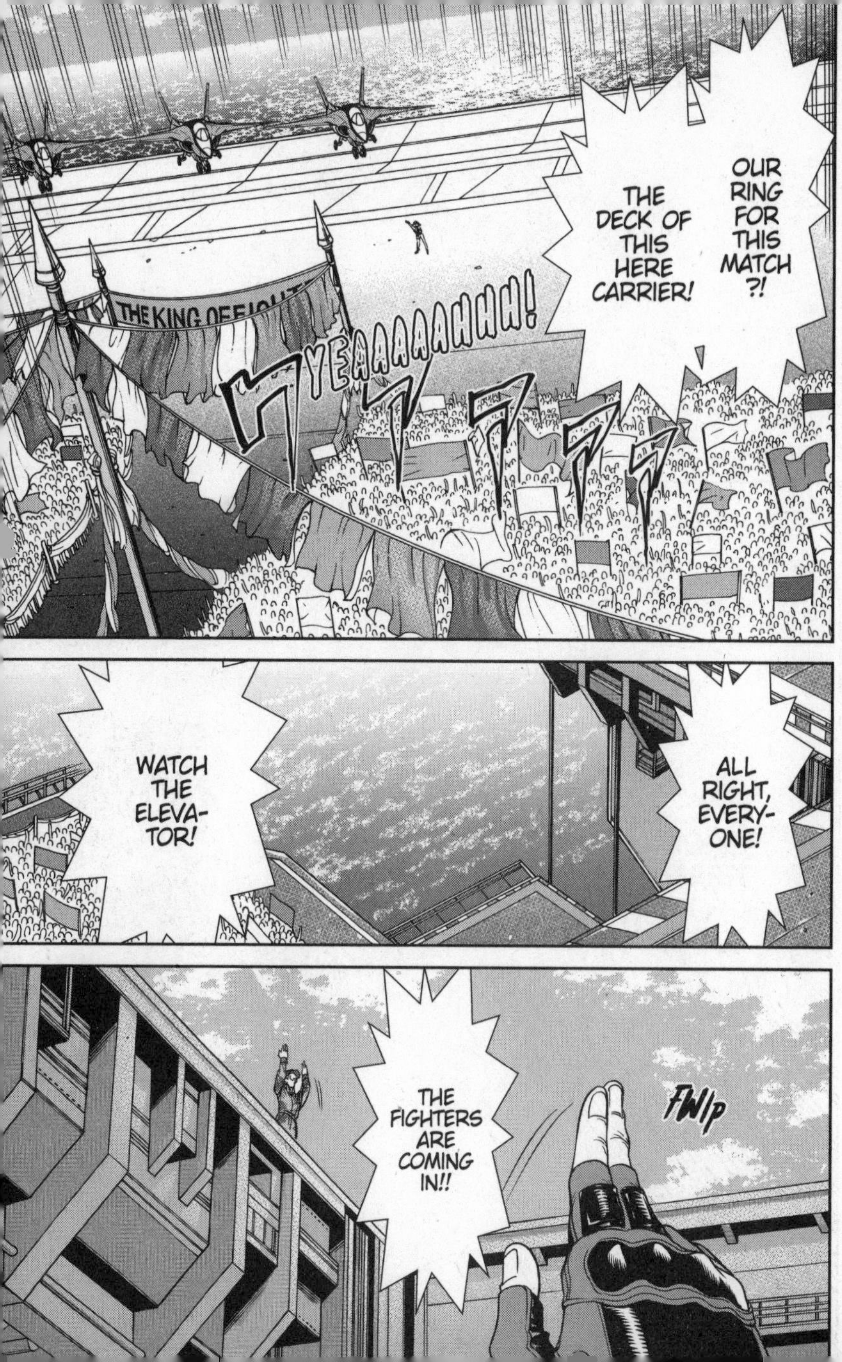
OUR RING FOR THIS MATCH ?!
THE DECK OF THIS HERE CARRIER!
YEAAAAAHHH!
ALL RIGHT, EVERY-ONE!
WATCH THE ELEVA-TOR!
THE FIGHTERS ARE COMING IN!!
FWIP

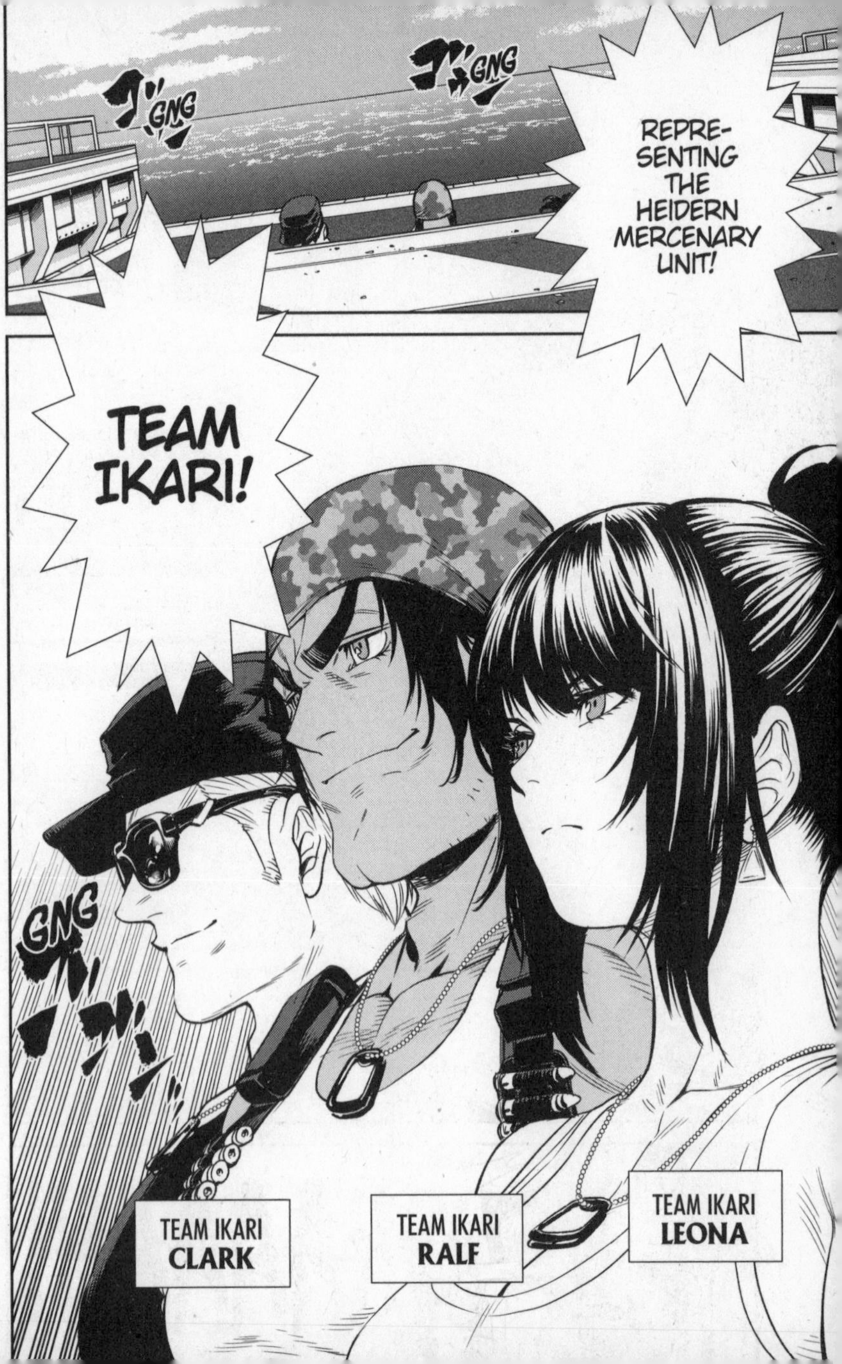
REPRE-
SENTING
THE
HEIDERN
MERCENARY
UNIT!
GNG
GNG
TEAM
IKARI!
GNG
TEAM IKARI
LEONA
TEAM IKARI
RALF
TEAM IKARI
CLARK

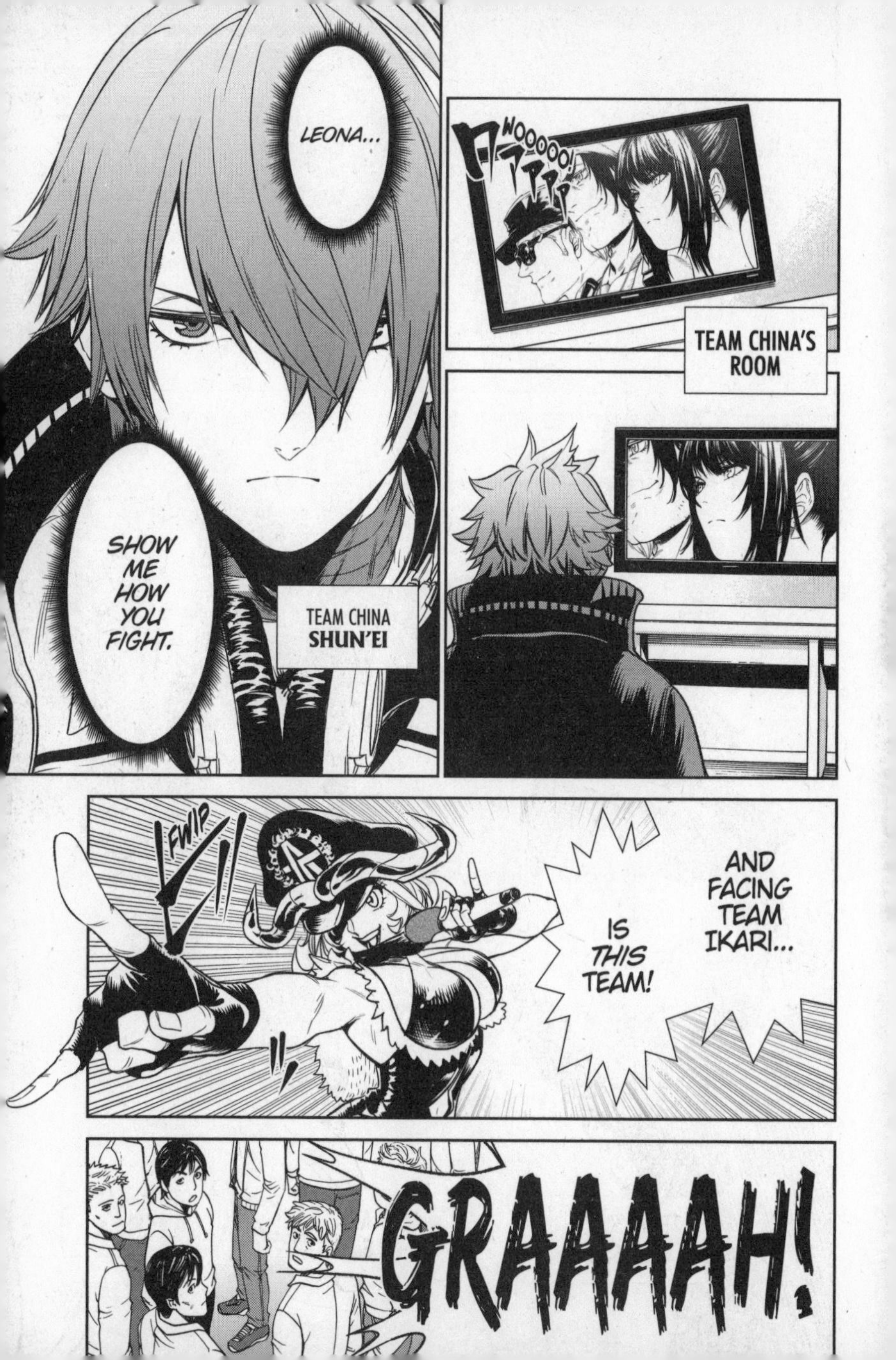
WOOOOOO!
TEAM CHINA'S ROOM
LEONA...
SHOW ME HOW YOU FIGHT.
TEAM CHINA SHUN'EI
AND FACING TEAM IKARI...
IS THIS TEAM!
FWIP
GRAAAAH!

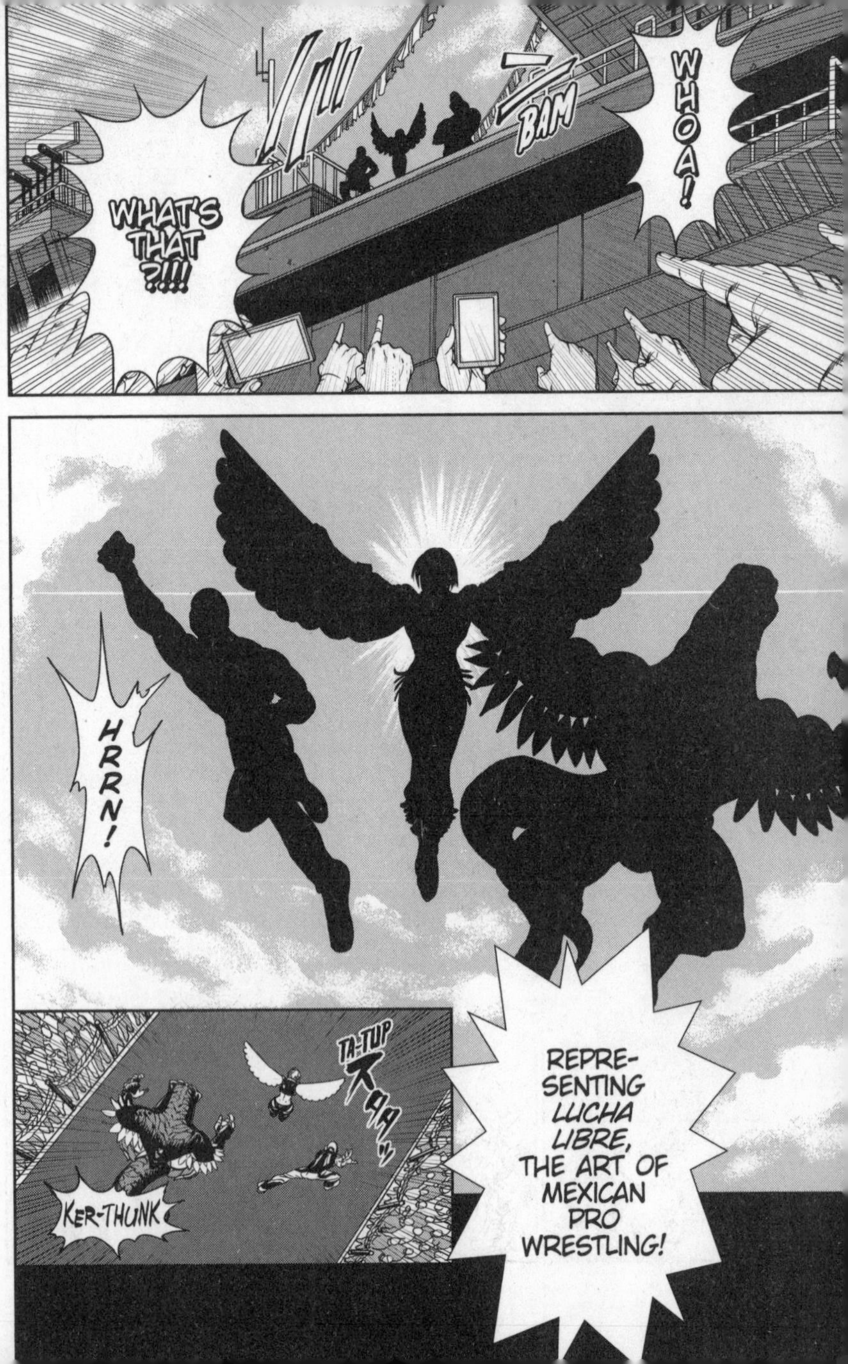
WHOA!
BAM
WHAT'S THAT ?!!!
HRRN!
REPRESENTING LUCHA LIBRE, THE ART OF MEXICAN PRO WRESTLING!
TA-TUP
KER-THUNK

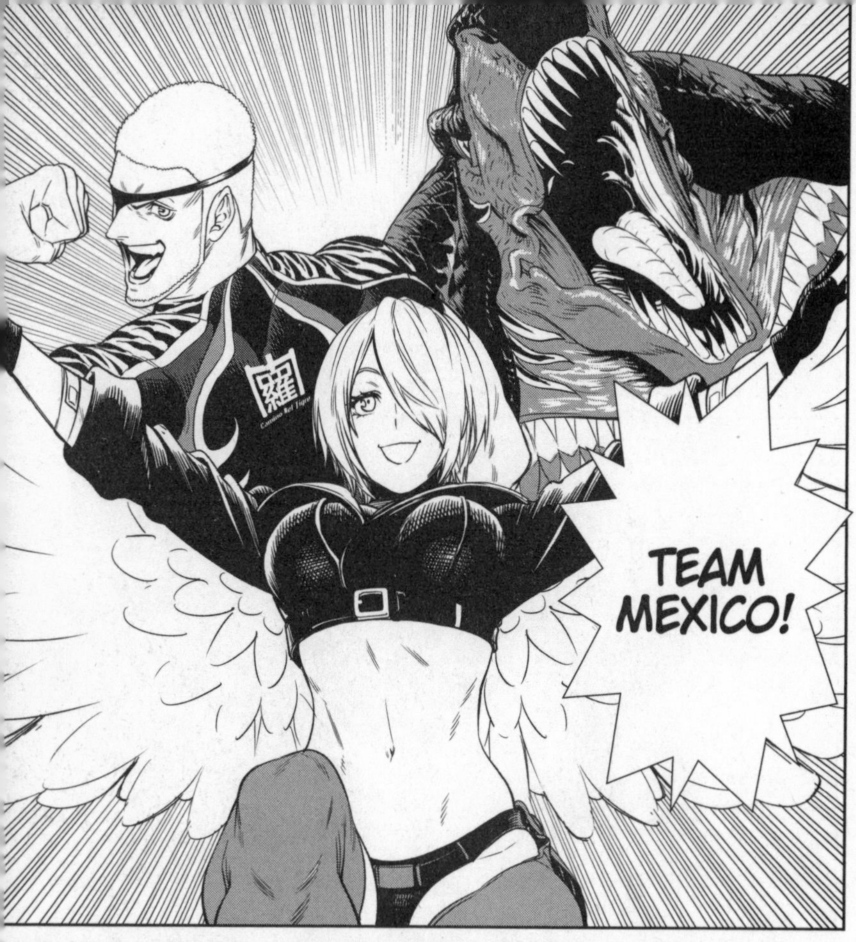
TEAM MEXICO!

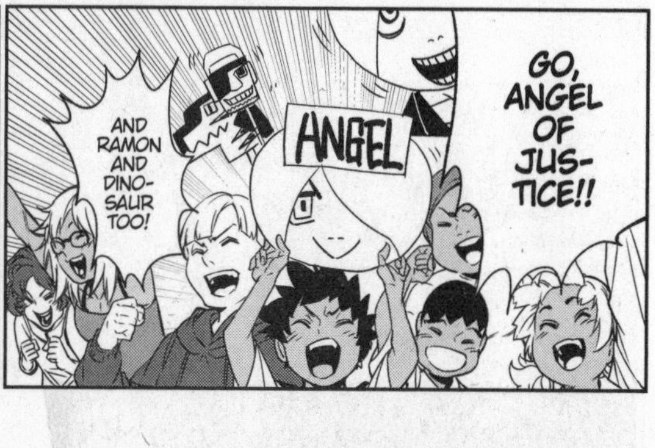
GO, ANGEL OF JUS-TICE!!
ANGEL
AND RAMON AND DINO-SAUR TOO!

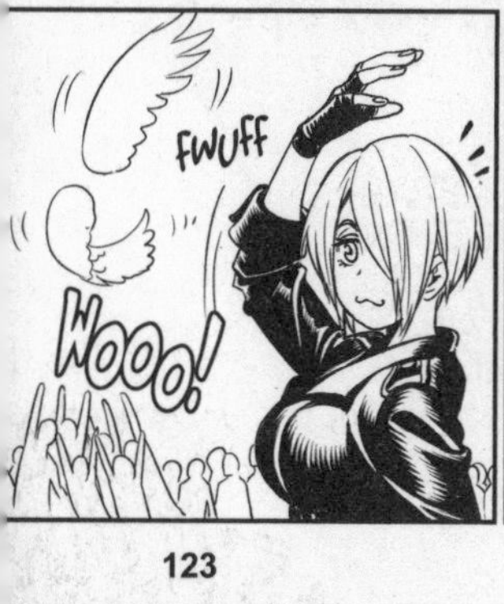
FWUFF
WOOO!

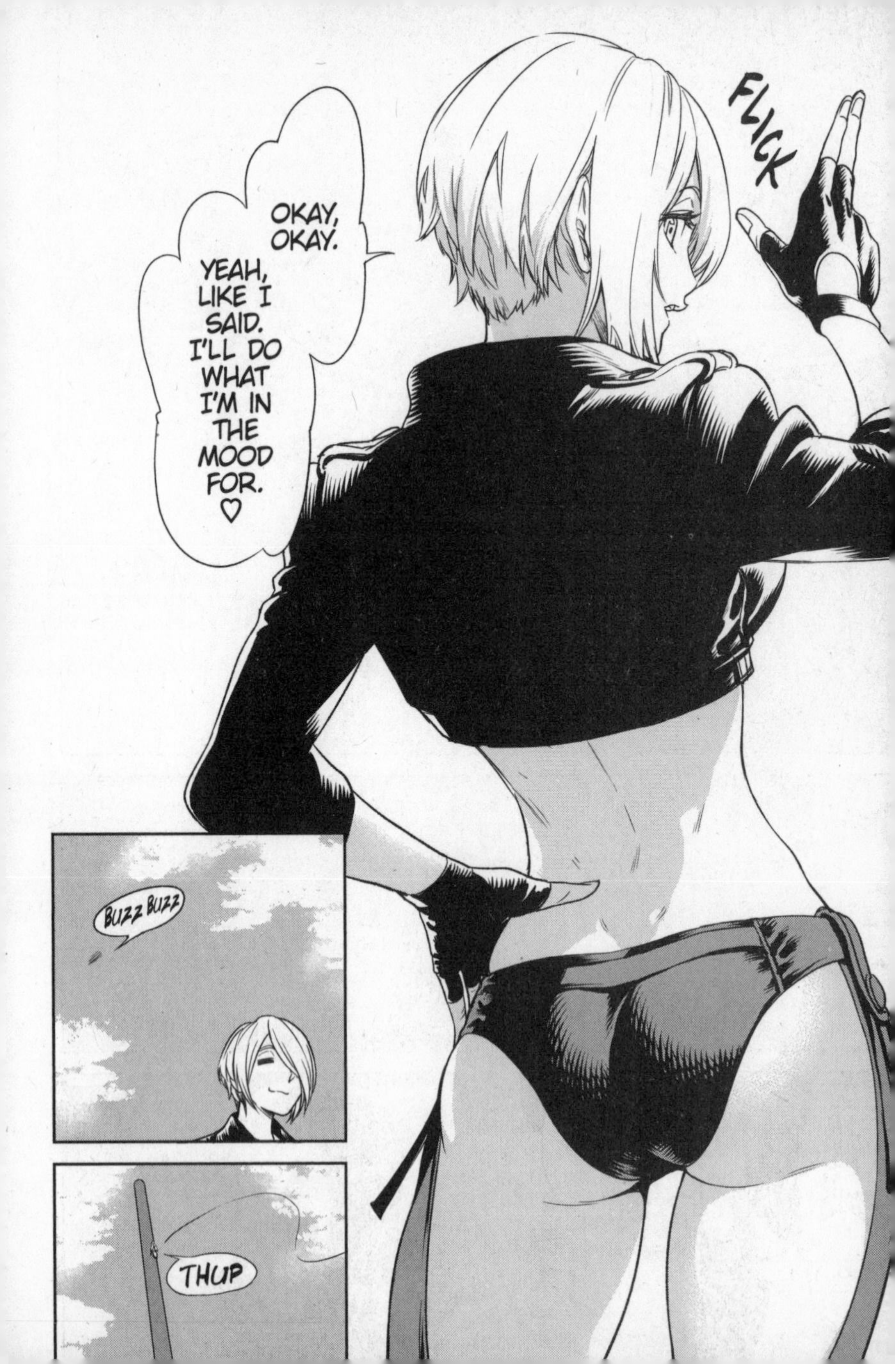
FLICK
OKAY, OKAY. YEAH, LIKE I SAID. I'LL DO WHAT I'M IN THE MOOD FOR. ♡
BUZZ BUZZ
THUP

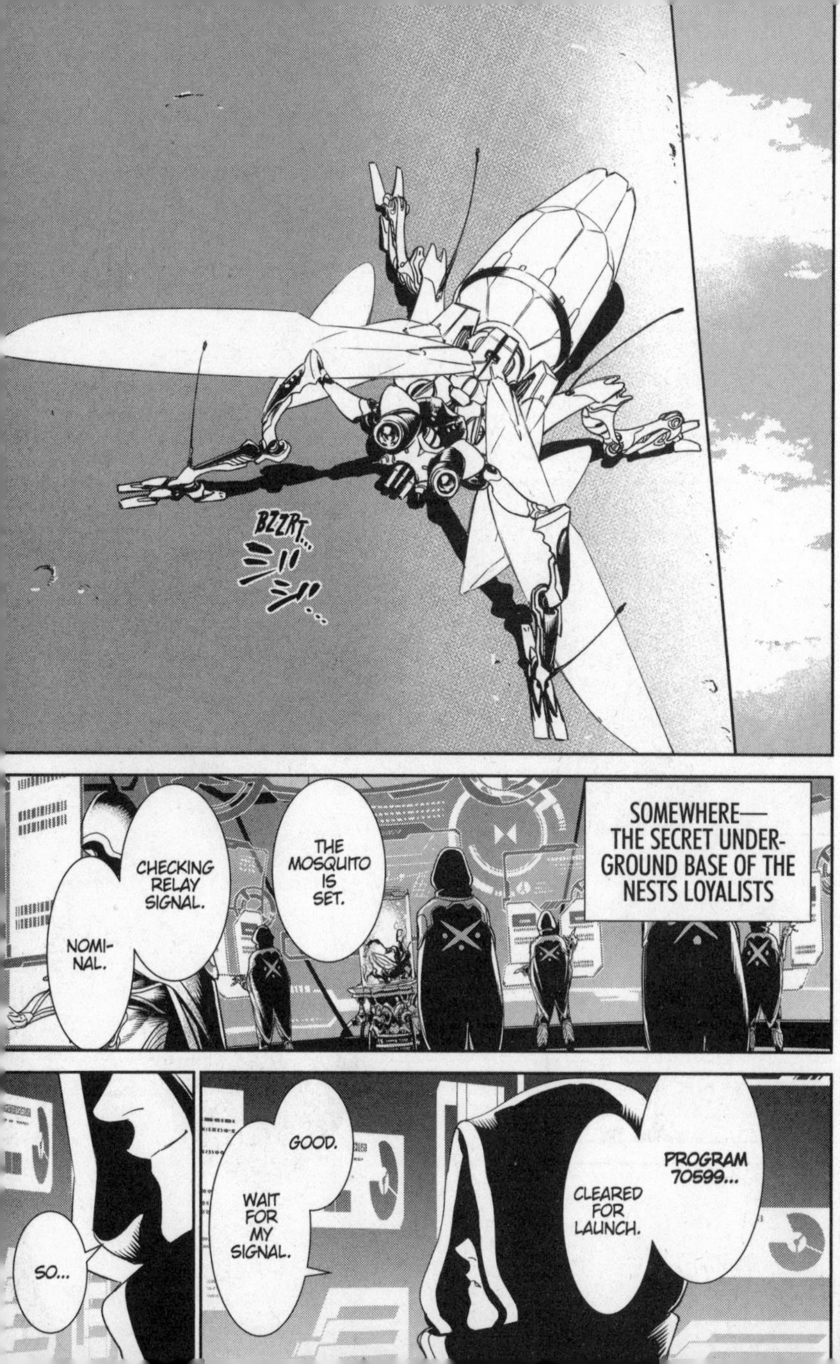
BZZRT...
SOMEWHERE—THE SECRET UNDER-GROUND BASE OF THE NESTS LOYALISTS
THE MOSQUITO IS SET.
CHECKING RELAY SIGNAL.
NOMI-NAL.
PROGRAM 70599...
CLEARED FOR LAUNCH.
GOOD.
WAIT FOR MY SIGNAL.
SO...

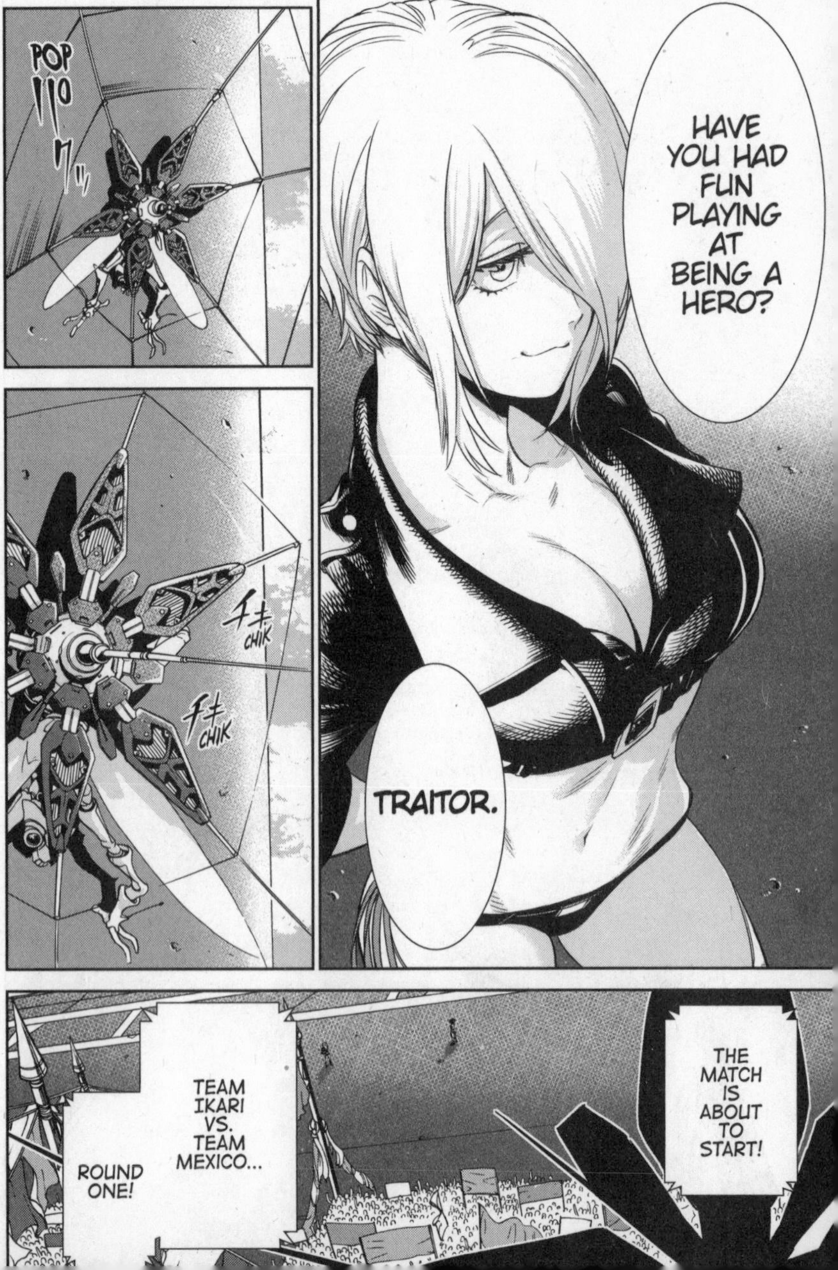
HAVE YOU HAD FUN PLAYING AT BEING A HERO?
TRAITOR.
POP
CHIK
CHIK
THE MATCH IS ABOUT TO START!
TEAM IKARI VS. TEAM MEXICO...
ROUND ONE!

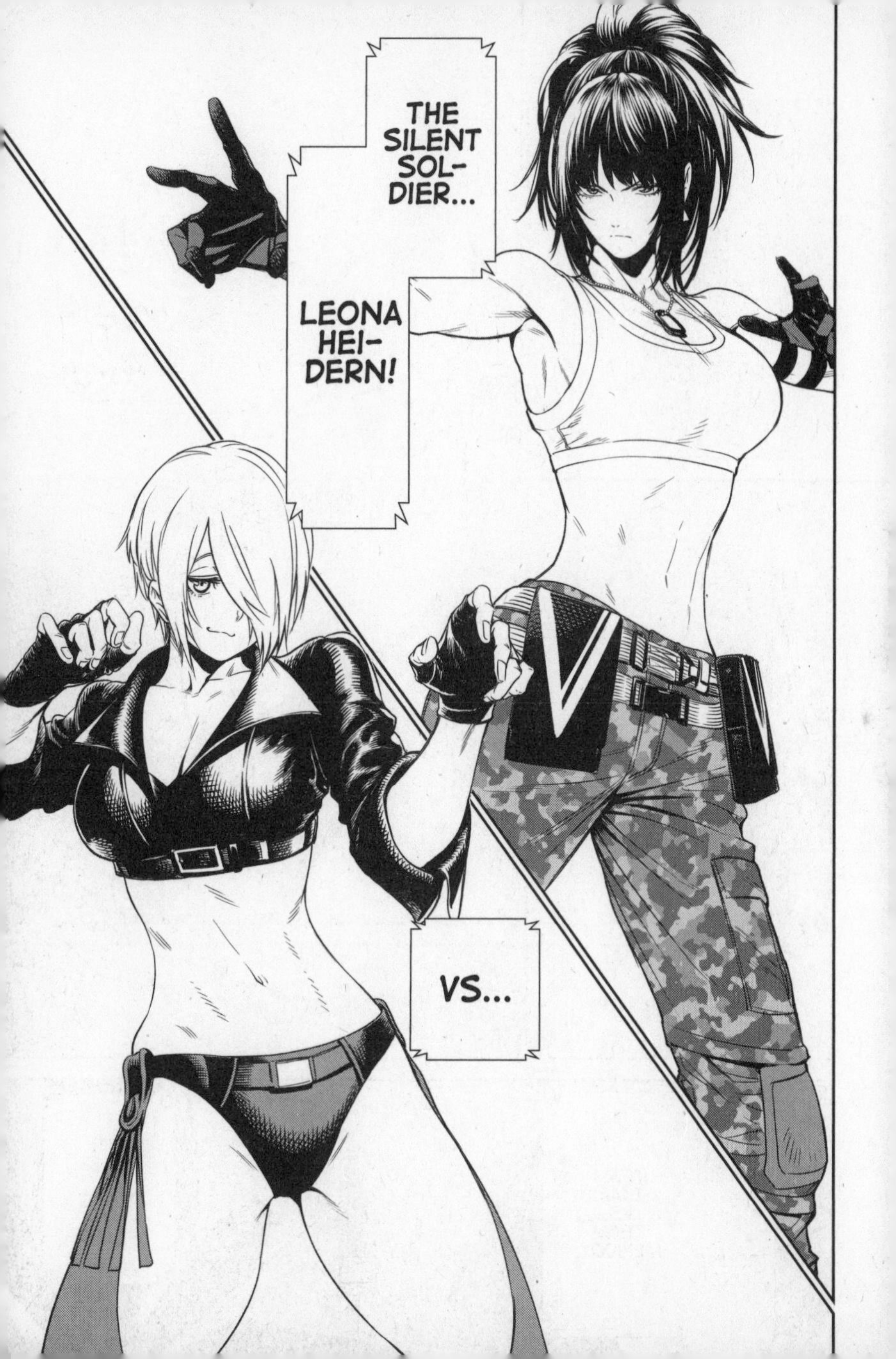
THE SILENT SOL-DIER...
LEONA HEI-DERN!
VS...

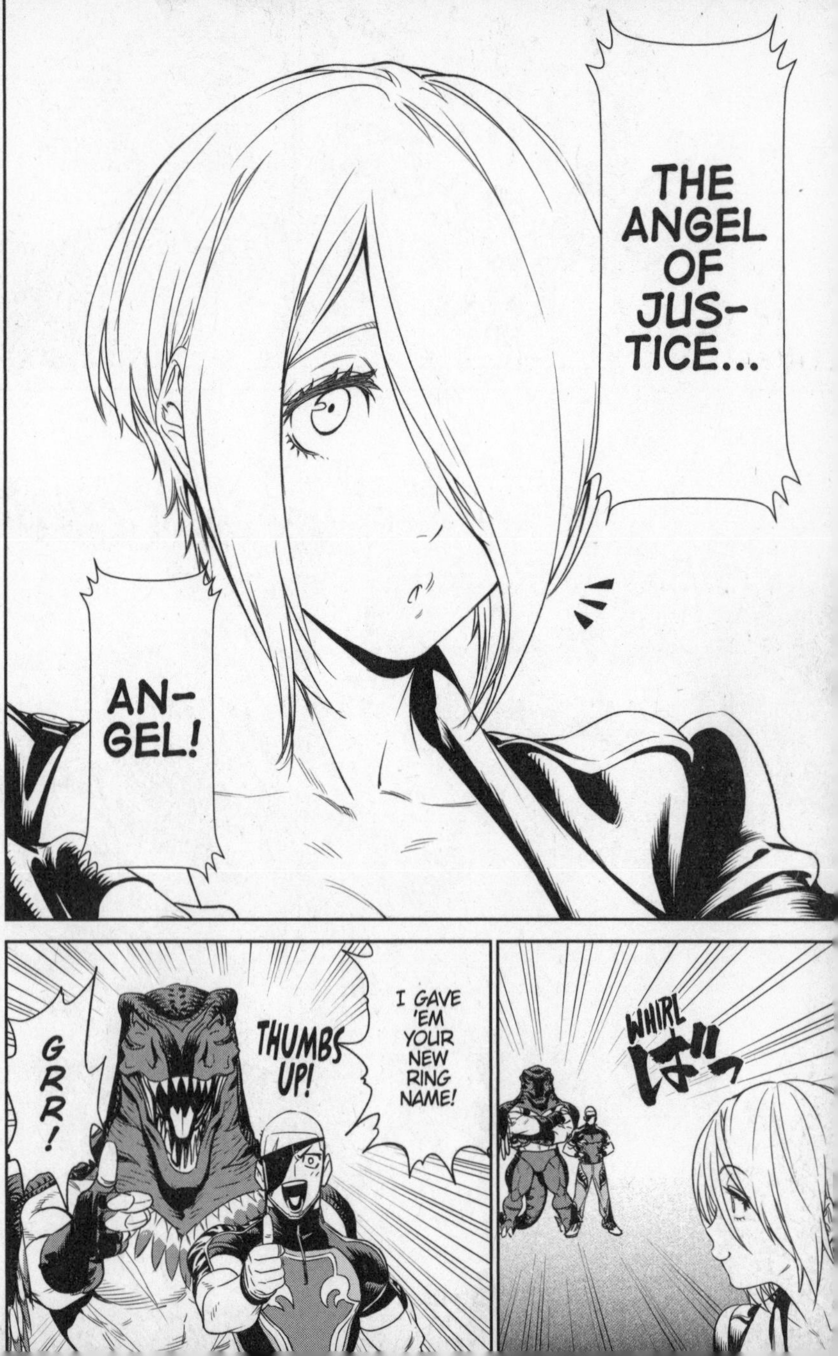
THE ANGEL OF JUSTICE...
ANGEL!
WHIRL
I GAVE 'EM YOUR NEW RING NAME!
THUMBS UP!
GRR!

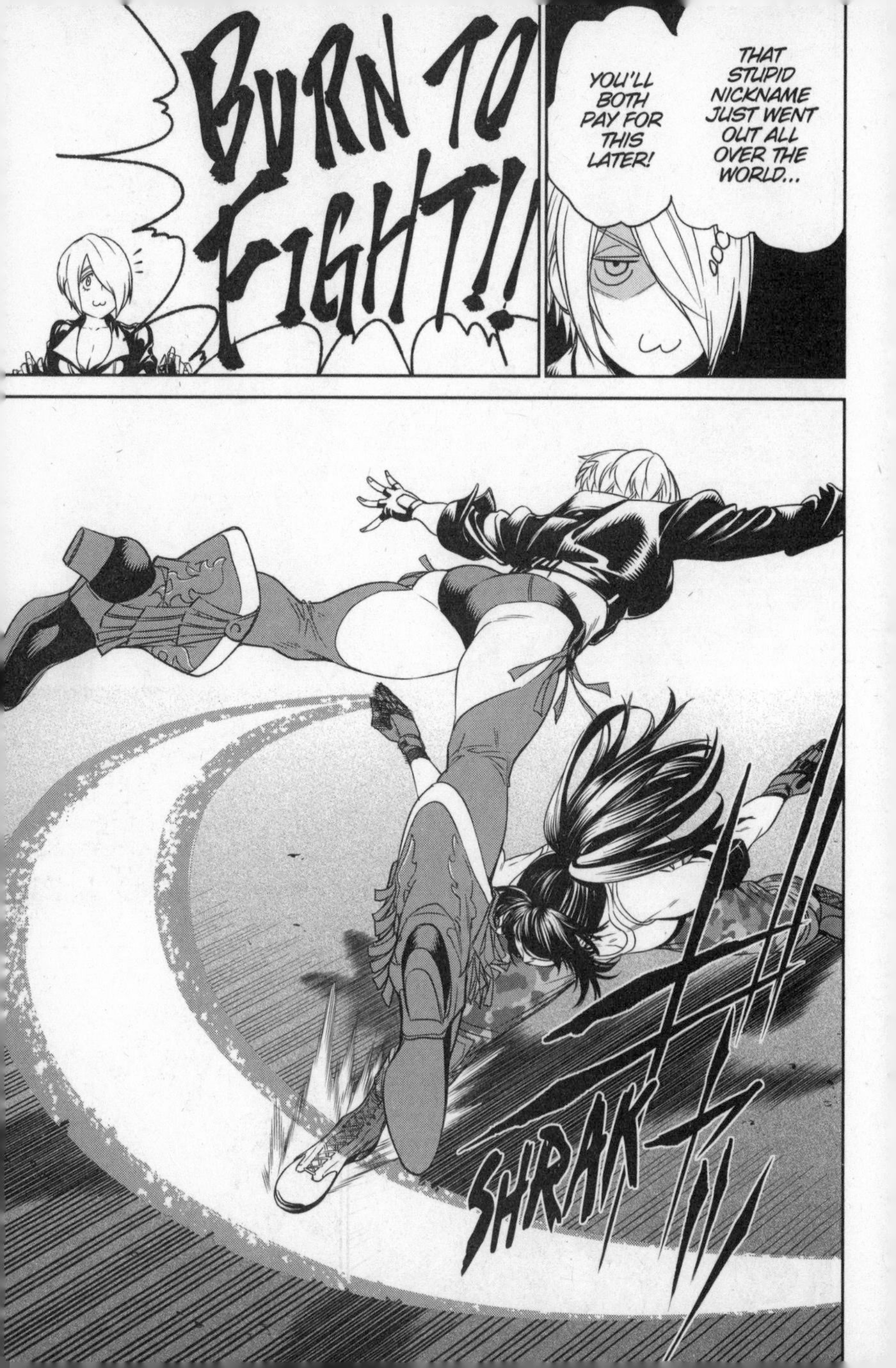
THAT STUPID NICKNAME JUST WENT OUT ALL OVER THE WORLD...
YOU'LL BOTH PAY FOR THIS LATER!
BURN TO FIGHT!!
SHRAK

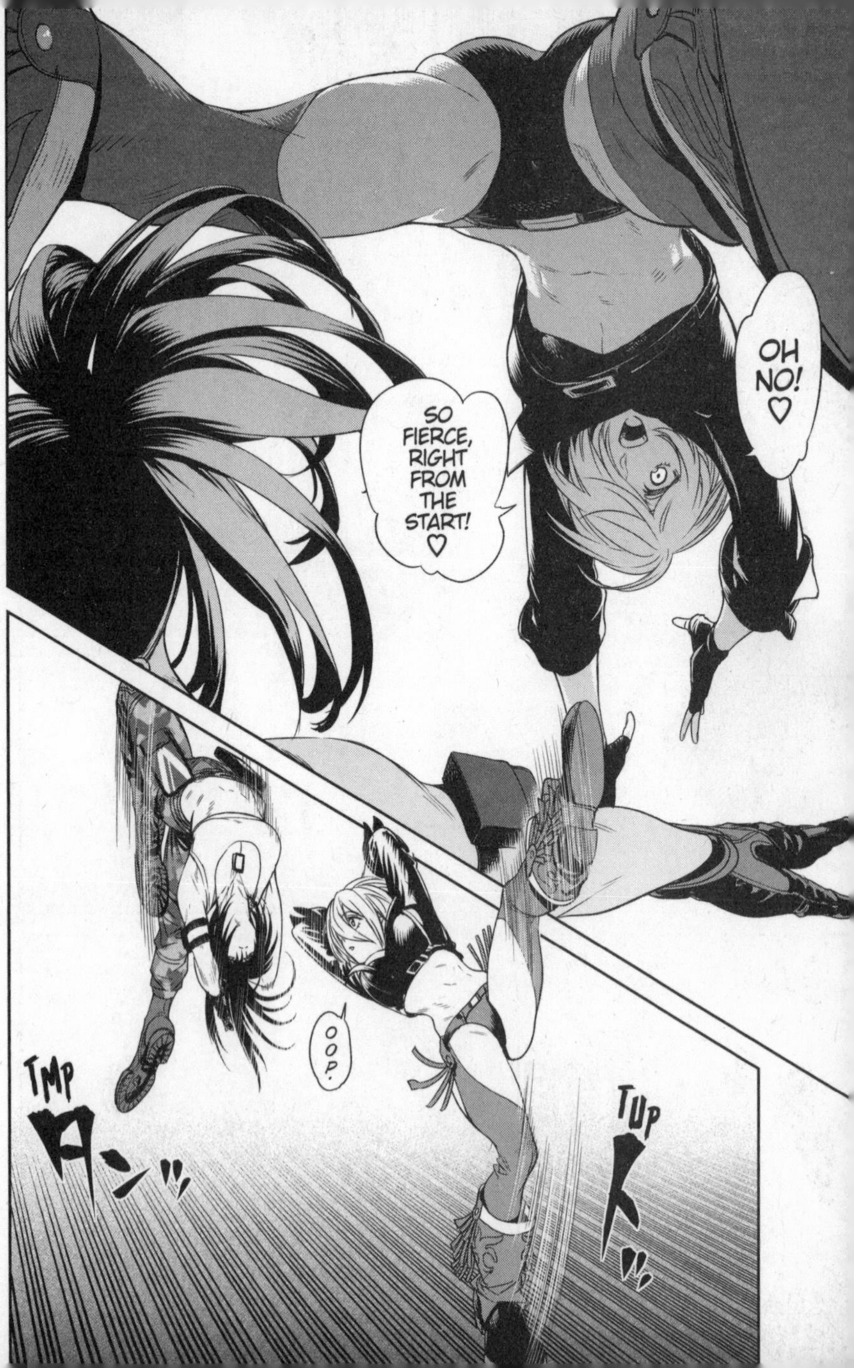
OH NO! ♡
SO FIERCE, RIGHT FROM THE START! ♡
OOP.
TUP
TMP

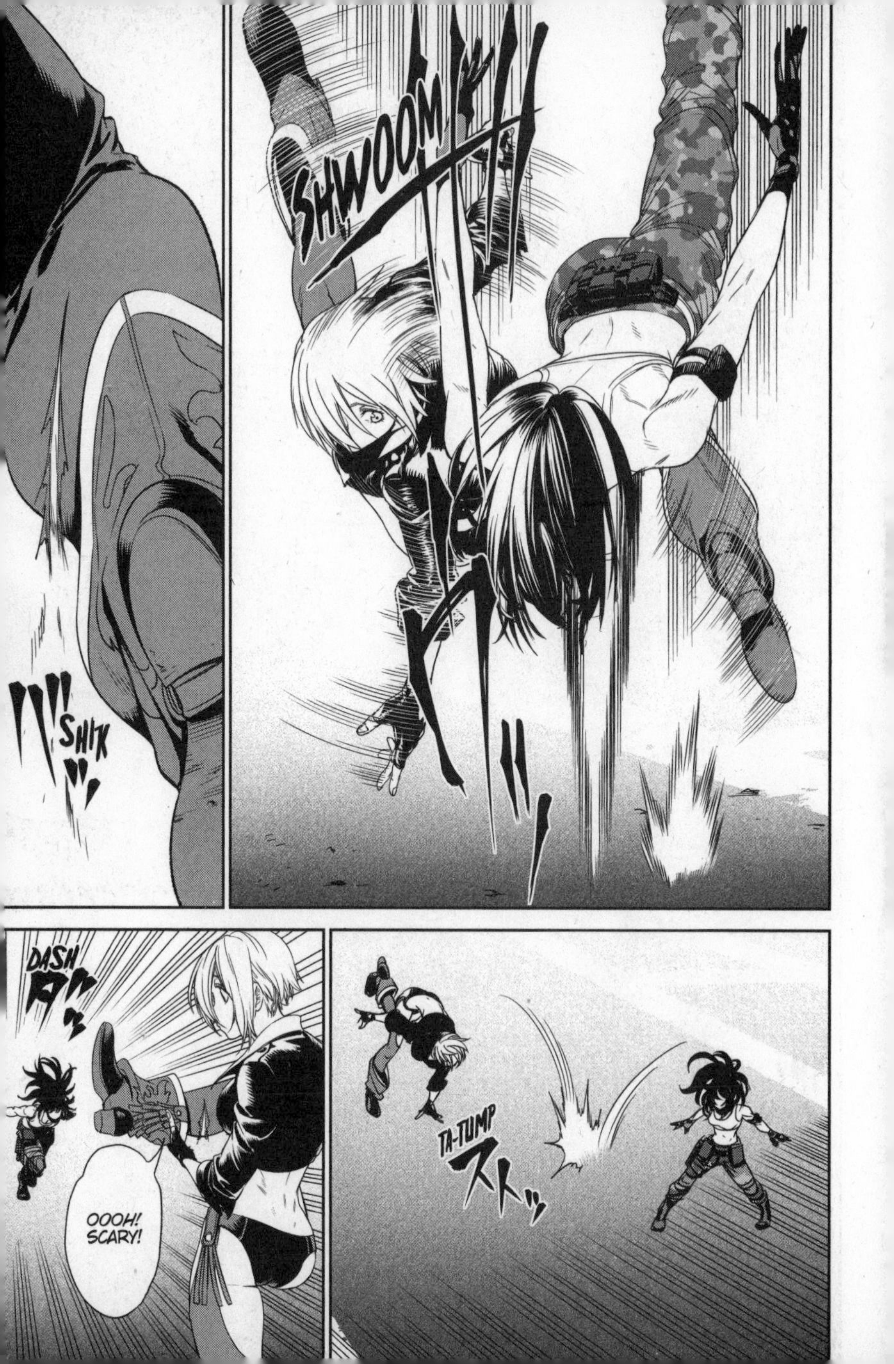
SHWOOM
SHIK
TA-TUMP
ストッ
DASH
ダッ
OOOH! SCARY!

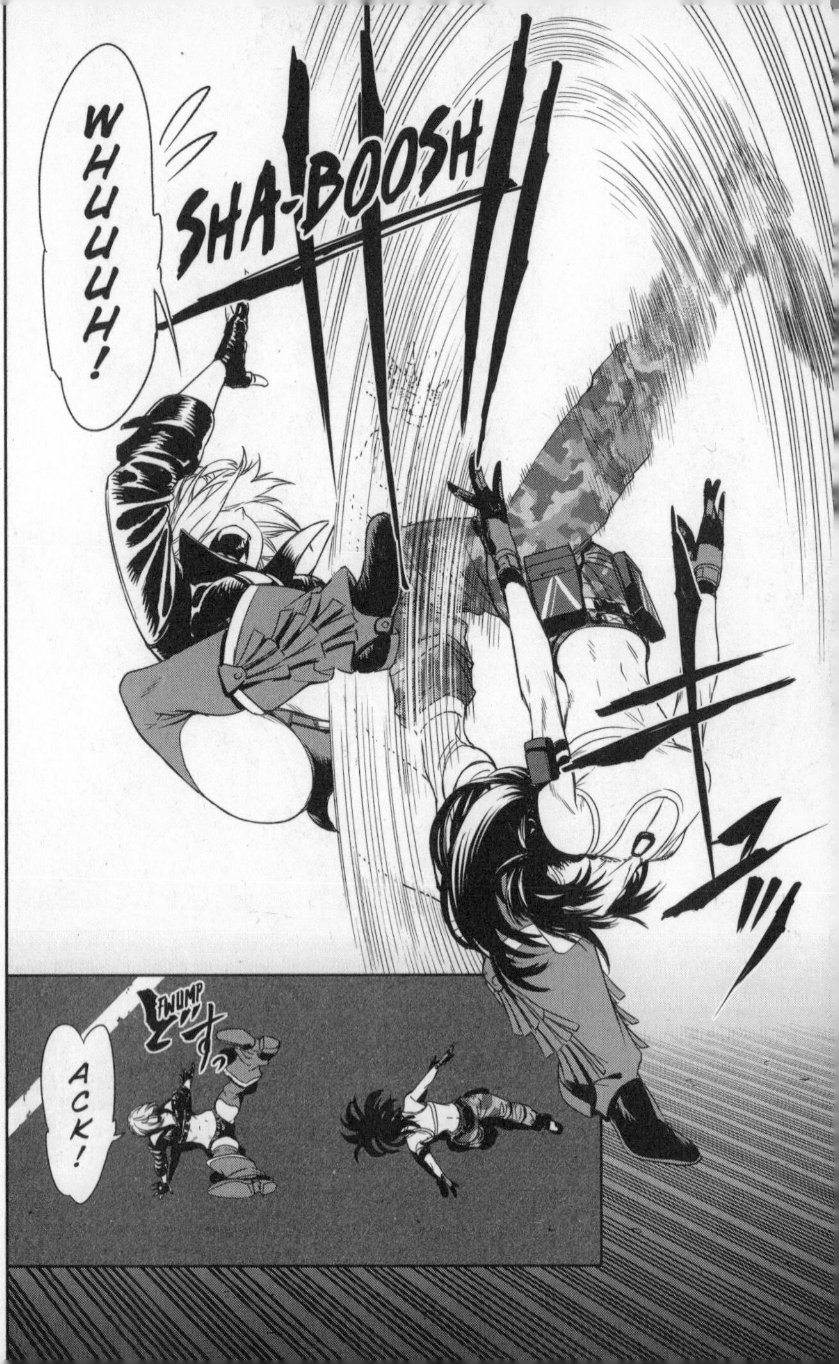
SHA-BOOSH
WHUUUUH!
FWUMP
どすっ
ACK!

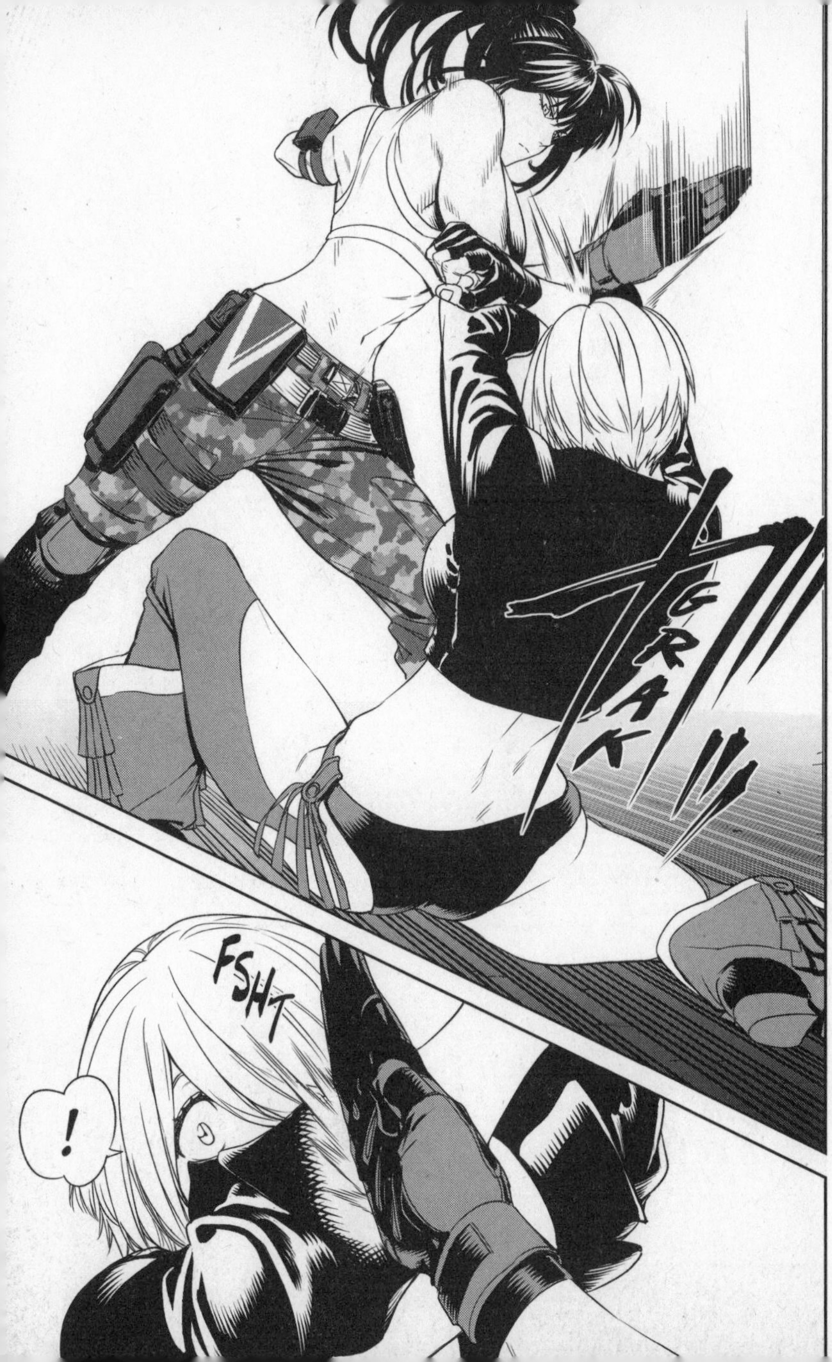
GRAK
FSHT
!

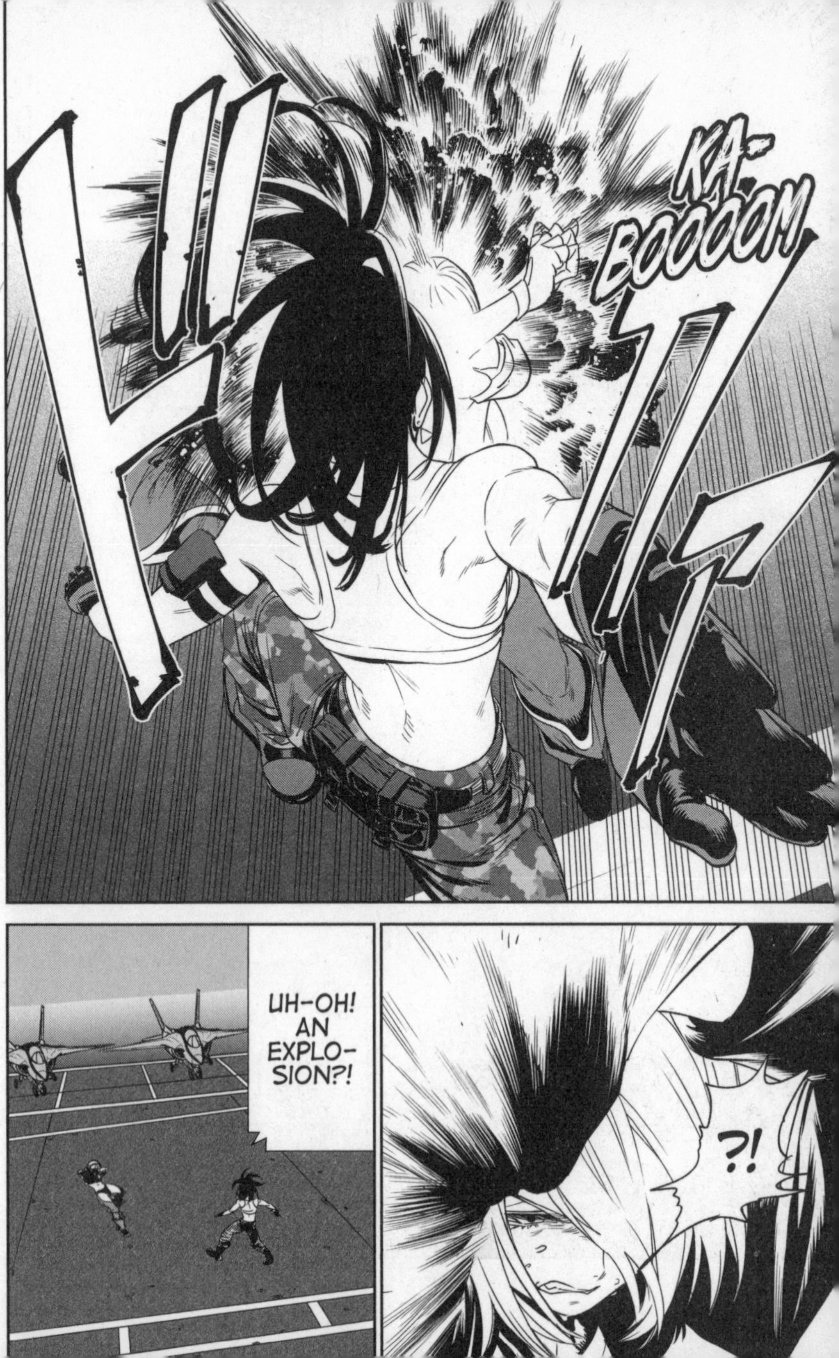
KA-BOOOOM
?!
UH-OH! AN EXPLO-SION?!

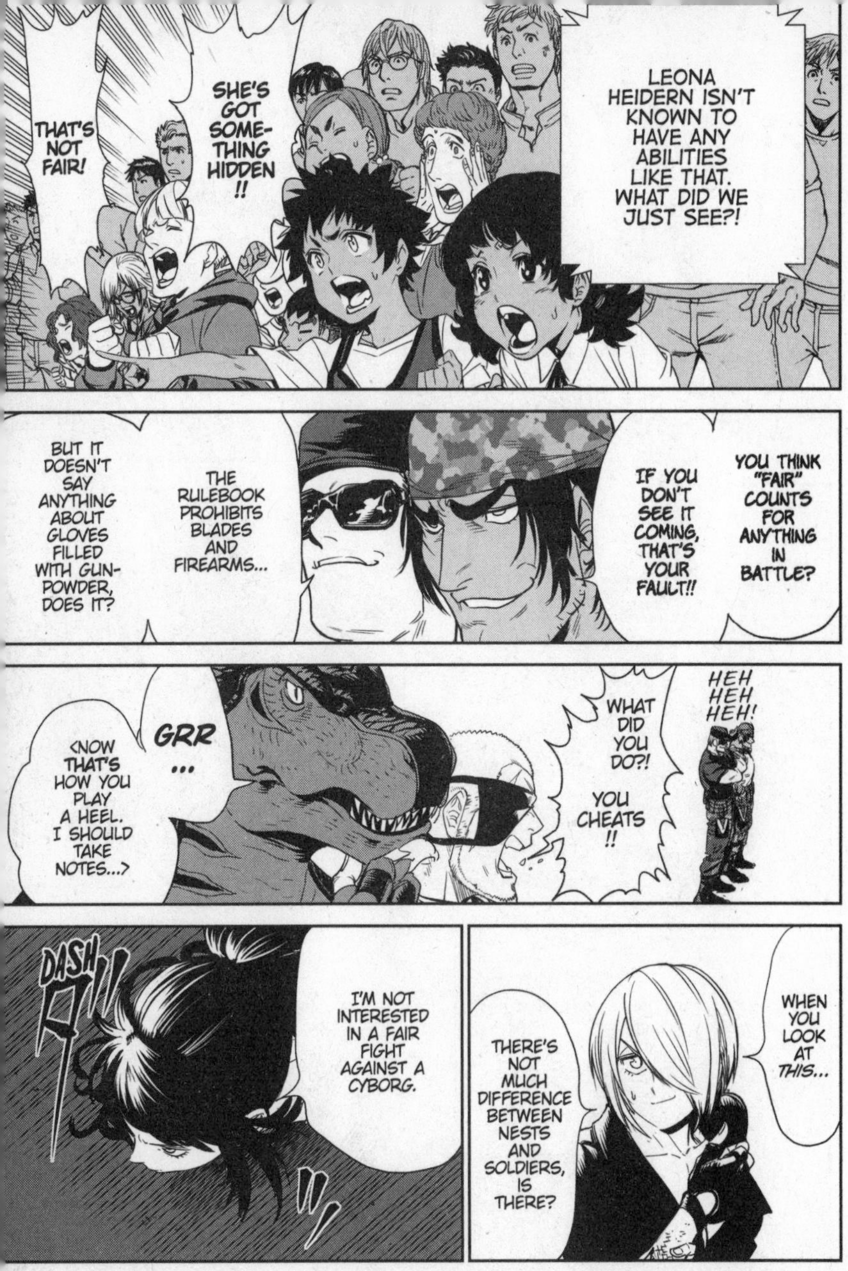
LEONA HEIDERN ISN'T KNOWN TO HAVE ANY ABILITIES LIKE THAT. WHAT DID WE JUST SEE?!
SHE'S GOT SOMETHING HIDDEN!!
THAT'S NOT FAIR!
YOU THINK "FAIR" COUNTS FOR ANYTHING IN BATTLE?
IF YOU DON'T SEE IT COMING, THAT'S YOUR FAULT!!
THE RULEBOOK PROHIBITS BLADES AND FIREARMS...
BUT IT DOESN'T SAY ANYTHING ABOUT GLOVES FILLED WITH GUNPOWDER, DOES IT?
HEH HEH HEH!
WHAT DID YOU DO?!
YOU CHEATS!!
GRR...
<NOW THAT'S HOW YOU PLAY A HEEL. I SHOULD TAKE NOTES...>
WHEN YOU LOOK AT *THIS*...
THERE'S NOT MUCH DIFFERENCE BETWEEN NESTS AND SOLDIERS, IS THERE?
I'M NOT INTERESTED IN A FAIR FIGHT AGAINST A CYBORG.
DASH!!

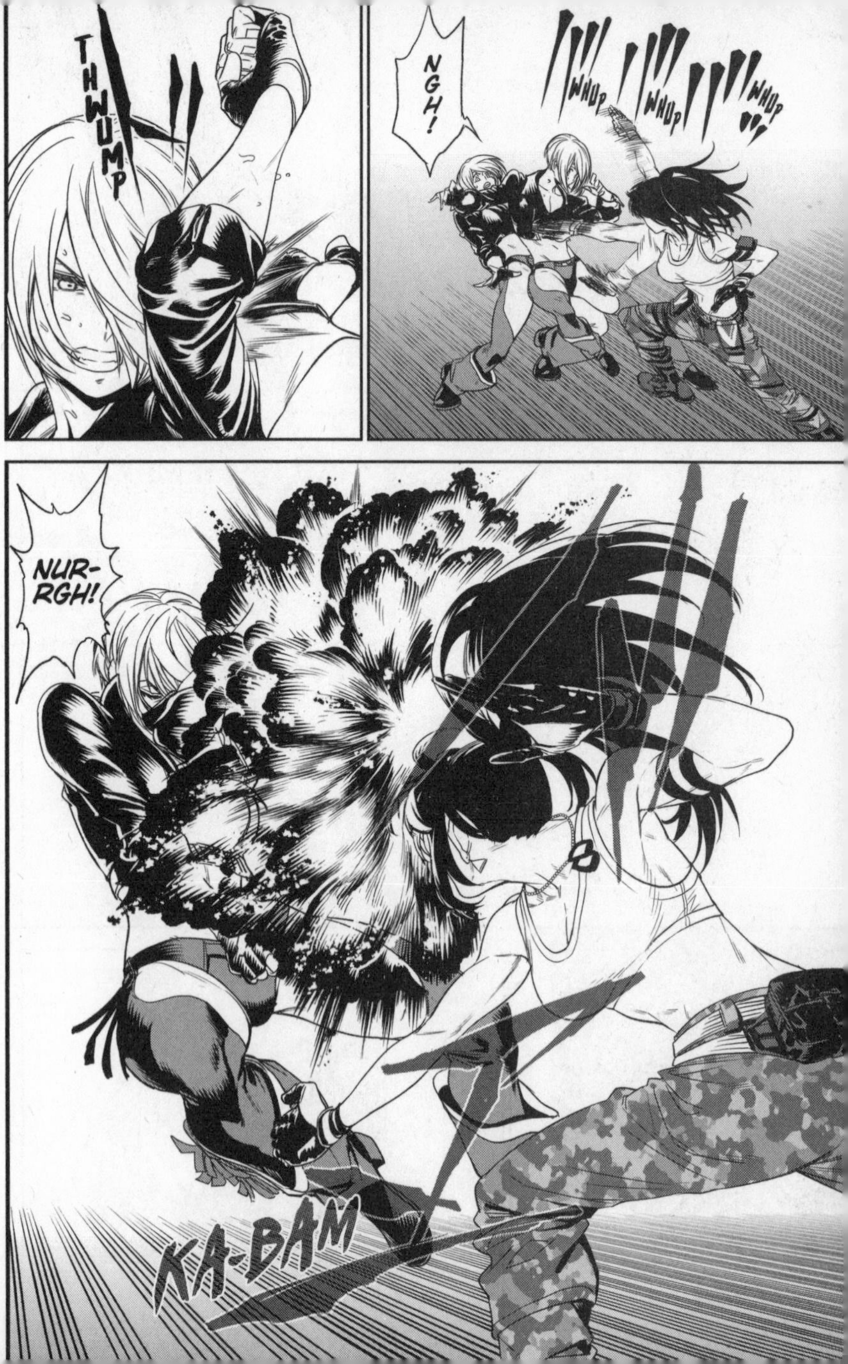
NGH!
WHUP
WHUP
WHUP
THWUMP
NUR-RGH!
KA-BAM

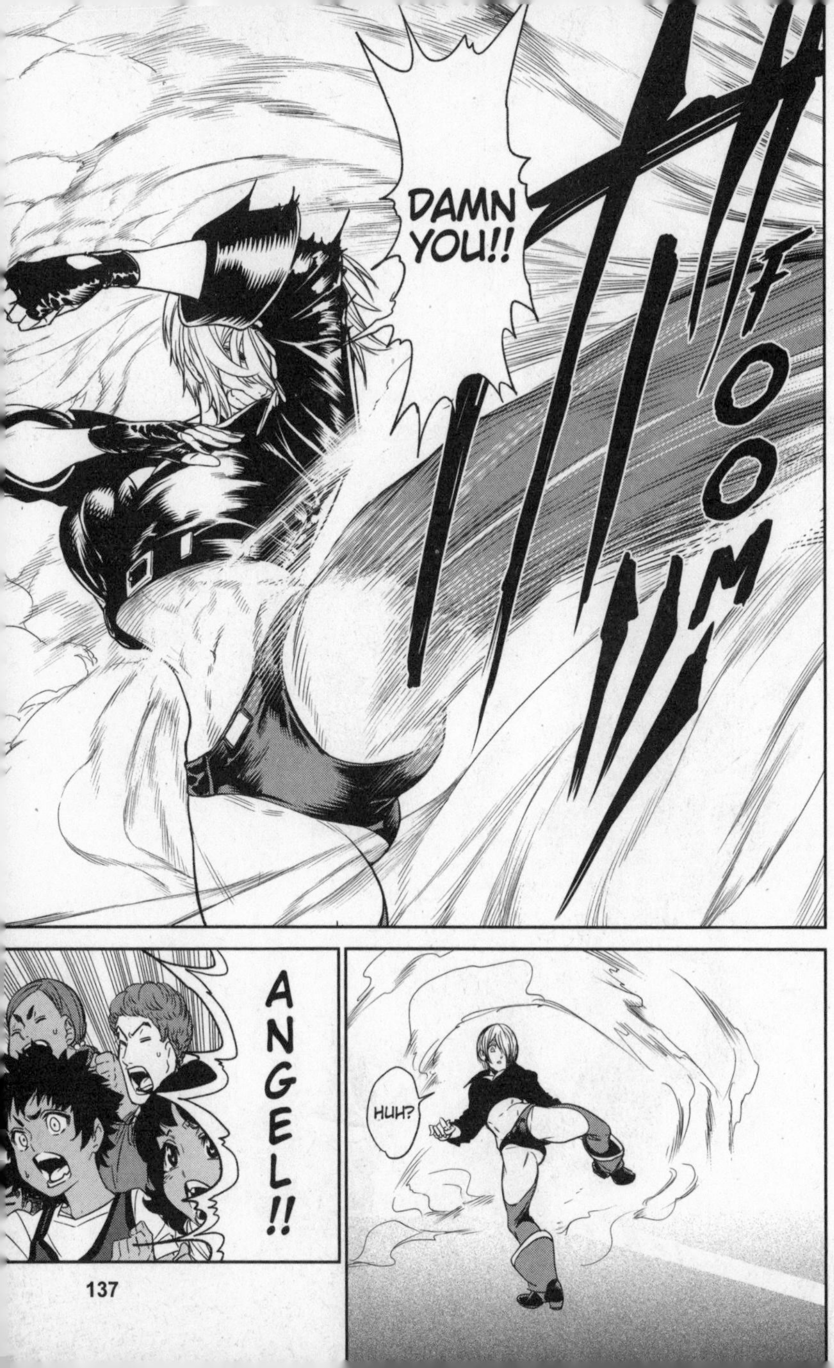
DAMN YOU!!
FOOM
HUH?
ANGEL!!

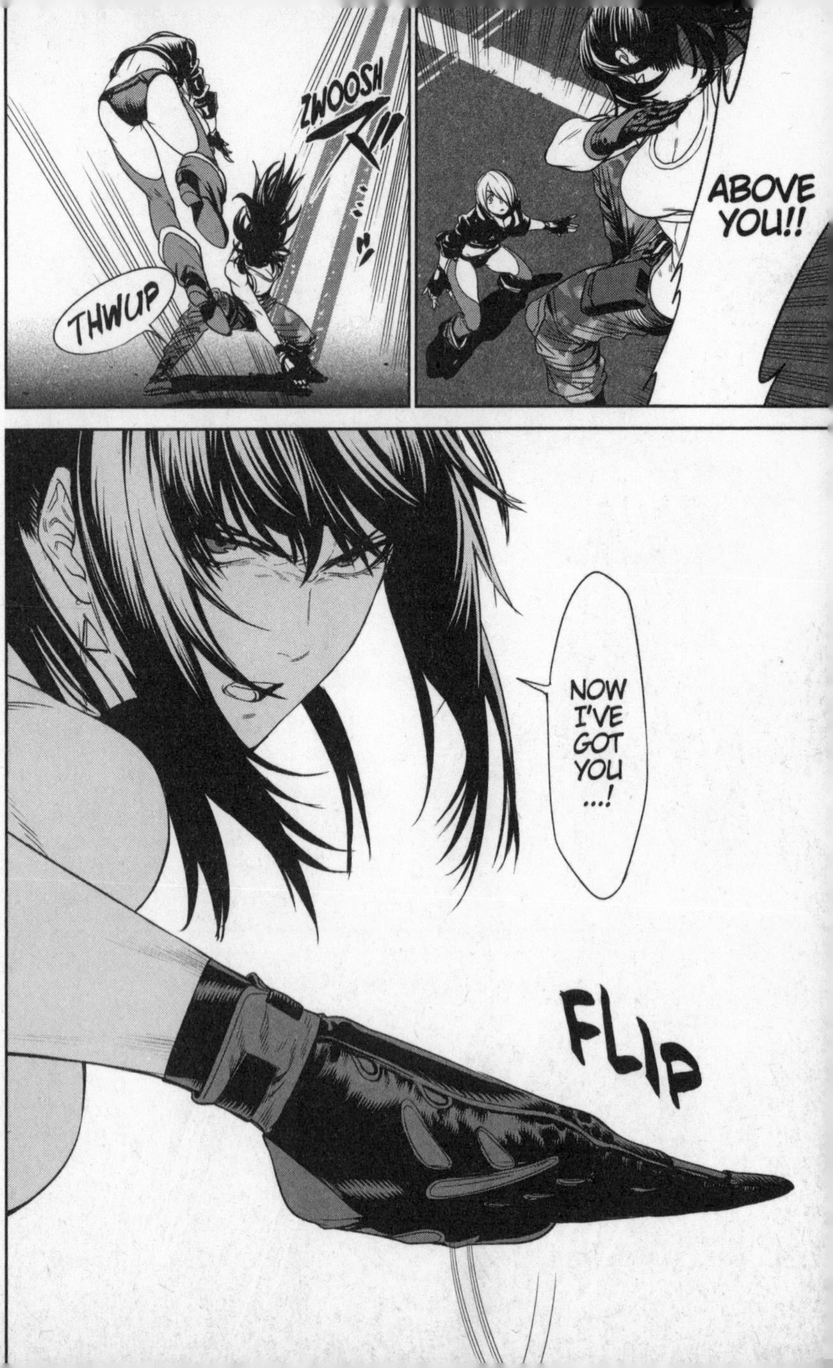
ABOVE YOU!!
ZWOOSH
THWUP
NOW I'VE GOT YOU ...!
FLIP

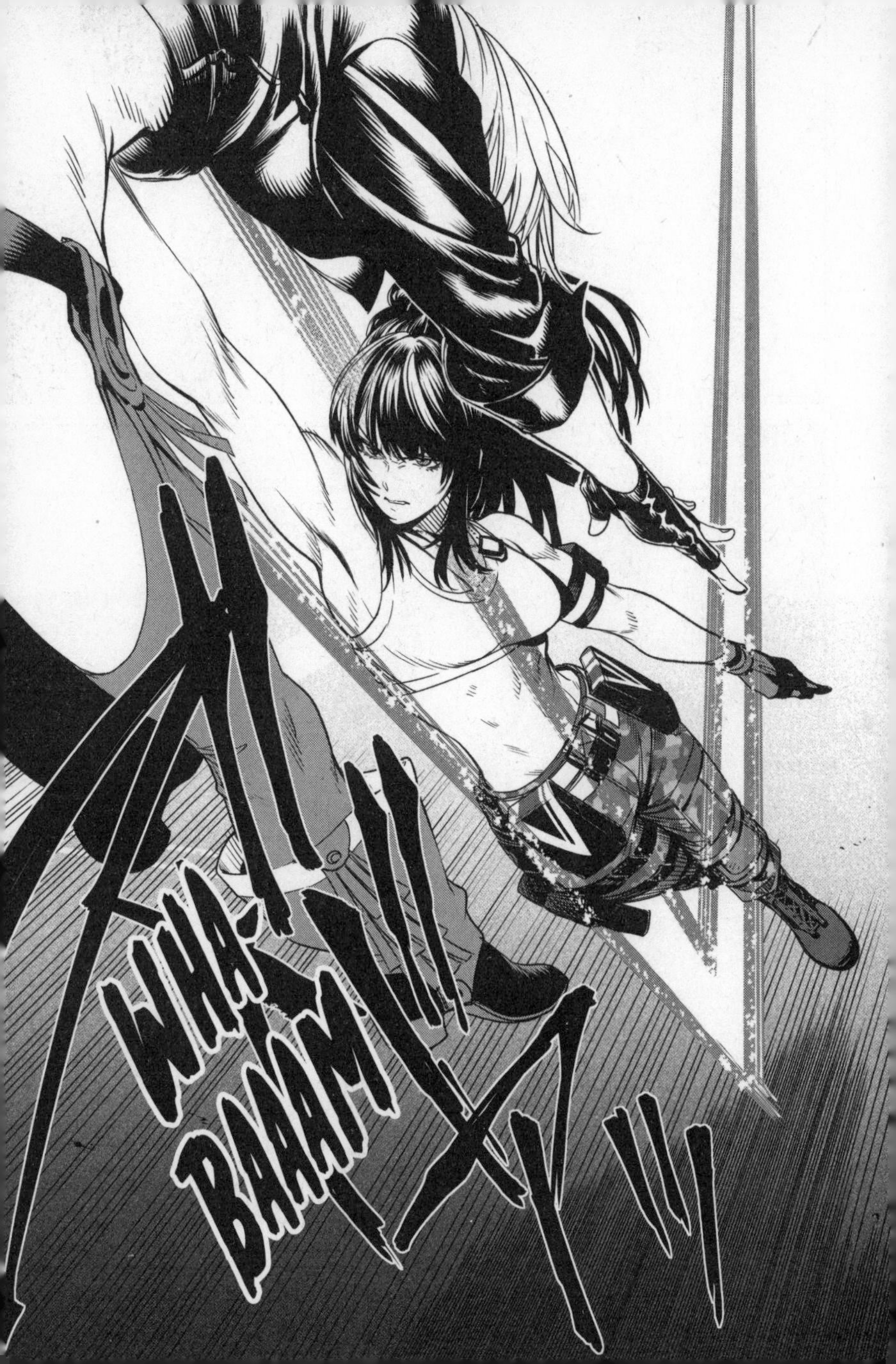
WHA
BAAM!!

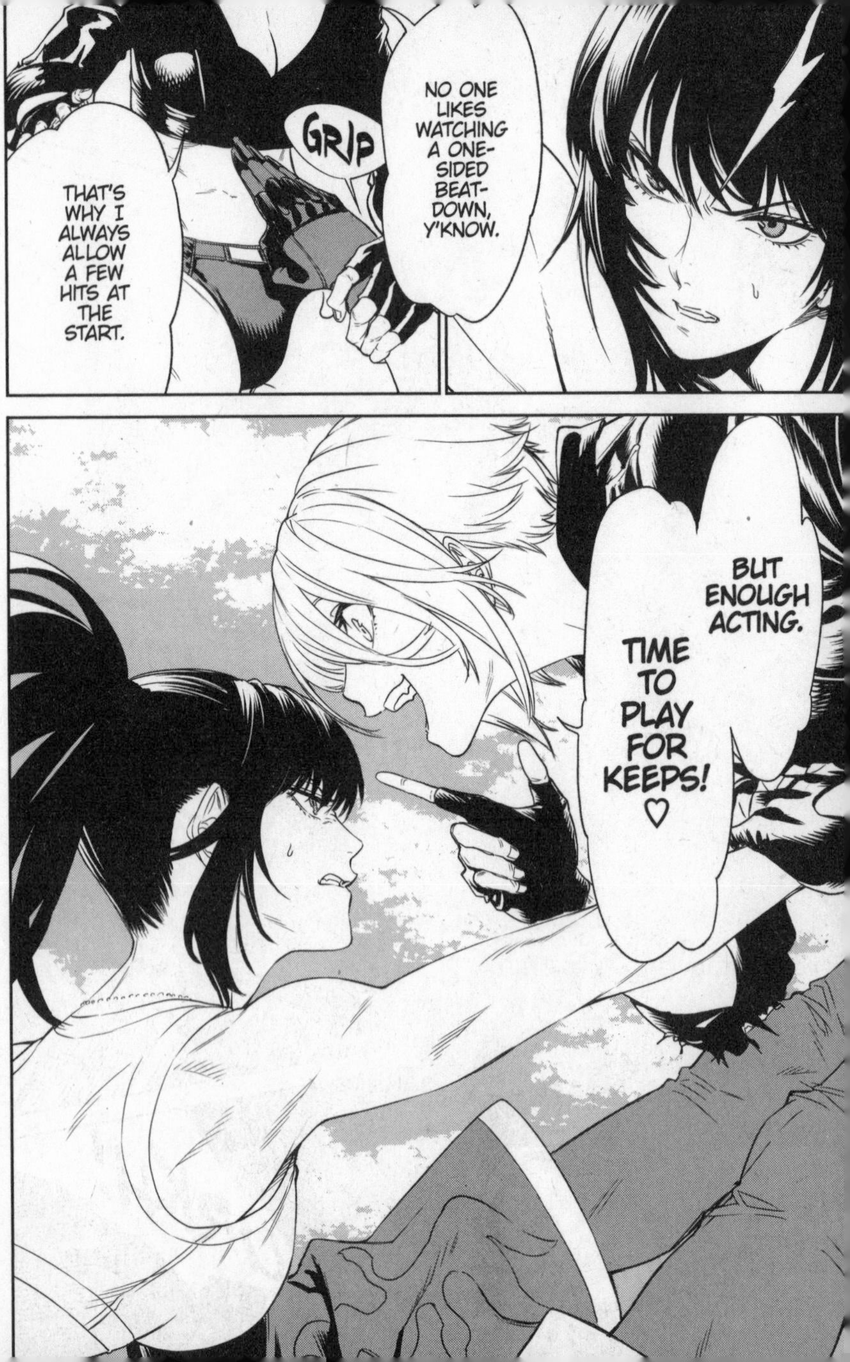
NO ONE LIKES WATCHING A ONE-SIDED BEAT-DOWN, Y'KNOW.
GRIP
THAT'S WHY I ALWAYS ALLOW A FEW HITS AT THE START.
BUT ENOUGH ACTING.
TIME TO PLAY FOR KEEPS! ♡

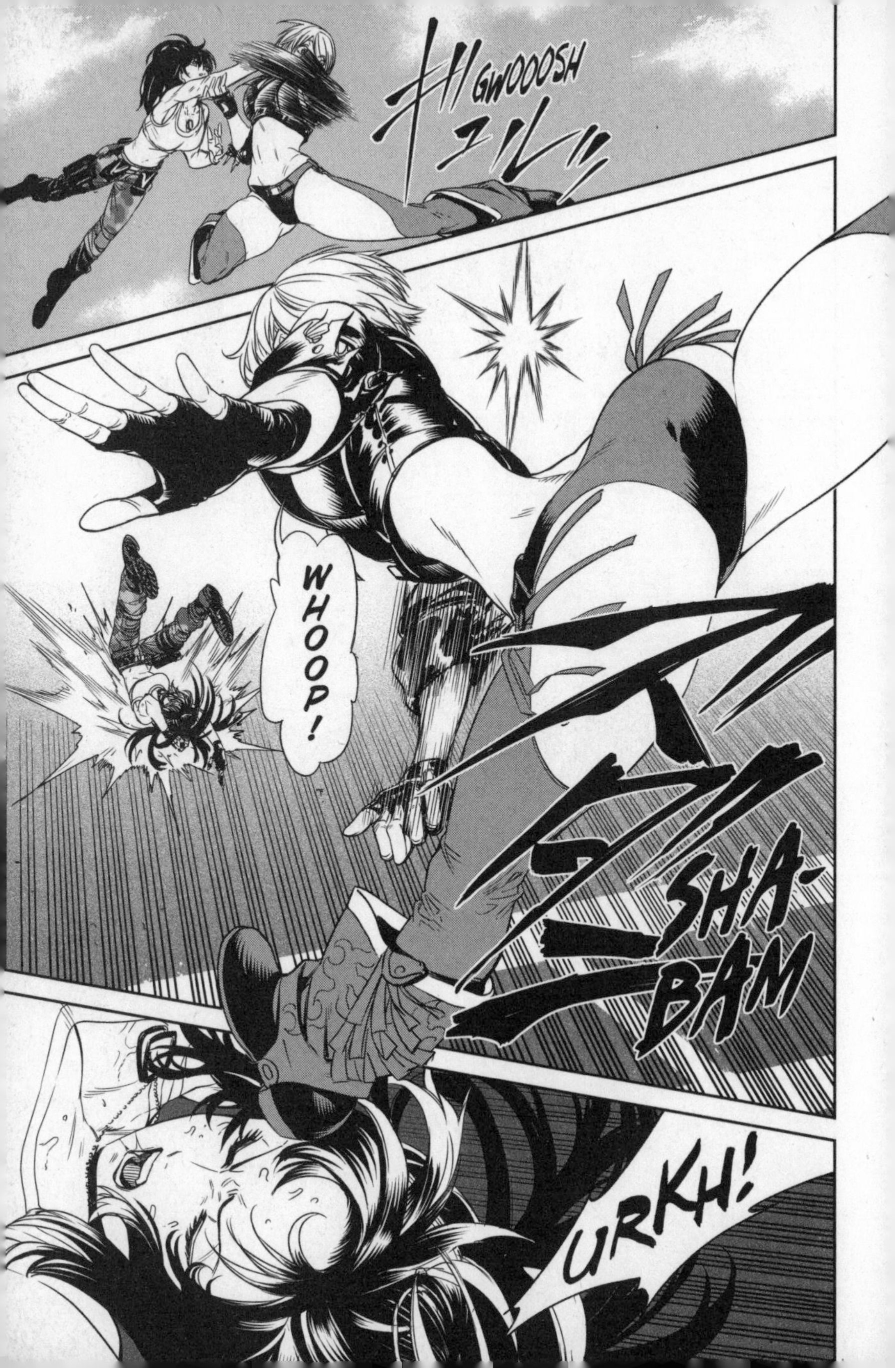
GWOOOSH
WHOOOP!
SHA-BAM
URKH!

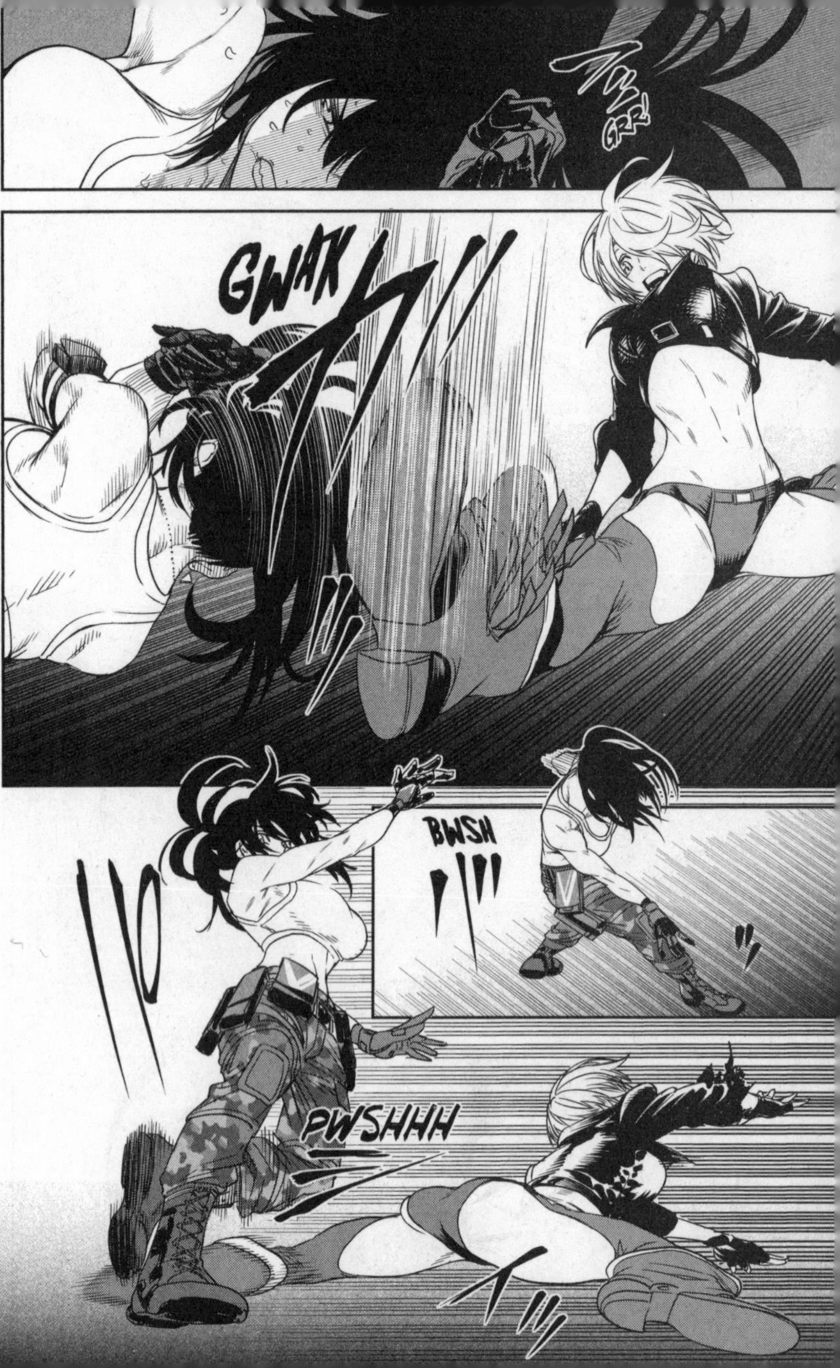
GRR!
GWAK
BWSH
PWSHHH

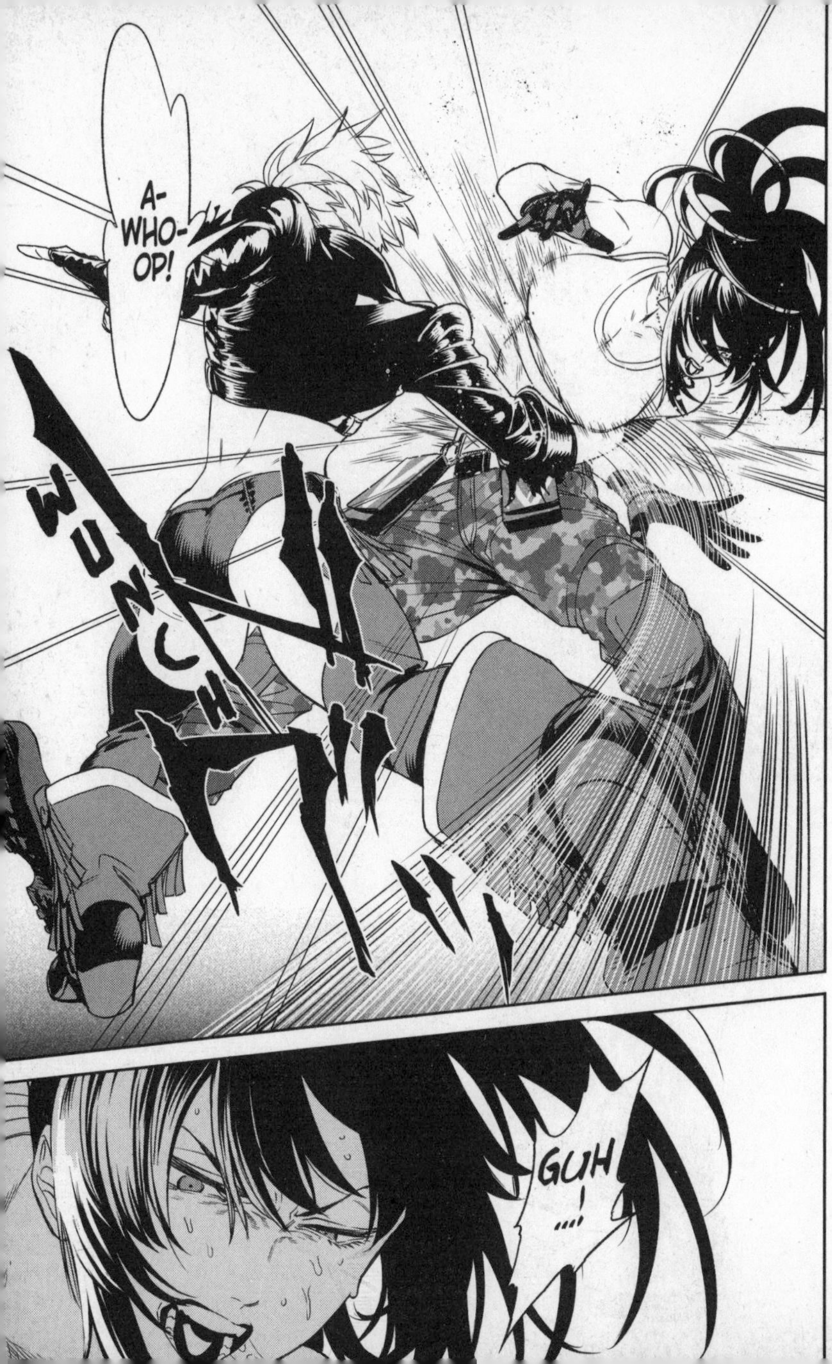
A-WHOO-OP!
WUNCH
GUH...!

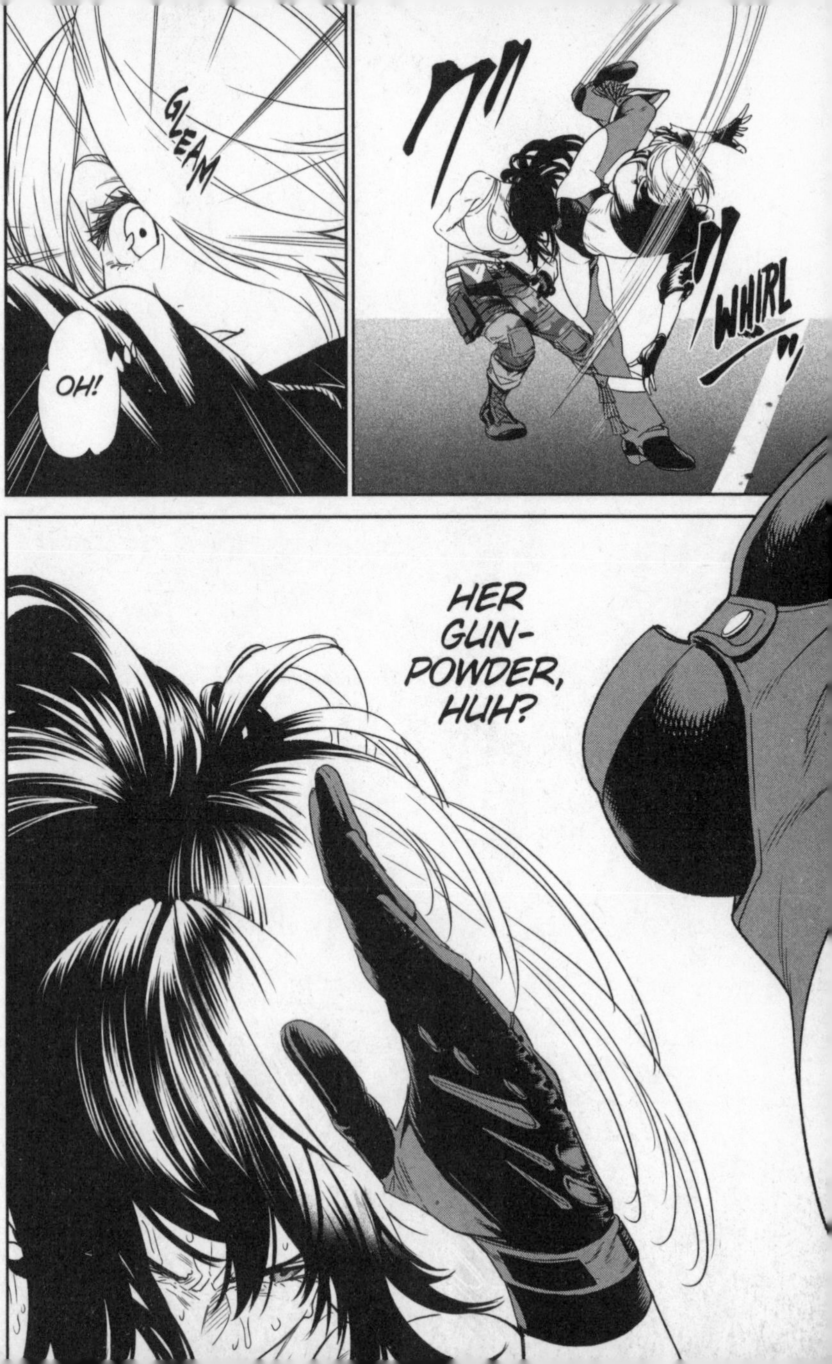
WHIRL
GLEAM
OH!
HER GUN-POWDER, HUH?

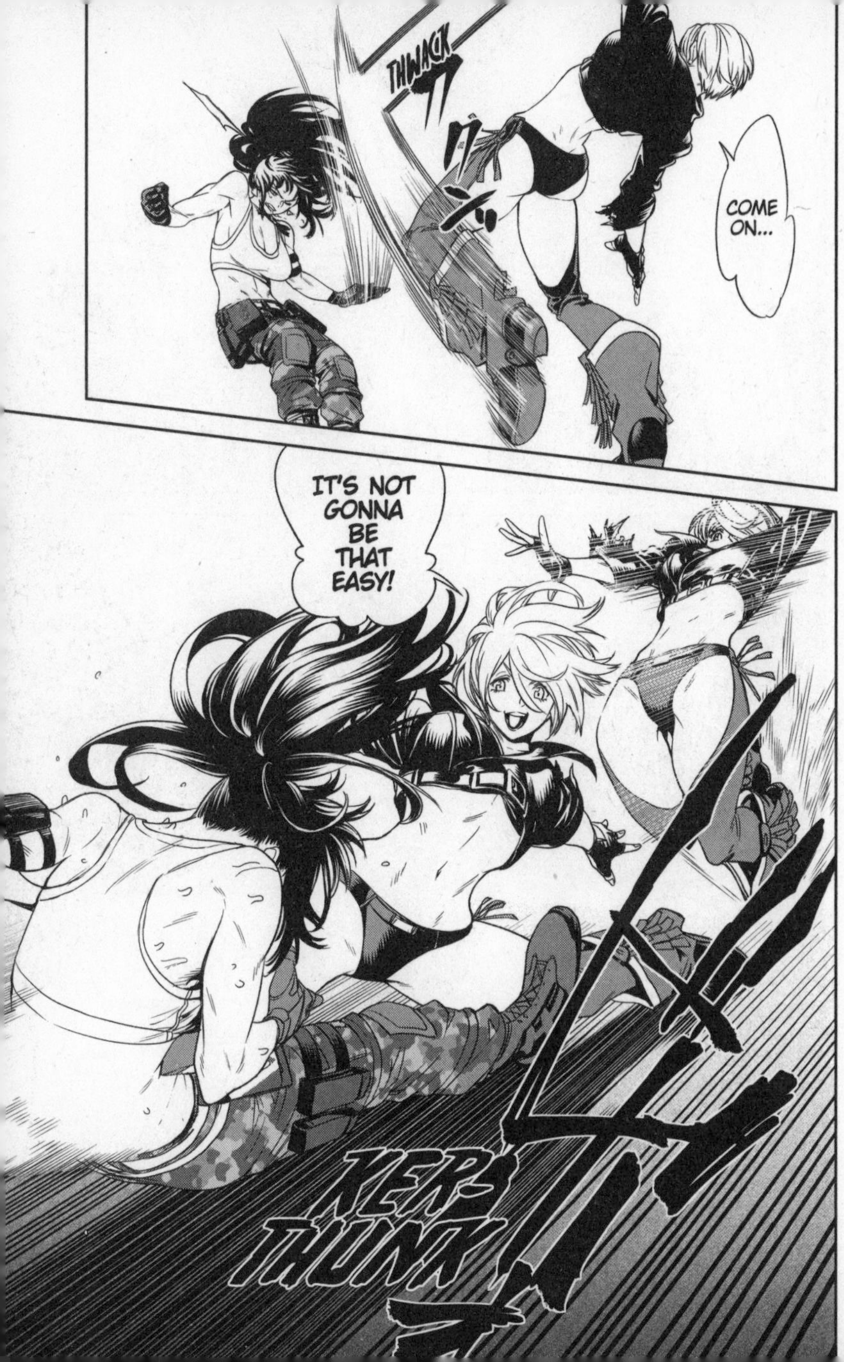
COME ON...
THWACK
IT'S NOT GONNA BE THAT EASY!
KER-THUNK

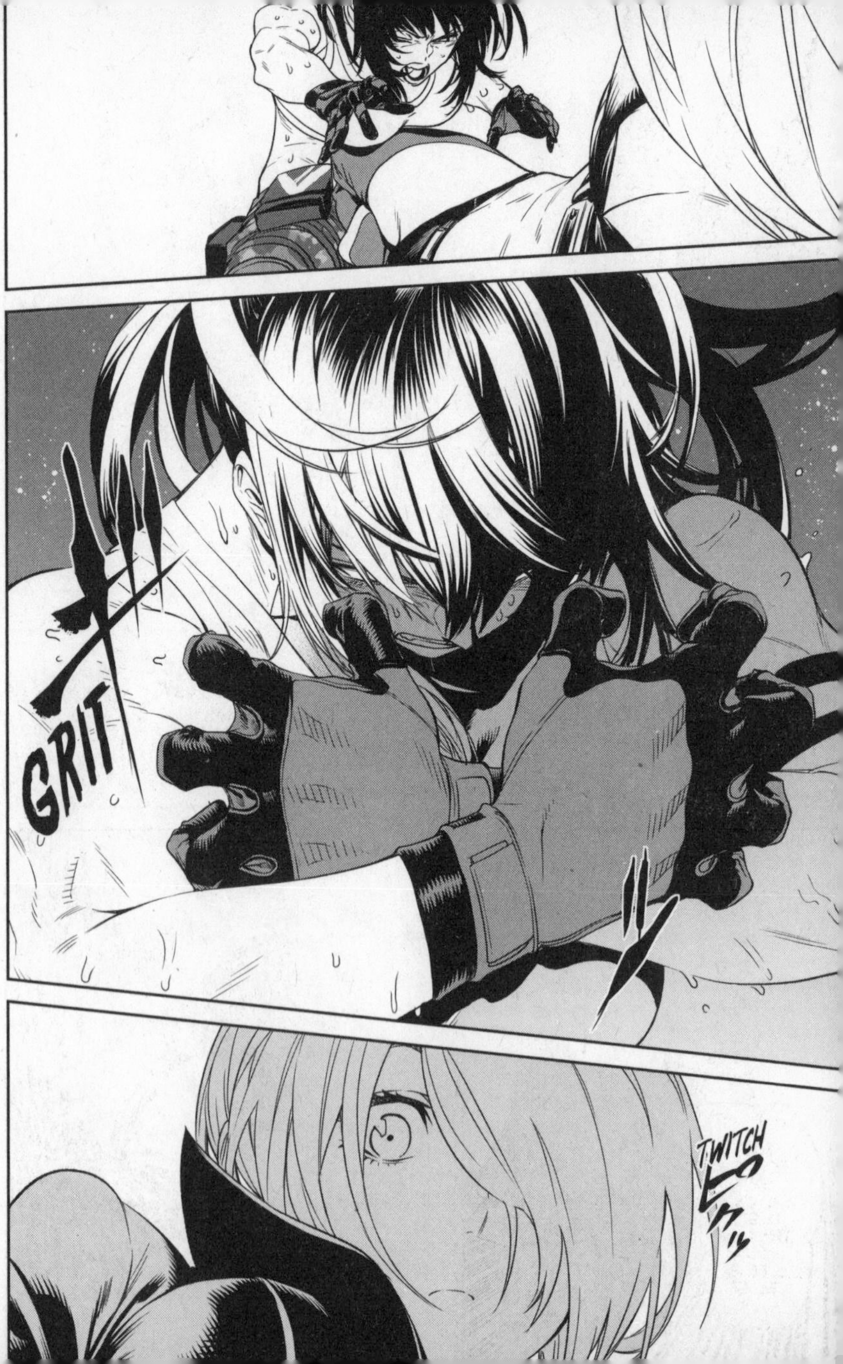
GRIT
TWITCH

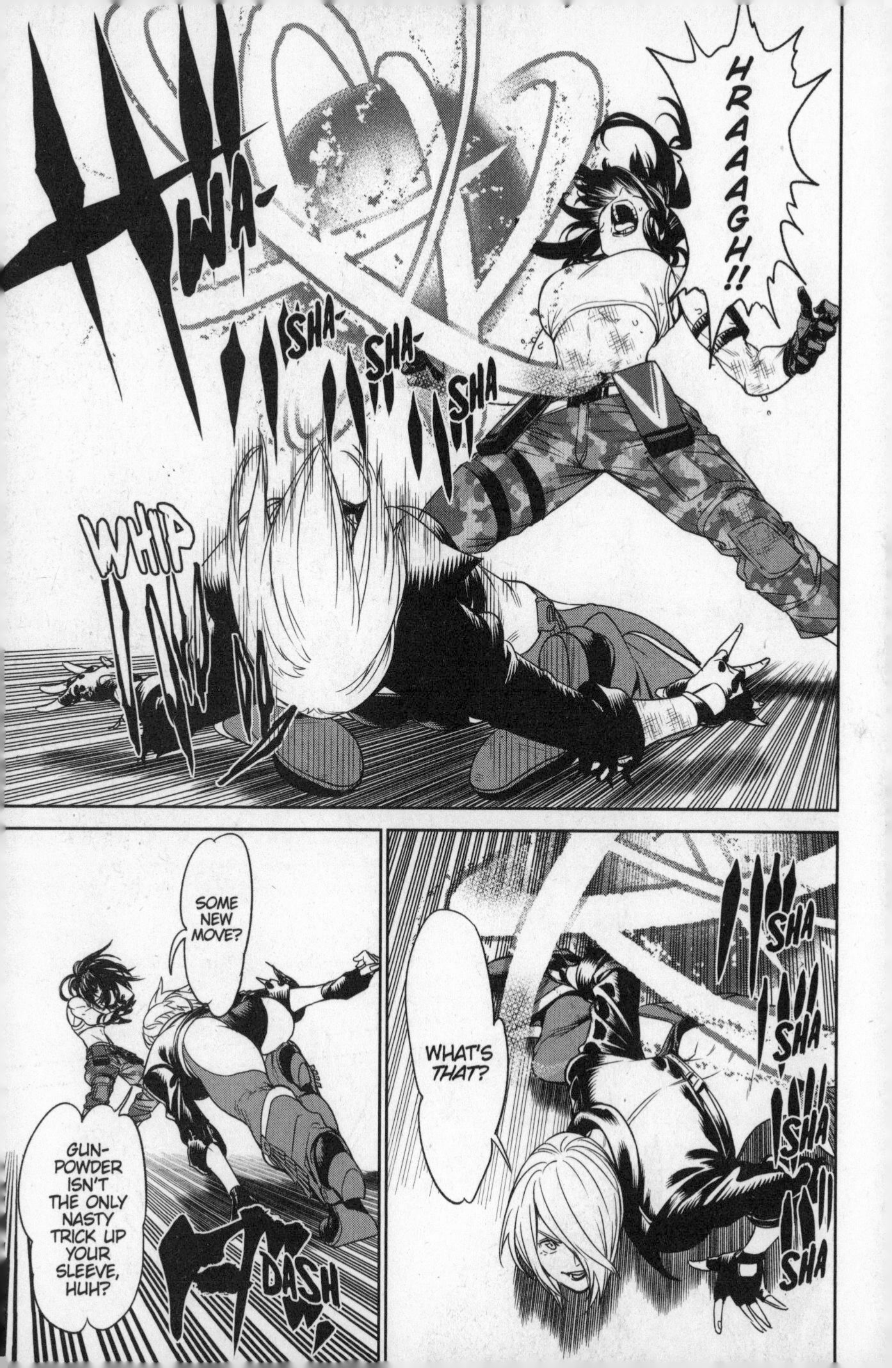
HRAAAAGH!!
HWA-
SHA- SHA- SHA
WHIP
SHA SHA SHA SHA
WHAT'S THAT?
SOME NEW MOVE?
GUN-POWDER ISN'T THE ONLY NASTY TRICK UP YOUR SLEEVE, HUH?
DASH

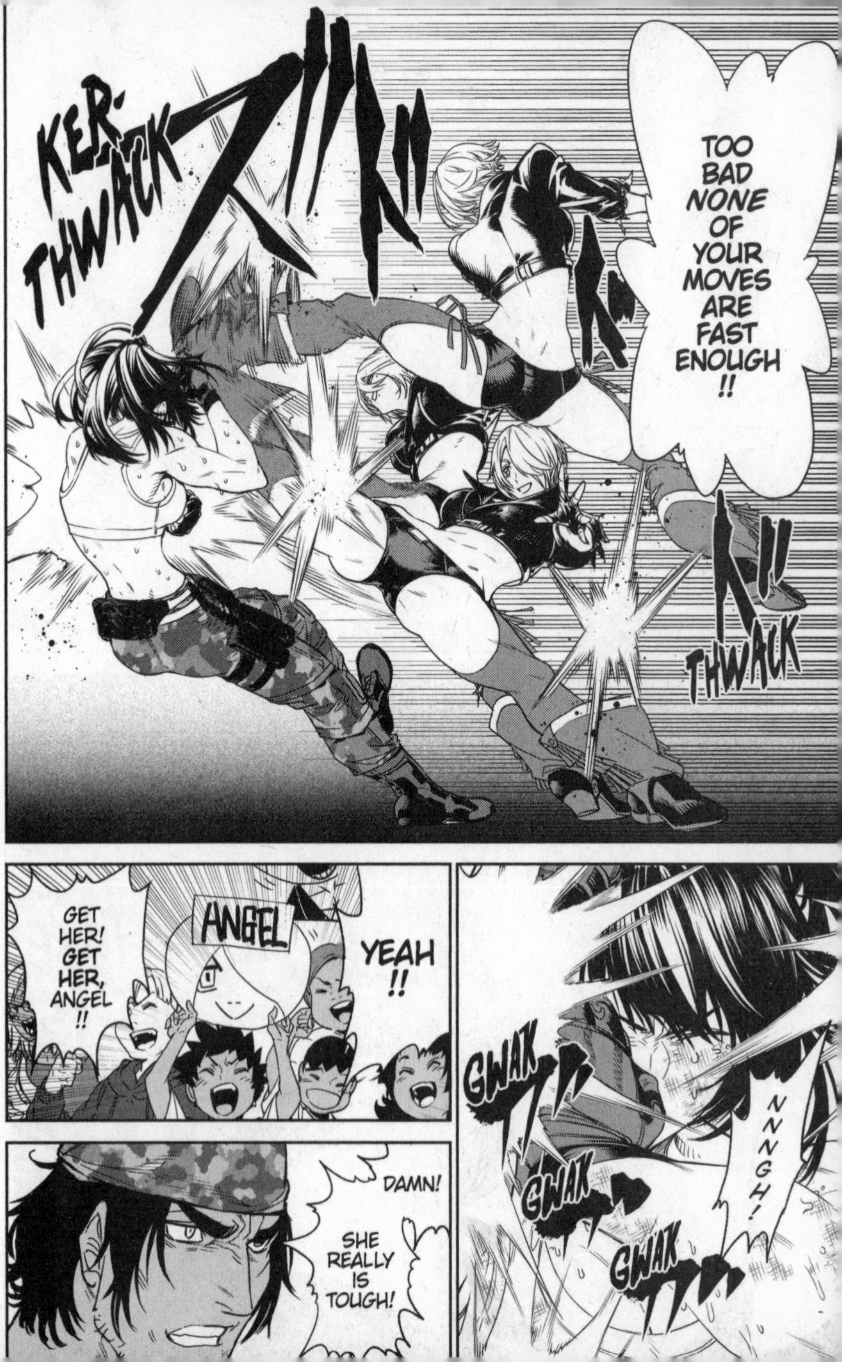
TOO BAD NONE OF YOUR MOVES ARE FAST ENOUGH!!
KER-THWACK
THWACK
NNNGH!
GWAK
GWAK
GWAK
YEAH!!
ANGEL
GET HER! GET HER, ANGEL!!
DAMN!
SHE REALLY IS TOUGH!

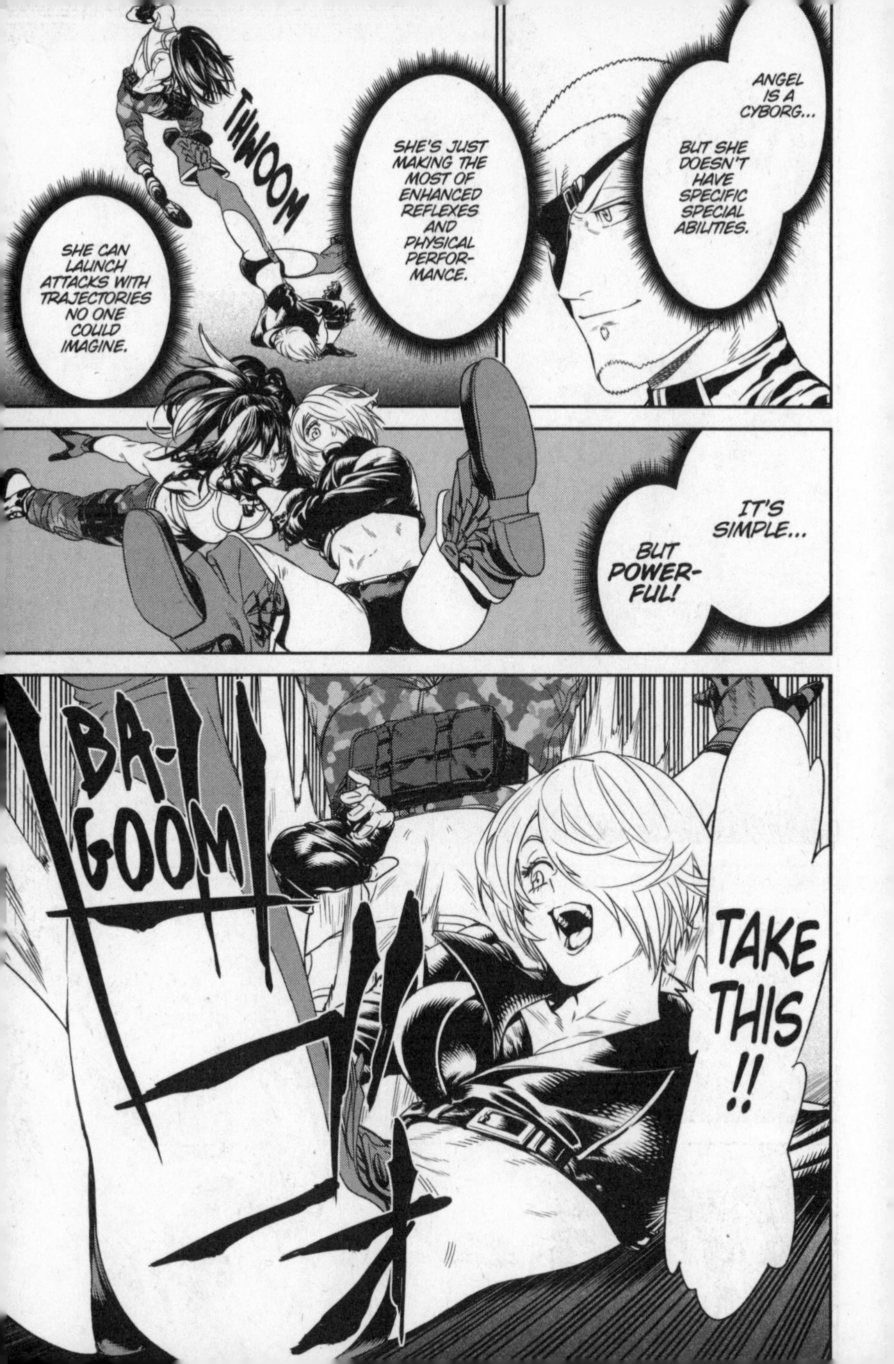
ANGEL IS A CYBORG...
BUT SHE DOESN'T HAVE SPECIFIC SPECIAL ABILITIES.
SHE'S JUST MAKING THE MOST OF ENHANCED REFLEXES AND PHYSICAL PERFOR-MANCE.
THWOOM
SHE CAN LAUNCH ATTACKS WITH TRAJECTORIES NO ONE COULD IMAGINE.
IT'S SIMPLE...
BUT POWER-FUL!
TAKE THIS!!
BA-GOOM

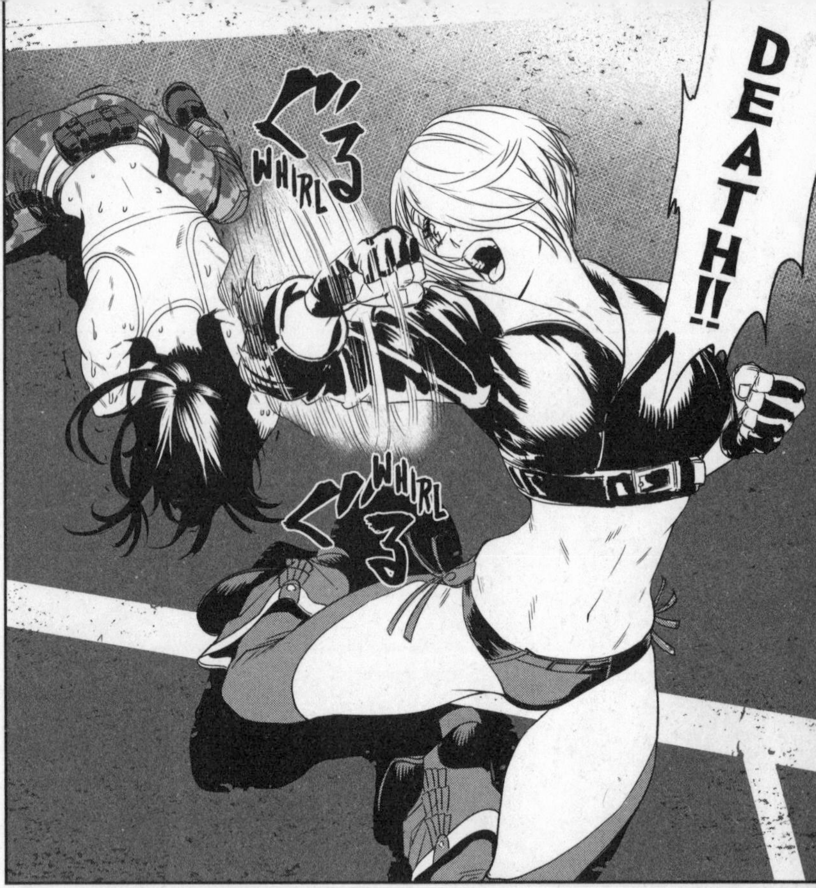
DEATH!!
WHIRL
WHIRL
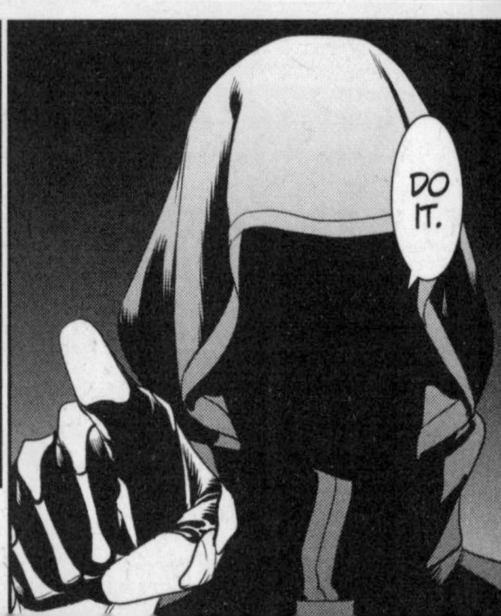
DO IT.
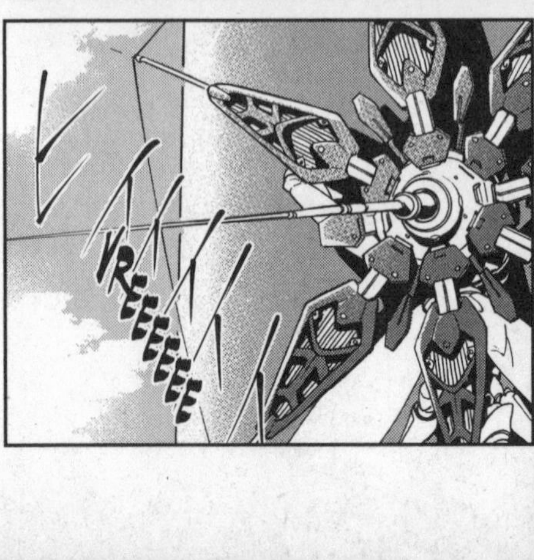
VREEEEEEE

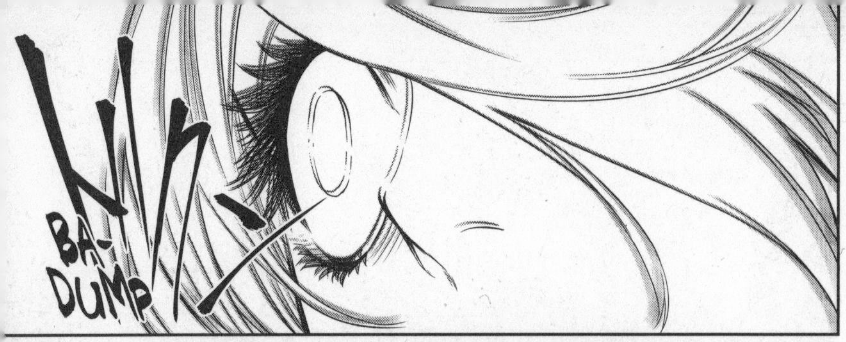
BA-DUMP
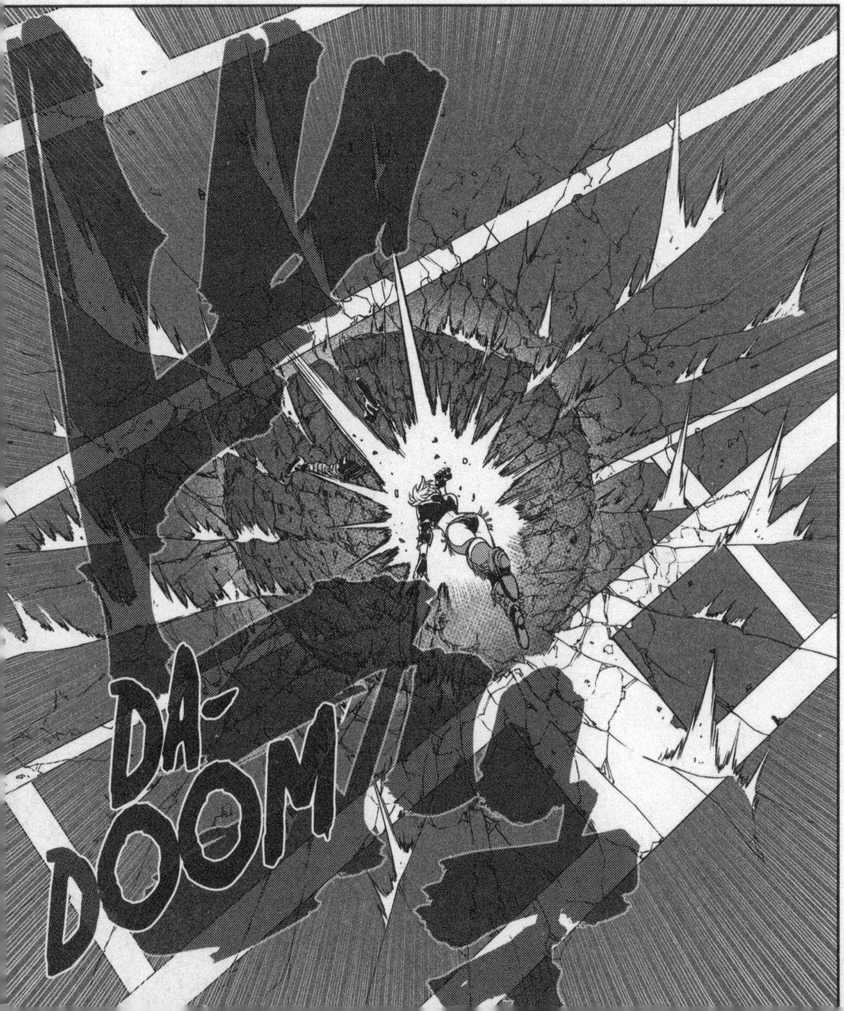
DA-DOOM!

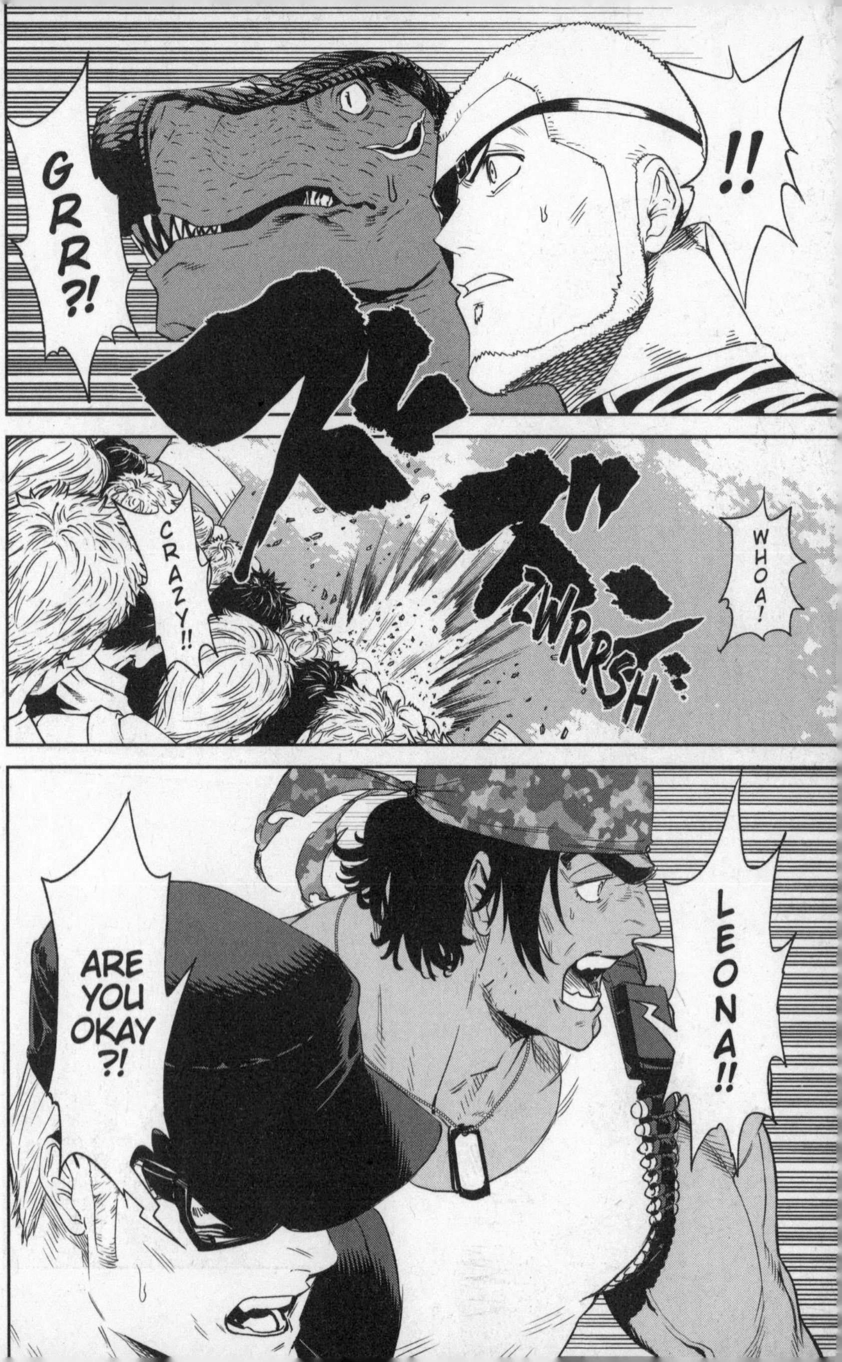
!!
GRR?!
WHOA!
ZWRRSH
CRAZY!!
LEONA!!
ARE YOU OKAY?!

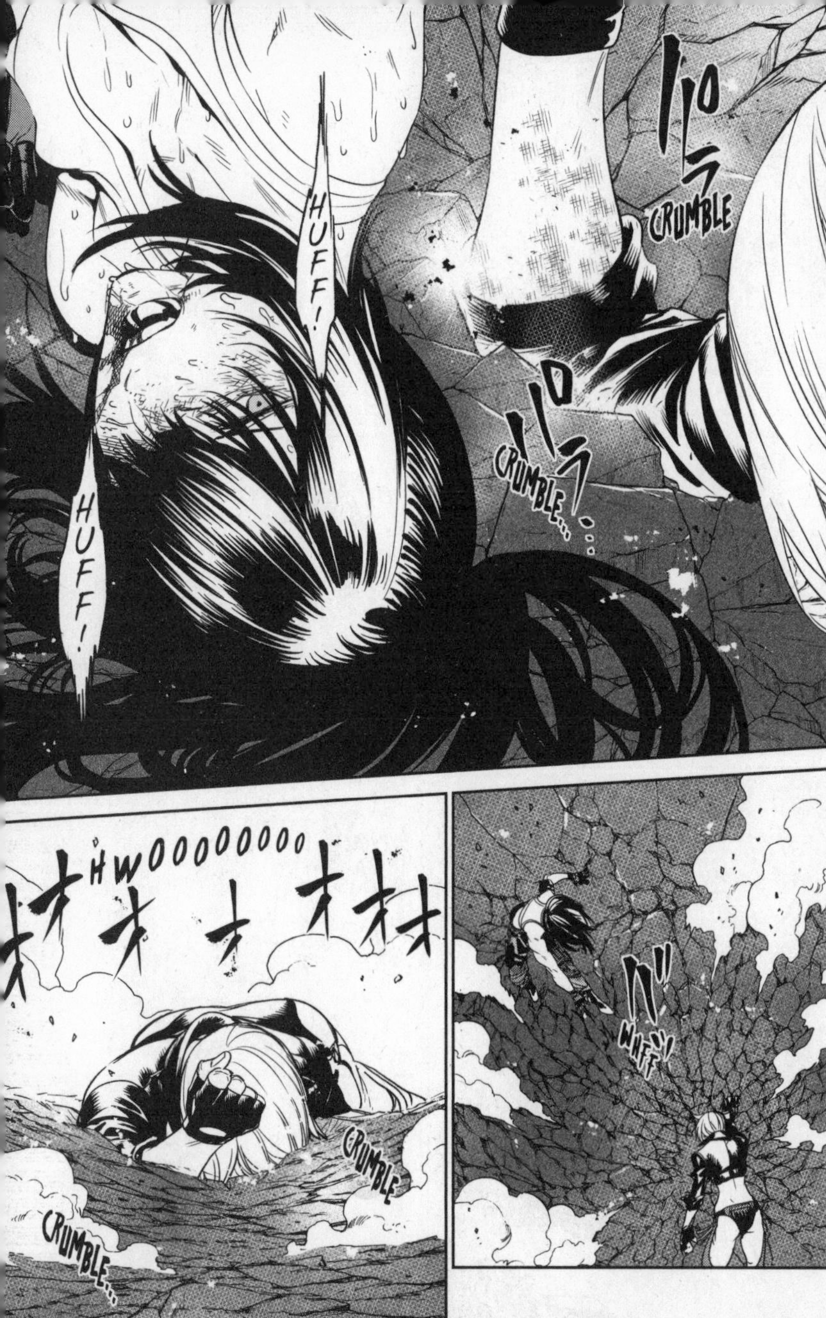
CRUMBLE
HUFF!
HUFF!
CRUMBLE...
WHFF
HWOOOOOOOO
CRUMBLE
CRUMBLE...

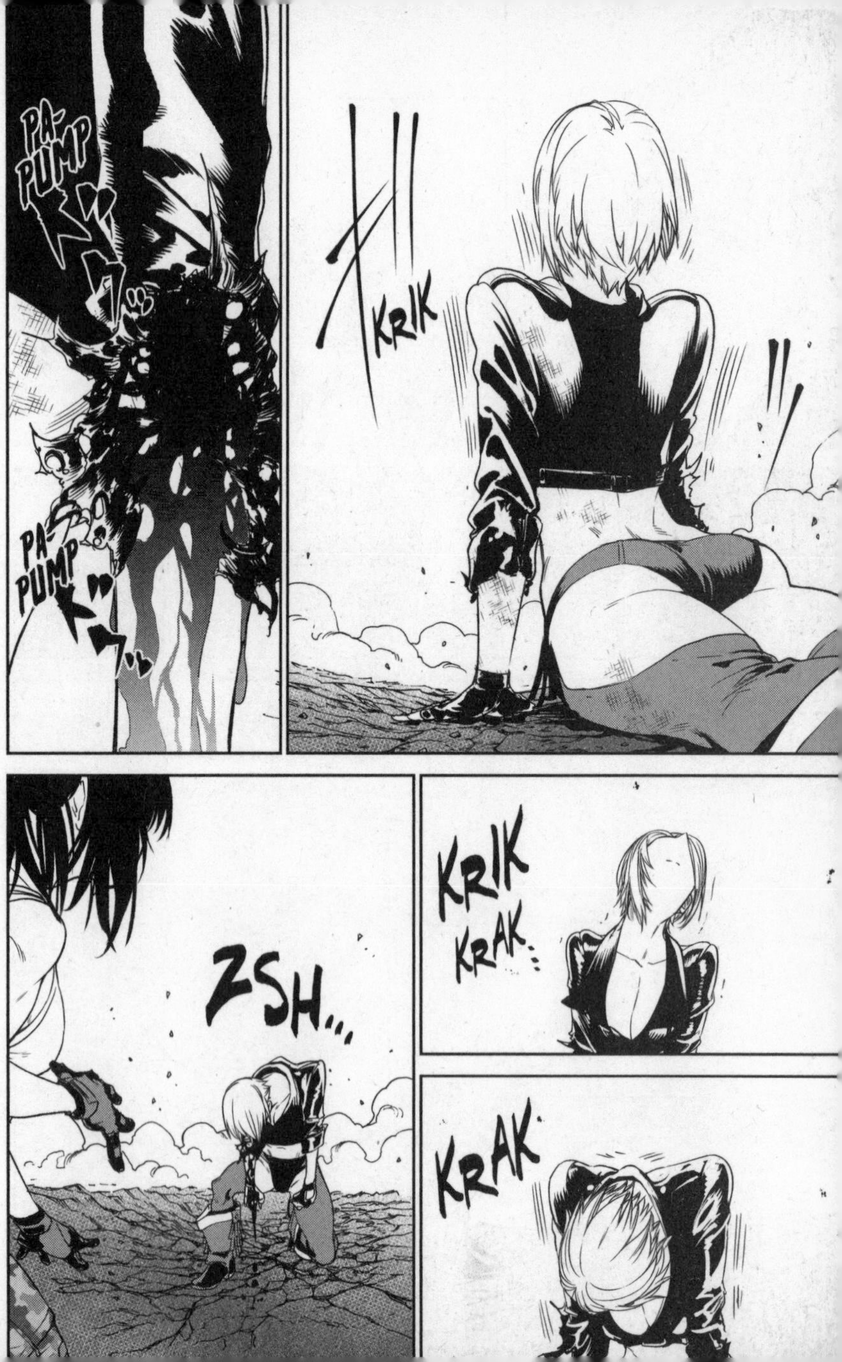
KRIK
PA-PUMP
PA-PUMP
KRIK KRAK...
KRAK
ZSH...

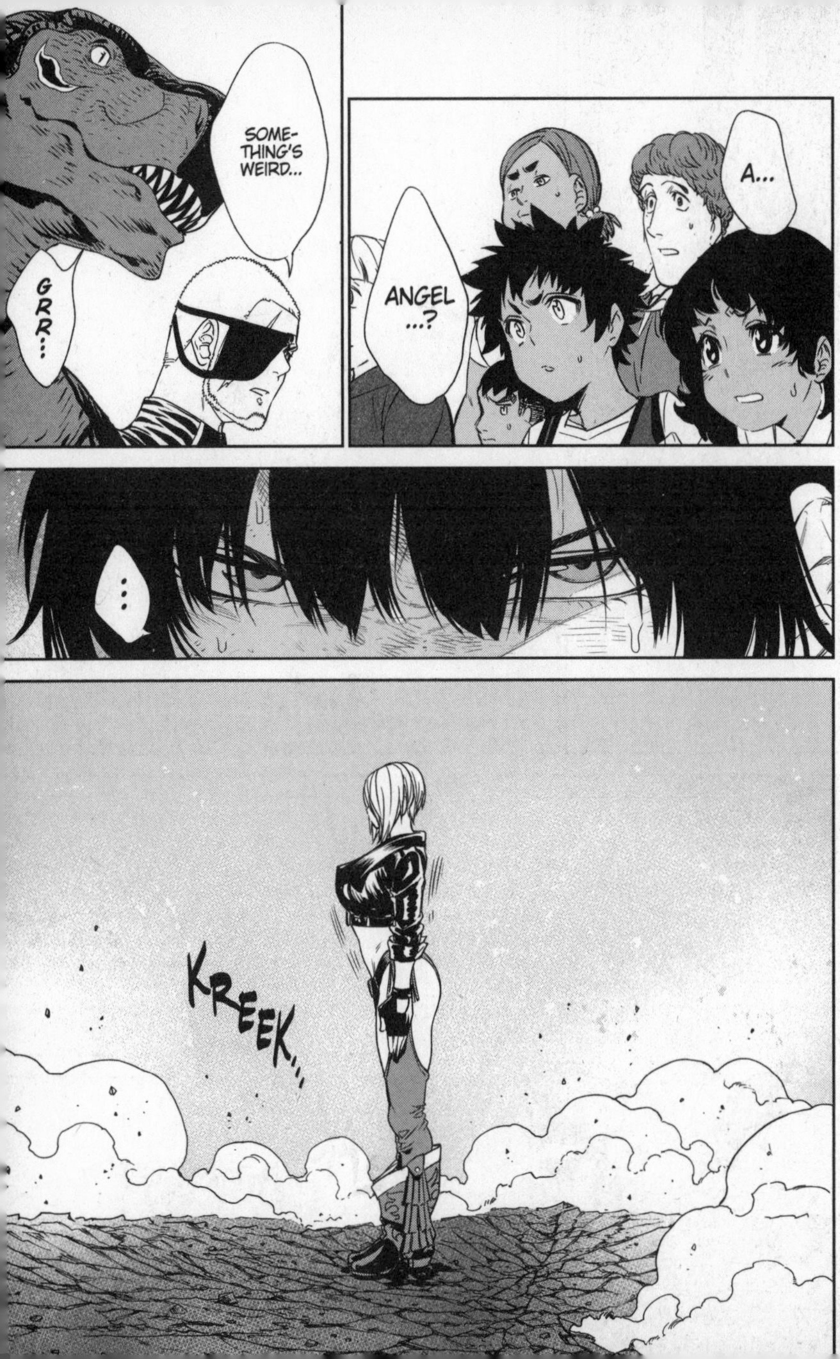
A...
ANGEL ...?
SOME-THING'S WEIRD...
GRR...
...
KREEK...

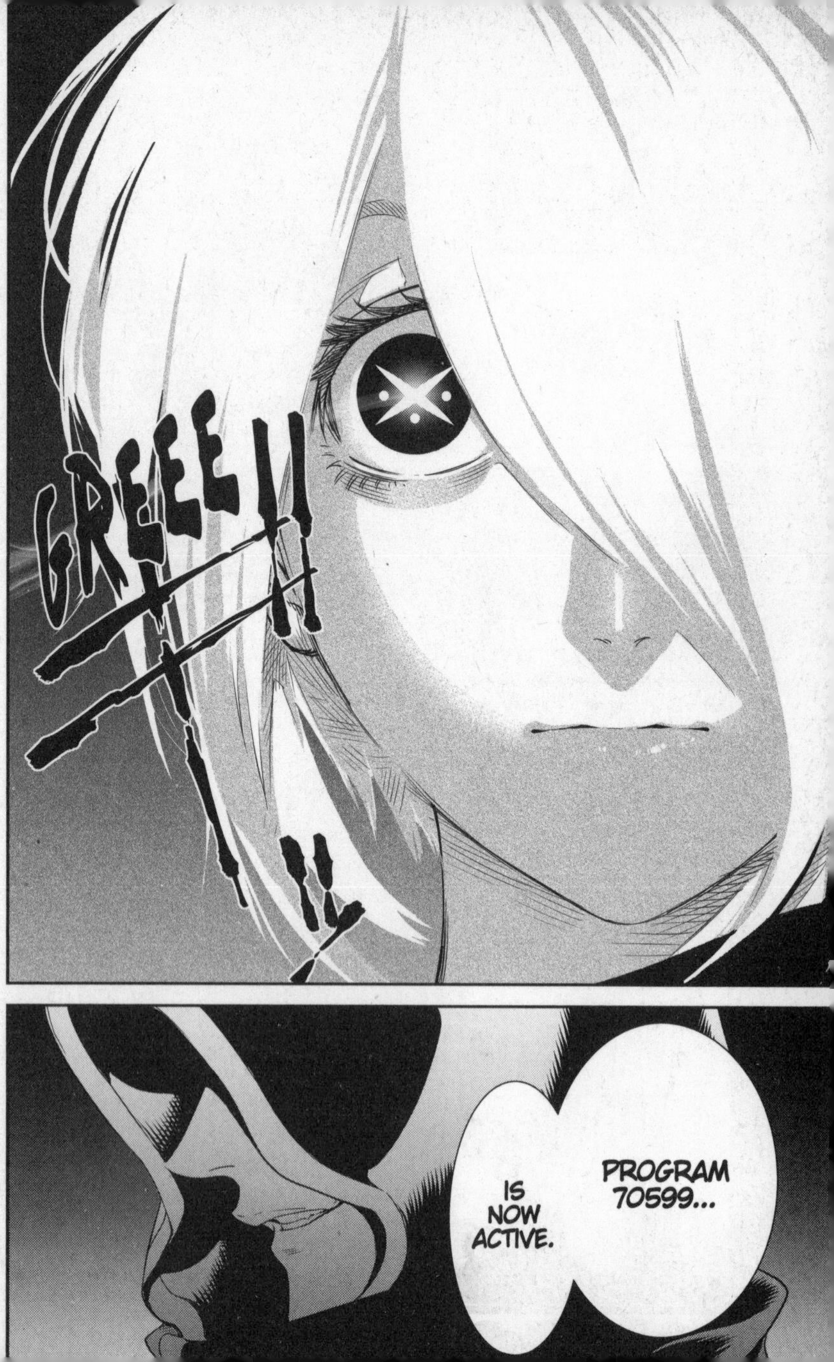
GREEE!!
PROGRAM 70599...
IS NOW ACTIVE.

MOVE LIST

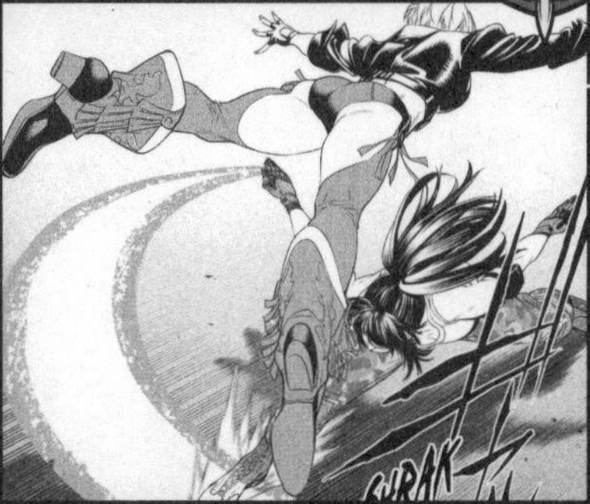

Grand Saber

A lowered charge leading into a horizontal chop.

User: Leona Heidern

Command:

← (hold) → + LK or HK

V-Slasher

A chop from the air followed immediately by a chop back upward from the ground. The overall path takes the shape of a V.

User: Leona Heidern

Command:

↓↘→↘↓↙← + LK or HK

※(in the air)

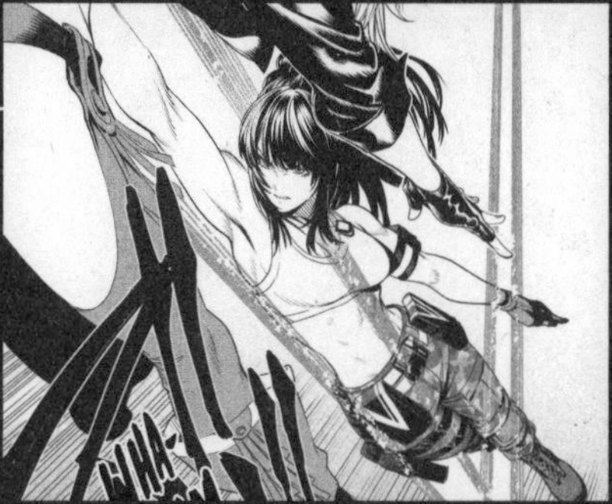

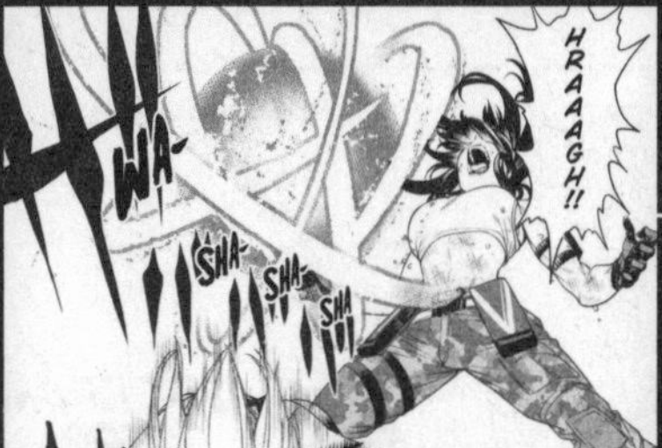
HRAAAAGH!!
WA-
SHA-
SHA-
SHA-

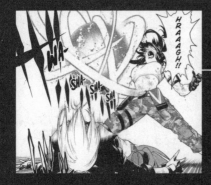

Baltic Launcher

A ball of light swirls in front and rips up those whom it touches mercilessly.

User: Leona Heidern

Command:

← (hold) → + LP or HP

MOVE LIST

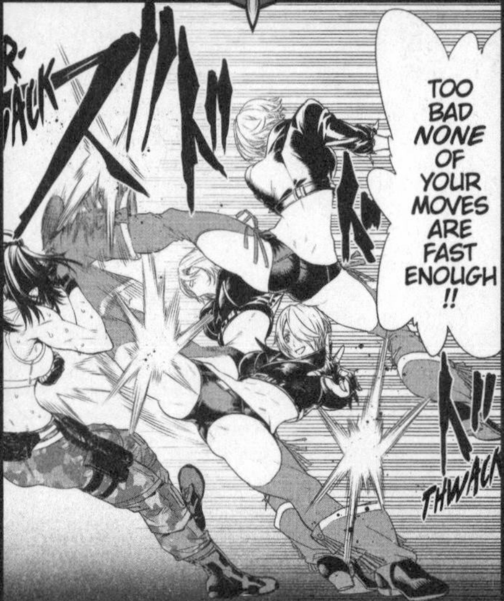
TOO BAD NONE OF YOUR MOVES ARE FAST ENOUGH !!

Unchain

A wild and capricious combo relying on enhanced reflexes and physical performance. It can branch into many variations, following a path impossible to predict.

User: Angel

Command:

[Unchain Start] [Unchain Circle] [Unchain Finish]

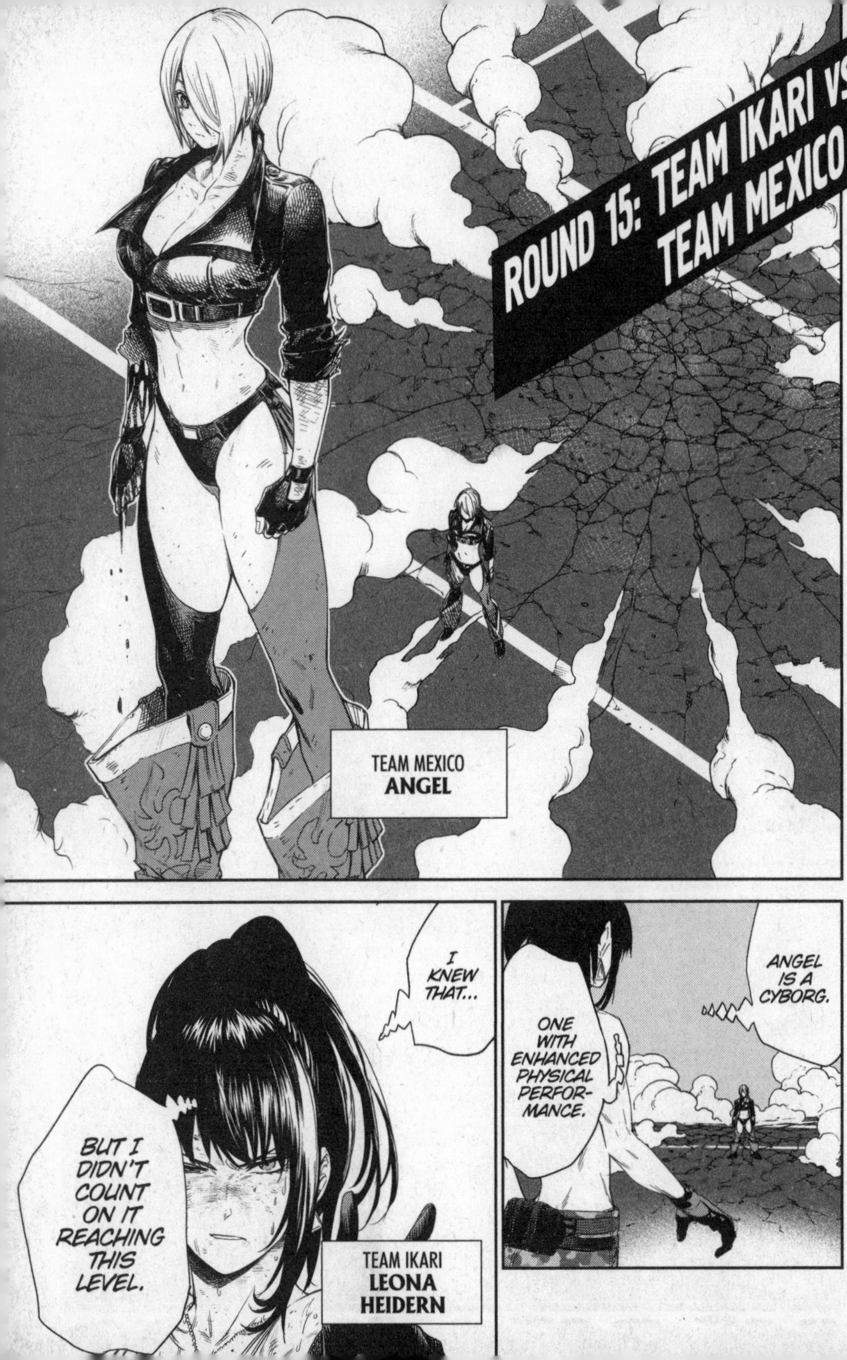
ROUND 15: TEAM IKARI VS. TEAM MEXICO (2
TEAM MEXICO
ANGEL
ANGEL IS A CYBORG.
ONE WITH ENHANCED PHYSICAL PERFOR-MANCE.
I KNEW THAT...
BUT I DIDN'T COUNT ON IT REACHING THIS LEVEL.
TEAM IKARI
LEONA HEIDERN

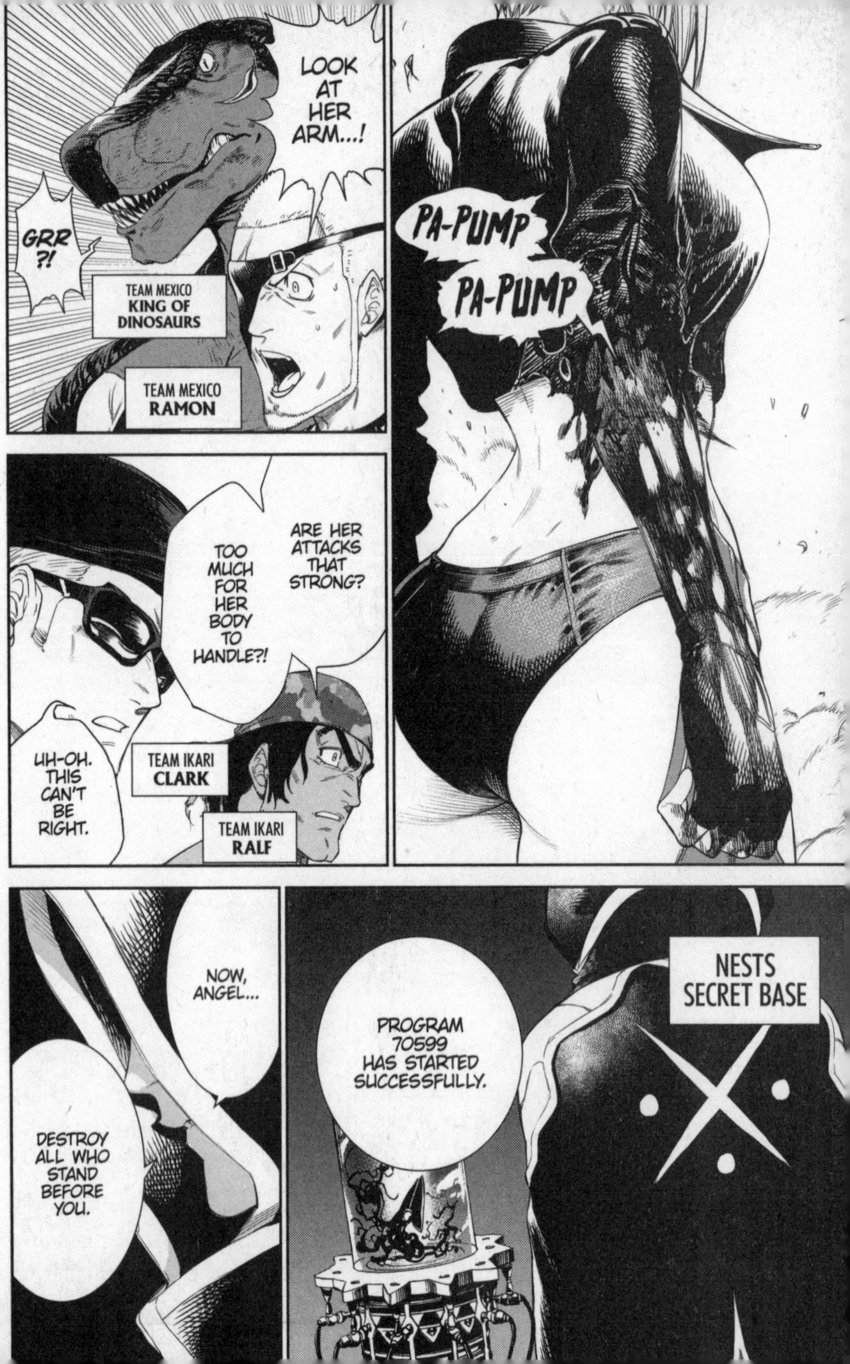
PA-PUMP
PA-PUMP
LOOK AT HER ARM...!
GRR ?!
TEAM MEXICO KING OF DINOSAURS
TEAM MEXICO RAMON
ARE HER ATTACKS THAT STRONG?
TOO MUCH FOR HER BODY TO HANDLE?!
UH-OH. THIS CAN'T BE RIGHT.
TEAM IKARI CLARK
TEAM IKARI RALF
NESTS SECRET BASE
PROGRAM 70599 HAS STARTED SUCCESSFULLY.
NOW, ANGEL...
DESTROY ALL WHO STAND BEFORE YOU.

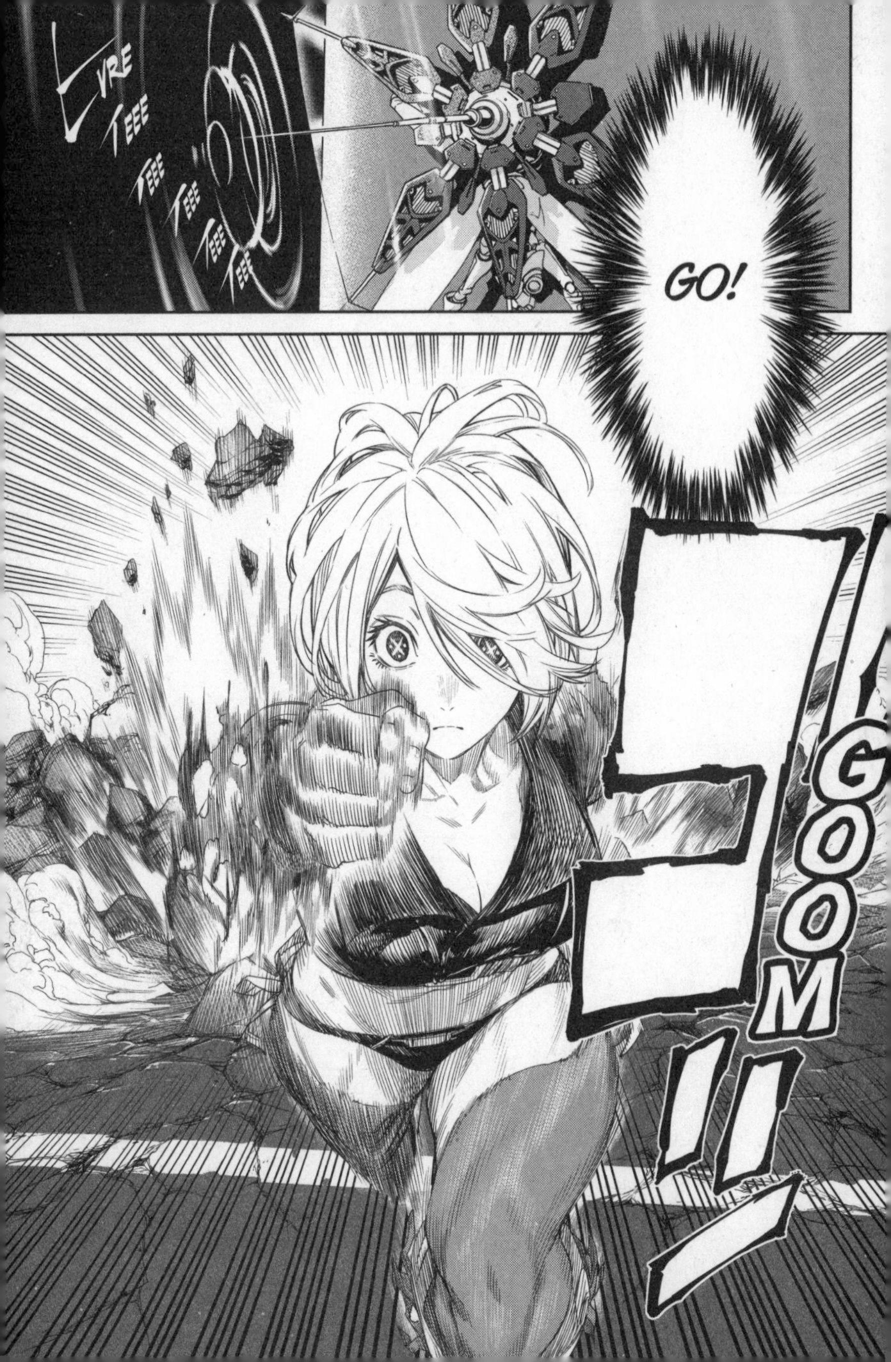

VREE TEEE TEEE TEEE TEEE TEEE
GO!
GOOOM!!

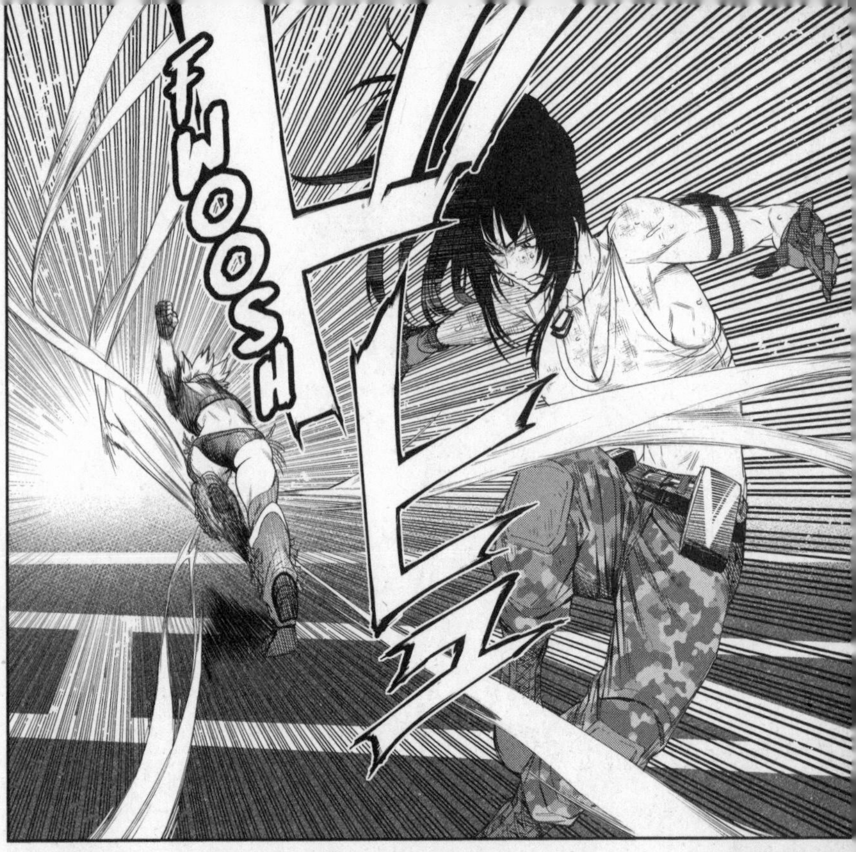
FWOOSH
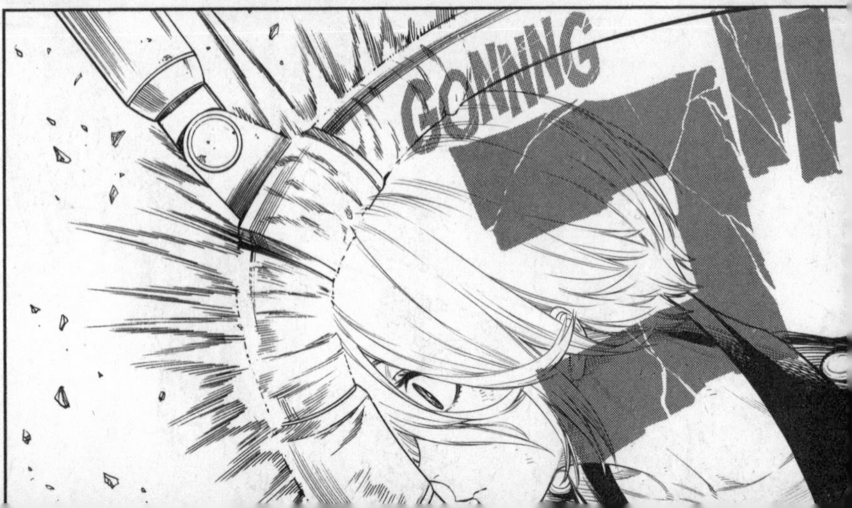
GONNNG

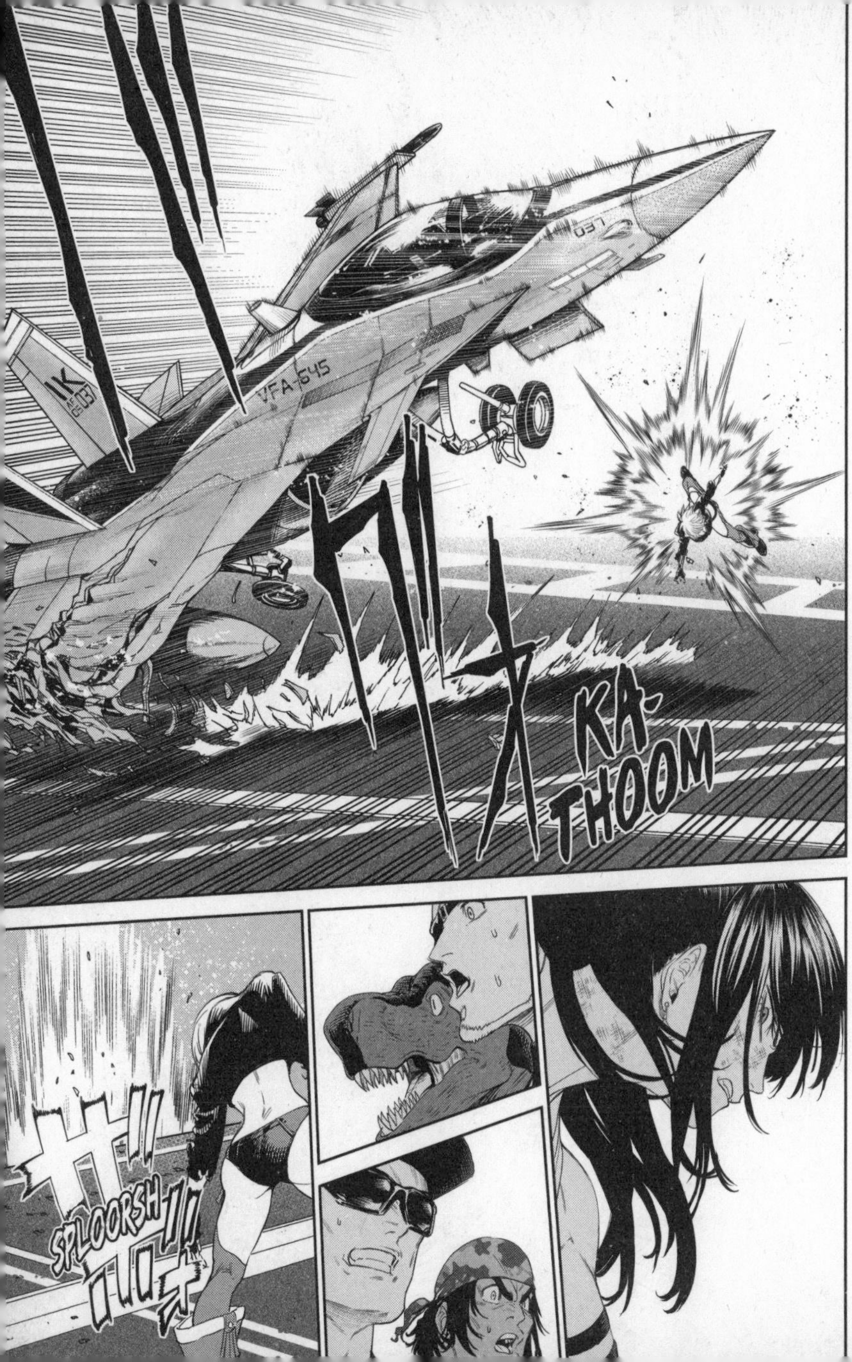
VFA-645
IK
KA-THOOM
SPLOORSH

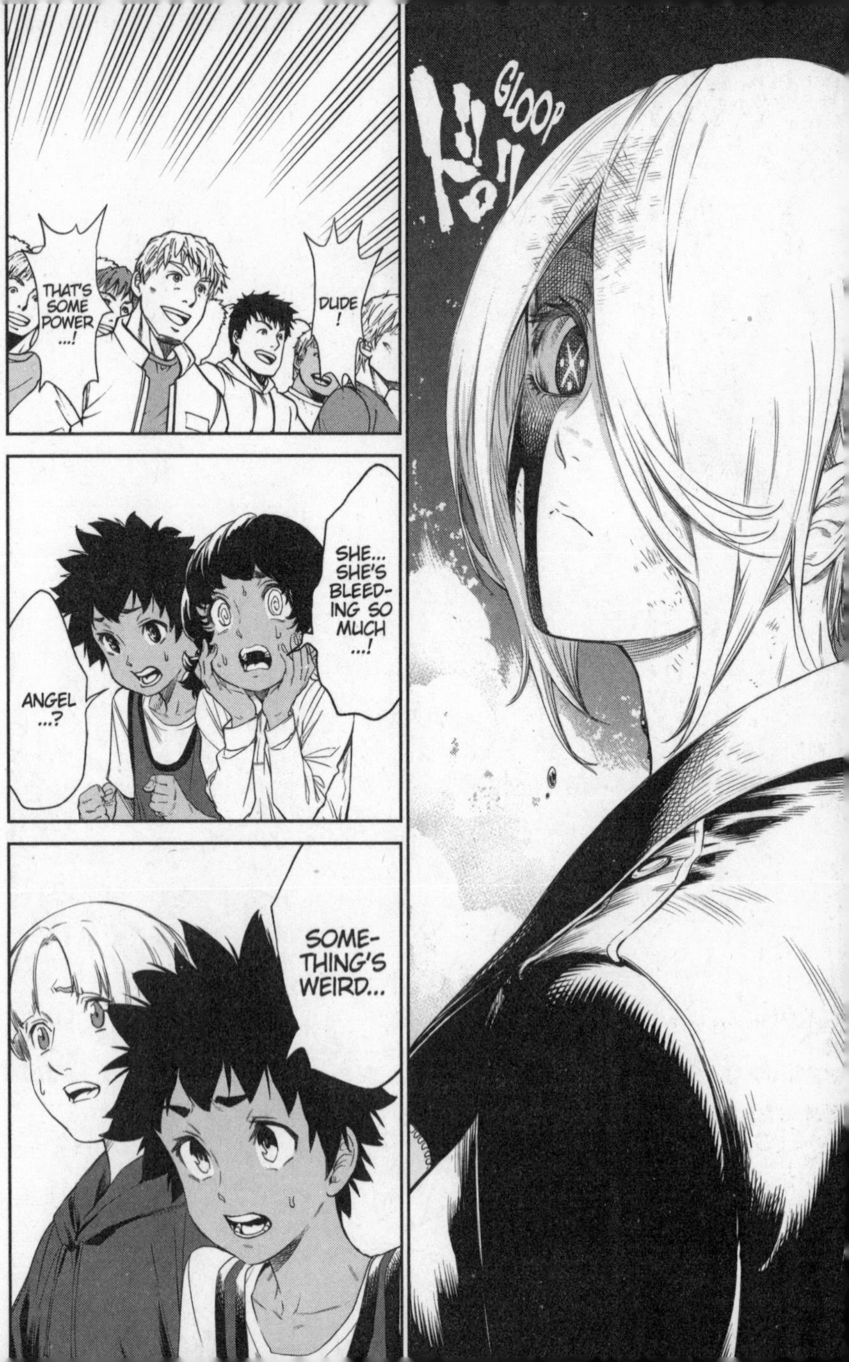
GLOOP
DUDE!
THAT'S SOME POWER ...!
SHE... SHE'S BLEEDING SO MUCH ...!
ANGEL ...?
SOMETHING'S WEIRD...

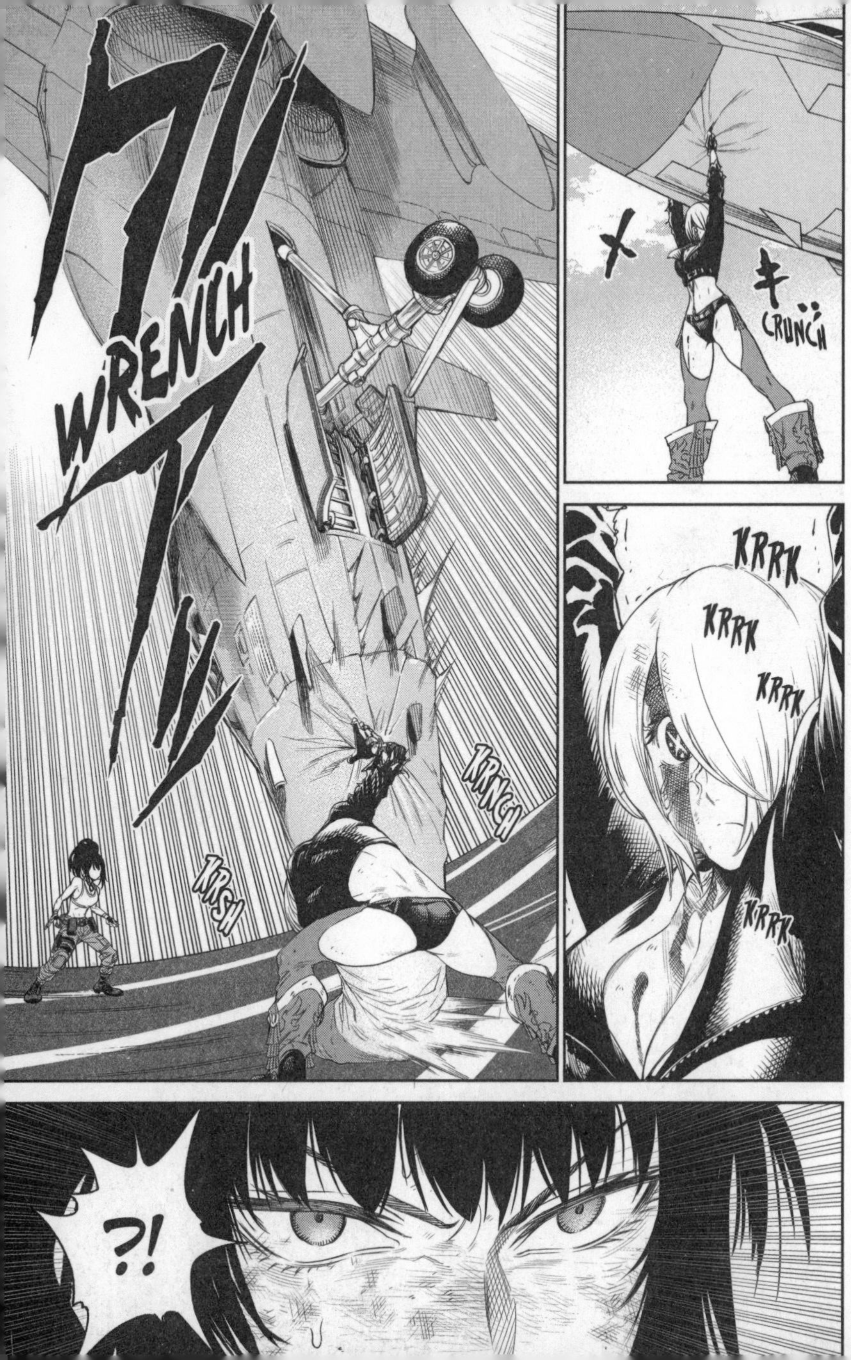
CRUNCH
KRRK
KRRK
KRRK
KRRK
WRENCH
KRNCH
KRSH
?!

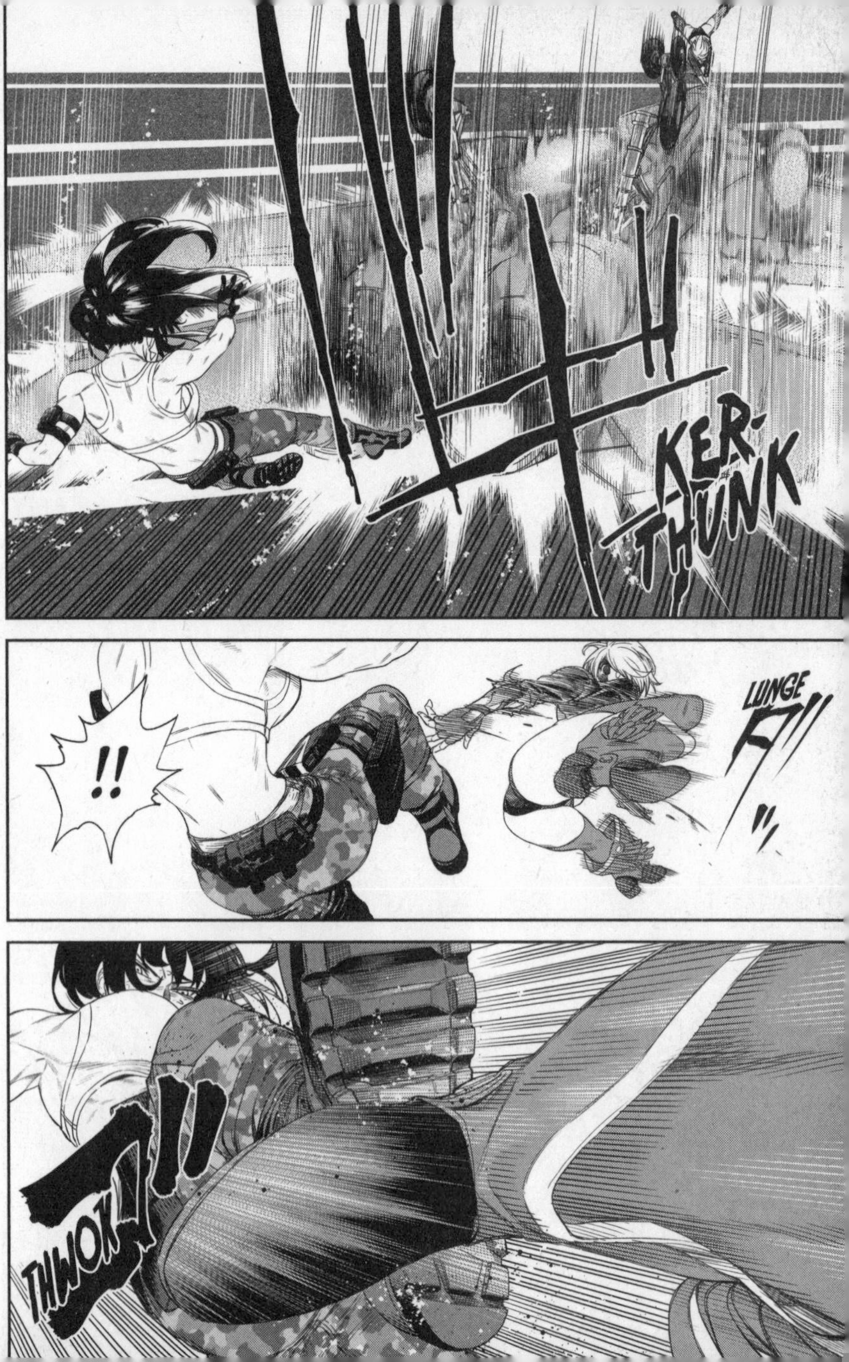
KER-THUNK
LUNGE
!!
THWOK!!

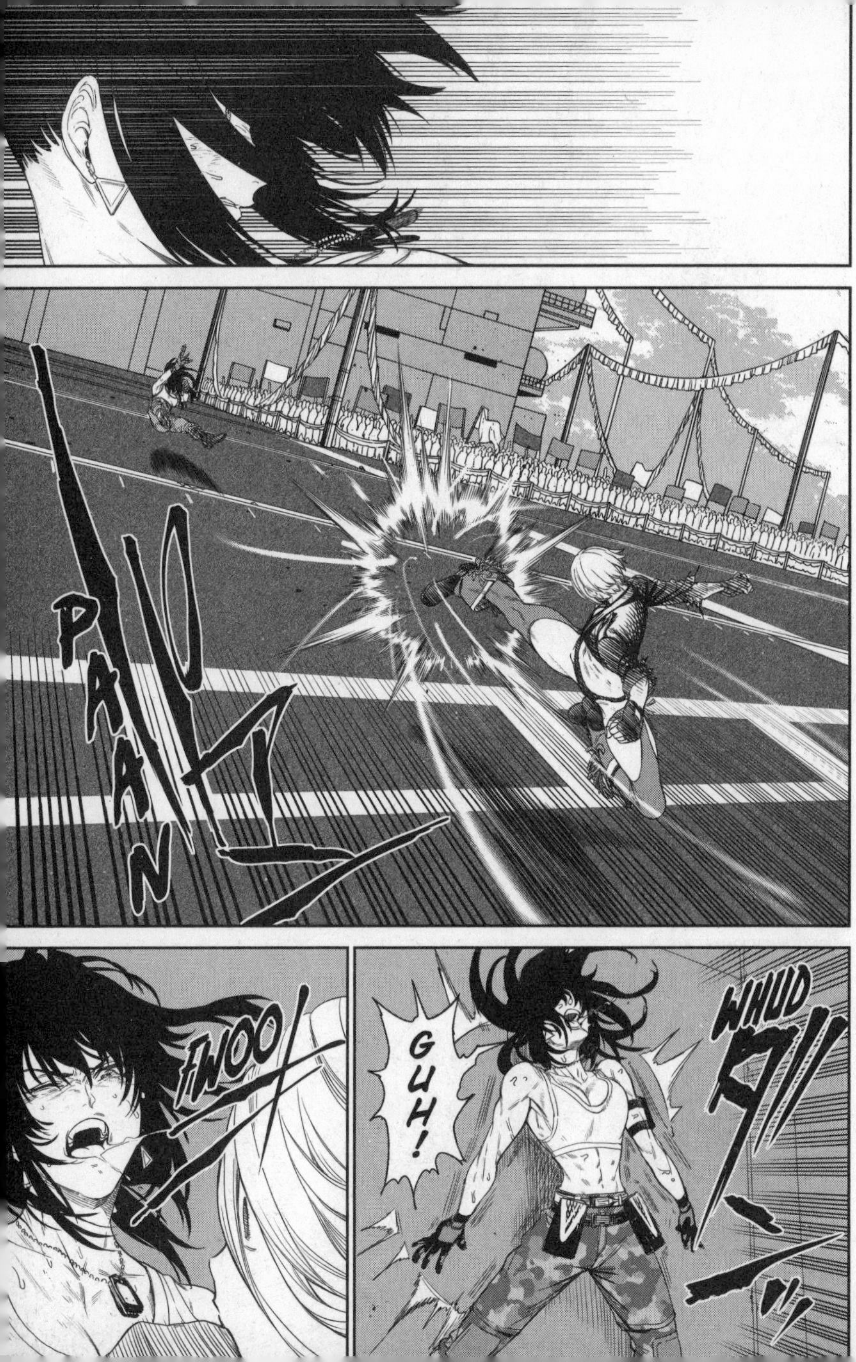
PAAAN
WHUD
GUH!
FWOO

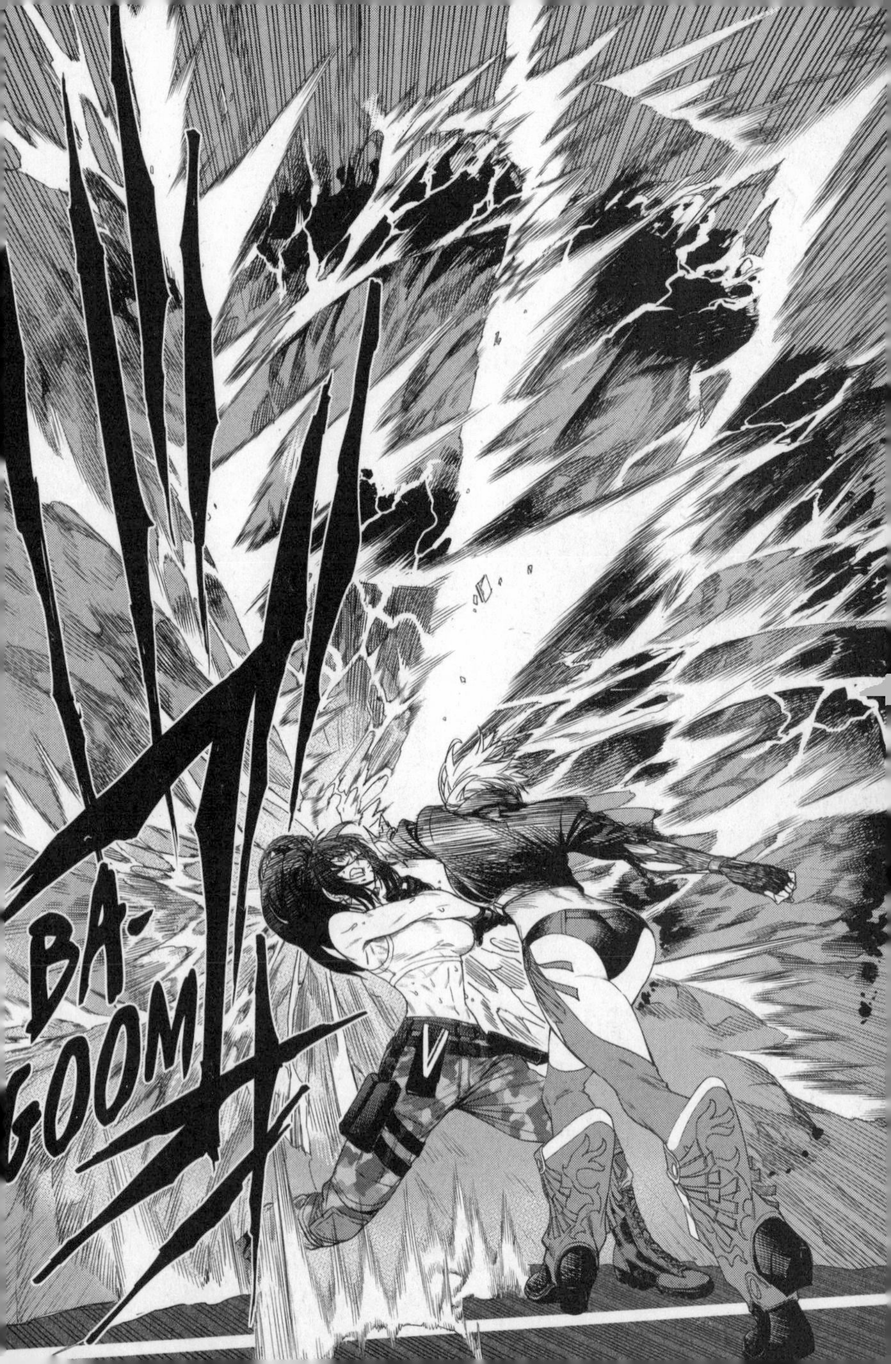
BA-GOOM

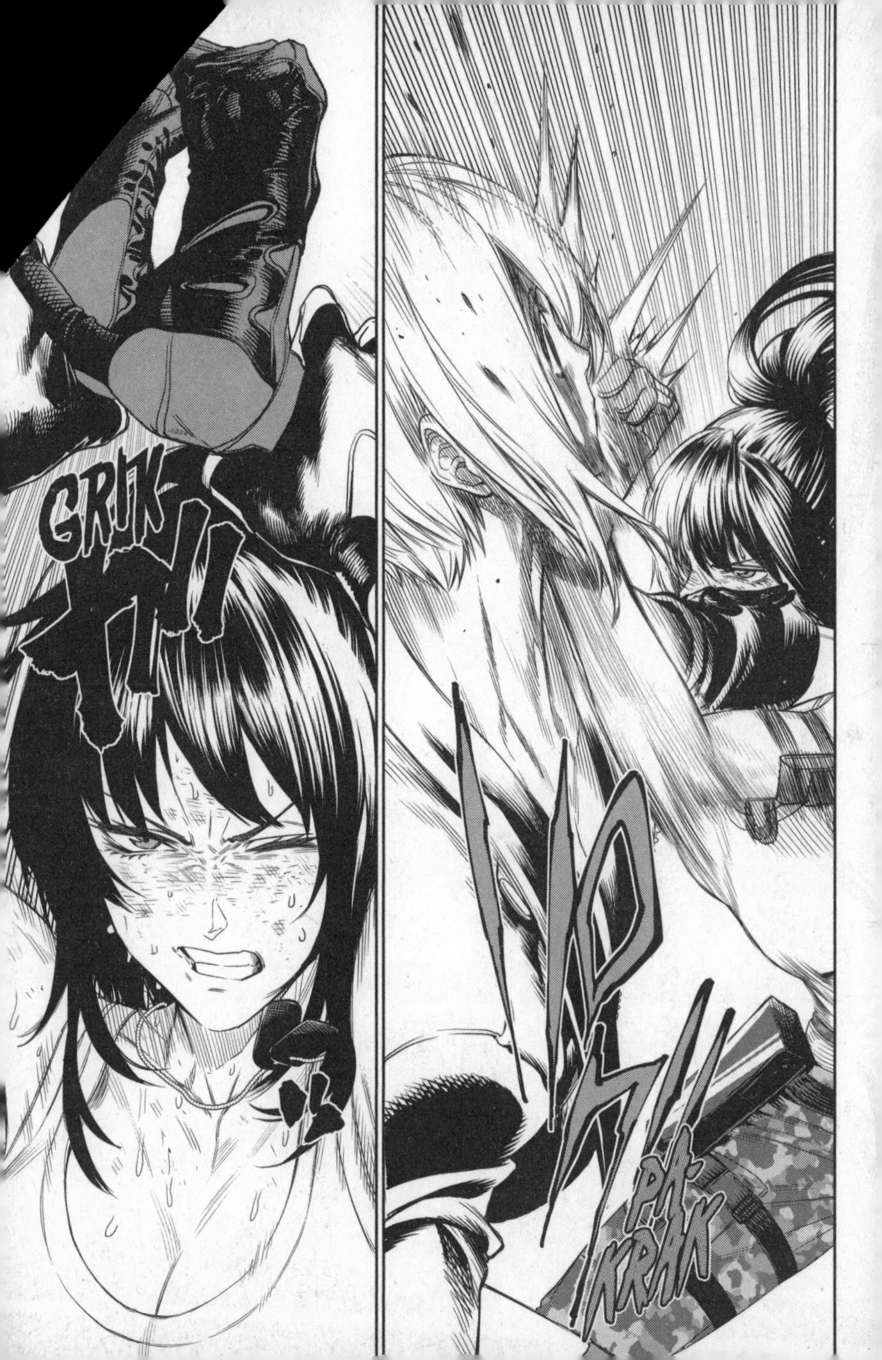
PA-KRAK
GRIK

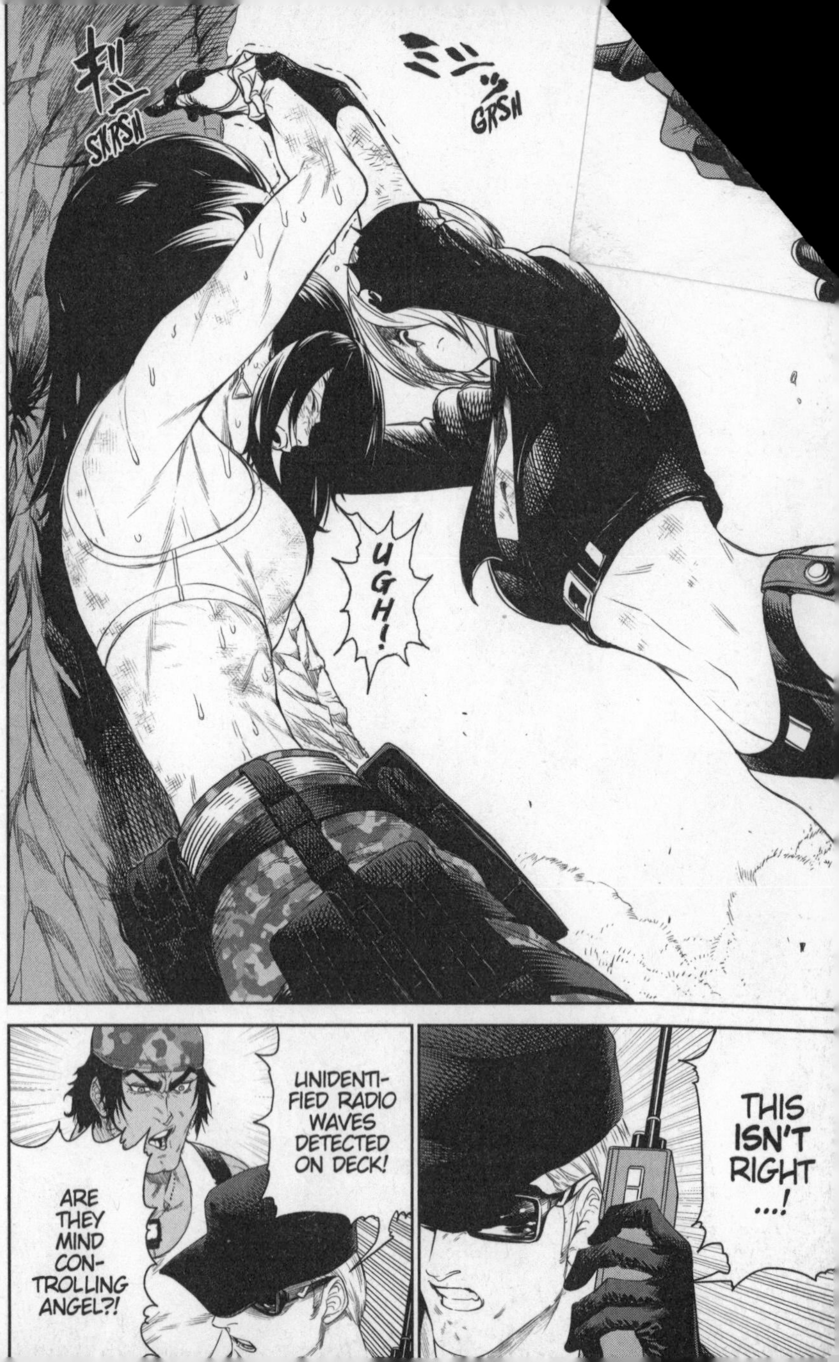
ミシッ
GRSH
ギリッ
SKRSH
UGH!
THIS ISN'T RIGHT ...!
UNIDENTI-FIED RADIO WAVES DETECTED ON DECK!
ARE THEY MIND CON-TROLLING ANGEL?!

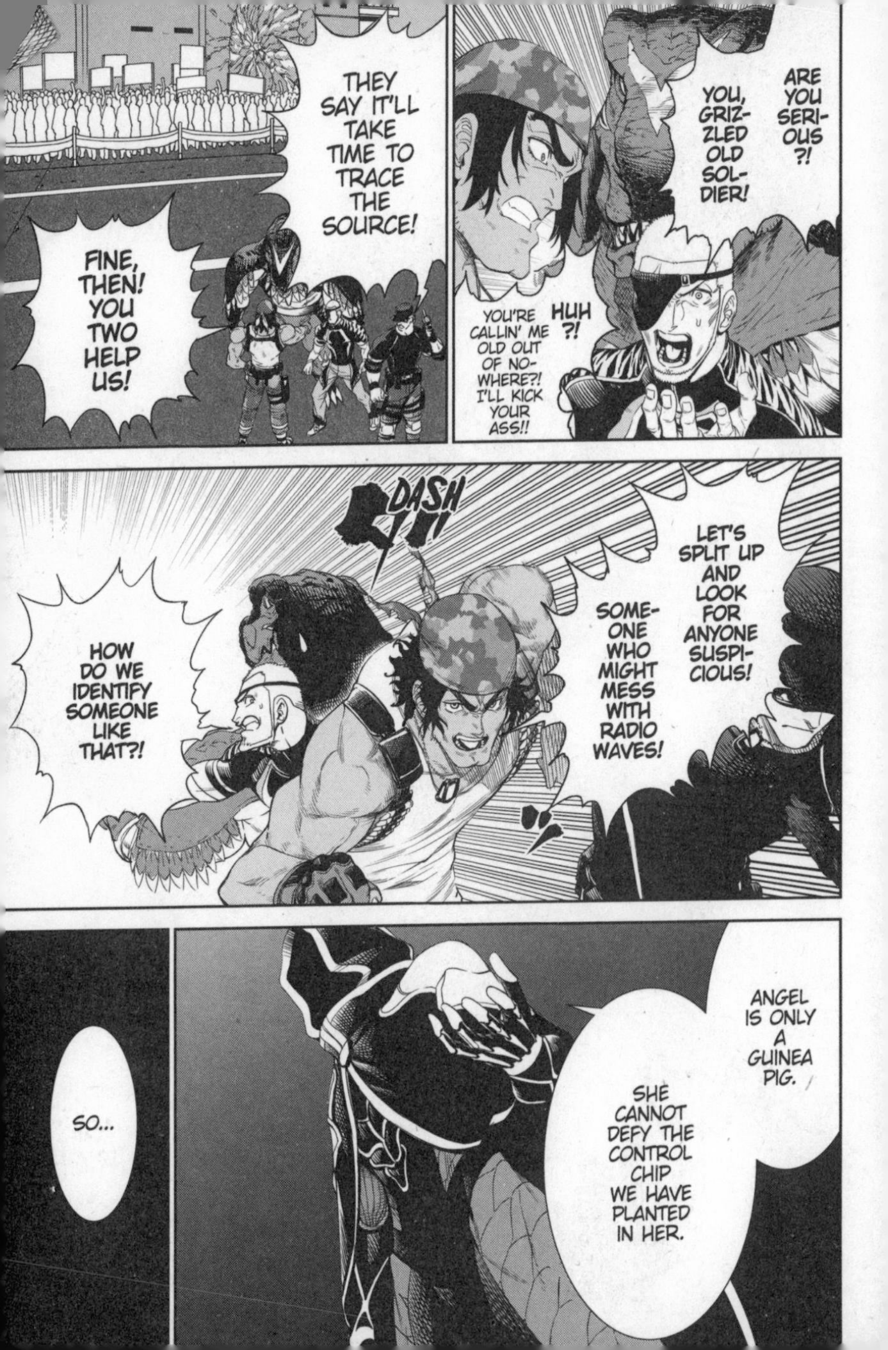
ARE YOU SERIOUS?!
YOU, GRIZZLED OLD SOLDIER!
HUH?!
YOU'RE CALLIN' ME OLD OUT OF NOWHERE?! I'LL KICK YOUR ASS!!
THEY SAY IT'LL TAKE TIME TO TRACE THE SOURCE!
FINE, THEN! YOU TWO HELP US!
DASH
LET'S SPLIT UP AND LOOK FOR ANYONE SUSPICIOUS!
SOMEONE WHO MIGHT MESS WITH RADIO WAVES!
HOW DO WE IDENTIFY SOMEONE LIKE THAT?!
ANGEL IS ONLY A GUINEA PIG.
SHE CANNOT DEFY THE CONTROL CHIP WE HAVE PLANTED IN HER.
SO...

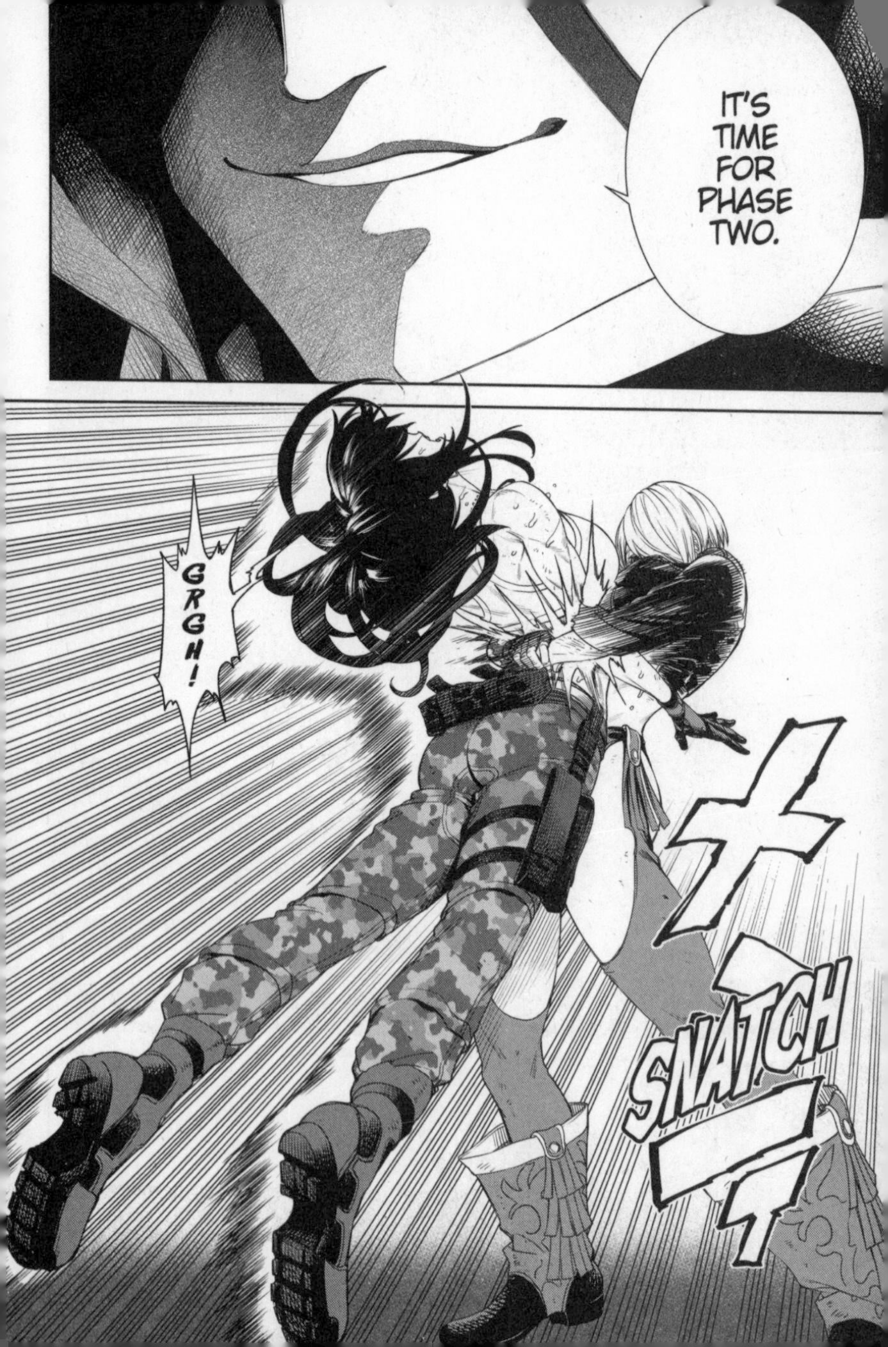
IT'S TIME FOR PHASE TWO.
GRGH!
SNATCH

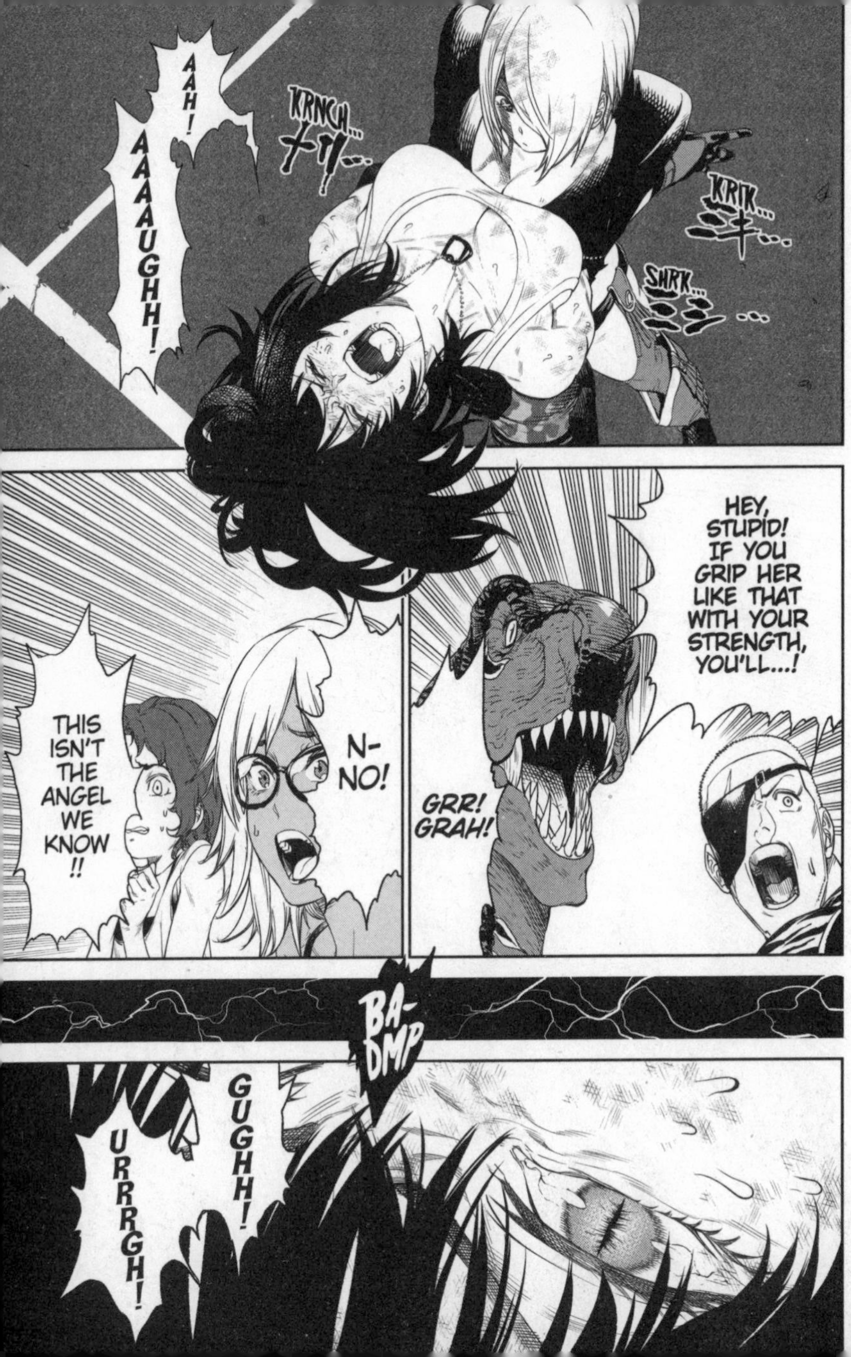
KRIK...
SHRK...
KRNCH...
AAH! AAAAAUGHH!
HEY, STUPID! IF YOU GRIP HER LIKE THAT WITH YOUR STRENGTH, YOU'LL...!
GRR! GRAH!
N-NO!
THIS ISN'T THE ANGEL WE KNOW!!
BA-DMP
GUGHH!
URRRGH!

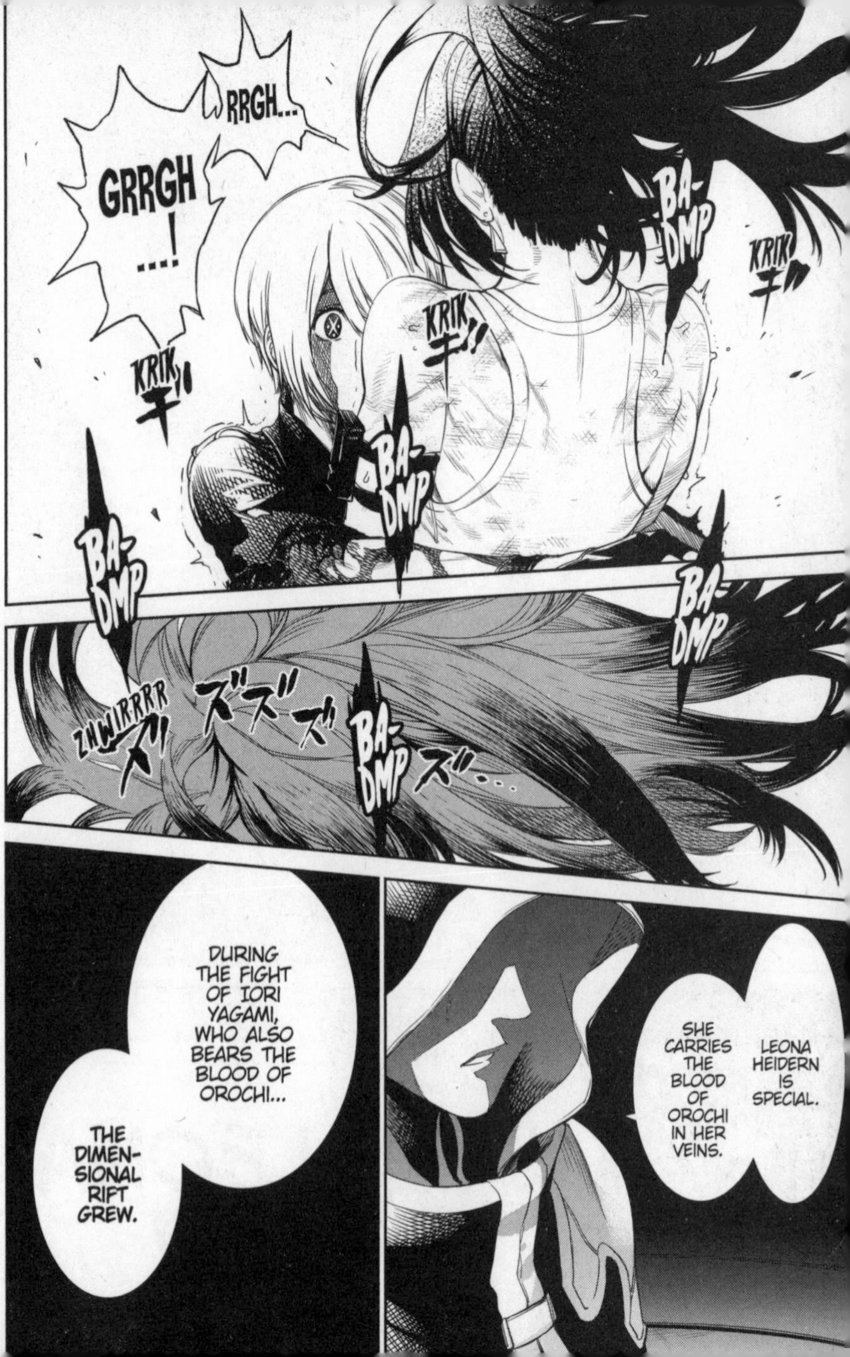

BA-DMP
KRIK
RRGH...
KRIK
GRRGH ...!
KRIK
BA-DMP
BA-DMP
BA-DMP
BA-DMP
ZHWIRRRR
LEONA HEIDERN IS SPECIAL.
SHE CARRIES THE BLOOD OF OROCHI IN HER VEINS.
DURING THE FIGHT OF IORI YAGAMI, WHO ALSO BEARS THE BLOOD OF OROCHI...
THE DIMENSIONAL RIFT GREW.

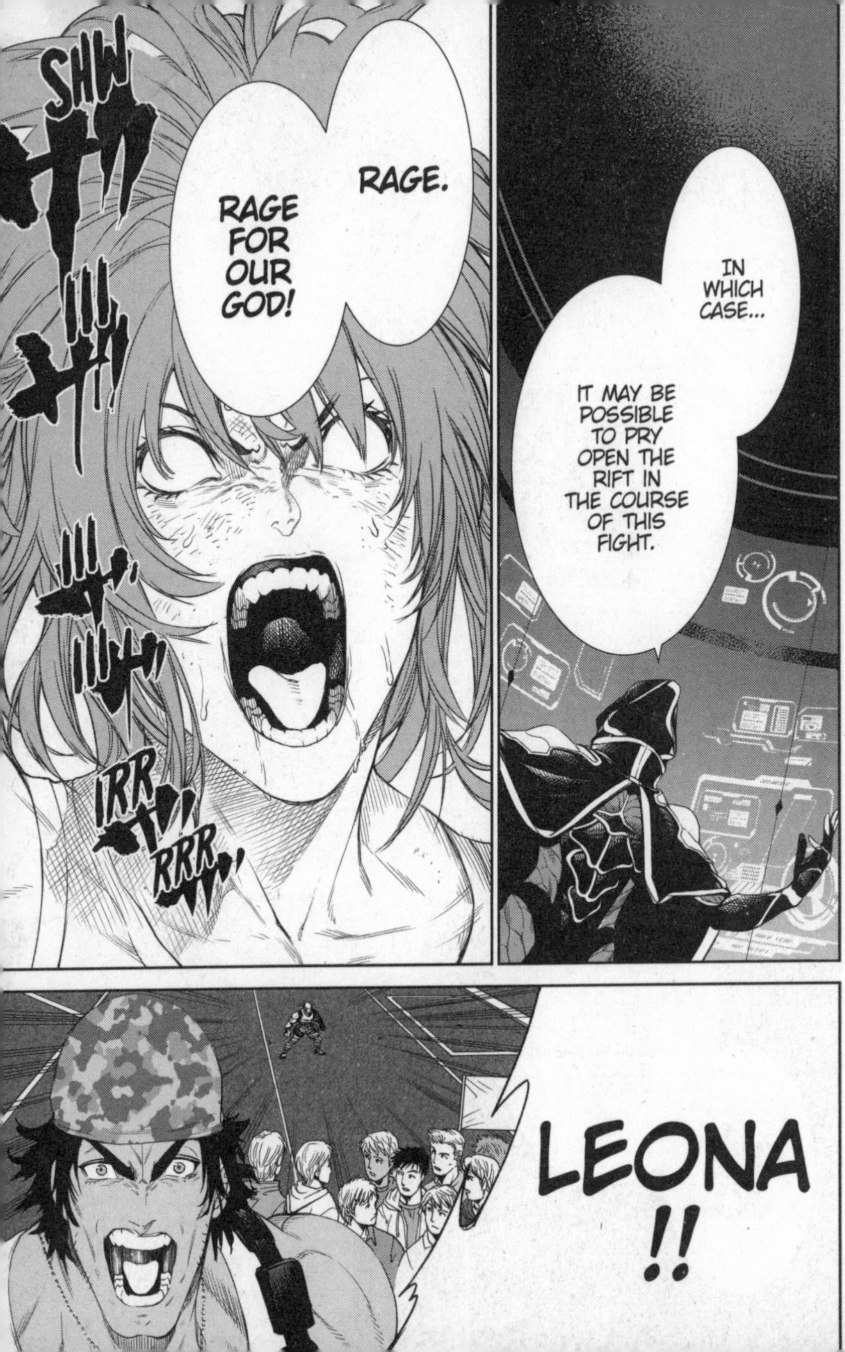
IN WHICH CASE...
IT MAY BE POSSIBLE TO PRY OPEN THE RIFT IN THE COURSE OF THIS FIGHT.
RAGE.
RAGE FOR OUR GOD!
SHW
IRR
RRR
LEONA!!

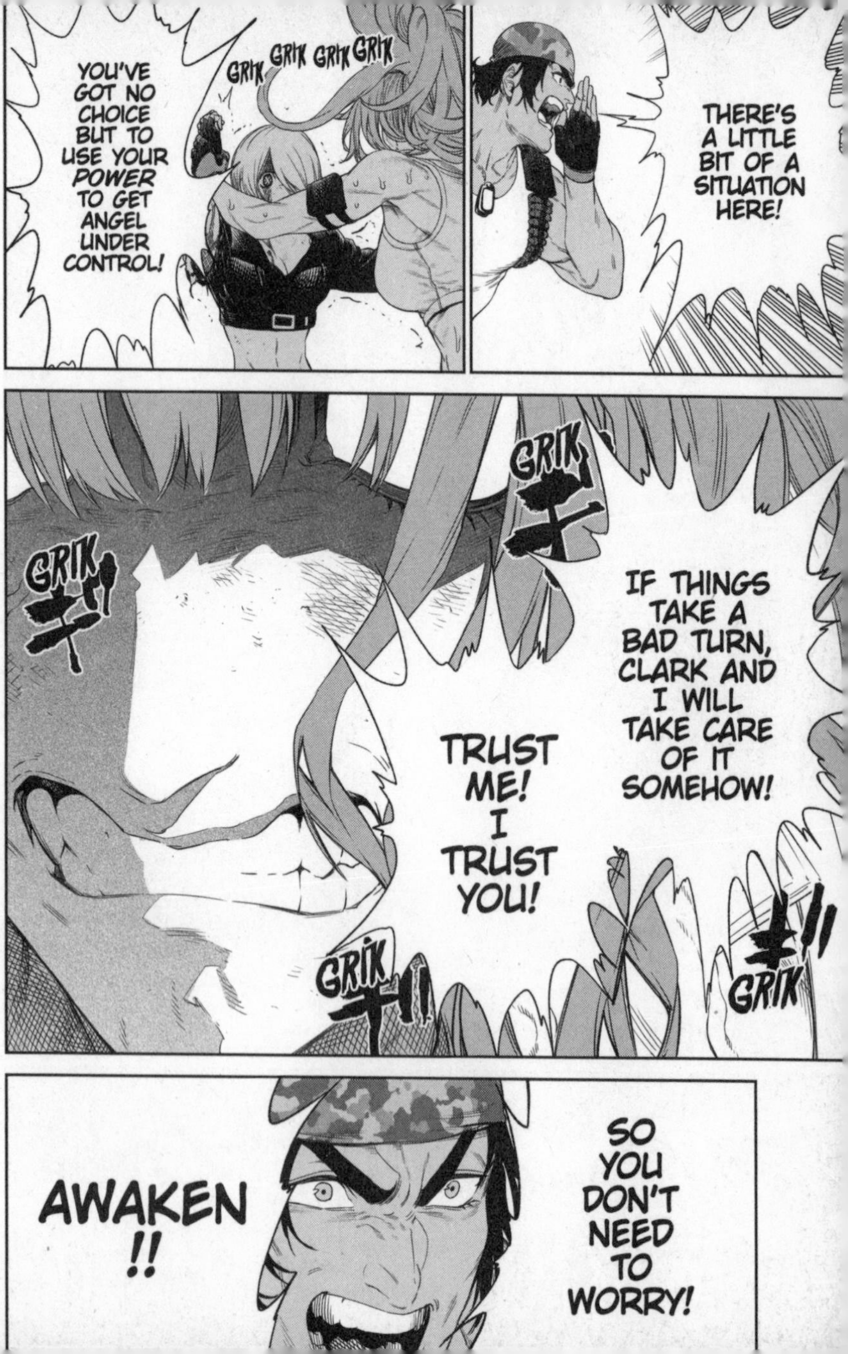
THERE'S A LITTLE BIT OF A SITUATION HERE!
GRIK GRIK GRIK GRIK
YOU'VE GOT NO CHOICE BUT TO USE YOUR POWER TO GET ANGEL UNDER CONTROL!
GRIK
IF THINGS TAKE A BAD TURN, CLARK AND I WILL TAKE CARE OF IT SOMEHOW!
TRUST ME! I TRUST YOU!
GRIK
GRIK
GRIK
SO YOU DON'T NEED TO WORRY!
AWAKEN !!

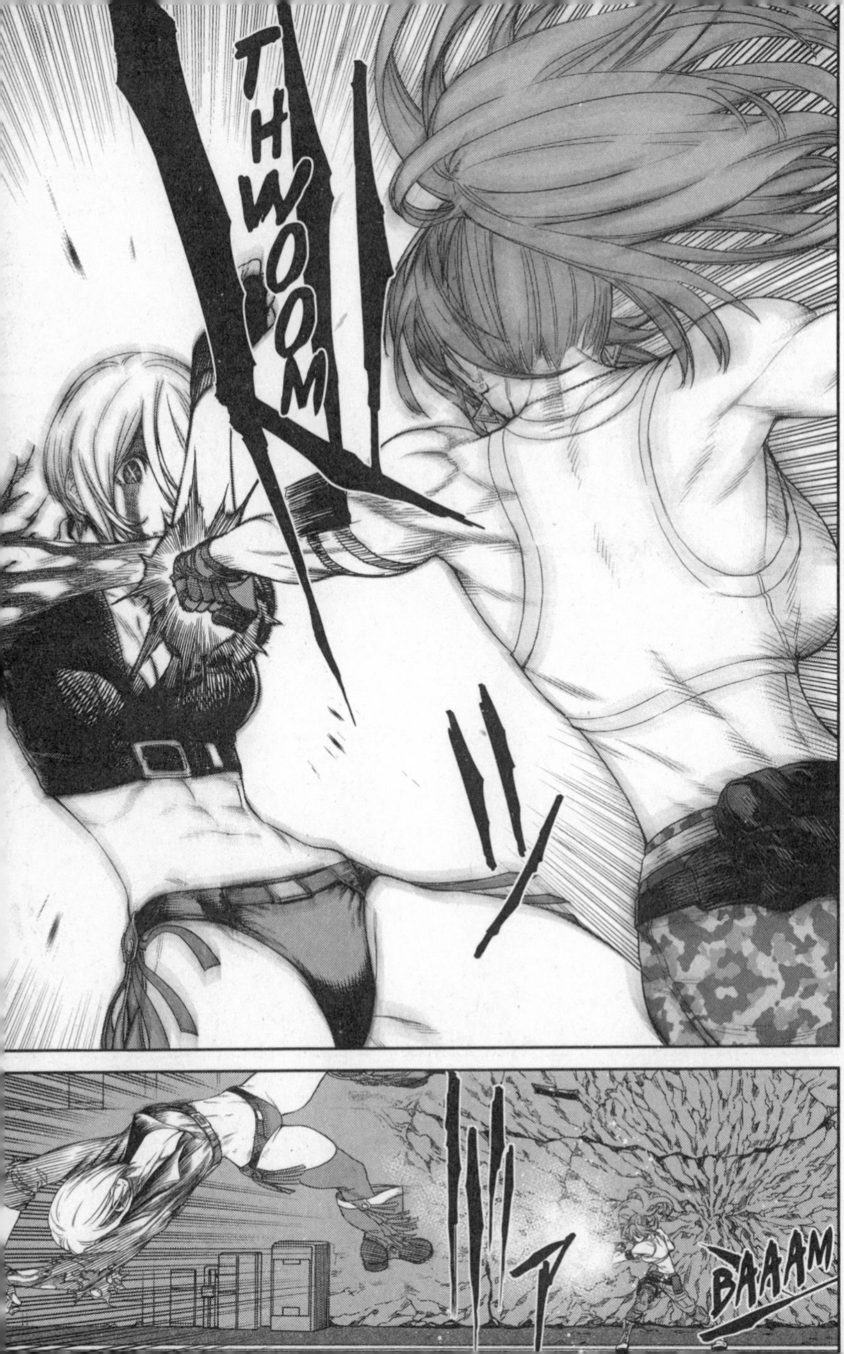
THWOOM
BAAAM

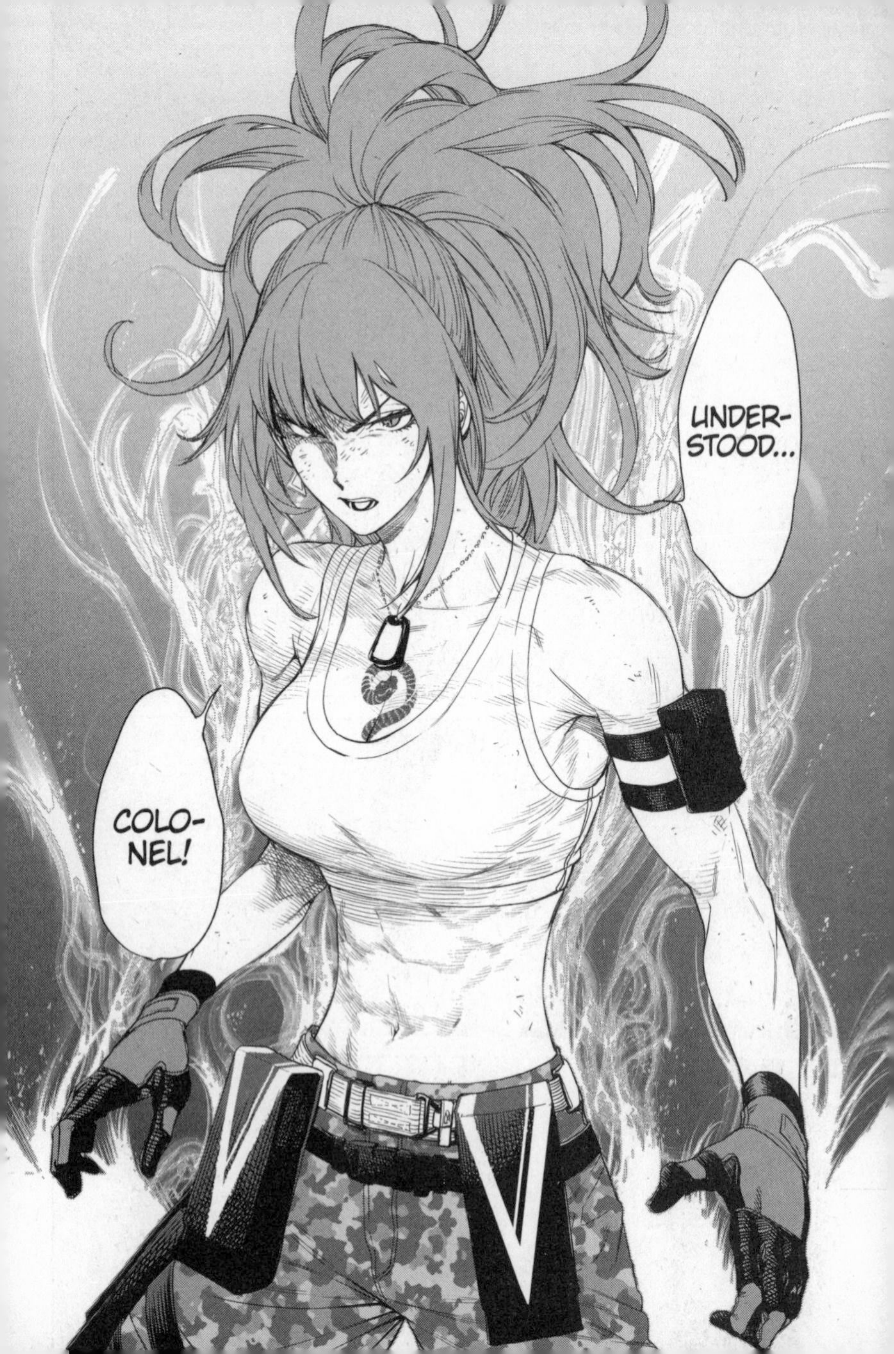
UNDER-STOOD...
COLO-NEL!

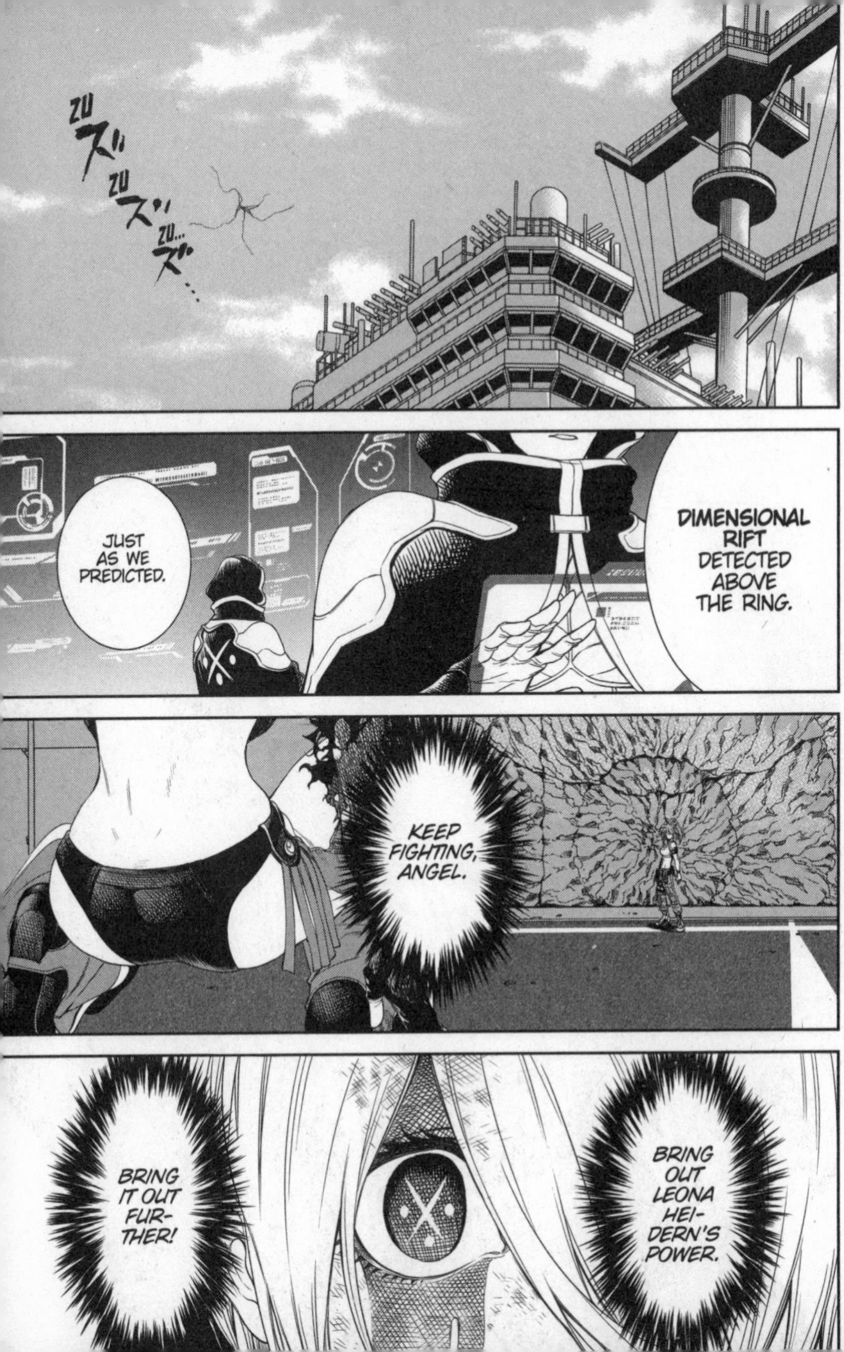
ZU
ZU
ZU...
DIMENSIONAL RIFT DETECTED ABOVE THE RING.
JUST AS WE PREDICTED.
KEEP FIGHTING, ANGEL.
BRING OUT LEONA HEI-DERN'S POWER.
BRING IT OUT FUR-THER!

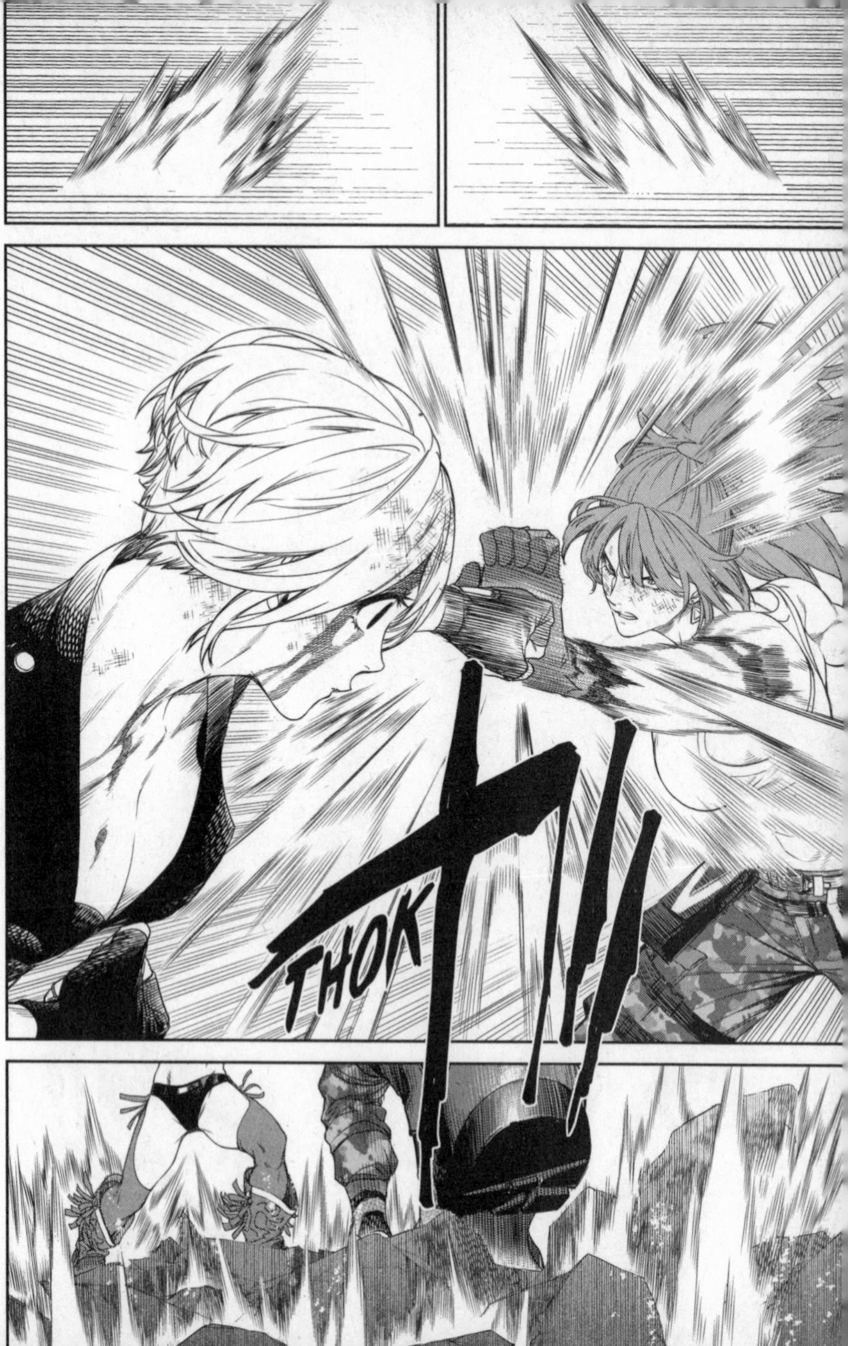
THOK

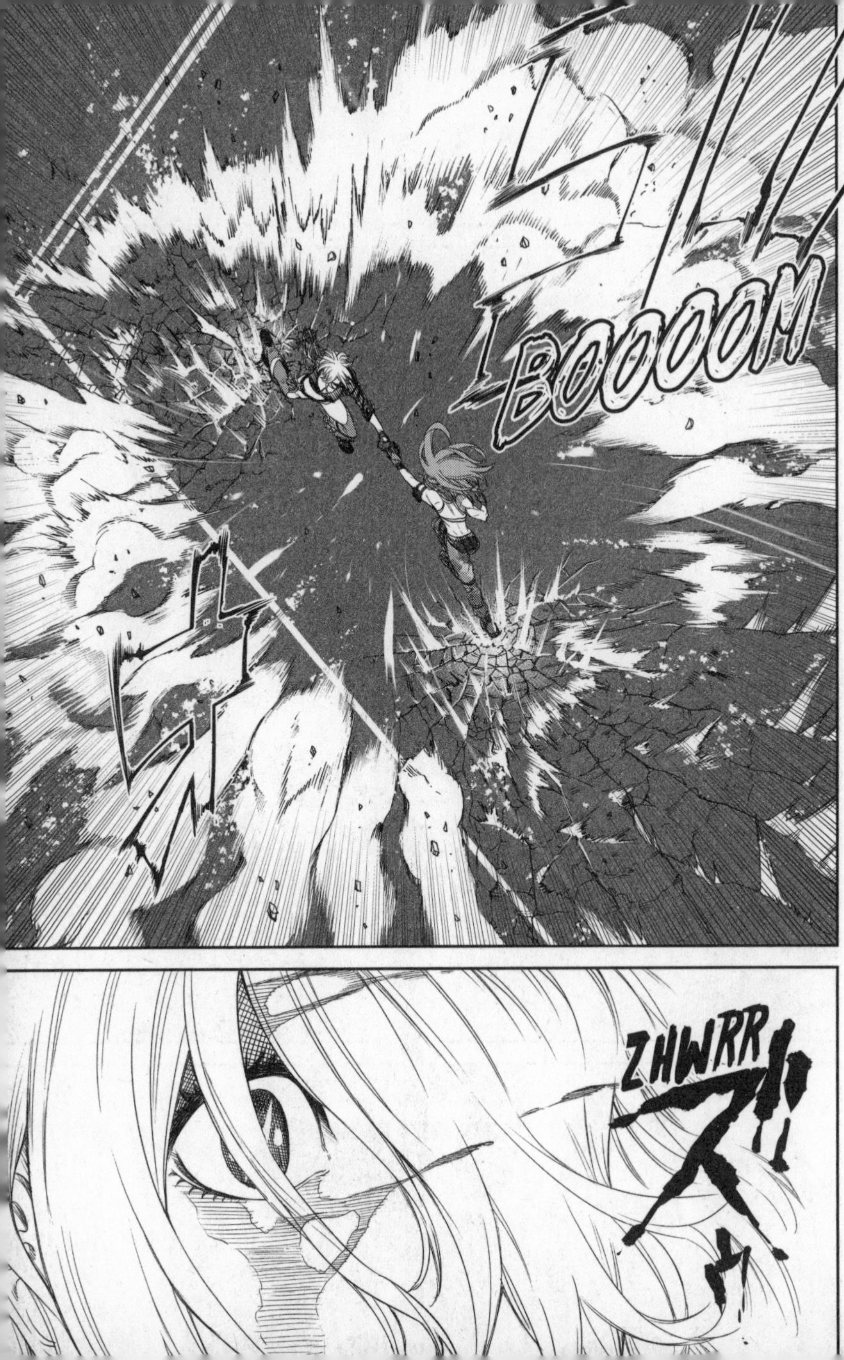
BOOOOM
ZHWRR

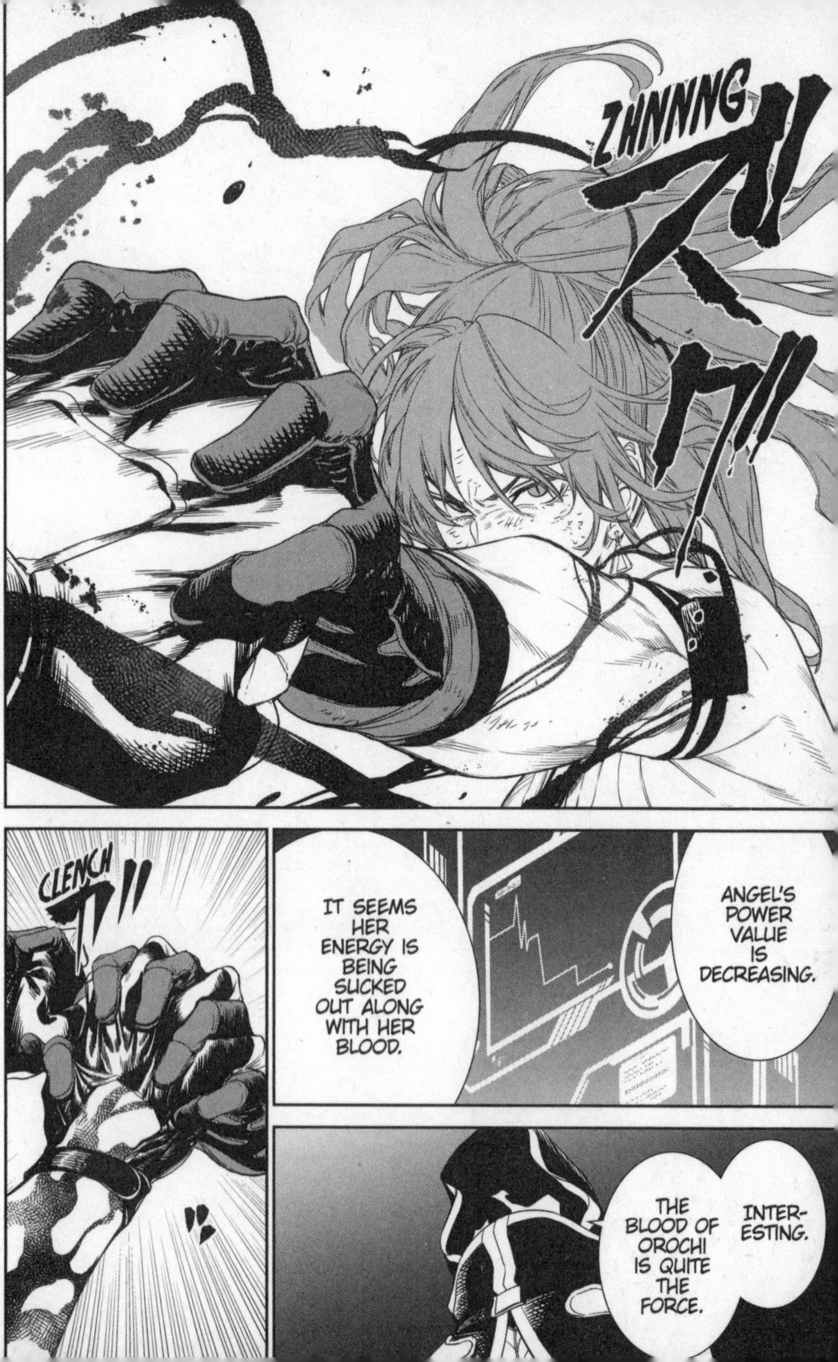
ZHINNNG
ANGEL'S POWER VALUE IS DECREASING.
IT SEEMS HER ENERGY IS BEING SUCKED OUT ALONG WITH HER BLOOD.
INTER-ESTING.
THE BLOOD OF OROCHI IS QUITE THE FORCE.
CLENCH

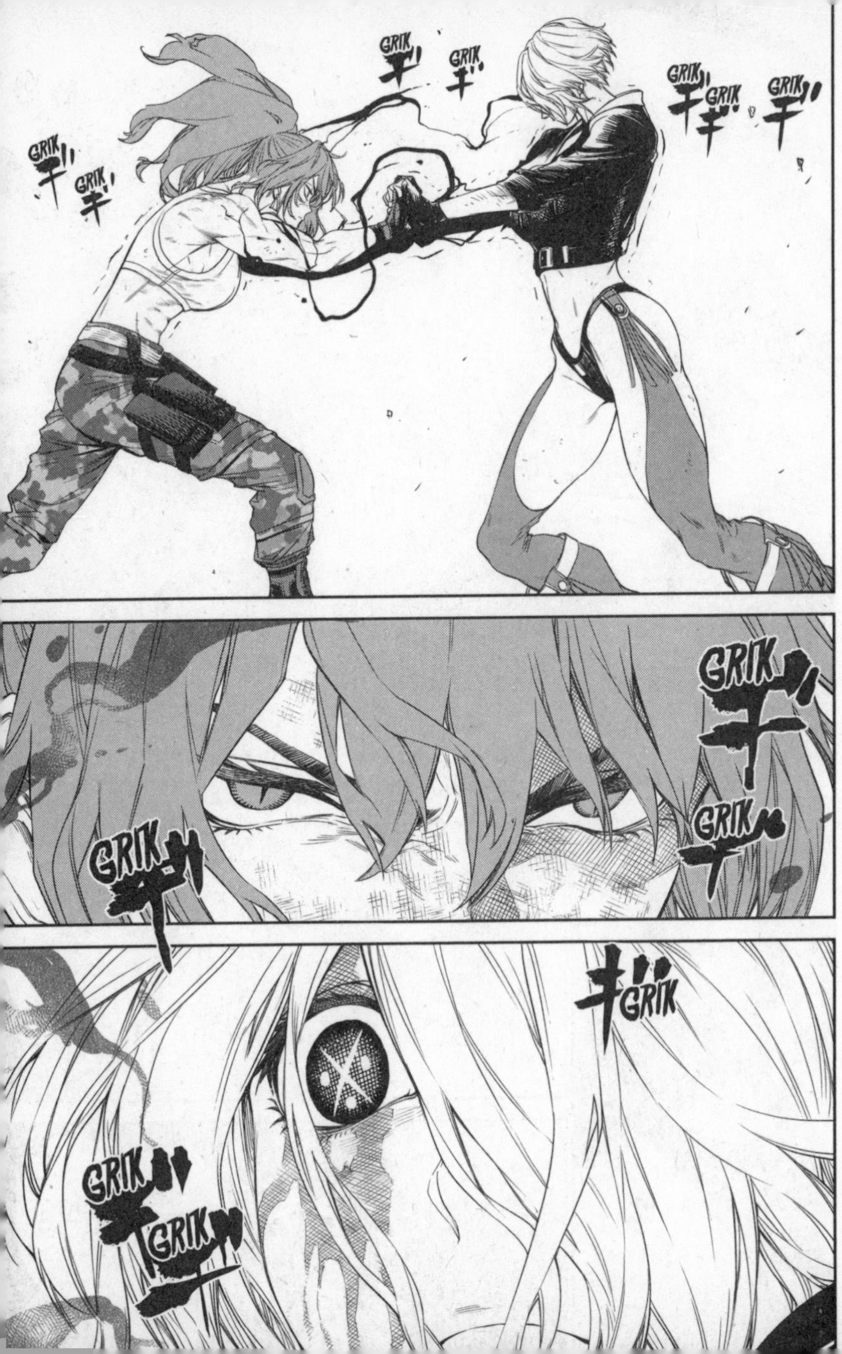

GRIK
GRIK
GRIK
GRIK
GRIK
GRIK
GRIK
GRIK
GRIK
GRIK
GRIK
GRIK
GRIK

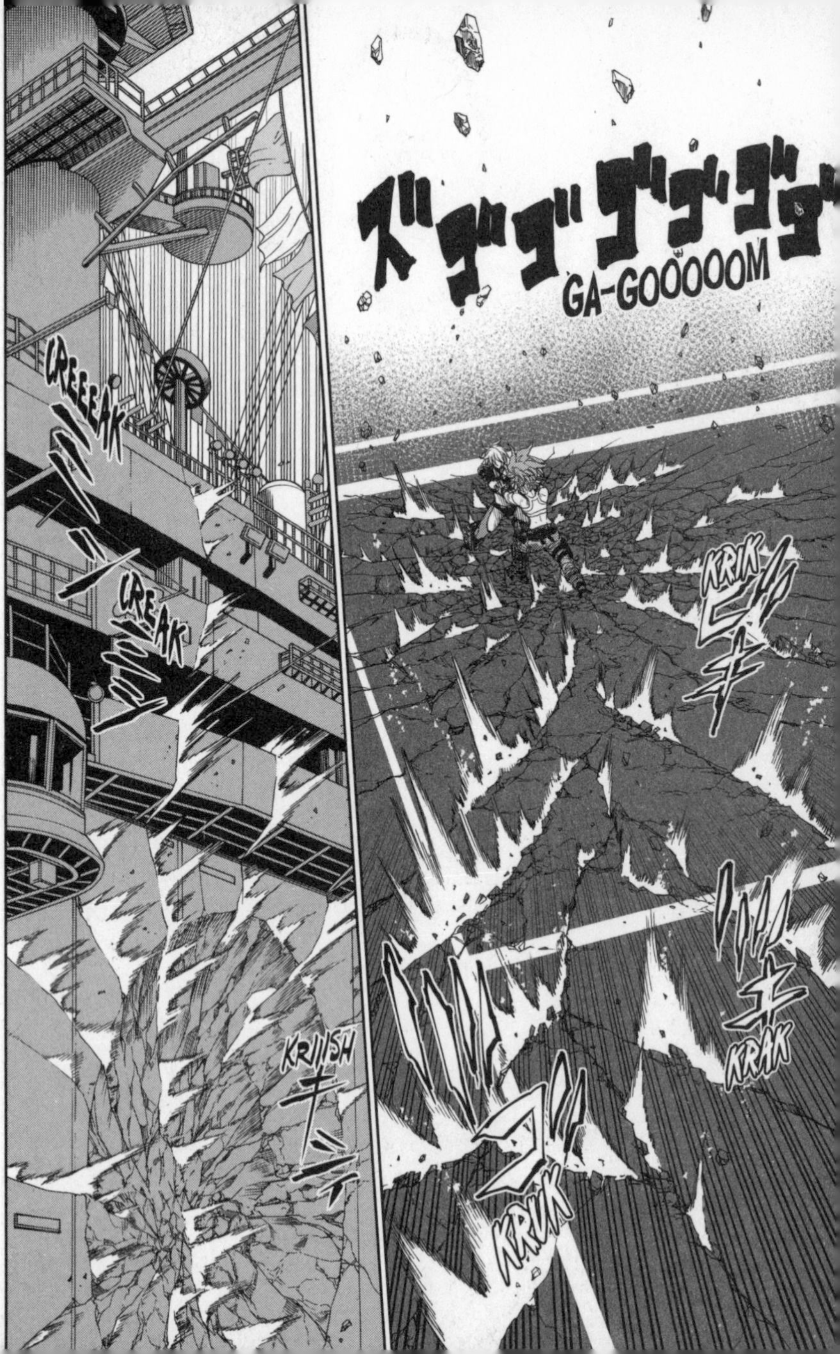
GA-GOOOOOM
KRIK
KRAK
KRUK
CREEEAK
CREAK
KRIISH

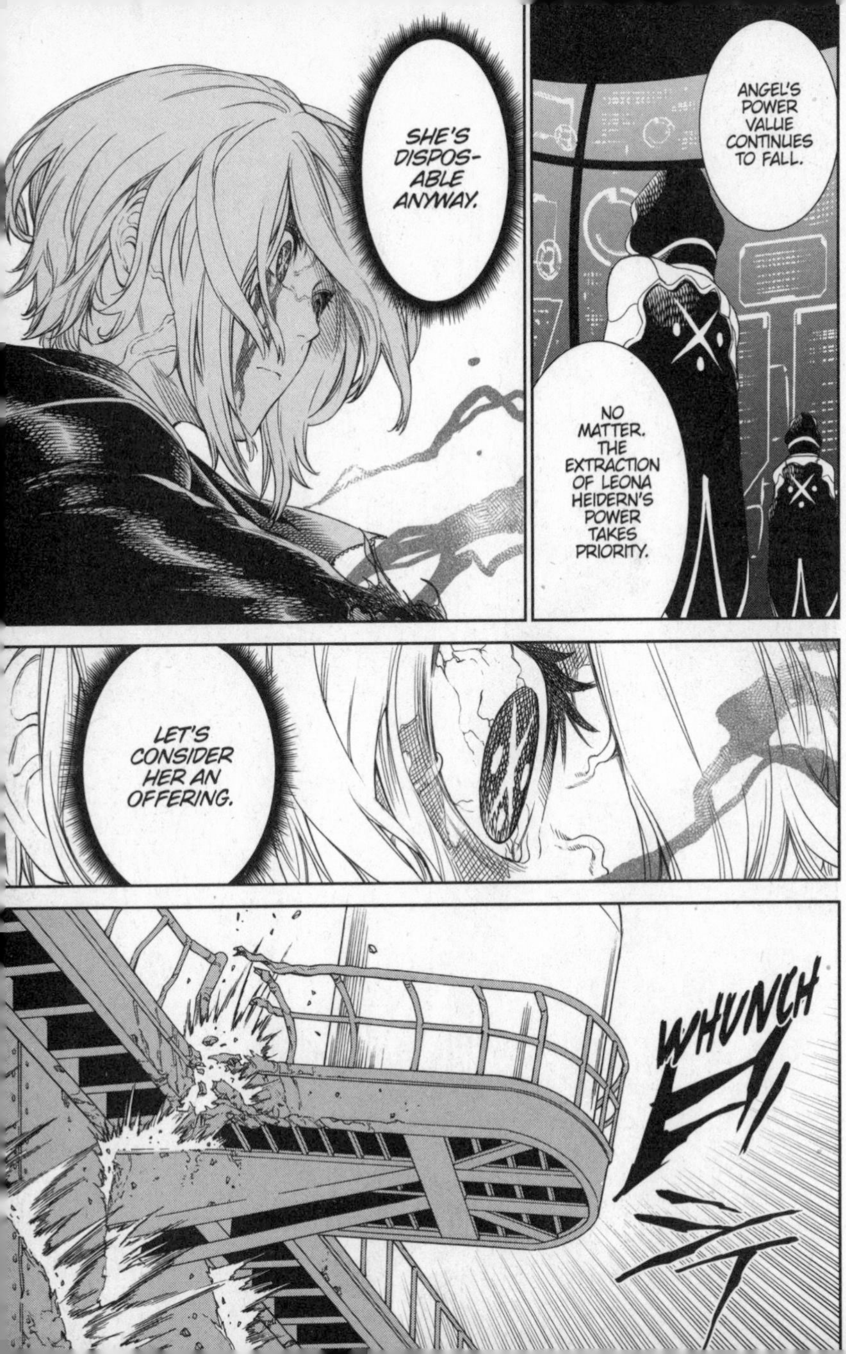
ANGEL'S POWER VALUE CONTINUES TO FALL.
NO MATTER. THE EXTRACTION OF LEONA HEIDERN'S POWER TAKES PRIORITY.
SHE'S DISPOSABLE ANYWAY.
LET'S CONSIDER HER AN OFFERING.
WHUNCH

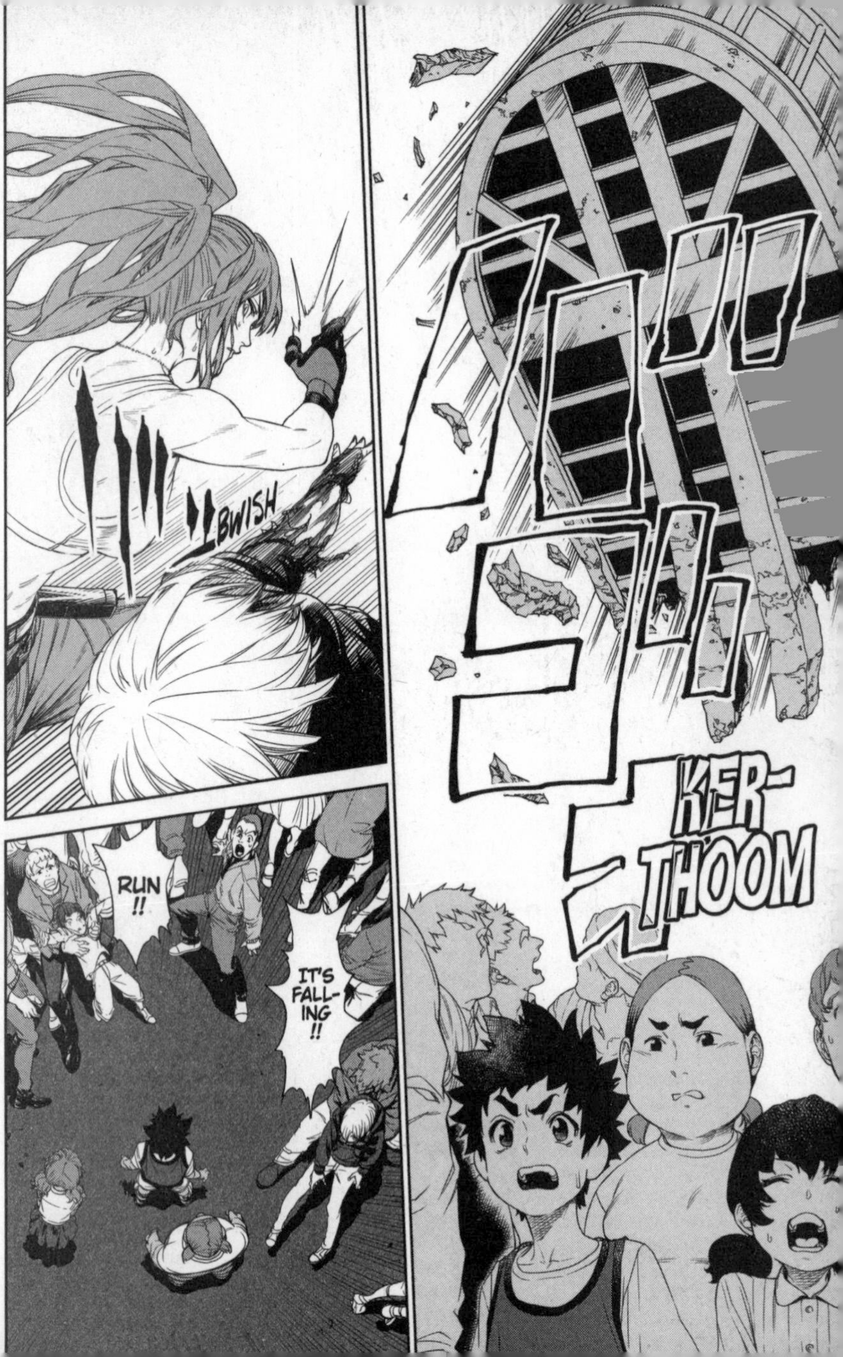
KER-
THOOM
BWISH
RUN
!!
IT'S
FALL-
ING
!!

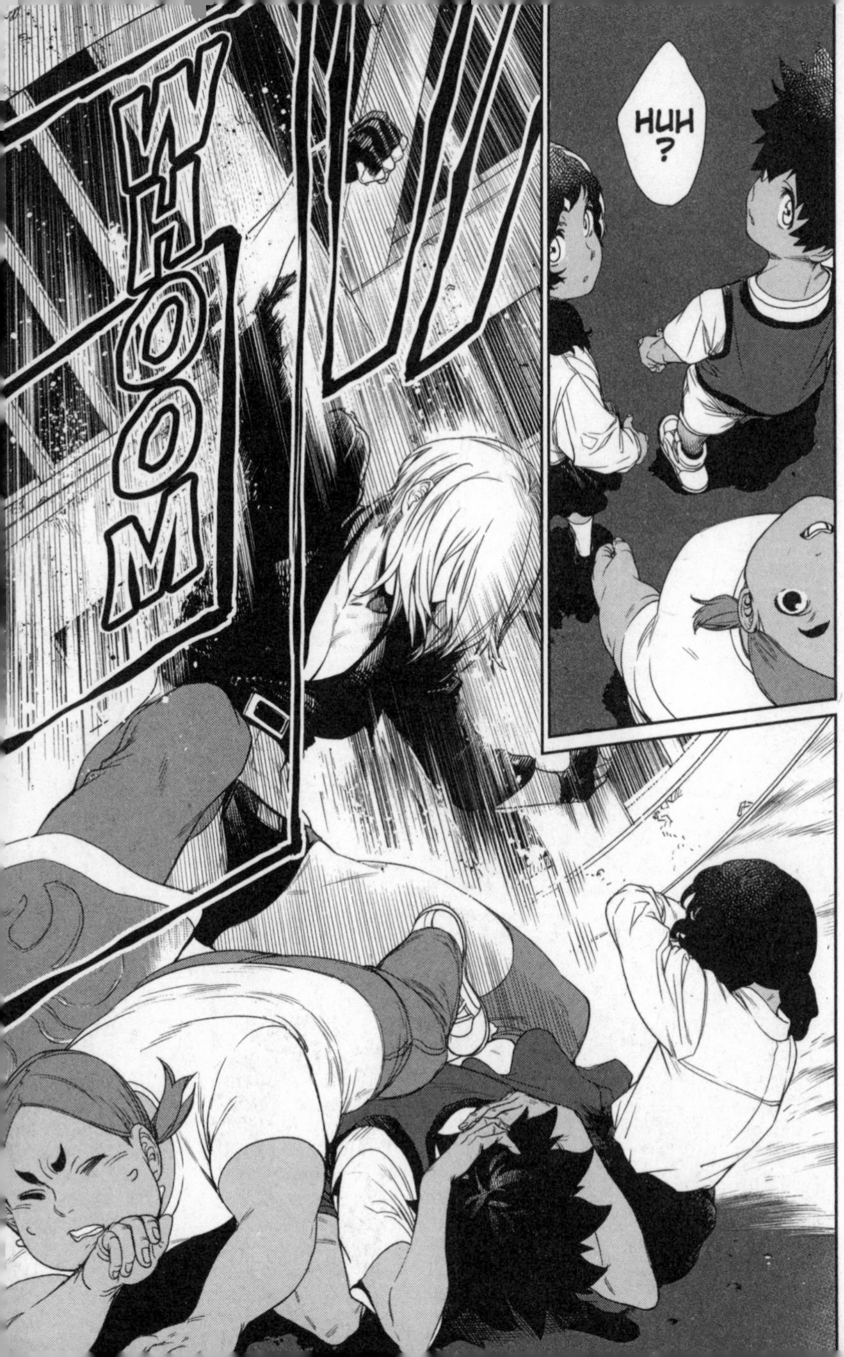
HUH?
WHOOM

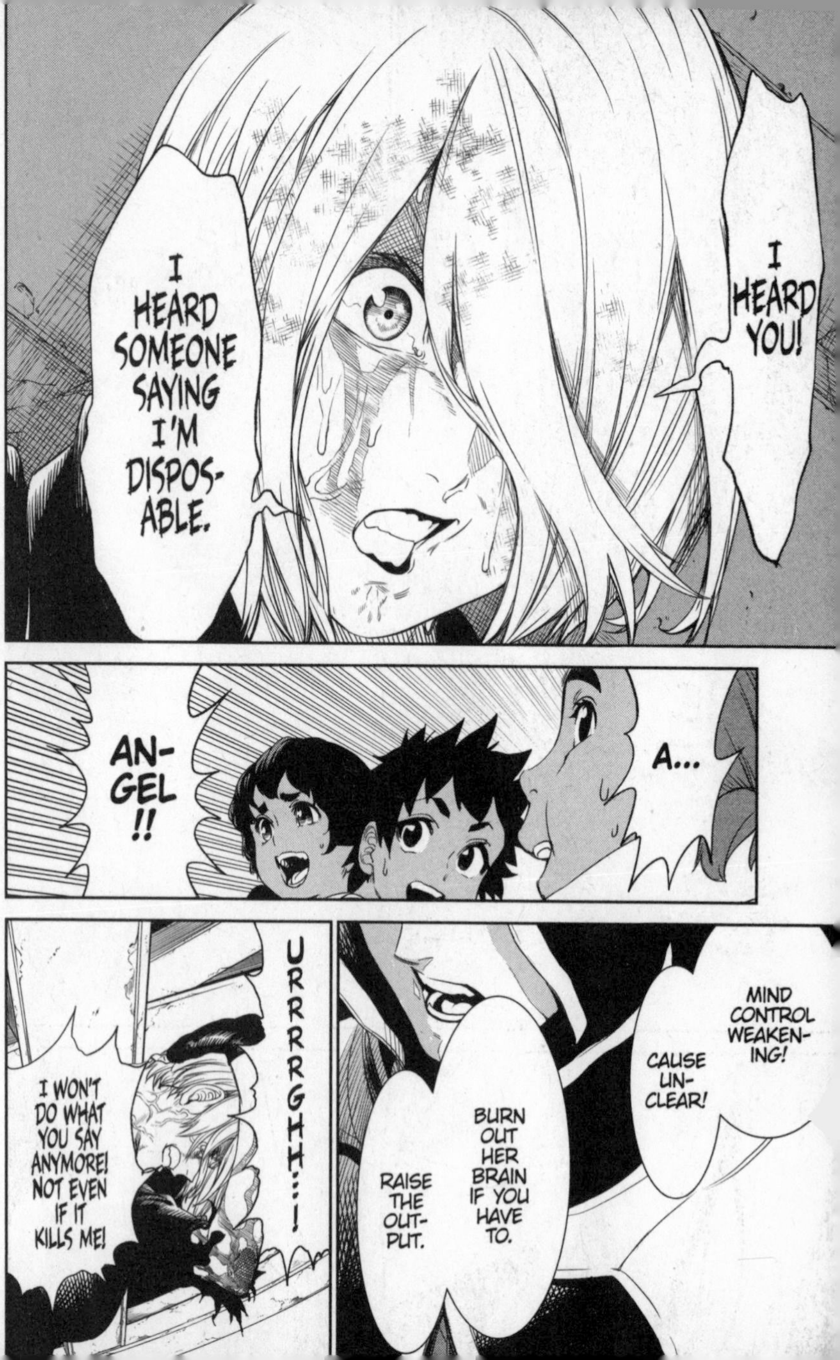
I HEARD YOU!
I HEARD SOMEONE SAYING I'M DISPOSABLE.
A...
AN-GEL!!
MIND CONTROL WEAKENING!
CAUSE UNCLEAR!
BURN OUT HER BRAIN IF YOU HAVE TO.
RAISE THE OUTPUT.
URRRRGHH...!
I WON'T DO WHAT YOU SAY ANYMORE! NOT EVEN IF IT KILLS ME!

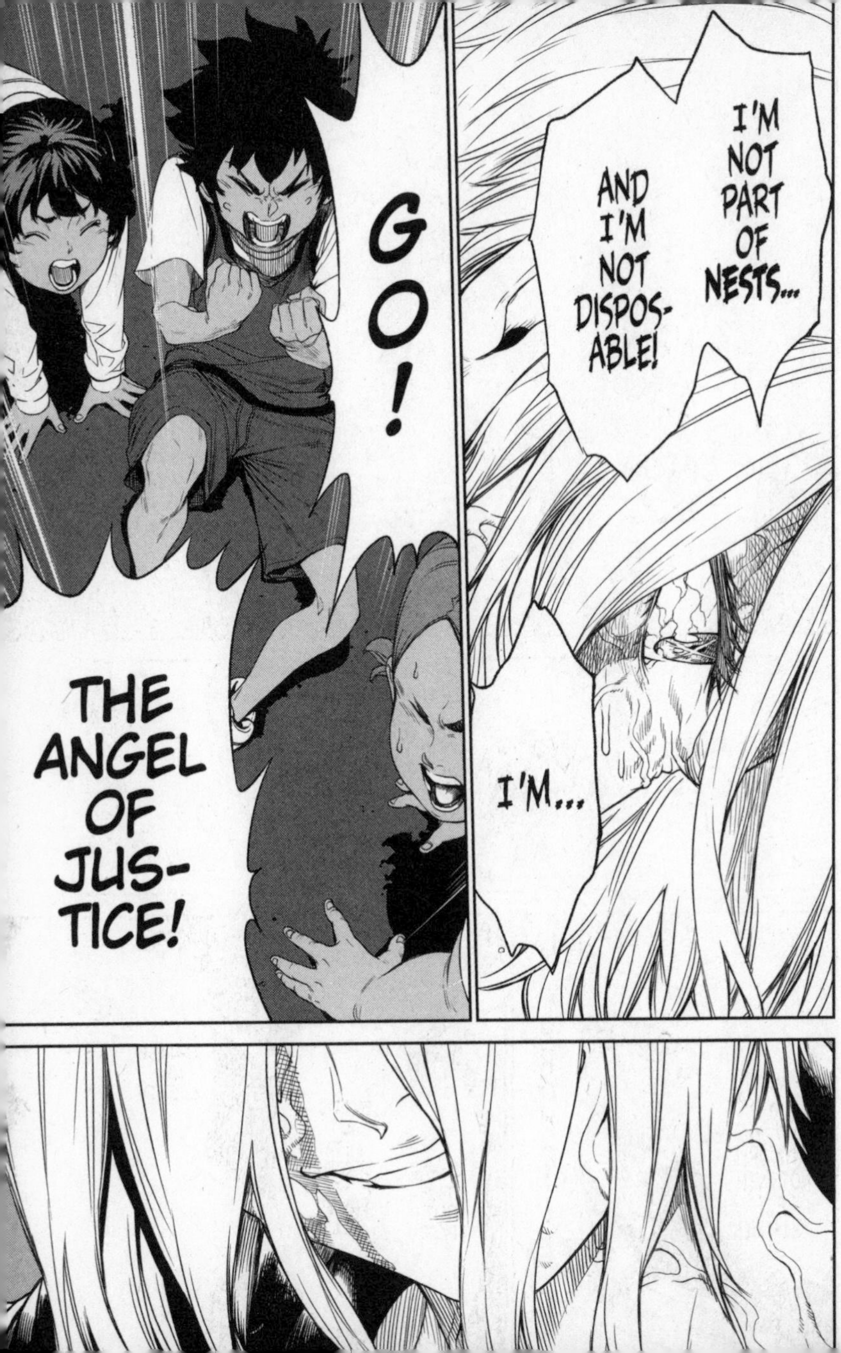
I'M NOT PART OF NESTS...
AND I'M NOT DISPOS-ABLE!
I'M...
GO!
THE ANGEL OF JUS-TICE!

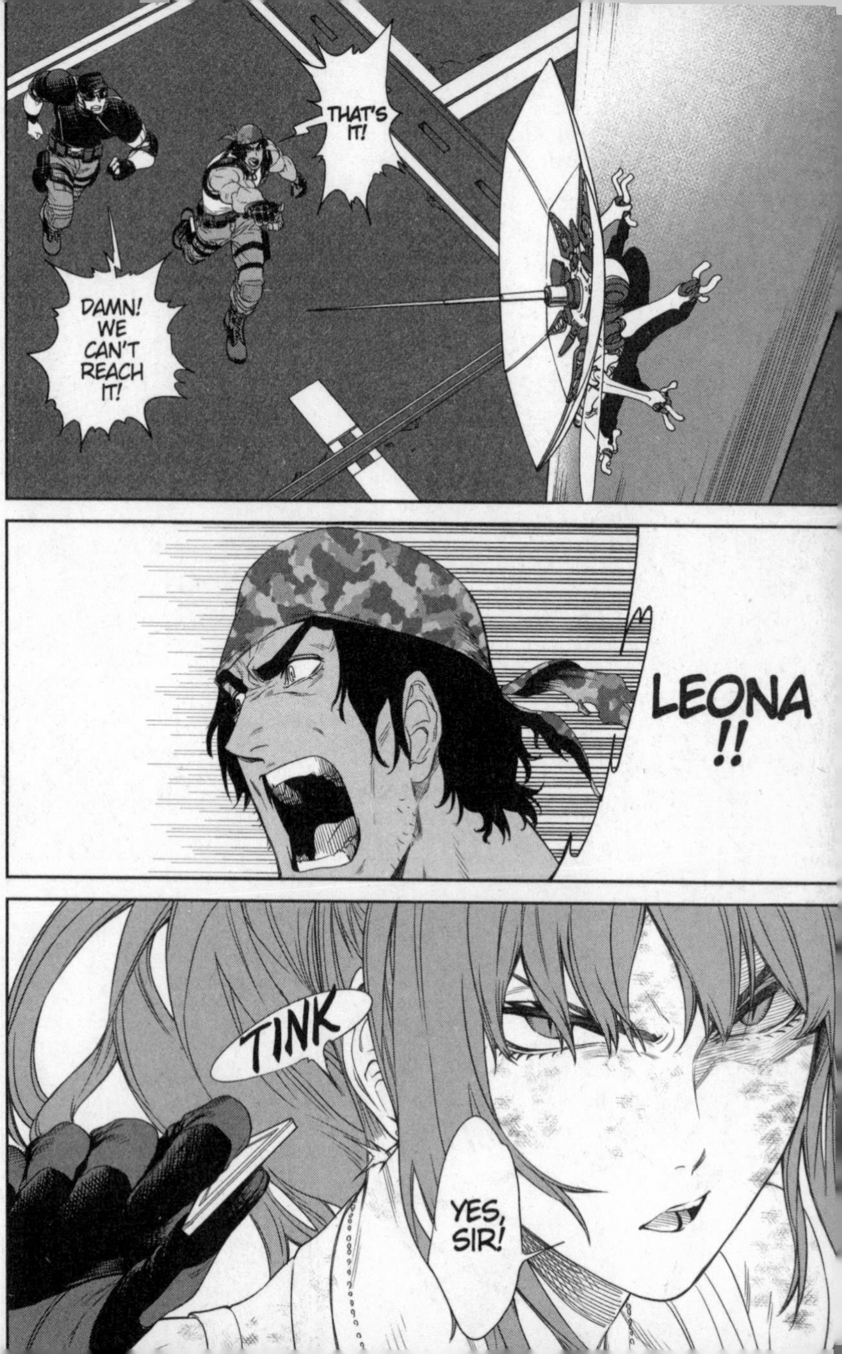
THAT'S IT!
DAMN! WE CAN'T REACH IT!
LEONA!!
TINK
YES, SIR!

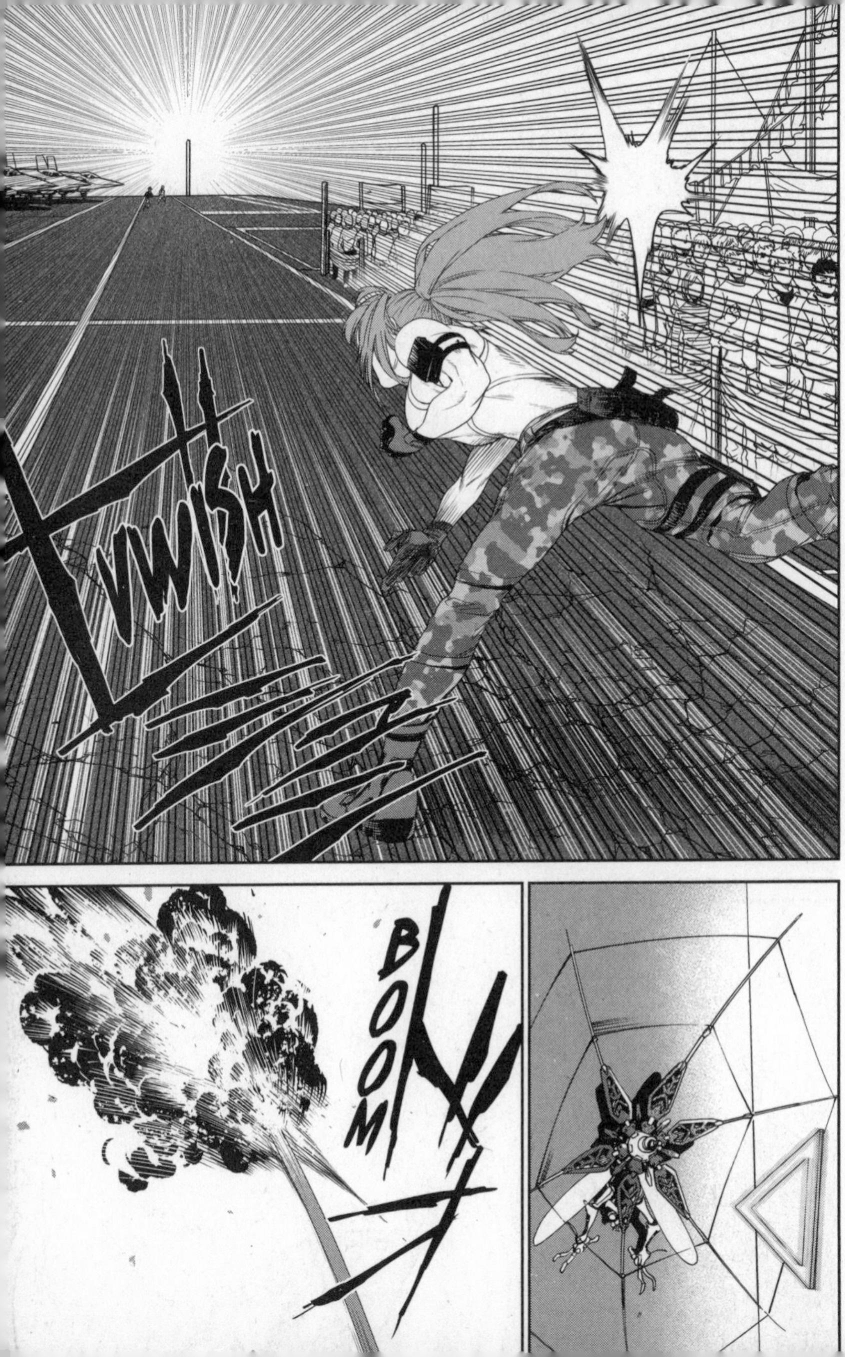
FVWISH
BOOOM

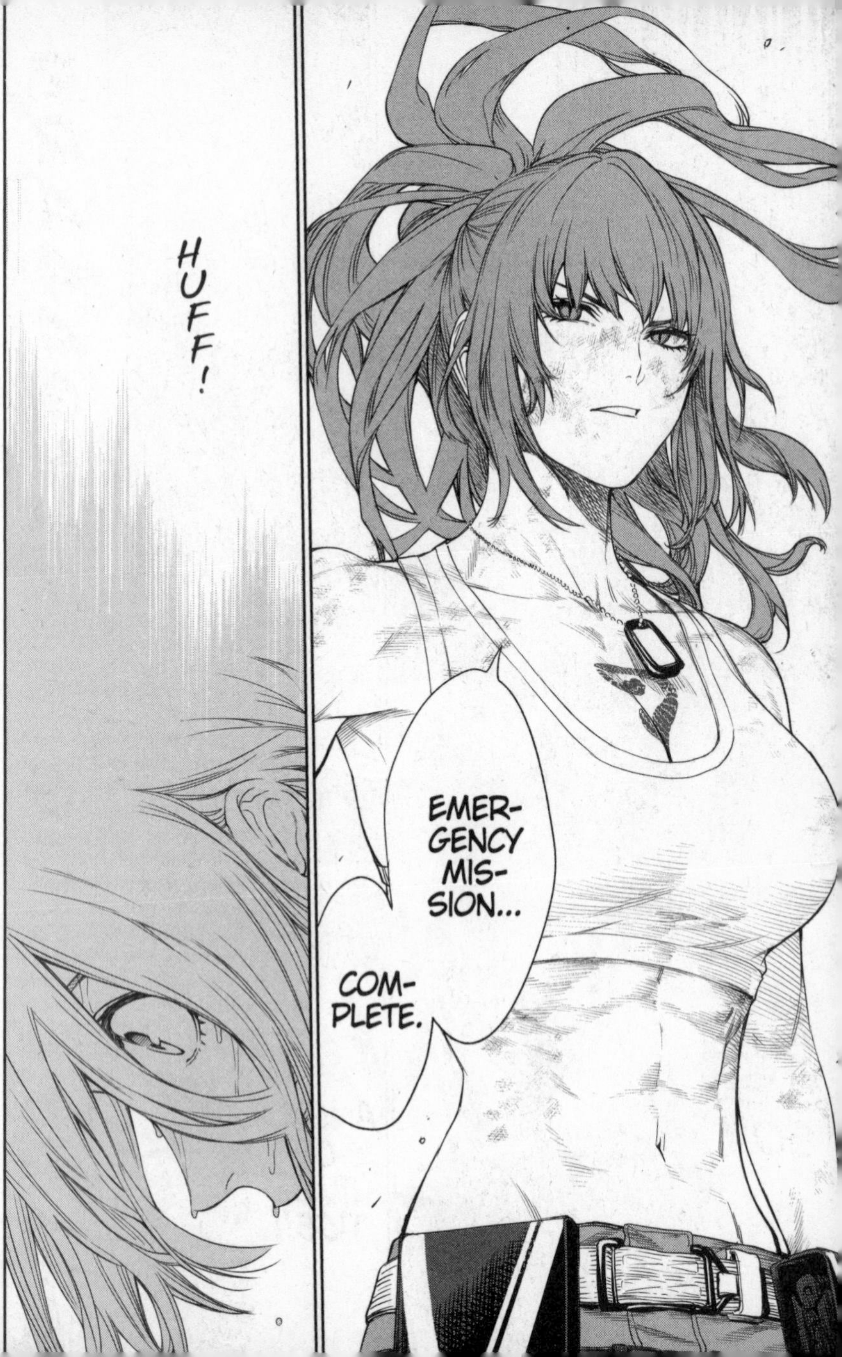
EMERGENCY MISSION... COMPLETE.
HUFF!

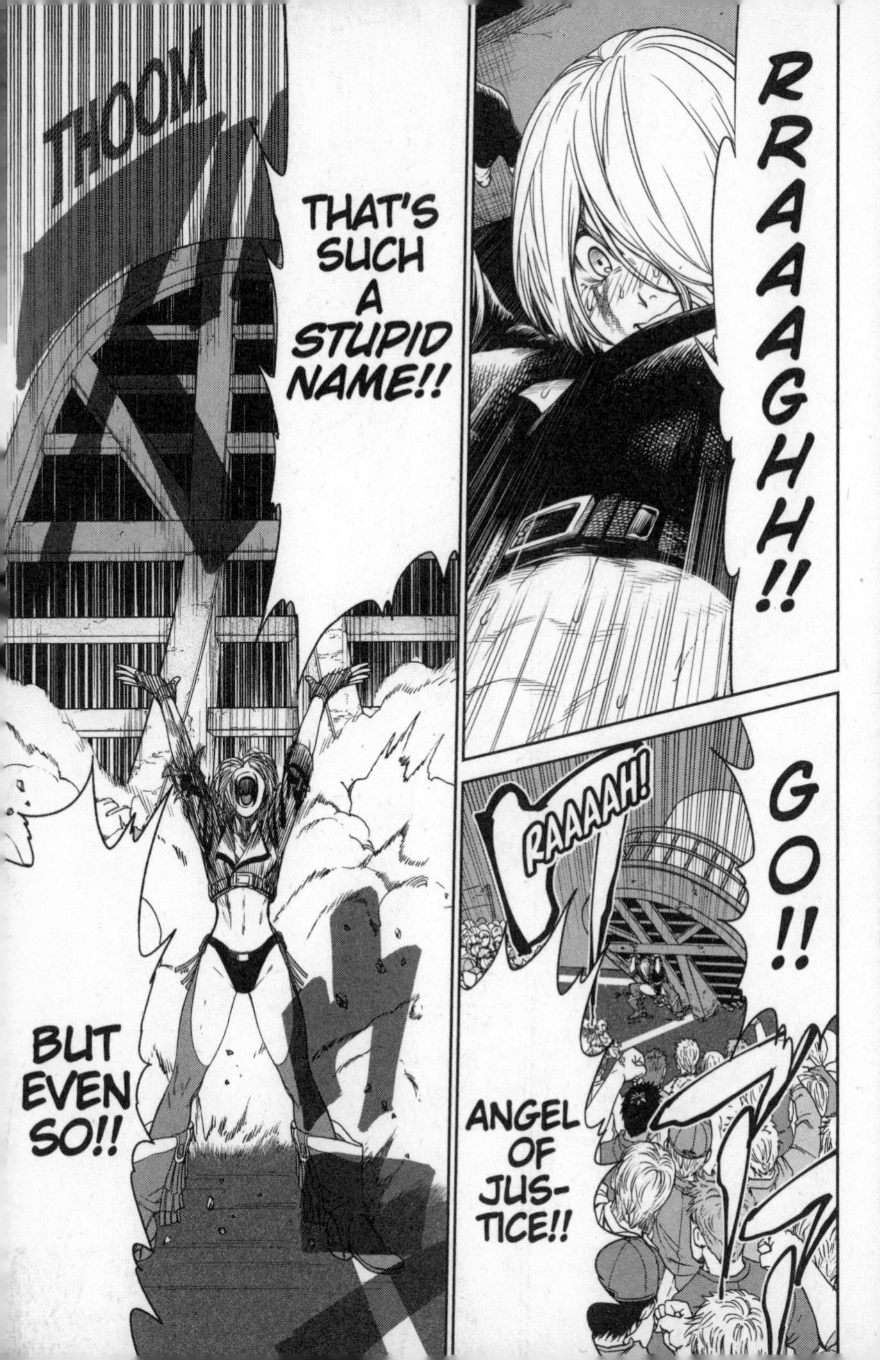
RRAAGHH!!
GO!!
RAAAAH!
ANGEL OF JUSTICE!!
THOOM
THAT'S SUCH A STUPID NAME!!
BUT EVEN SO!!

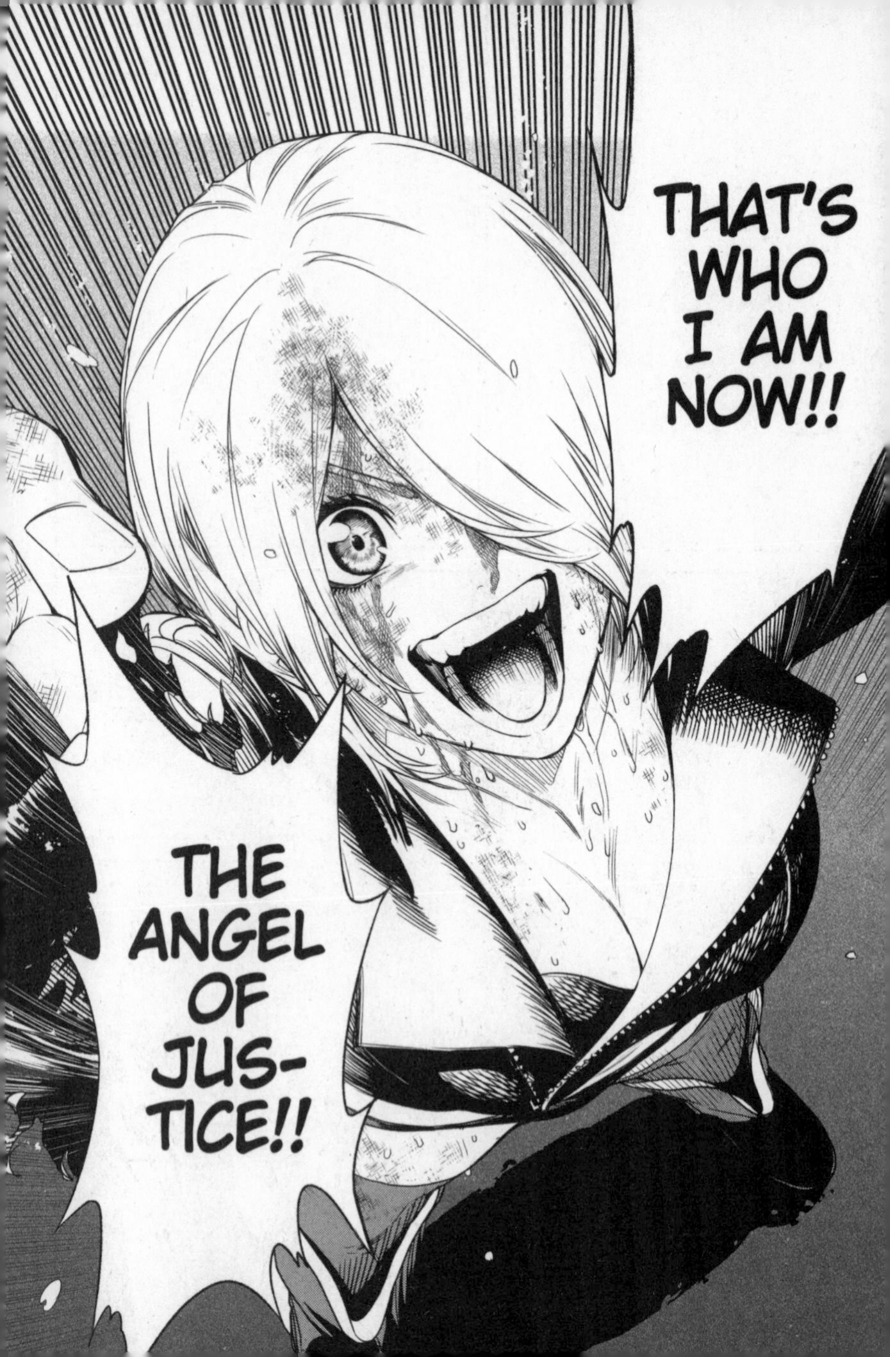
THAT'S WHO I AM NOW!!
THE ANGEL OF JUS-TICE!!

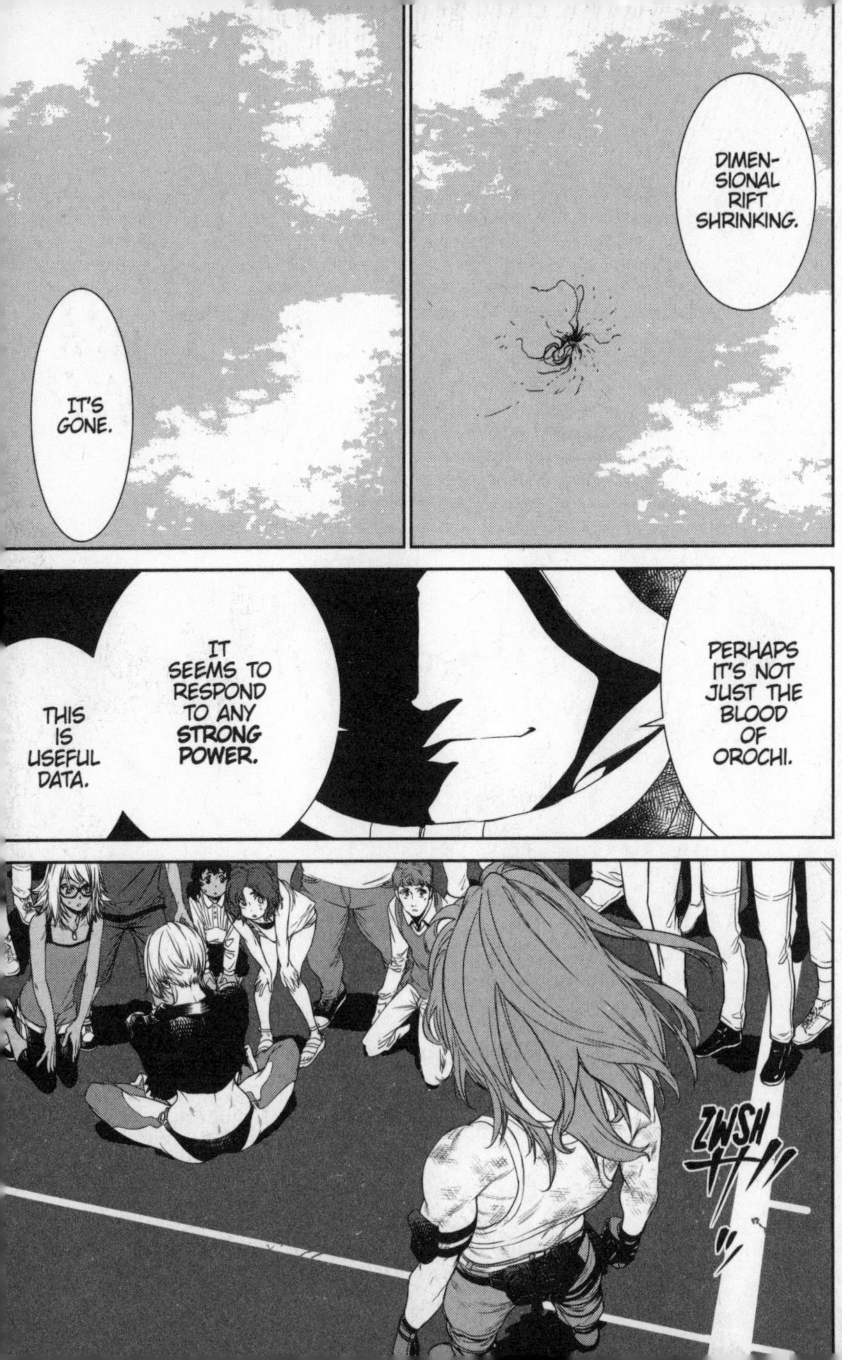
DIMEN-
SIONAL
RIFT
SHRINKING.
IT'S GONE.
PERHAPS IT'S NOT JUST THE BLOOD OF OROCHI.
IT SEEMS TO RESPOND TO ANY STRONG POWER.
THIS IS USEFUL DATA.
ZWSH

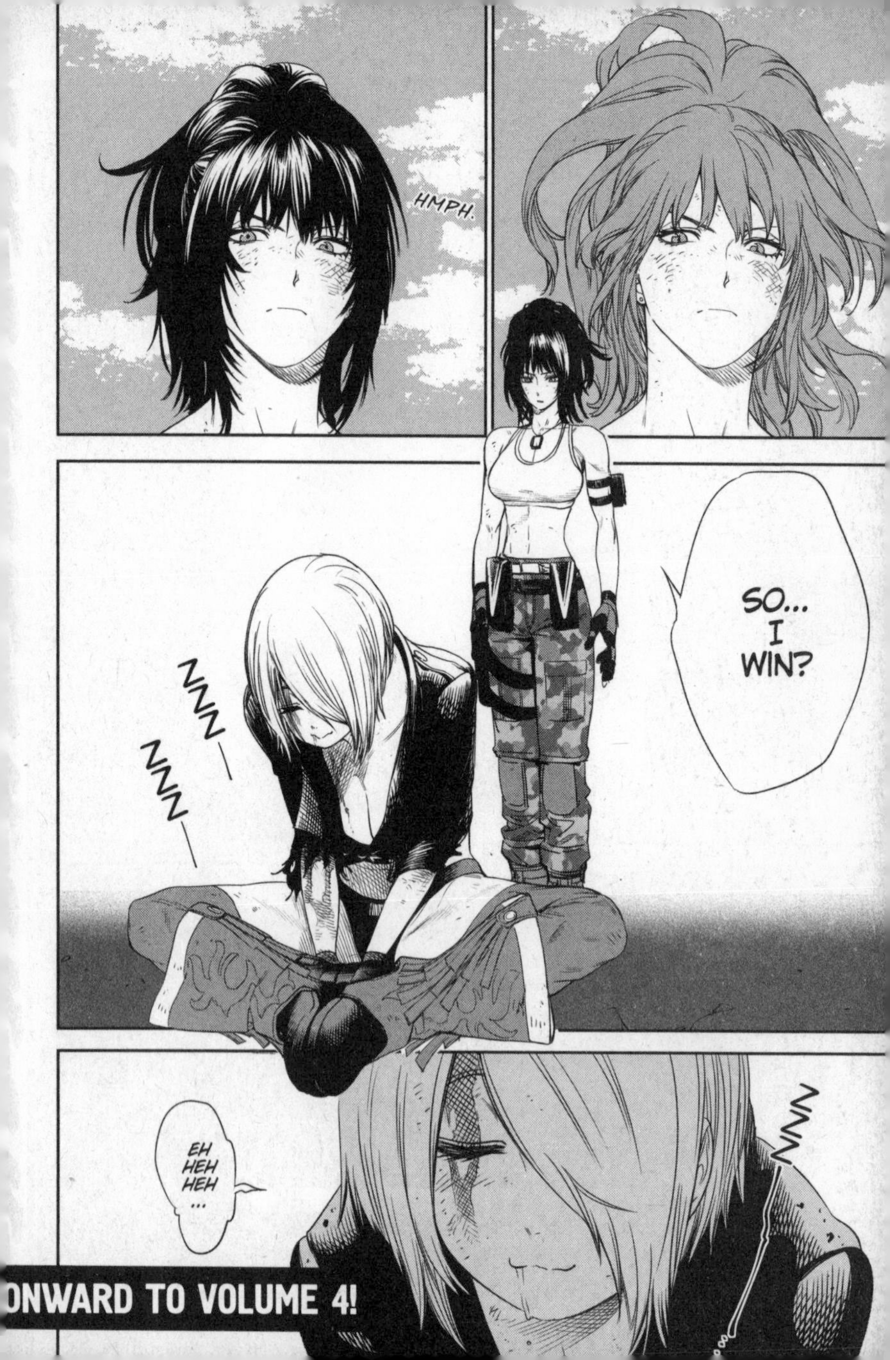
HMPH.
SO... I WIN?
ZZZ—
ZZZ—
NNN
EH HEH HEH ...
ONWARD TO VOLUME 4!

MOVE LIST

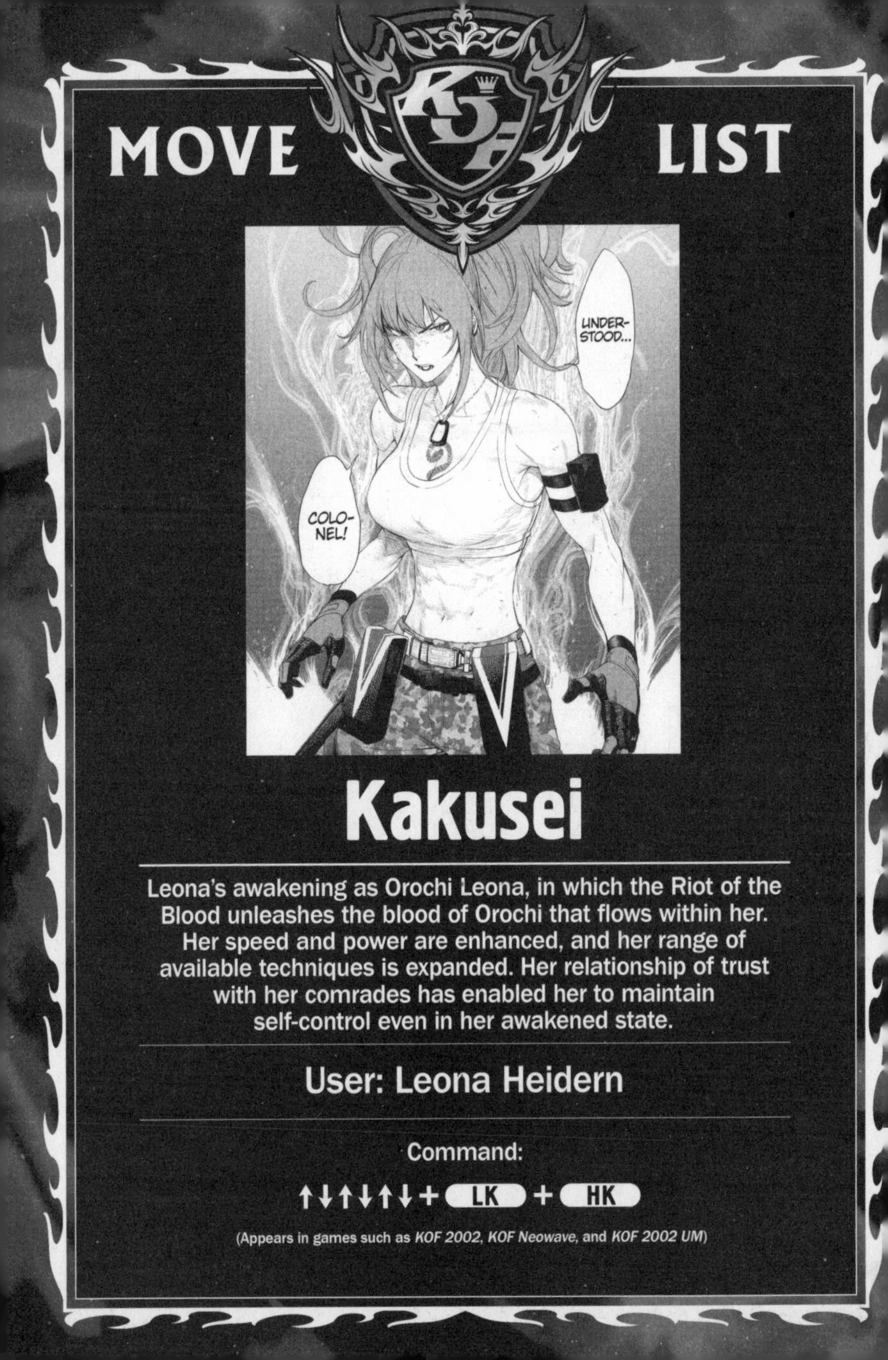
UNDER-
STOOD...
COLO-
NEL!

Kakusei

Leona's awakening as Orochi Leona, in which the Riot of the Blood unleashes the blood of Orochi that flows within her. Her speed and power are enhanced, and her range of available techniques is expanded. Her relationship of trust with her comrades has enabled her to maintain self-control even in her awakened state.

User: Leona Heidern

Command:

↑↓↑↓↑↓ + LK + HK

(Appears in games such as *KOF 2002*, *KOF Neowave*, and *KOF 2002 UM*)

MOVE LIST

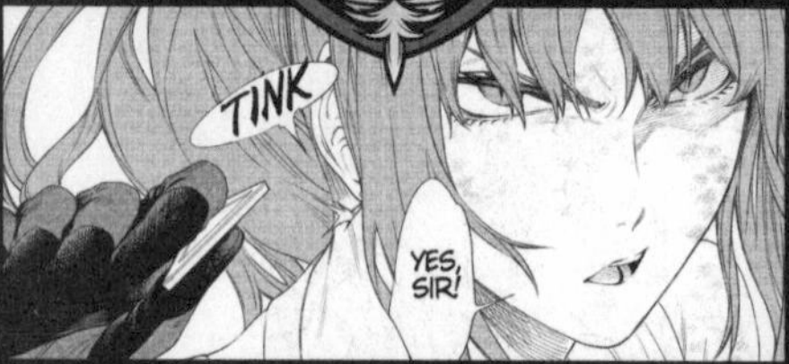
TINK
YES, SIR!

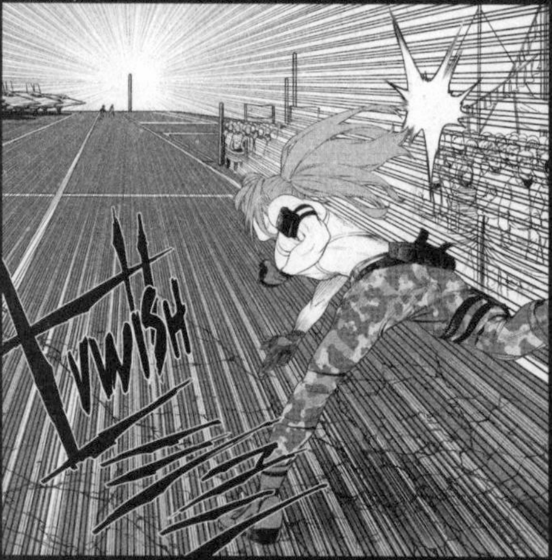
VWISH

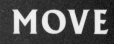

Earring Bomb

Leona throws an explosive earring.

User: Leona Heidern

Command:

↓↙← + LK or HK

Advertisement illustration from the June 2018 issue of *Shonen Sirius*.

KOF ILLUSTRATION GALLERY

Art by
Kyoutarou Azuma

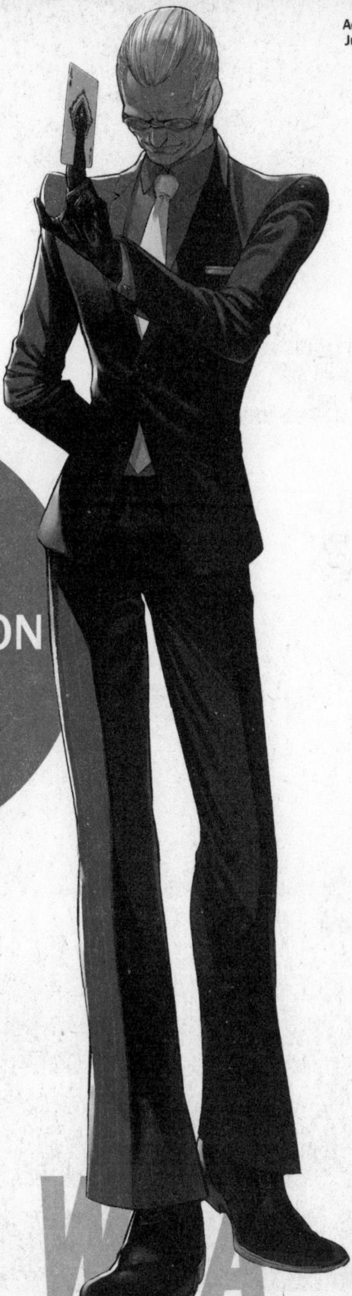

オズワルド

OSWALD

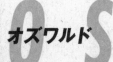

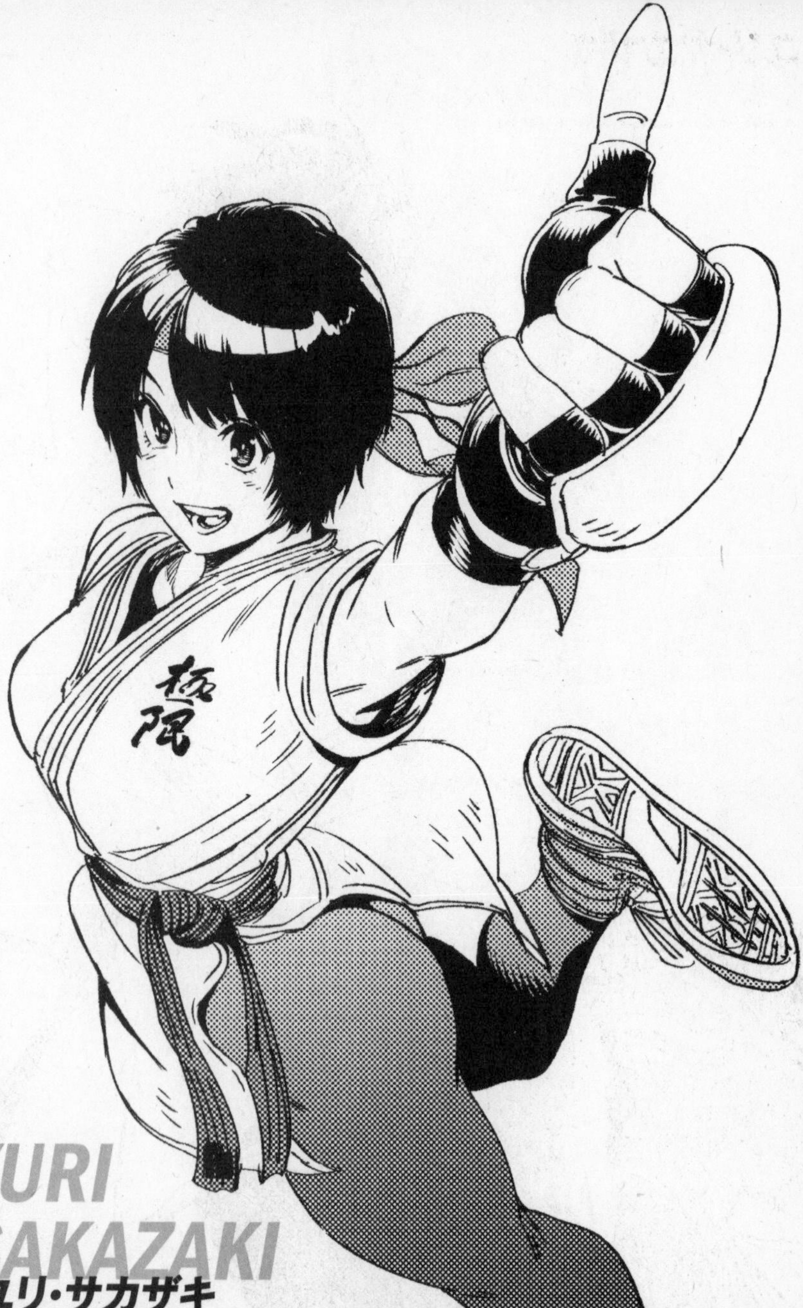
極限

YURI
SAKAZAKI
ユリ・サカザキ

Vol. 2 Store-Exclusive Bonus Illustration (for Animate)

ユリ・サカザキ
YURI SAKAZAKI

Vol. 2 Store-Exclusive Bonus Illustration (for Gamers)

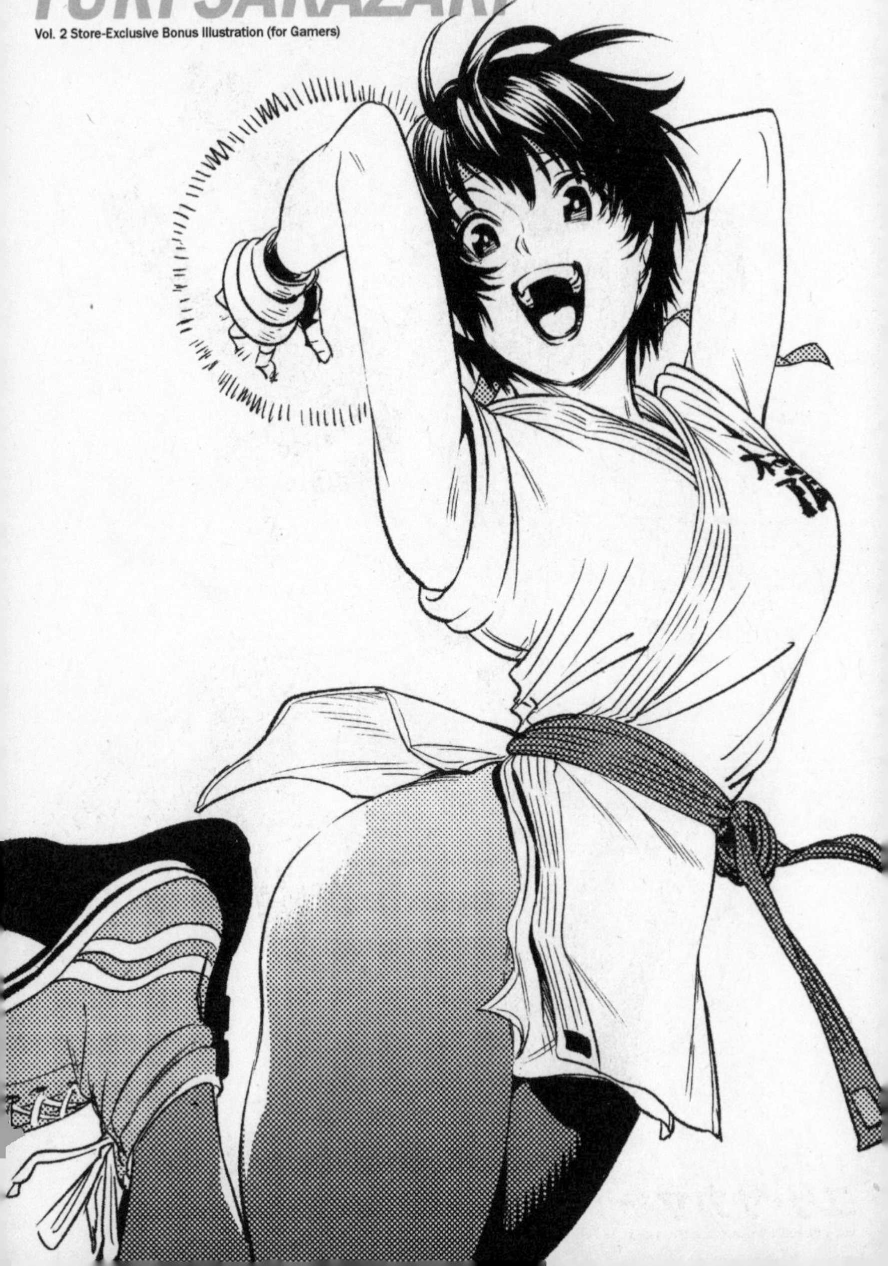

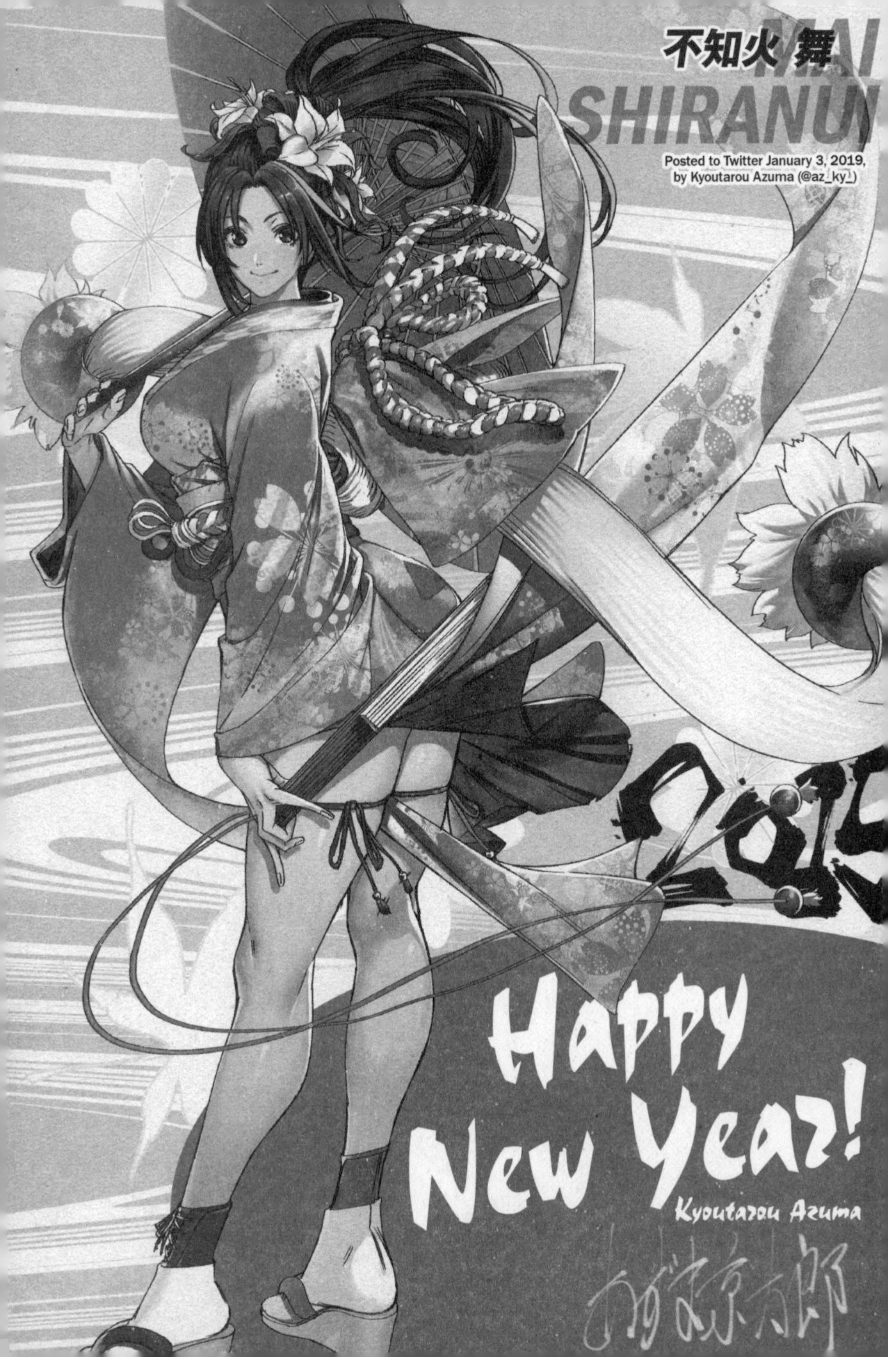
不知火 舞
MAI SHIRANUI
Posted to Twitter January 3, 2019, by Kyoutarou Azuma (@az_ky_)
Happy New Year!
Kyoutarou Azuma

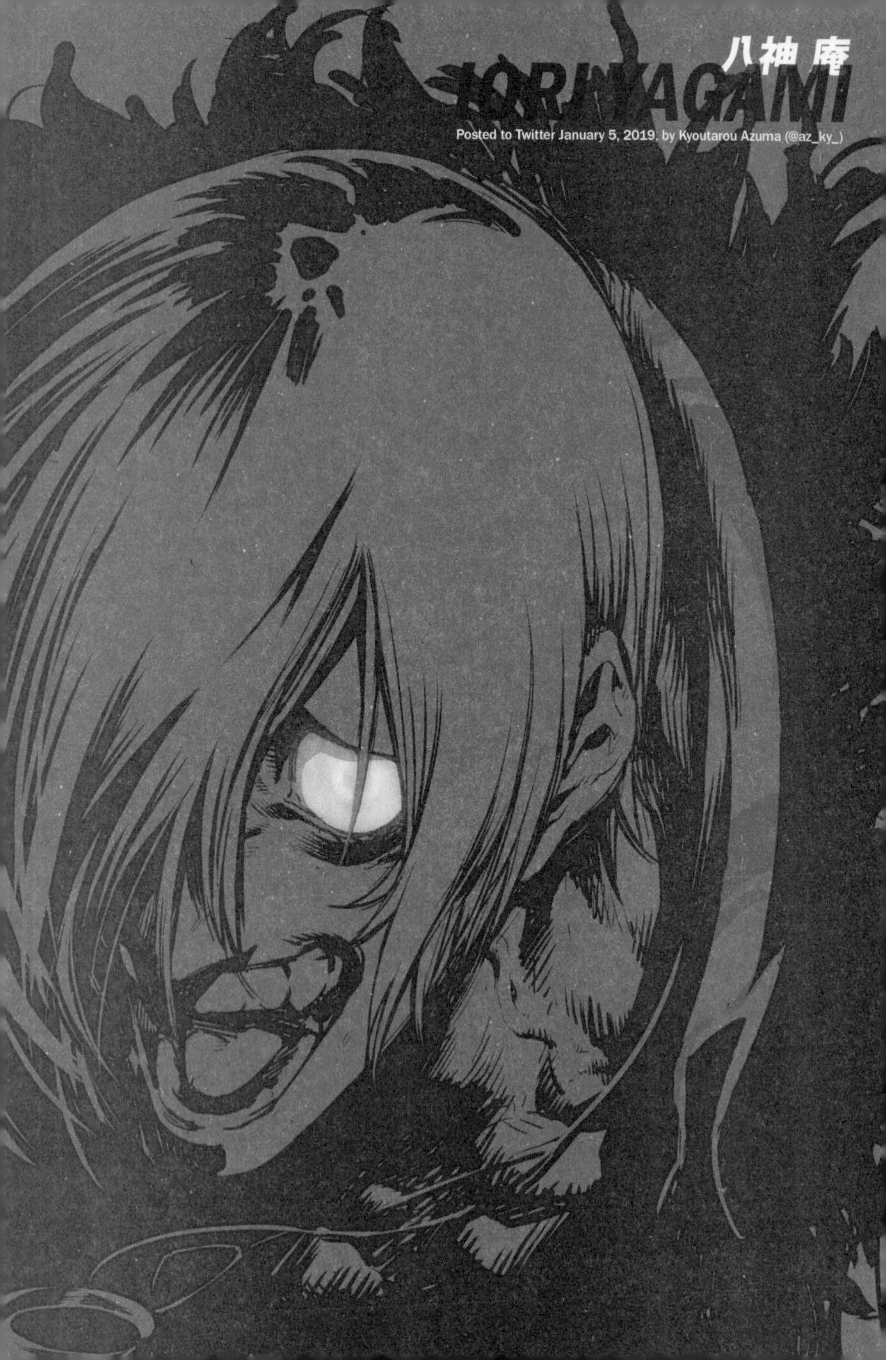
八神庵
IORI YAGAMI
Posted to Twitter January 5, 2019, by Kyoutarou Azuma (@az_ky_)

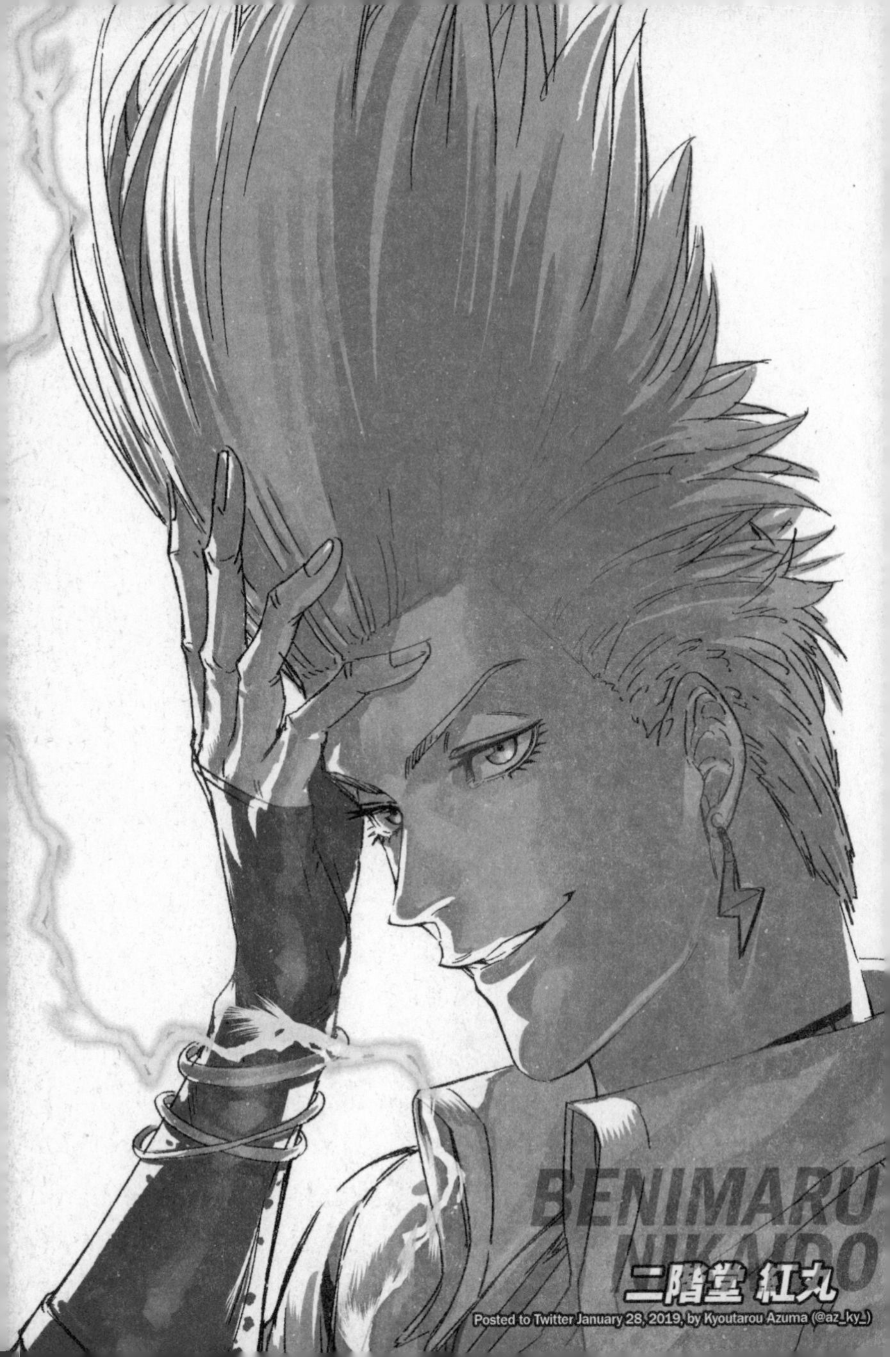
BENIMARU NIKAIDO
二階堂 紅丸
Posted to Twitter January 28, 2019, by Kyoutarou Azuma (@az_ky_)

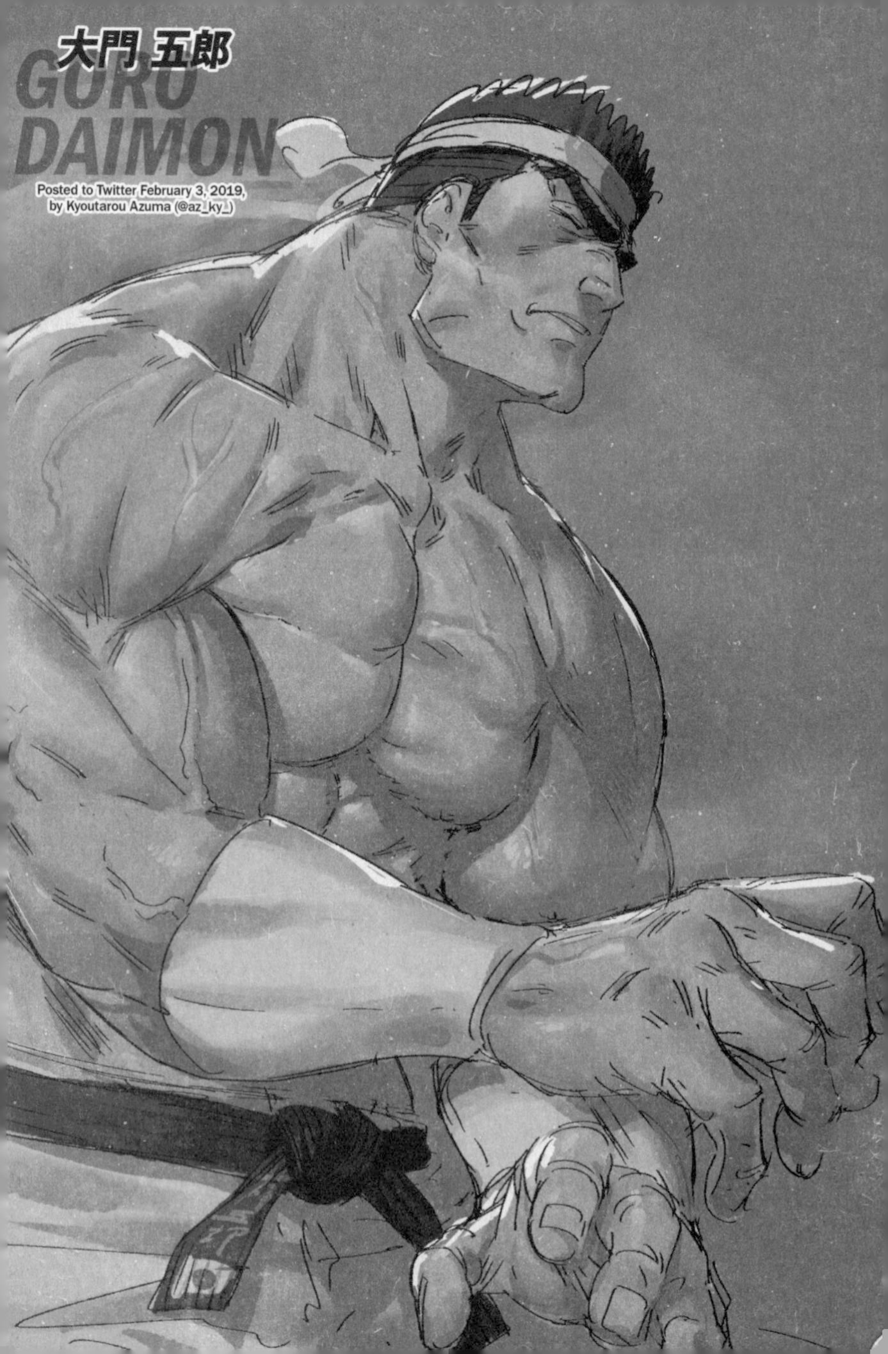
大門 五郎
GORO
DAIMON

Posted to Twitter February 3, 2019,
by Kyoutarou Azuma (@az_ky_)